ASIAN DEVELOPMENT OUTLOOK 2020 UPDATE

WELLNESS IN WORRYING TIMES

SEPTEMBER 2020

ADB

ASIAN DEVELOPMENT BANK

© 2020 Asian Development Bank
6 ADB Avenue, Mandaluyong City, 1550 Metro Manila, Philippines
Tel +63 2 8632 4444; Fax +63 2 8636 2444
www.adb.org

Some rights reserved. Published in 2020.

ISBN 978-92-9262-361-6 (print); 978-92-9262-362-3 (electronic); 978-92-9262-363-0 (ebook)
ISSN 1655-4809 (print)
Publication Stock No. FLS200256-3
DOI: http://dx.doi.org/10.22617/FLS200256-3

The views expressed in this publication are those of the authors and do not necessarily reflect the views and policies of the Asian Development Bank (ADB) or its Board of Governors or the governments they represent.

ADB does not guarantee the accuracy of the data included in this publication and accepts no responsibility for any consequence of their use. The mention of specific companies or products of manufacturers does not imply that they are endorsed or recommended by ADB in preference to others of a similar nature that are not mentioned.

By making any designation of or reference to a particular territory or geographic area, or by using the term "country" in this document, ADB does not intend to make any judgments as to the legal or other status of any territory or area.

Corrigenda to ADB publications may be found at http://www.adb.org/publications/corrigenda.

Notes:
In this publication, "$" refers to US dollars.
ADB recognizes "Hong Kong" as Hong Kong, China; "China" as the People's Republic of China; "Korea" and "South Korea" as the Republic of Korea; and "Vietnam" as Viet Nam.

Cover design by Anthony Victoria.

Cover artwork by Atsuko Yamagata/2020.

Contents

Foreword   iv
Acknowledgments   v
Definitions and assumptions   vi
Abbreviations   vii

ADO 2020 Update—Highlights   ix

Part 1 A precarious path to recovery   1

Recent developments: Asia falters as COVID-19 spreads   5
Outlook: Partial recovery after contraction in 2020   24
Risks: Looming threats in an unsettled new normal   34
Annex: Global economy plunges as pandemic rages   42

Part 2 Wellness in worrying times   53

A pandemic brings wellness to the fore   56
Contours of wellness in Asia   63
Holistic pathway to physical wellness   73
Leveraging Asian traditions for mental wellness   94
Wellness for happiness and inclusion   111
Policies for physical and mental wellness   117

Part 3 Economic trends and prospects in developing Asia   139

Central Asia   141
East Asia   154
South Asia   168
Southeast Asia   193
The Pacific   225

Statistical appendix   241

Foreword

Asia's path to recovery remains precarious half a year into the COVID-19 pandemic. Unfortunately, the regional economy will contract this year as the virus continues to spread and as ill effects linger from border restrictions, quarantines, and stay-at-home orders. Deterioration is far more widespread than during the Asian financial crisis of 1997–1998, reaching every corner of Asia and the Pacific. Conditions are also grim for our major trade partners, with GDP in the euro area and the US likewise stumbling and making it hard for our region to recover.

The sustained spread of COVID-19 remains the major risk to economies around the world. A prolonged pandemic and global slowdown will severely harm not just those economies struggling with significant outbreaks at home, but also those that depend on tourism, commodity exports, or other forms of external demand. Softer demand and falling food and fuel prices will ease the inflation burden on most Asian consumers, but supply disruption stemming from mobility and transport restrictions may pose particular inflation risk in some economies. This merits close monitoring.

In these worrying times, maintaining physical and mental health becomes even more essential than usual. We believe wellness is critical for post-pandemic recovery—especially in Asia and the Pacific. Wellness not only maintains happy and productive societies but can be an important driver of growth, tapping into our wealth of Asian wellness traditions. Indeed, the provision of wellness has become an important segment of the Asian economy, generating more than a tenth of regional output and growing in recent years by over 10% annually. Wellness policies to boost physical and mental health should be inclusive to benefit the whole spectrum of Asian society. Policies should create healthy living environments, encourage physical activity and healthy diets, and enhance workplace wellness.

With this *Update* to the *Asian Development Outlook 2020*, we in the Asian Development Bank sincerely strive once more to provide to policy makers in Asia and the Pacific a unique service that combines astute economic analyses for the near term with well-considered and thought-provoking policy advice for the medium and long term. In these uncertain times, as regional governments steer their economies toward recovery, we hope our insights and recommendations will help to make each regional economy and society even more resilient, innovative, and inclusive.

MASATSUGU ASAKAWA
President
Asian Development Bank

Acknowledgments

Asian Development Outlook 2020 Update was prepared by staff of Asian Development Bank (ADB) regional departments and resident missions under the guidance of the Economic Research and Regional Cooperation Department (ERCD). Representatives of these departments met regularly as the Regional Economic Outlook Task Force to coordinate and develop consistent forecasts for the region.

Economists in ERCD, led by Abdul Abiad, director of the Macroeconomics Research Division, coordinated the production of the publication, assisted by Edith Laviña. Technical and research support was provided by Shiela Camingue-Romance, Nedelyn Magtibay-Ramos, Pilipinas Quising, Dennis Sorino, Priscille Villanueva, and Mai Lin Villaruel. Additional research support was provided by Emmanuel Alano, Rosa Mia Lasam Arao, Christian Regie Jabagat, Jesson Pagaduan, Reizle Jade Platitas, Rene Cris Rivera, and Michael Timbang. Inputs provided by Liming Chen, Jesus Felipe, Rana Hasan, and Aiko Kikkawa Takenaka are much appreciated. Economic editorial advisors Robert Boumphrey, Eric Clifton, Joshua Greene, Henry Ma, Srinivasa Madhur, Richard Niebuhr, and Reza Vaez-Zadeh made substantive contributions to the country chapters and regional outlook.

A team of economists prepared the theme chapter, led by Donghyun Park, principal economist of the Macroeconomics Research Division of ERCD. In addition to contributors named in the byline and authors of background papers, the theme chapter benefited from valuable feedback and inputs from Abdul Abiad, Benno Ferrarini, Soon Chan Hong, Manbar Singh Khadka, Utsav Kumar, Tshering Lhamo, Shalini Mittal, Masato Nakane, Dominik Peschel, and Lei Lei Song. Support and guidance from Yasuyuki Sawada, Joseph E. Zveglich, Jr., and Edimon Ginting throughout production is gratefully acknowledged. Special thanks are due to former ADB president Takehiko Nakao for initially suggesting the theme. Margarita Debuque-Gonzales provided editorial advice on the theme chapter and the regional outlook. Map illustrations were created by Abraham Villanueva and Angel Villarez.

Authors who contributed the sections are bylined in each chapter. The subregional coordinators were Kenji Takamiya, Lilia Aleksanyan, and Fatima Catacutan for Central Asia; Akiko Terada-Hagiwara for East Asia; Lei Lei Song and Lani Garnace for South Asia; Thiam Hee Ng and Dulce Zara for Southeast Asia; and Rommel Rabanal and Cara Tinio for the Pacific.

Peter Fredenburg advised on ADB style and English usage. Alvin Tubio handled typesetting and graphics generation, in which he was assisted by Heili Ann Bravo, Elenita Pura, and Angel Love Roque. Art direction for the cover was by Anthony Victoria, with artwork by Atsuko Yamagata. Critical support for printing and publishing the report was provided by the Printing Services Unit of the ADB Office of Administrative Services and by the publications and web teams of the ADB Department of Communications. Rhia Bautista-Piamonte and Fermirelyn Cruz provided administrative and secretarial support. Colleagues in the Department of Communications, including Vicky Tan, David Kruger, and Ami Takagawa planned and coordinated the dissemination of *Asian Development Outlook 2020 Update*; and Kevin Peter Nellies, Ma. Melissa Enojado, and Ralph Romero redesigned the landing page of the *ADO* and its background papers.

Definitions and assumptions

The economies discussed in *Asian Development Outlook 2020 Update* are classified by major analytic or geographic group. For the purposes of this publication, the following apply:

- **Association of Southeast Asian Nations** (ASEAN) comprises Brunei Darussalam, Cambodia, Indonesia, the Lao People's Democratic Republic, Malaysia, Myanmar, the Philippines, Singapore, Thailand, and Viet Nam. In this report, the ASEAN-5 are Indonesia, Malaysia, the Philippines, Thailand, and Viet Nam.
- **Developing Asia** comprises the 46 members of the Asian Development Bank listed below.
- **Newly industrialized economies** comprise Hong Kong, China; the Republic of Korea; Singapore; and Taipei,China.
- **Central Asia** comprises Armenia, Azerbaijan, Georgia, Kazakhstan, the Kyrgyz Republic, Tajikistan, Turkmenistan, and Uzbekistan.
- **East Asia** comprises Hong Kong, China; Mongolia; the People's Republic of China; the Republic of Korea; and Taipei,China.
- **South Asia** comprises Afghanistan, Bangladesh, Bhutan, India, Maldives, Nepal, Pakistan, and Sri Lanka.
- **Southeast Asia** comprises Brunei Darussalam, Cambodia, Indonesia, the Lao People's Democratic Republic, Malaysia, Myanmar, the Philippines, Singapore, Thailand, Timor-Leste, and Viet Nam.
- **The Pacific** comprises the Cook Islands, the Federated States of Micronesia, Fiji, Kiribati, the Marshall Islands, Nauru, Niue, Palau, Papua New Guinea, Samoa, Solomon Islands, Tonga, Tuvalu, and Vanuatu.

Unless otherwise specified, the symbol "$" and the word "dollar" refer to US dollars.

A number of assumptions have been adopted for the projections presented in the *Asian Development Outlook 2020 Update*: The established policies of national authorities are maintained. Real effective exchange rates remain constant at their average from 20 July to 28 August 2020. The average price of oil is $42.50/barrel in 2020 and $50.00/barrel in 2021. The 6-month London interbank offered rate (Libor) for US dollar deposits averages 0.4% in 2020 and 0.1% in 2021, the European Central Bank refinancing rate averages 0.0% in both years, and the Bank of Japan overnight call rate averages –0.1% in both years.

Asian Development Outlook 2020 Update is generally based on information available to **31 August 2020**.

Abbreviations

ADB	Asian Development Bank
ADO	*Asian Development Outlook*
ASEAN	Association of Southeast Asian Nations
COVID-19	Coronavirus Disease 2019
FSM	Federated States of Micronesia
FY	fiscal year
GDP	gross domestic product
GFC	global financial crisis of 2008–2009
H	half
ICT	information and communication technology
IMF	International Monetary Fund
GTF	garments, travel goods, and footwear
GVA	gross value added
Lao PDR	Lao People's Democratic Republic
Libor	London interbank offered rate
M2	money that includes cash and highly liquid accounts
M3	broad money that adds time accounts to M2
mbd	million barrels per day
MSME	micro, small, or medium-sized enterprise
NCD	noncommunicable disease
NIE	newly industrialized economy
NPL	nonperforming loan
OECD	Organisation for Economic Co-operation and Development
OPEC	Organization of the Petroleum Exporting Countries
PMI	purchasing managers' index
PNG	Papua New Guinea
PRC	People's Republic of China
Q	quarter
ROK	Republic of Korea
R(t)	reproduction number
US, USA	United States of America

ADO 2020 Update—Highlights

Economic prospects in developing Asia have worsened. As the COVID-19 pandemic continues to disrupt global economic activity, gross domestic product (GDP) forecasts have been downgraded from *Asian Development Outlook 2020.* The region is now expected to contract by 0.7% in 2020, the first regional recession in nearly 6 decades. GDP is projected to grow by 6.8% in 2021, but this will still leave it smaller than forecast before COVID-19. Excluding high-income newly industrialized economies, regional GDP is expected to also contract by 0.5% this year before growing by 7.2% next year.

Softening demand and subdued food prices will keep inflation benign. The headline inflation forecast is revised down from 3.2% to 2.9% for 2020 and maintained at 2.3% for 2021.

The threat of a prolonged COVID-19 pandemic is the main risk to the outlook. A return to more stringent containment measures could slow or even derail recovery and possibly trigger financial turmoil. While economies in developing Asia remain resilient, continued policy support is needed to underpin recovery.

Physical and mental health is vital to post-pandemic recovery. The theme chapter in this report explores wellness, or the deliberate pursuit of activities that bring holistic health. Wellness is a large and growing segment of the Asian economy, providing 11% of regional output. Further, Asia has a wealth of wellness traditions that are valuable assets for enhancing economic development and public health. Government interventions such as building recreation centers in poor neighborhoods can promote wellness for all Asians. More generally, wellness policies can help Asians navigate these uncertain, stressful times toward a better new normal after the pandemic.

Yasuyuki Sawada
Chief Economist
Asian Development Bank

A precarious path to recovery

■ **The global pandemic persists, and is at varying stages in developing Asia.** The curve showing the number of new Coronavirus Disease 2019 (COVID-19) cases daily is rising in some regional economies, flattening or subsiding in others, and reviving in still others in second or third waves. In response to the outbreaks, Asian governments imposed a range of containment measures, their stringency differing across economies and over time. These restrict mobility outside of the home and so economic activity. Containment measures have been eased in most economies across developing Asia and are now less strict than in the second quarter of 2020.

■ **Second-quarter growth slumped under containment restrictions regionally and globally.** Economies in the euro area contracted by 14.7% year on year, and the US economy by 9.1%. Growth in developing Asia also collapsed, with several regional economies recording quarterly contraction for the first time since the Asian financial crisis of 1997–1998. Signs of bottoming out have appeared as leading economic indicators improved, though they remain below pre-pandemic readings in most economies. Consumer and investor confidence remain suppressed across the region. Inflation in developing Asia has been kept in check by depressed demand and declining food prices.

■ **Nascent recovery in the PRC contrasts with continued fragility in India.** After containing its domestic outbreak relatively rapidly, the People's Republic of China (PRC) saw growth recover from 6.8% contraction in the first quarter to 3.2% growth in the second. By contrast, the outbreak in India has intensified since April, spreading fast from cities to rural areas. The hard and prolonged lockdown caused output to contract by 23.9% in the April–June quarter, and various high-frequency indicators, while improving somewhat, show continued economic weakness.

■ **Trade plummeted then bottomed out, with Asia's trade falling by less than global trade.** In line with plummeting global trade and economic activity, developing Asia's exports also contracted, but not as badly as global exports. As aggregate exports plunged almost across the board, they picked up for health supplies, particularly from the PRC. Stronger demand for devices, amid increased digitalization, boosted exports from some producers of electrical and electronic devices and optical equipment.

■ **Capital flows, financial markets, and currencies recovered after an initial nosedive.** Foreign portfolio investment in developing Asia suffered large outflows in March–April as global financial markets reacted to the intensifying pandemic, battering Asian currencies. But policy responses, including measures to contain the virus and liquidity injections to sustain finance, reinforced robust fundamentals and quickly stabilized regional financial markets. Portfolio flows into Asia resumed since May, and most regional currencies have recovered. However, risk sentiment in equity and bond markets has not fully returned to pre-pandemic readings.

■ **Asian governments pledged wide-ranging crisis response.** The value of policy support packages announced to the end of August amounted in aggregate to $3.6 trillion, about 15% of regional GDP, and is fairly evenly divided between direct income support and measures to shore up liquidity and credit. Since March, the authorities in the major advanced economies and Asia have eased their monetary policies. Financing conditions in some segments nevertheless remain tight. An Asian Development Bank survey conducted in four Southeast Asian economies found more than half of micro, small, and medium-sized enterprises facing severe shortages of working capital and inadequate access to formal financial services. This raises concerns about debt-service capacity and business sustainability.

■ **Regional GDP will contract this year for the first time in 6 decades.** As the pandemic persists, developing Asia is projected to contract by 0.7% in 2020—the first regional GDP contraction since the early 1960s. Developing Asia excluding the newly industrialized economies will also contract by 0.5%. Growth is forecast to rebound to 6.8% in 2021, but this will still leave GDP next year substantially below expectations before COVID-19. Thus, the regional recovery will be L-shaped or "swoosh-shaped" rather than V-shaped.

■ **Depressed demand and lower oil prices will contain regional inflation.** The 2020 inflation forecast for the whole region is revised down from 3.2% to 2.9% as the slowdown in demand is expected to outweigh inflationary supply-side disruptions, and with the abatement of last year's food price shocks. More muted inflation expectations do not apply to South or Central Asia, however, where inflation forecasts are revised up on supply disruption due to the pandemic and, in some economies, currency depreciation. Inflation in 2021 is expected to ease further to 2.3%.

■ **The current account surplus is projected stable in 2020 and 2021.** The regional current account surplus will hold steady at the equivalent of 1.4% of aggregate GDP in 2020 and 2021. With supply disruption and waning global demand, trade will shrink further in 2020 but is projected to recover in 2021 as regional and global economic activity picks up. Surpluses are expected little changed in East and Southeast Asia, as both exports and imports decline. South Asia's current account deficit will narrow marginally as imports plummet along with domestic demand before widening again. Central Asia's deficit will widen as commodity exports decline. Surpluses in the Pacific will narrow due to subdued tourism.

■ **Risks tilt to the downside and center on COVID-19.** A prolonged pandemic—either an extended first wave in some economies or recurrent waves in others—is the main risk to the outlook, as it would require protracted caution and containment measures, with consequent disruption to both supply and demand. Protracted weakness induced by COVID-19 could trigger crises in some countries with debt sustainability issues or financial vulnerabilities. Another risk would be worsening geopolitical tensions, most notably potential for US–PRC friction over trade and technology to intensify.

Outlook by subregion

■ **Developing Asia stalls in 2020 but will start to recover in 2021.** Aggregate economic output will contract by 0.7% in 2020 and rebound by 6.8% in 2021. The downturn is across the board, with almost three-fourths of the region's economies—but not the heavily weighted PRC—expected to contract this year. Consequently, 2020 growth forecasts for all subregions are revised down from *ADO 2020* and for all but East Asia further downgraded from the June *ADO Supplement*. Looking ahead to 2021, the subregions with upgraded growth forecasts are East, South, and Southeast Asia.

■ **East Asia is slowing more this year but will rebound higher next year.** The subregional forecast is for growth in both years, at 1.3% in 2020 and 7.0% in 2021. Expansion in the PRC will weaken from 6.1% in 2019 to 1.8% this year, as anticipated in the June *ADO Supplement*, after broad restrictions on movement and economic activity induced sharp contraction in the first quarter. With this and other public health measures having contained the COVID-19 virus, the PRC economy is now expected to gather momentum in the second half of this year and grow by 7.7% next year, above previous projections. Taipei,China will similarly avoid GDP shrinkage this year owing to accommodative policies and should rebound robustly next year. The rest of East Asia will see output contract in 2020 as the pandemic continues to take a huge toll but will likewise see stronger growth in 2021. Hong Kong, China—already pushed into recession in 2019 by political turmoil at home and trade tensions between the US and the PRC, will suffer the subregion's sharpest output decline this year but looks set to grow by 5.1% in 2021. Similarly, Mongolia and the Republic of Korea will contract this year, much as forecast in the June *ADO Supplement*, and return to growth next year. Inflation forecasts for East Asia are tweaked, to reflect diminished demand, down to 2.6% in 2020 and 1.7% in 2021.

■ **South Asia sees economic woes deepen as COVID-19 spreads.** The subregion is now expected to shrink by a steep 6.8% in 2020 and rebound by 7.1% in 2021. India began its fiscal year with April–June quarterly GDP contracting by a record 23.9% as a pandemic lockdown clobbered consumer and business spending. The economy having weakened even before the pandemic struck, the government enjoyed little fiscal space with which to respond. Indian GDP is expected to fall by 9.0% in the whole of this fiscal year and then grow by 8.0% in the next. Maldives and Sri Lanka, heavily dependent on tourism, will be among the hardest hit. Output in Maldives is expected to shrink by a fifth in 2020, the sharpest GDP forecast revision in the subregion, then grow by 10.5% in 2021. Growth expectations for Afghanistan have also worsened, with output forecast to decline by 5.0% this year. Output will inch up by 1.5% next year as the country continues to grapple with political and security instability. Bangladesh, Bhutan, and Nepal managed to grow in their recently completed fiscal years because COVID-19 affected only their tail end. They are set to continue expanding in the current fiscal year, though only minimally for Bhutan and Nepal. Inflationary pressures have begun to intensify in South Asia, especially in India, as supply chain disruption pushed up food prices. The 2020 inflation forecast for the subregion is thus adjusted upward, with prices now expected to rise by 5.2%. The subregional inflation forecast for 2021 is revised up marginally to 4.5%.

■ **Southeast Asia retrenches, waging tough battles with the virus.** Strict quarantines and travel restrictions inflicted brutal second-quarter economic declines in the subregion, requiring steep downgrades to 2020 GDP growth forecasts for almost every economy. The quarter featured double-digit contractions in Malaysia, the Philippines, Singapore, and Thailand, all of which are now expected to shrink by 5% or more this year. Projected subregional GDP is thus revised down by nearly 5 percentage points to 3.8% contraction in 2020, with the forecast rebound revised up by nearly 1 point to 5.5% growth in 2021, enabled crucially by domestic stimulus. As COVID-19 infections continue to rise in some countries, notably Indonesia and the Philippines, and surprise outbreaks reappear elsewhere in the subregion, most prominently Viet Nam, economic recovery will continue to be slow and painful, largely determined by developments in world trade and the global economy. Resilient exports of petrochemicals from Brunei Darussalam, agricultural products from Myanmar, and work-from-home electronics from Viet Nam are forecast to keep these three source economies in growth territory this year. As slow demand and low world oil prices continue to dampen price pressure in the subregion, inflation is forecast to dip by half to 1.0% in 2020—with deflation in Malaysia, Singapore, and Thailand—and revive to trend at 2.3% in 2021.

■ **Central Asian economic prospects continue to dim.** Subregional GDP forecasts are downgraded from low growth to 2.1% contraction in 2020 and tepid 3.9% growth in 2021. *ADO 2020* output projections for all economies in Central Asia are revised down as quarantines and mobility restrictions have greatly weakened economic activity. GDP in Kazakhstan, the subregion's largest economy, is now projected to contract by 3.2% in 2020, as the pandemic response hits services hard, and then recover by 2.8% in 2021. GDP decline in the Kyrgyz Republic is expected to be far worse, by 10.0% this year, with growth at 4.0% next year. As low global oil prices generate further headwinds for hydrocarbon exporters, Azerbaijan is now expected to contract by 4.3% this year, rather than hold its own as previously forecast, then post fragile 1.2% growth in 2021. Tourism-dependent Armenia and Georgia and remittance-dependent Tajikistan will contract this year, leaving only Turkmenistan and Uzbekistan able to grow in 2020. Supply constraints under lockdown and, in some economies, currency depreciation will likely stir inflation. The forecast for subregional inflation is therefore adjusted significantly upward to 8.3% this year and less so to 6.6% next year, despite GDP projected to grow in all Central Asian economies in 2021.

■ **The Pacific suffers crippling economic contraction this year.** As measures in the Pacific and beyond to address the COVID-19 public health crisis weigh heavily on the subregion, its forecast GDP is revised down substantially, to 6.1% contraction this year and only minimal growth in 2021. Risks to forecasts persist on the downside. Fiji, the second largest economy in the Pacific, suffers the steepest downward revision and, with tourist arrivals ground to a halt, is forecast to contract by nearly a fifth in 2020, followed by just 1.0% growth in 2021. Other tourism-dependent economies in the subregion are similarly buffeted, with the Cook Islands, Palau, and Vanuatu contracting substantially in 2020 and likely to falter further in 2021. In their current fiscal year—the first fully encompassed by the pandemic—the Cook Islands and Palau are forecast to sink deeper with double-digit GDP declines.

As quarantine requirements on shipping disrupt transport and trade, output in Papua New Guinea, the subregion's largest economy, is now projected to shrink by 2.9% in 2020 and expand by just 2.5% in 2021. Similarly, constraints on air transport have weakened tuna transhipment in the Federated States of Micronesia and the Marshall Islands, converting growth forecasts to contraction, though easing in 2021. Weaker remittance inflows, weather shocks, and other public health issues deepened contraction in Samoa and Tonga in their recently completed fiscal years, while infrastructure and other project delays push Nauru into contraction this year and impede activity in Kiribati and Tuvalu, the only two economies in the Pacific still forecast to grow in 2020. Average inflation is expected to stay benign at 2.8% in 2020, little changed from 2019 or the *ADO 2020* forecast, and at 3.1% in 2021, revised down on account of continuing economic doldrums.

Wellness in worrying times

Summary

❖ ***Wellness is vital for post-pandemic recovery in developing Asia.*** *COVID-19 underlines the importance of wellness, or the deliberate pursuit of activities that bring holistic health, happiness, and well-being. Public health, both physical and mental, has taken a beating during this pandemic. In Asia, as elsewhere, wellness can revive the human body, mind, and spirit, which are the first steps toward rebuilding the economy and society.*

❖ ***Wellness is a large and growing part of the Asian economy.*** *Even before COVID-19, Asians demanded more wellness as their incomes rose, chronic lifestyle diseases became more prevalent, and the population aged. A result has been a rapidly growing wellness economy, comprising industries that enable consumers to incorporate wellness activities into their daily lives. The wellness economy provides 11% of output in Asian countries, having grown annually by 10% in recent years. COVID-19 is likely to further boost demand in the coming years and support a strong recovery.*

❖ ***Asian wellness traditions can serve both well-being and the economy.*** *Although modern wellness industries originated in Western countries, Asia has a wealth of wellness traditions. Those traditions are productive assets for the wellness economy. At the same time, tapping these traditions can promote mental and physical health in the lives of Asians. As such, the present is the opportune time for Asia to rediscover its wellness roots.*

❖ ***Wellness policies should be comprehensive and target all Asians.*** *Government efforts to boost physical and mental well-being fall into four policy domains: create a healthy urban environment, enable and support physical activity, encourage healthy diets, and enhance wellness in the workplace. Because healthy aging begins in childhood, a lifelong wellness policy framework such as Japan's 100-Year Life Program should complement the four policy domains. And, because the poor have fewer opportunities for wellness activities, governments must invest in wellness infrastructure that benefits them.*

COVID-19 brings wellness to the fore

■ **Wellness is conceptually distinct from happiness and well-being.** It is the active pursuit of activities, choices, and lifestyles that lead to a state of holistic health. Whereas happiness and well-being are subjective conditions when one feels happy or in a state of well-being, wellness arises from the process of actively choosing options that enable optimal health and well-being. Wellness is related to but distinct from medical health. The two overlap in preventive health care, but medical care focuses primarily on treating and curing illness, while wellness aims to improve on neutral health to achieve optimal health by, most notably, exercising, eating healthy food, and meditating. Wellness is thus multidimensional and holistic in that it has physical, mental, emotional, and social dimensions.

■ **The pandemic spotlights both physical and mental wellness.** Medical evidence indicates much higher risk from COVID-19 for individuals with underlying physical health conditions such as obesity, asthma, or diabetes, as well as for the elderly.

Meanwhile, pandemic-induced isolation, fear, uncertainty, and economic hardship are causing a lot of stress and anxiety around the world. A recent United Nations report warns of a global mental health crisis, with current rates of mental distress at 35% in the PRC and 45% in the US. The crisis thus strengthens the case for individuals to take action to strengthen their own physical and mental health.

■ **Demand for wellness reflects three broad, long-term trends.** These trends are higher incomes, the rising prevalence of chronic lifestyle diseases, and aging populations. Decades of rapid economic growth have left many Asians much richer than their forebears. Consequently, they are more aware of the benefits of healthier lifestyles as, most starkly, hunger for more calories gives way to a quest for better nutrition. The rise of conditions such as heart disease, stroke, diabetes, and cancer—as well as maladies caused by worsening pollution in the region—encourages Asians to exercise more, eat better, and make healthier life choices. In addition, Asia's population is aging, and older populations are vulnerable to chronic diseases, loneliness, and mental health issues.

■ **Wellness is pro-poor and contributes to sustainable development.** Wellness, or the active pursuit of well-being, aligns with the United Nations Sustainable Development Goals, in particular the third goal: Ensure healthy lives and promote well-being for all at all ages. A focus on wellness promises to bring a more balanced and holistic view of development than does measuring its progress simply as increased income per capita. In principle, many wellness activities such as physical exercise are available to all. In practice, though, the poor are disadvantaged by their relative lack of money and time to devote to wellness, of access to health facilities, and of ready knowledge of nutritious food. These gaps can be narrowed with public investment in wellness infrastructure such as community recreation centers and green parks in poor neighborhoods, as well as health education campaigns.

The contours of wellness in Asia

■ **Wellness in developing Asia is on a par with the rest of world.** This report constructs the Wellness Index designed to compare wellness across countries and regions. The index measures four pillars of wellness—physical, intellectual, social, and environmental—using a number of outcome indicators. The Wellness Index reading for developing Asia is 47, close to the global figure of 52. Substantial differences across Asia only partly reflect variation in development stage. To be sure, rich countries such as the Republic of Korea tend to have higher wellness scores, but so do some lower-income countries, notably Bhutan.

■ **Wellness is a large and growing part of the regional economy.** The Global Wellness Institute describes the wellness economy as industries that enable consumers to incorporate wellness activities and lifestyles into their daily lives. It estimates the global wellness economy at $4.5 trillion in 2018, equal to 5% of global GDP. It is an even bigger part of the economy of developing Asia. ADB estimates that the wellness economy provided 11% of regional GDP in 2017 and that it has been growing by about 10% annually in recent years. The rapid growth of the wellness economy reflects Asians' growing demand for wellness.

Demand is likely to expand further in the wake of the COVID-19 pandemic, which has restricted physical exercise and caused a lot of anxiety and stress.

Holistic pathway to physical wellness

- **Physical inactivity is a worsening threat to regional public health.** Physical inactivity is a key lifestyle risk factor for chronic disease. While 33.2% of Asians regularly participate in recreational physical activity, this is somewhat below the global average of 35.5%. Inactivity rates are generally worse in South Asia and better in East Asia, Southeast Asia, and the Pacific. Asia has one of the world's largest and most diverse physical activity markets, valued at $240 billion in 2018, with sports and active recreation being the most popular activities. That said, many Asians spend little or nothing when pursuing leisure-time physical activity on the streets, at home, or in public parks, plazas, and free sporting facilities. Governments can support participation in physical activity after COVID-19 recedes by investing in venues for sports and physical recreation.

- **Asia can ill afford its increasingly unwell workplace.** The region accounted for over two-thirds of the 2.8 million people estimated to have died worldwide in 2017 from work-related accidents or disease. Workplace wellness is still a little-known concept in Asia, benefiting primarily those who work for multinational corporations or live in the region's wealthiest countries and cities. Only 5.2% of all employed workers in Asia stand to benefit from some form of workplace wellness program—barely half of the low 9.8% of workers globally. To be effective, a workplace wellness framework must be holistic and focus first on wellness challenges that arise within the workplace. Today, staying well while working from home is emerging as a new priority under widespread COVID-19 restrictions.

- **Community planning, zoning, and infrastructure can promote wellness.** When human health and wellness are central to urban planning, real estate, and infrastructure development, the result is wellness real estate—a $134 billion industry in 2017, with Asia and the Pacific accounting for $47 billion. Public investment can similarly focus built environments on wellness. For example, governments can invest in infrastructure that encourages physical activity: pedestrian sidewalks, paths and trails, and public parks. Such planning approaches create neighborhoods and communities that are healthier for residents and that enhance their well-being and the quality of life.

- **The double burden of malnutrition is a growing risk to health.** Food has become more readily available across the region, reducing malnutrition but encouraging unhealthy eating as poor choices of calories sources bring too much sugar, salt, and fat. As a result, the region has become a global hotspot for the double burden of malnutrition: concurrent undernutrition and obesity. Poor nutrition inflicts significant economic costs. Direct medical costs from obesity, for instance, are estimated to absorb 0.8% of regional GDP. Policies can favor healthy foods, as through targeted taxes that drive down demand for sugary drinks. Public education on nutrition can guide consumers toward better diets and minimize the burden on the public health-care system.

Leveraging Asian traditions for mental wellness

- **The path to mental well-being is self-managed and evidence-based.** The five pillars of mental wellness are emotional well-being, psychological well-being, resilience and balance, optimal functioning, and social well-being. Poor mental health—evidenced by depression, is the third-biggest cause of years lost to disability, after lower-back pain and headache. Yet many Asian economies have fewer than one mental health professional per 100,000 population. Evidence supports the benefits to mental wellness from healthy everyday habits such as eating well and seeking social support, as well as such specialized wellness enablers as meditation, tai chi, yoga, dance, and social laughter. Benefits are amplified if wellness is practiced in tune with local culture by, for example, basing optimal nutrition on local cuisine.

- **Asians can draw from a plethora of established wellness traditions.** Asia's two major systems of traditional health knowledge—Chinese and ayurvedic medicine—are grounded on principles of healthy living and wellness through the whole of life. These two systems have influenced not only the wellness traditions of East and South Asia, where they arose, but also Southeast Asia. Lifestyle is given primary emphasis over medicine. Individual wellness practices that leverage these traditions offer a low-cost avenue to mental and overall wellness that is culturally relevant, evidence-based, and self-managed. A growing body of scientific evidence confirms the wellness benefits of Asian wellness traditions. As a bonus, these traditions can reduce public health care costs and provide new economic opportunities.

- **An aging Asian population makes healthy aging an urgent priority.** The share of developing Asia's population aged 65 or older is rising, from 6% in 2010 to 9% in 2020 and a projected 18% in 2050. Evidence indicates that older populations generate greater demand for wellness. For example, a 1% increase in the share of population aged 65 or older boosts hot spring revenues by 0.29%. While mental and physical health naturally deteriorates with age, eating healthier food, including traditional Asian food, and exercising regularly can improve how well populations age. Optimizing home design helps, as does reducing isolation through technology and social support. The evidence is mixed about the impact of retirement on wellness, but it is clear that wellness in old age depends on staying mentally and physically active and fit, whether retired or not.

- **Wellness tourism is a growing segment of the tourism industry.** While almost all tourism activities encourages rest and relaxation and is thus beneficial to mental wellness, a key driver of rapid tourism growth in Asia is wellness tourism, which lies at the intersection of the $2.7 trillion global tourism industry and the $4.5 trillion global wellness industry. Wellness tourism, defined as travel designed to maintain or enhance personal well-being, generated $639 billion in revenue globally in 2017 and $137 billion in Asia and the Pacific. Global tourism has been hit very hard by COVID-19. Beyond the short term, countries with post-COVID recovery strategies that strengthen the sustainability of wellness tourism will be among those that benefit the most from global economic recovery.

Wellness for happiness and inclusiveness

■ **Subjective happiness is low in Asia relative to other regions.** Sustained rapid growth has lifted developing Asia's living standards in recent decades. Yet research indicates that higher income does not necessarily translate into greater happiness. As a result, happiness has recently attracted a lot of attention. The rise of positive psychology as a field of enquiry indicates burgeoning academic interest, and Bhutan's famous gross national happiness index is emblematic of growing interest among policy makers. The *World Happiness Report 2019* states that, despite rapid economic growth, self-reported happiness in Asia averages 5.17 on a scale of 0 to 10, substantially lower than in every other region except Africa and the Middle East and the global average of 5.46. Some poorer countries such as Pakistan and the Philippines are relatively happy countries.

■ **Empirical evidence associates wellness with happiness.** The wellness economy can, in principle, generate greater well-being. Recreational physical therapy, workplace wellness programs, and spa therapy are examples of wellness enterprise geared toward better health outcomes, which are central to well-being. Empirical analysis across 146 countries confirms a significant positive association between wellness and happiness. Thus, if annual spending per capita on workplace wellness doubled from the current world average of $11 to $22, happiness would improve by 0.15 units on a scale of 0 to 10.

■ **The wellness economy can promote inclusive growth.** Developing Asia has a large, fast-growing wellness economy. Wellness tourism expenditure in the region grew by 11% annually from 2015 to 2017, reaching $137 billion as the industry directly employed 3.74 million in India, 1.78 million in the PRC, and 0.53 million in Thailand. In addition, demand for many wellness products, such as local and traditional culinary experiences and goods, can encourage micro or small enterprises to leverage local heritage and indigenous ingredients toward their creation. As many wellness-related occupations, such as complementary medicine practitioners, are dominated by women, growth in the wellness economy contributes to female employment. In these ways, the wellness economy can enable inclusive growth and reduce poverty.

Policies for physical and mental wellness

■ **Government policies that promote wellness offer broad benefits.** Individuals, the economy, and society as a whole benefit where wellness makes people happier and more productive and wellness industries are a growing part of the economy. Yet, because wellness is poorly understood by governments, they do not incorporate it into policy making as an overarching framework or explicit priority. Meanwhile, wellness can bring an important perspective to policy making that complements public health, health policy, and the emerging field of happiness. Wellness policies are those that nudge people to proactively make healthy choices and live healthy lifestyles, while also creating living environments that support and encourage healthy behavior and lifestyles. Such policies are most effective if they address four cross-cutting domains and take a lifespan approach, as explained below.

■ **Wellness policies span four cross-cutting policy domains.** First, Asian governments can help create a healthy built environment by, for example, prioritizing walkability and physical movement in urban and regional planning. Second, policy makers can enable and support physical activity by funding public infrastructure, facilities, and programs for it. Third, governments can encourage healthy eating by improving consumer awareness of nutrition and diet. Finally, Asian policy makers can enhance wellness in the workplace by ensuring a safe and healthy physical work environment. Taken together, policies in these four cross-cutting domains can promote mental and physical wellness.

■ **A lifespan approach safeguards mental and physical health from birth.** Healthy aging begins in childhood and progresses through an overarching lifespan framework such as Japan's 100-Year Life Program. Preventive interventions in an individual's first 1,000 days bring lifelong benefits. Further, wellness is worth adding to the formal education system, embedded in curricula and in learning and social environments. Finally, a range of policies can support healthy aging, including lifelong learning, reskilling, personal growth and transformation, and, for seniors, better nutrition and safe homes that enable wellness. In conjunction with cross-cutting wellness policies, lifelong wellness policies can help Asians navigate the uncertain, stressful COVID-19 world toward a better new normal after the pandemic.

GDP growth rate, % per year

	2019	2020			2021		
		April ADO 2020	*June ADOS*	*September Update*	*April ADO 2020*	*June ADOS*	*September Update*
Central Asia	4.9	2.8	−0.5	−2.1	4.2	4.2	3.9
Armenia	7.6	2.2	−3.5	−4.0	4.5	3.5	3.5
Azerbaijan	2.2	0.5	−0.1	−4.3	1.5	1.2	1.2
Georgia	5.1	0.0	−5.0	−5.0	4.5	5.0	4.5
Kazakhstan	4.5	1.8	−1.2	−3.2	3.6	3.4	2.8
Kyrgyz Republic	4.5	4.0	−5.0	−10.0	4.5	4.0	4.0
Tajikistan	7.5	5.5	−3.6	−0.5	5.0	7.0	6.0
Turkmenistan	6.3	6.0	3.2	3.2	5.8	5.8	5.8
Uzbekistan	5.6	4.7	1.5	0.5	5.8	6.5	6.5
East Asia	5.4	2.0	1.3	1.3	6.5	6.8	7.0
Hong Kong, China	−1.2	−3.3	−6.5	−6.5	3.5	5.1	5.1
Mongolia	5.1	2.1	−1.9	−2.6	4.6	4.7	5.1
People's Republic of China	6.1	2.3	1.8	1.8	7.3	7.4	7.7
Republic of Korea	2.0	1.3	−1.0	−1.0	2.3	3.5	3.3
Taipei,China	2.7	1.8	0.8	0.8	2.5	3.5	3.5
South Asia	4.3	4.1	−3.0	−6.8	6.0	4.9	7.1
Afghanistan	3.0	3.0	−4.5	−5.0	4.0	3.0	1.5
Bangladesh	8.2	7.8	4.5	5.2	8.0	7.5	6.8
Bhutan	4.4	5.2	2.4	2.4	5.8	1.7	1.7
India	4.2	4.0	−4.0	−9.0	6.2	5.0	8.0
Maldives	5.9	−3.0	−11.3	−20.5	7.5	13.7	10.5
Nepal	7.0	5.3	2.3	2.3	6.4	3.1	1.5
Pakistan	1.9	2.6	−0.4	−0.4	3.2	2.0	2.0
Sri Lanka	2.3	2.2	−6.1	−5.5	3.5	4.1	4.1
Southeast Asia	4.4	1.0	−2.7	−3.8	4.7	5.2	5.5
Brunei Darussalam	3.9	2.0	1.4	1.4	3.0	3.0	3.0
Cambodia	7.1	2.3	−5.5	−4.0	5.7	5.9	5.9
Indonesia	5.0	2.5	−1.0	−1.0	5.0	5.3	5.3
Lao People's Democratic Republic	5.0	3.5	−0.5	−2.5	6.0	4.5	4.5
Malaysia	4.3	0.5	−4.0	−5.0	5.5	6.5	6.5
Myanmar	6.8	4.2	1.8	1.8	6.8	6.0	6.0
Philippines	6.0	2.0	−3.8	−7.3	6.5	6.5	6.5
Singapore	0.7	0.2	−6.0	−6.2	2.0	3.2	4.5
Thailand	2.4	−4.8	−6.5	−8.0	2.5	3.5	4.5
Timor-Leste	3.4	−2.0	−3.7	−6.3	4.0	4.0	3.3
Viet Nam	7.0	4.8	4.1	1.8	6.8	6.8	6.3
The Pacific	3.5	−0.3	−4.3	−6.1	2.7	1.6	1.3
Cook Islands	5.3	−2.2	−9.0	−7.0	1.0	−15.4	−15.4
Federated States of Micronesia	1.2	1.6	−2.0	−5.4	3.0	−1.5	−1.9
Fiji	−1.3	−4.9	−15.0	−19.8	3.0	−0.7	1.0
Kiribati	2.4	1.6	0.6	0.6	1.8	1.8	1.8
Marshall Islands	3.8	2.5	−5.5	−5.5	3.7	−1.4	−1.4
Nauru	1.0	0.4	−1.7	−1.7	1.1	0.8	0.5
Niue	...	...	...	...	...	...	...
Palau	−1.8	−4.5	−9.5	−9.5	1.2	−12.8	−12.8
Papua New Guinea	5.0	0.8	−1.5	−2.9	2.8	2.9	2.5
Samoa	3.5	−3.0	−5.0	−5.0	0.8	−2.0	−9.7
Solomon Islands	1.2	1.5	−6.0	−6.0	2.7	2.5	1.0
Tonga	0.7	0.0	−3.0	−3.0	2.5	−4.0	−8.0
Tuvalu	4.1	2.7	2.0	2.0	3.2	2.5	2.5
Vanuatu	2.9	−1.0	−9.8	−9.8	2.5	2.0	1.0
Developing Asia	5.1	2.2	0.1	−0.7	6.2	6.2	6.8
Developing Asia excluding the NIEs	5.6	2.4	0.4	−0.5	6.7	6.6	7.2

... = unavailable, ADOS = ADO Supplement, GDP = gross domestic product, NIEs = newly industrialized economies (Hong Kong, China; the Republic of Korea; Singapore; and Taipei,China).

Inflation, % per year

	2019	2020			2021		
		April ADO 2020	June ADOS	September Update	April ADO 2020	June ADOS	September Update
Central Asia	7.5	7.6	8.0	8.3	6.3	6.6	6.6
Armenia	1.4	2.8	1.2	1.4	2.2	2.5	2.2
Azerbaijan	2.6	2.5	2.8	3.8	3.5	3.5	3.2
Georgia	4.9	4.5	5.0	6.0	3.0	3.5	4.5
Kazakhstan	5.3	6.0	7.9	7.7	5.7	6.2	6.2
Kyrgyz Republic	1.1	3.5	7.0	7.0	3.0	5.0	5.0
Tajikistan	8.0	9.0	10.0	9.5	8.0	8.5	8.5
Turkmenistan	13.4	13.0	8.0	10.0	8.0	8.0	8.0
Uzbekistan	14.6	13.0	13.0	13.0	10.0	10.0	10.0
East Asia	2.6	3.2	2.9	2.6	1.8	1.8	1.7
Hong Kong, China	2.9	2.0	1.5	1.5	2.5	2.5	2.5
Mongolia	7.3	6.6	6.4	5.6	7.9	8.2	8.2
People's Republic of China	2.9	3.6	3.3	3.0	1.9	1.9	1.8
Republic of Korea	0.4	0.9	0.5	0.5	1.3	1.3	1.3
Taipei,China	0.6	0.4	0.2	0.2	0.8	0.8	0.8
South Asia	5.0	4.1	4.0	5.2	4.4	4.5	4.5
Afghanistan	2.3	2.3	5.0	5.0	3.5	4.5	4.5
Bangladesh	5.5	5.6	5.6	5.7	5.5	5.5	5.5
Bhutan	2.8	3.8	2.8	3.0	4.0	4.0	4.0
India	4.8	3.0	3.0	4.5	3.8	4.0	4.0
Maldives	0.2	1.0	1.0	0.5	1.2	1.2	1.5
Nepal	4.6	6.0	6.6	6.2	5.5	6.5	5.5
Pakistan	6.8	11.5	11.0	10.7	8.3	8.0	7.5
Sri Lanka	4.3	5.0	4.0	4.5	4.8	4.2	4.2
Southeast Asia	2.1	1.9	1.0	1.0	2.2	2.3	2.3
Brunei Darussalam	-0.4	-0.2	0.4	1.4	0.1	0.4	1.0
Cambodia	1.9	2.1	2.1	2.1	1.8	1.8	1.8
Indonesia	2.8	3.0	2.0	2.0	2.8	2.8	2.8
Lao People's Democratic Republic	3.3	4.0	5.5	5.5	4.5	5.0	5.0
Malaysia	0.7	1.0	-1.5	-1.5	1.3	2.5	2.0
Myanmar	8.6	7.5	6.0	6.0	7.5	6.0	6.0
Philippines	2.5	2.2	2.2	2.4	2.4	2.4	2.6
Singapore	0.6	0.7	-0.2	-0.3	1.3	0.8	1.0
Thailand	0.7	-0.9	-1.3	-1.6	0.4	0.7	0.8
Timor-Leste	1.5	1.3	1.3	1.0	1.8	1.8	1.0
Viet Nam	2.8	3.3	3.0	3.3	3.5	3.5	3.5
The Pacific	3.0	2.7	2.9	2.8	3.8	3.8	3.1
Cook Islands	0.8	1.5	1.5	1.5	1.7	1.7	1.7
Federated States of Micronesia	-1.0	0.5	0.5	1.6	1.0	1.0	1.9
Fiji	1.8	1.5	1.2	0.5	3.5	3.0	1.3
Kiribati	-1.8	1.0	1.0	1.0	1.1	1.1	1.1
Marshall Islands	0.1	0.3	0.3	0.3	0.5	0.5	0.5
Nauru	3.9	2.8	1.5	1.5	2.3	1.7	1.7
Niue	...	...	...	...	...	...	...
Palau	0.6	0.4	0.4	0.4	0.8	0.8	0.8
Papua New Guinea	3.6	3.3	3.3	3.3	4.4	4.4	3.8
Samoa	2.2	2.0	2.8	1.9	2.5	2.5	2.2
Solomon Islands	1.6	2.0	4.5	6.0	2.3	3.0	3.0
Tonga	3.2	1.3	1.3	1.6	2.2	1.8	2.0
Tuvalu	3.3	3.5	3.0	3.0	3.5	3.0	3.0
Vanuatu	2.8	1.5	4.0	3.0	2.0	2.2	2.2
Developing Asia	2.9	3.2	2.9	2.9	2.3	2.4	2.3
Developing Asia excluding the NIEs	3.3	3.6	3.2	3.2	2.5	2.5	2.5

... = unavailable, ADOS = ADO Supplement, NIEs = newly industrialized economies (Hong Kong, China; the Republic of Korea; Singapore; and Taipei,China).

1

A PRECARIOUS PATH
TO RECOVERY

A precarious path to recovery

Developing Asia's growth results and prospects have further deteriorated since Asian Development Outlook 2020 (ADO 2020) *was published in April. As Coronavirus Disease 2019 (COVID-19) continued to expand regionally and globally, containment measures to counter the pandemic stifled economic activity. Domestic demand and production plummeted, and plunging global economic activity slashed external demand. Governments in the region responded with diverse policy measures. After nosediving at first, capital flows, financial markets, and currencies have recovered. Recent data suggest that the crisis may have bottomed out, but the picture across the region is mixed. In particular, the two largest economies in the region are diverging as nascent recovery in the People's Republic of China (PRC) contrasts with continued fragility in India.*

With aggregate gross domestic product (GDP) forecast to contract by 0.7% in 2020, developing Asia will suffer contraction this year for the first time since the early 1960s (Figure 1.0.1A). The downturn is across the board, with almost three-fourths of regional economies projected to contract— the largest such share in the past 6 decades (Figure 1.0.1B). Growth projected at 6.8% in 2021 will still leave the level of GDP substantially smaller than forecast before COVID-19. Depressed demand and lower oil prices will keep regional inflation muted. The regional current account surplus will remain stable despite weakened global trade.

Geopolitical tensions—most notably the persistent friction between the PRC and the United States over trade and technology—are a concern, but the prospect of a prolonged pandemic through extended first waves or recurrent outbreaks casts the largest shadow over the outlook. Prolonged containment measures would stifle economic activity and could trigger financial crises where vulnerability exists.

Figure 1.0.1A GDP growth in developing Asia

Developing Asia is now expected to contract this year...

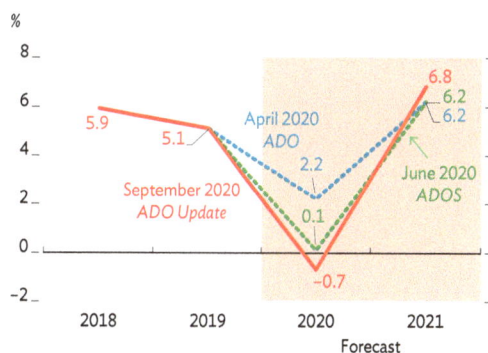

Source: *Asian Development Outlook* database.

This section was written by Abdul Abiad, Shiela Camingue-Romance, Matteo Lanzafame (lead), Irfan Qureshi, Arief Ramayandi, Marcel Schroder, Dennis Sorino, Shu Tian, Priscille Villanueva, and Mai Lin Villaruel of the Economic Research and Regional Cooperation Department, ADB, Manila, and Michael Timbang, consultant, Economic Research and Regional Cooperation Department, ADB, Manila.

Figure 1.0.1B Regional GDP growth and the share of individual economies contracting

...it is the region's first contraction in nearly six decades, and it is broad-based.

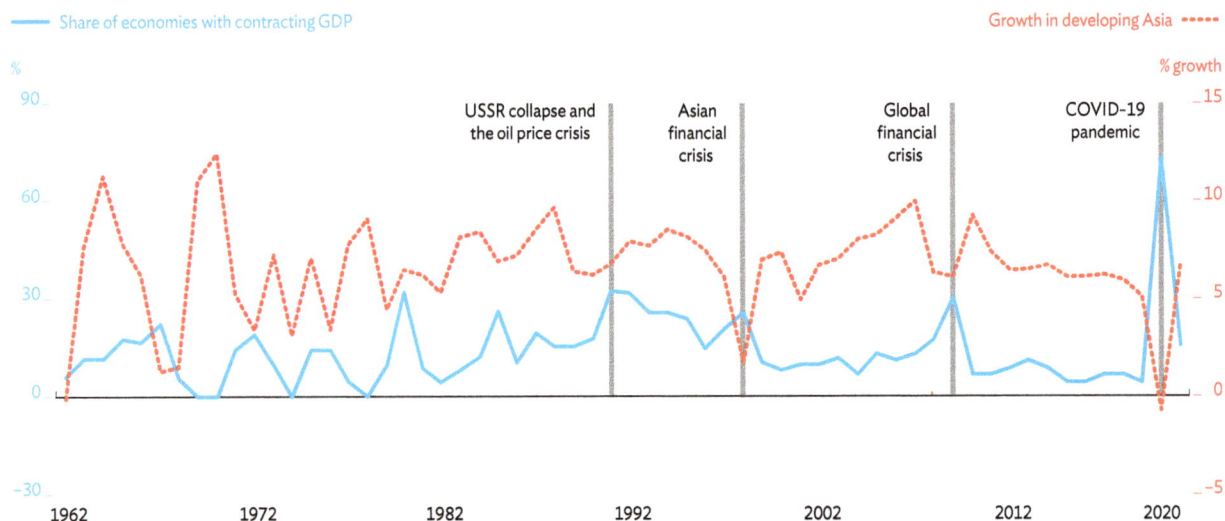

COVID-19 = Coronavirus Disease 2019, GDP = gross domestic product, USSR = Union of Soviet Socialist Republics.

Notes: The period 1962–1969 includes 17 economies: Bangladesh; China, People's Republic of; Fiji; Hong Kong, China; Georgia; India; Indonesia; Malaysia; Myanmar; Nepal; Pakistan; Papua New Guinea; the Philippines; the Republic of Korea; Singapore; Sri Lanka; and Thailand. Three economies are added in 1970 to 1979: Kiribati; Taipei,China; and Solomon Islands. Thirteen economies are added in 1980–1989: Bhutan; Cambodia; the Kyrgyz Republic, the Lao People's Democratic Republic; Marshall Islands; Micronesia, Federated States of; Samoa; Tajikistan; Tonga; Turkmenistan; Uzbekistan; Vanuatu; and Viet Nam. Nine were added in 1990–2000: Armenia, Azerbaijan, Brunei Darussalam, Cook Islands, Kazakhstan, Maldives, Mongolia, Palau, and Tuvalu. Timor-Leste was added in 2001, Afghanistan in 2003; Niue in 2004, and Nauru in 2005, bringing the total to 46.

Sources: World Bank World Development Indicators database; *Asian Development Outlook* database (accessed 31 August 2020).

1.1 Recent developments: Asia falters as COVID-19 spreads

The COVID-19 pandemic continues its global and regional spread. As of the end of August 2020, the 7-day moving average of new cases diagnosed daily exceeded 80,000 in developing Asia and 75,000 in Latin America, while the number in the US had declined from a peak of almost 70,000 to about 40,000. Europe, which was the pandemic epicenter in March and April, managed to flatten its curve but has recently seen infections rising again (Figure 1.1.1A). While the number of new cases in developing Asia is still on the rise, subregions show substantial heterogeneity. New infections daily are concentrated in South Asia, having risen to over 75,000; stabilizing in Southeast Asia at about 6,000; declining in Central Asia to 1,500, and flattened in East Asia at less than 500 (Figure 1.1.1B). Pacific island countries have remained largely free of COVID-19 but with a small number of cases recently appearing there as well.

Economies that successfully contained their outbreaks were able to achieve sustained declines in the number of new cases daily (Figure 1.1.2A). They include many economies in East Asia but also in other subregions, including Thailand in Southeast Asia and Sri Lanka in South Asia. The intensity of the authorities' containment responses to the virus has differed widely (Figure 1.1.2B), with containment measures generally more stringent where the incidence of COVID-19 cases was high or rising. Concluding that lockdowns were economically unsustainable, many governments started to loosen measures after an initial period of maximum stringency, even where domestic outbreaks had not yet been fully contained.

Stringent lockdowns have reduced mobility outside the home, impeding economic activity (Figure 1.1.3). Containment measures were less strict in parts of East Asia, where economies such as the Republic of Korea and Taipei,China relied more on massive testing, extensive contact tracing, and localized quarantines aiming to isolate virus outbreaks while still allowing continued mobility and economic activity. At the other extreme were many economies in South Asia, as well as the Philippines in Southeast Asia, that relied more heavily on stay-at-home policies and workplace and school closures, and kept them in place for longer periods. Some of these economies saw their largest contractions in the second quarter (Q2) of 2020.

Figure 1.1.1 COVID-19 daily cases

The virus continues to spread globally...

A. Global

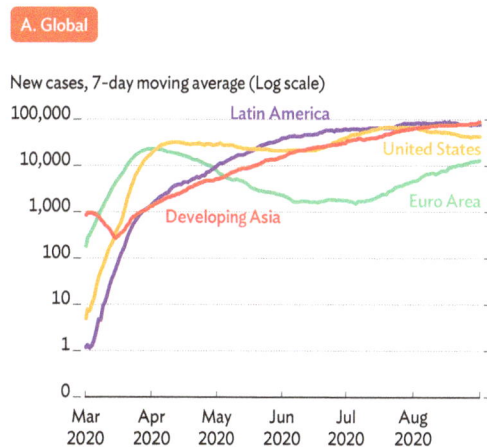

...and in developing Asia, with South Asia as the regional epicenter.

B. Developing Asia

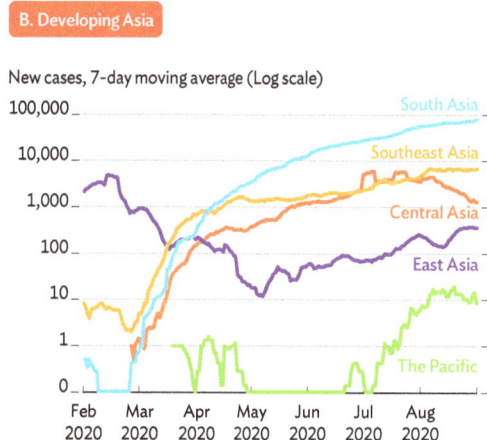

Notes: Latin America includes Argentina, Bolivia, Brazil, Chile, Colombia, Costa Rica, Cuba, the Dominican Republic, El Salvador, Guatemala, Haiti, Honduras, Mexico, Nicaragua, Panama, Paraguay, Peru, Uruguay, and Venezuela. Data as of 31 August 2020.
Sources: European Centre for Disease Prevention and Control; Johns Hopkins University; *Telegraph* UK; Worldometer (accessed 8 September 2020).

Figure 1.1.2A Change in new cases of COVID-19, selected economies

Sustained declines in new cases flattened the curve in some economies...

Weekly change in the 7-day moving average, %

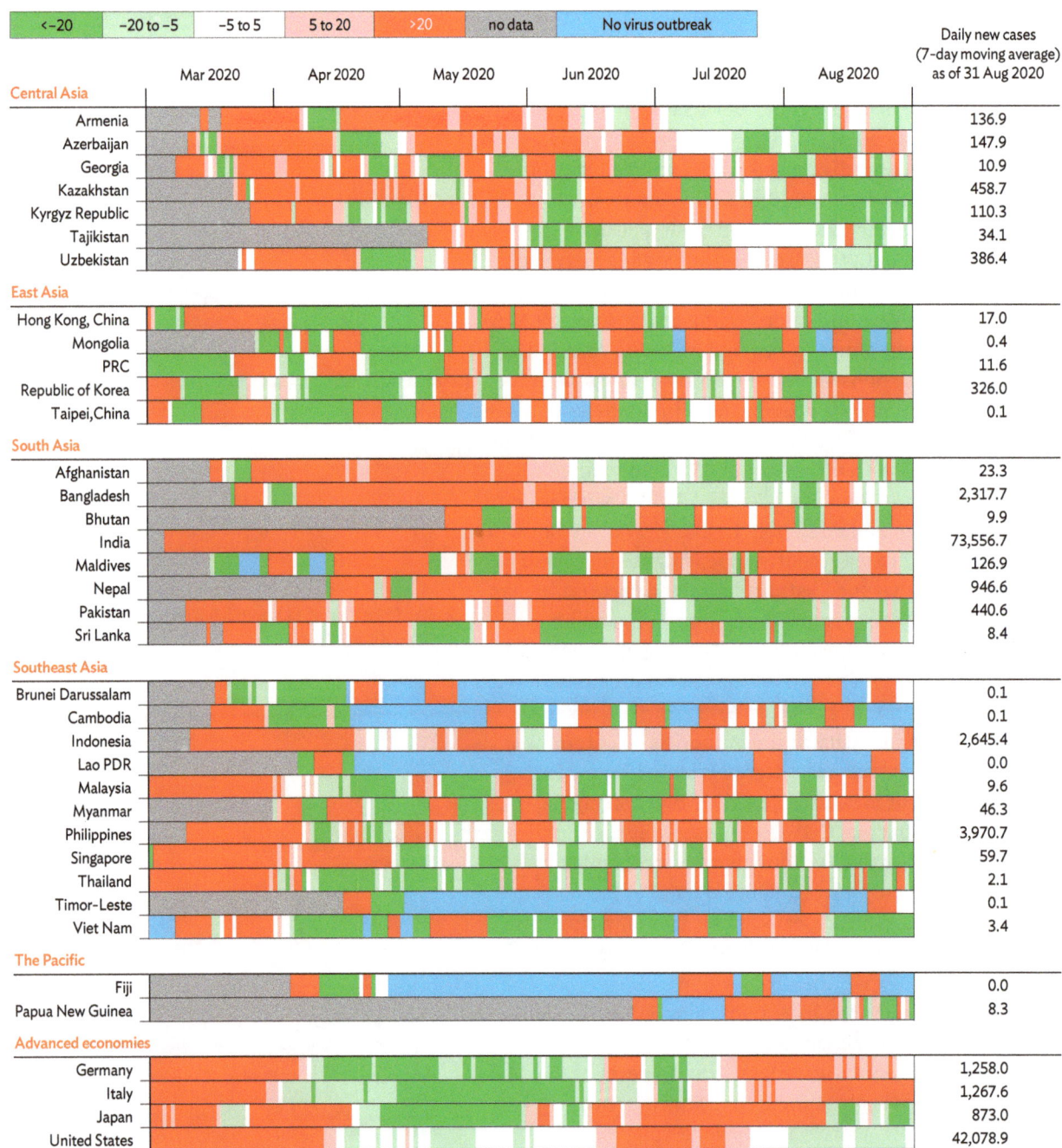

<-20	-20 to -5	-5 to 5	5 to 20	>20	no data	No virus outbreak

Time axis: Mar 2020 — Apr 2020 — May 2020 — Jun 2020 — Jul 2020 — Aug 2020

Economy	Daily new cases (7-day moving average) as of 31 Aug 2020
Central Asia	
Armenia	136.9
Azerbaijan	147.9
Georgia	10.9
Kazakhstan	458.7
Kyrgyz Republic	110.3
Tajikistan	34.1
Uzbekistan	386.4
East Asia	
Hong Kong, China	17.0
Mongolia	0.4
PRC	11.6
Republic of Korea	326.0
Taipei,China	0.1
South Asia	
Afghanistan	23.3
Bangladesh	2,317.7
Bhutan	9.9
India	73,556.7
Maldives	126.9
Nepal	946.6
Pakistan	440.6
Sri Lanka	8.4
Southeast Asia	
Brunei Darussalam	0.1
Cambodia	0.1
Indonesia	2,645.4
Lao PDR	0.0
Malaysia	9.6
Myanmar	46.3
Philippines	3,970.7
Singapore	59.7
Thailand	2.1
Timor-Leste	0.1
Viet Nam	3.4
The Pacific	
Fiji	0.0
Papua New Guinea	8.3
Advanced economies	
Germany	1,258.0
Italy	1,267.6
Japan	873.0
United States	42,078.9

Lao PDR = Lao People's Democratic Republic, PRC = People's Republic of China.

Note: Data as of 31 August 2020.

Source: European Centre for Disease Prevention and Control; Johns Hopkins University; *Telegraph* UK; Worldometer (accessed 7 September 2020).

Figure 1.1.2B Government response stringency index

...as containment measures of varying stringency were imposed in Asia, which are now being gradually relaxed.

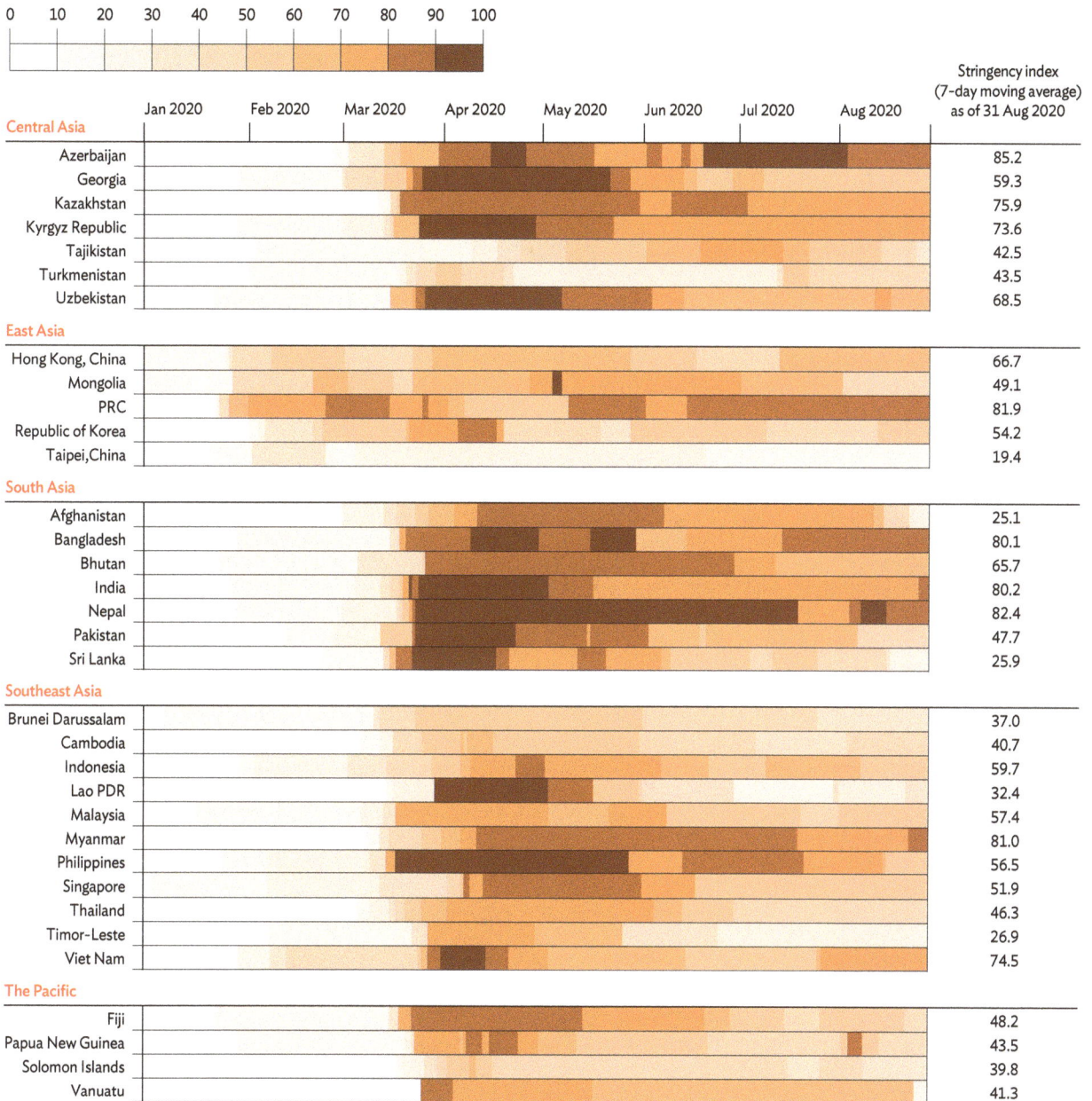

Lao PDR = Lao People's Democratic Republic, PRC = People's Republic of China.

Note: The Government Response Stringency Index is a composite measure of nine response indicators including school closure, workplace closure, and travel bans, rescaled to a value from 0 to 100, with 100 being the strictest response.

Source: Hale, T., N. Angrist, E. Cameron-Blake, L. Hallas, B. Kira, S. Majumdar, A. Petherick, T. Phillips, H. Tatlow, and S. Webster. 2020. Oxford COVID-19 Government Response Tracker. Blavatnik School of Government. University of Oxford (accessed 7 September 2020).

Figure 1.1.3 Stringency, mobility, and economic activity in developing Asia

More stringent lockdowns reduced mobility outside the home....

- ■ East Asia
- ♦ Central Asia
- ▲ South Asia
- ● Southeast Asia
- ✳ The Pacific
- ── Linear (Trend line)

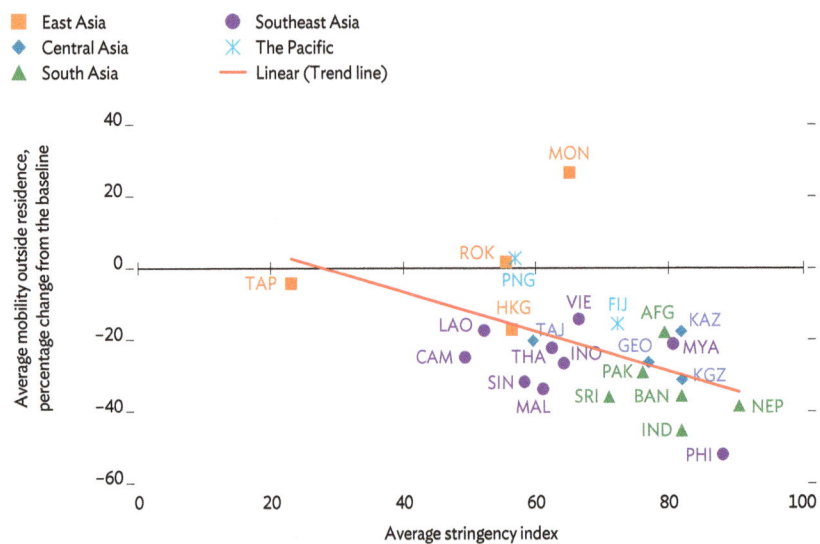

AFG = Afghanistan, BAN = Bangladesh, CAM = Cambodia, FIJ = Fiji, GEO = Georgia, HKG = Hong Kong, China, IND = India, INO = Indonesia, KAZ = Kazakhstan, KYR = Kyrgyz Republic, LAO = Lao People's Democratic Republic, MAL = Malaysia, MON = Mongolia, MYA = Myanmar, NEP = Nepal, PAK = Pakistan, PNG = Papua New Guinea, PHI = Philippines, ROK = Republic of Korea, SIN = Singapore, SRI = Sri Lanka, TAJ = Tajikistan, TAP = Taipei,China, THA = Thailand, VIE = Viet Nam.

Note: The baseline is the median value, for the corresponding day of the week, during the 5-week period 3 January–6 February 2020.

Sources: ADB estimates using data from University of Oxford. Our World in Data. https://ourworldindata.org/grapher/covid-stringency-index; Google LLC. Community Mobility Reports. https://www.google.com/covid19/mobility/.

...which caused steep declines in economic activity.

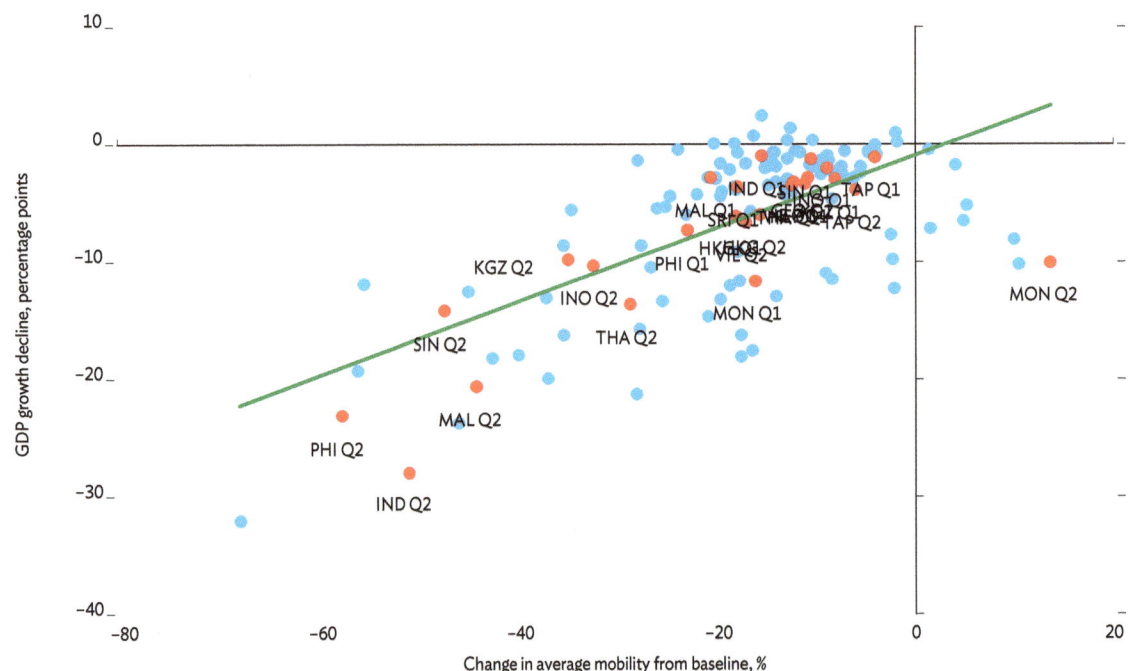

GEO = Georgia, HKG = Hong Kong, China, IND = India, INO = Indonesia, KGZ = Kyrgyz Republic, MAL = Malaysia, MON = Mongolia, NEP = Nepal, PHI = Philippines, Q = quarter, ROK = Republic of Korea, SIN = Singapore, SRI = Sri Lanka, TAP = Taipei,China, THA = Thailand, VIE = Viet Nam.

Notes: Red dots are ADB developing member economies. GDP growth year on year relative to GDP growth in Q4 of 2019.

Sources: CEIC Data Company; ADB estimates using data from University of Oxford. Our World in Data. https://ourworldindata.org/grapher/covid-stringency-index; Google LLC. Community Mobility Reports. https://www.google.com/covid19/mobility/.

Asian Development Bank (ADB) analysis shows different types of containment having different impacts on COVID-19 transmission rates. Transmission is typically measured by the reproduction number R(t), which indicates the average number of people that contract the virus from one infected person. An outbreak will expand if R(t) > 1 and recede if R(t) < 1. The analysis suggests that gathering bans are more effective in reducing R(t) than workplace or public transit closure (Figure 1.1.4). While stay-at-home orders can reduce R(t)—albeit at great economic cost—they are less effective in countries with larger households. Mask use and mass testing can help, and contact tracing is particularly effective in economies that provide paid sick leave. Paid sick leave provides potentially infected or exposed workers the incentive to accurately disclose information about symptoms or illness, which is key for implementing isolation protocols and establishing actual contact patterns to restrict the spread of the disease. In the absence of paid sick leave benefits, workers may prefer to not reveal their true health status, and report to work in order to get paid. The ADB analysis also found school and workplace closures associated with larger declines in GDP, and gathering bans, mass testing, and contact tracing associated with smaller output losses.

Figure 1.1.4 **Estimated impact of various policy measures on outbreak transmission R(t)**

Containment measures are not all equally effective at stemming outbreak transmission.

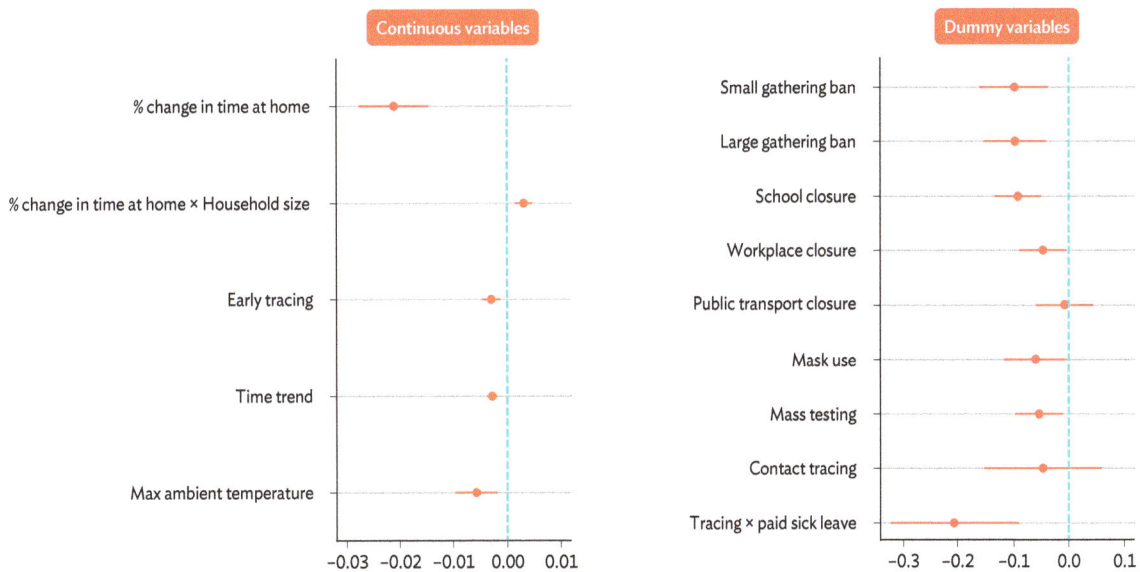

Notes: The figure plots coefficients and corresponding 90% confidence intervals of explanatory variables. The dependent variable is the daily effective reproductive rate of COVID-19, or R(t). "% change in time at home × Household size" is the interaction of percentage change in time spent at home and country average household size, and "Tracing × paid sick leave" is the interaction of contact tracing and paid sick leave. See Chen et al. (forthcoming) for further details.

Source: Chen et al. forthcoming.

The global pandemic also hit Asia's major trading partners hard. In the major advanced economies, the COVID-19 pandemic caused unprecedented GDP declines in Q2 (Figure 1.1.5). The drop in the euro area was a seasonally adjusted annualized rate of 39.4%, or 14.7% year on year, and in the US was 31.7%, or 9.1% year on year. However, leading indicators suggest that global activity may have already bottomed out. Global manufacturing and composite purchasing managers' indexes have edged up substantially from lows in April and exceeded the contraction threshold at 50 in August.

The combination of domestic outbreaks and lockdowns and a gloomy global environment hit growth hard in developing Asia. Growth rates in the first half of 2020 were substantially below 2019 growth rates in most economies, many of which actually contracted (Figure 1.1.6). Private consumption—normally a stable source of demand and the bulwark of regional growth for the past decade—contracted in the first half in most economies. Investment also took a hit, particularly in India and the Philippines. Sharp contraction in imports in India and the Philippines made net exports contributors to growth, but in economies that rely heavily on exports—such as Hong Kong, China; Singapore; and tourism-dependent Thailand—net exports dragged on growth.

The region's two largest economies, the PRC and India, both slowed significantly but then diverged markedly (Figure 1.1.7). Much of the divergence reflects how the outbreak has evolved in the two countries. The PRC outbreak peaked in Q1, and since April the 7-day moving average of new COVID-19 cases has been around or less than 100. This allowed the economy to reopen and, after 6.8% contraction in Q1, GDP grew by 3.2% in Q2. By contrast, the outbreak in India intensified from April, spreading fast from cities to rural areas. As of end-August, new cases daily exceeded 75,000 and are still rising. The hard and prolonged lockdown from late March to late May caused output to contract by 23.9% in April–June, the first quarter of the Indian fiscal year 2020. Various high-frequency indicators, while improving somewhat, show continued economic weakness.

Monthly data suggest that the regional economy is improving from its April nadir—and that the PRC has resumed economic expansion. In April, industrial production contracted by 7.2% in developing Asia; almost 30% in Indonesia, Malaysia, the Philippines, Thailand, and Viet Nam; and a staggering 60% in India (Figure 1.1.8). Since then the picture has improved, providing evidence of bottoming out. And in the PRC, which had its outbreak and containment earlier than others, industrial production has resumed expansion, by 4.8% in June.

Figure 1.1.5 Global activity indicators

As the pandemic spread, second quarter GDP growth in advanced economies slumped...

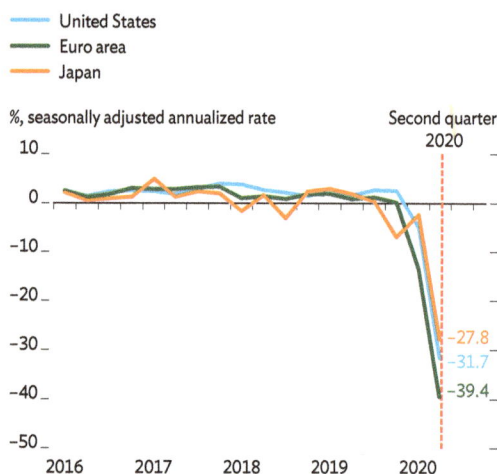

Source: Haver Analytics (accessed 28 August 2020).

... but high-frequency indicators suggest that global activity may have already bottomed out.

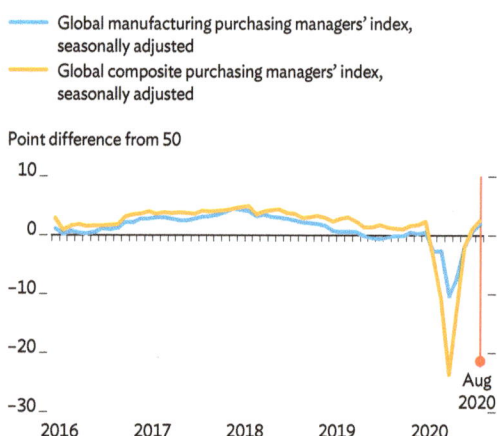

Source: ADB estimates based on data from CEIC Data Company; CPB Netherlands Bureau for Economic Policy Analysis. https://www.cpb.nl/en/worldtrademonitor (both accessed 7 September 2020).

Figure 1.1.6 Growth and demand-side contributions in selected economies

The global crisis and widespread lockdowns hit growth hard in developing Asia.

- ◻ Consumption
- ◻ Investment
- ◻ Net exports
- ● GDP growth

Percentage points

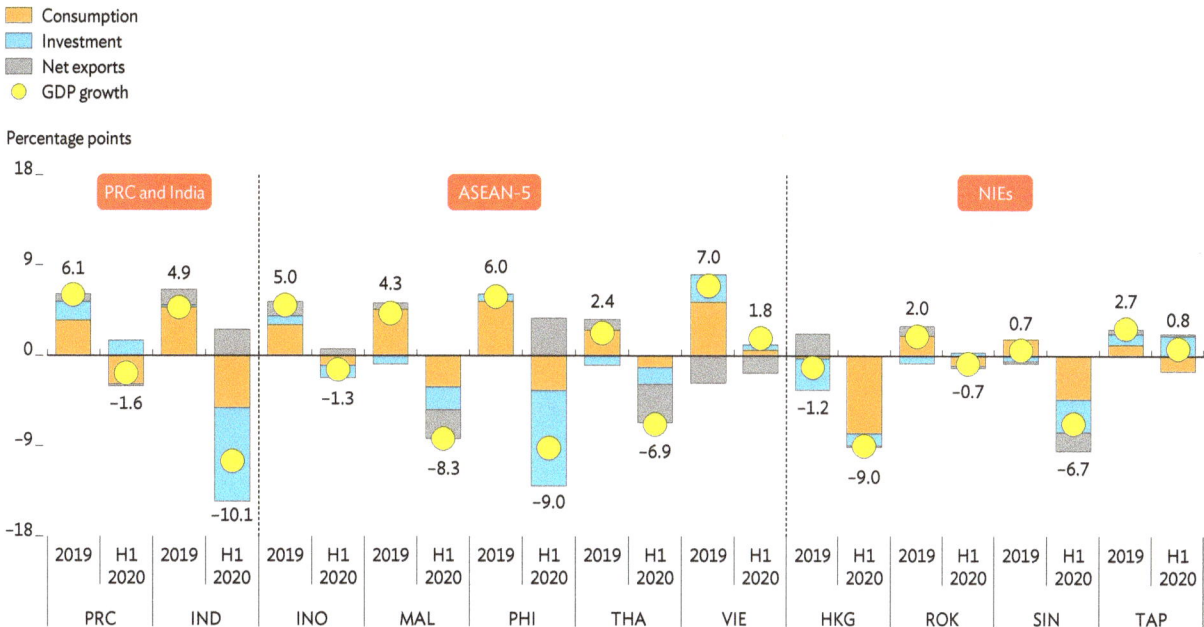

ASEAN = Association of Southeast Asian Nations, GDP = gross domestic product, H1 = first half, HKG = Hong Kong, China, IND = India, INO = Indonesia, MAL = Malaysia, NIEs = newly industrialized economies, PHI = Philippines, PRC = People's Republic of China, ROK = Republic of Korea, SIN = Singapore, TAP = Taipei,China, THA = Thailand, VIE = Viet Nam.

Notes: Data for all economies including India are by calendar year. Details may not sum precisely because of statistical discrepancy.

Sources: Haver Analytics (accessed 1 September 2020); ADB estimates.

Figure 1.1.7 Outbreaks and GDP growth in India and the PRC

The region's two giants are on divergent paths. While COVID-19 has been contained in the PRC, India is now the epicenter of the pandemic in the region...

...so, while growth is rebounding in the PRC, recovery in India will take longer.

A. New cases of COVID-19 daily

New cases, 7-day moving average (Log scale)

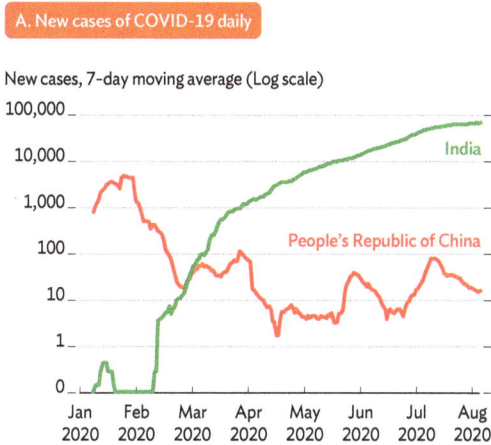

Source: Johns Hopkins University.

B. GDP growth

% change year on year

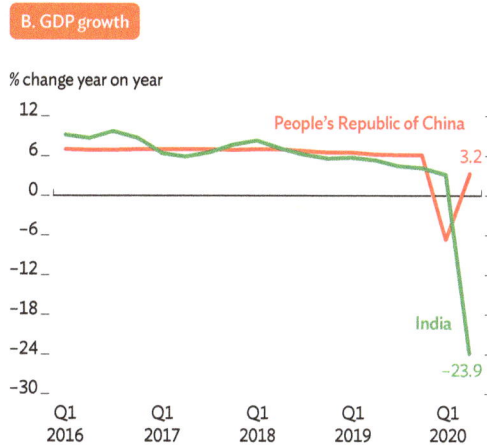

Sources: CEIC Data Company (accessed 31 August 2020), ADB estimates.

A similar pattern of hitting bottom in April and recovery since then is evident in purchasing managers' indexes (Table 1.1.1), although some heterogeneity and plateauing can also be observed. In particular, the August readings for Manufacturing PMI are lower than in July for Malaysia, the Philippines, and Viet Nam. This is partly due to softness in new export orders, as uncertainty about the duration of the pandemic led to postponement of purchases. Renewed lockdown also played a role in the Philippines.

Meanwhile, inflation was kept in check as food price inflation declined. Headline inflation in developing Asia declined from 5.0% in January to 2.6% in June, primarily as food price pressures abated, such as for pork in the PRC (Figure 1.1.9). This development was not uniform across subregions. In Central Asia, headline inflation rose slightly to 6.9% in June, and food inflation to 11.3%. The picture across the regions is mixed in terms of core inflation, which excludes food and energy prices. The deflationary impact of the pandemic-induced demand shock seems to have outweighed any supply-side disruption in East and Southeast Asia, as inflation decelerated moderately in these two subregions, while it remained benign in South Asia. Central Asia, by contrast, has seen core inflation increase by about 1 percentage point since January, reflecting a combination of supply-side constraints and currency depreciation in some economies.

Figure 1.1.8 Growth in industrial production, selected economies

Industrial activity in the PRC is now growing, and elsewhere contractions are off their April lows...

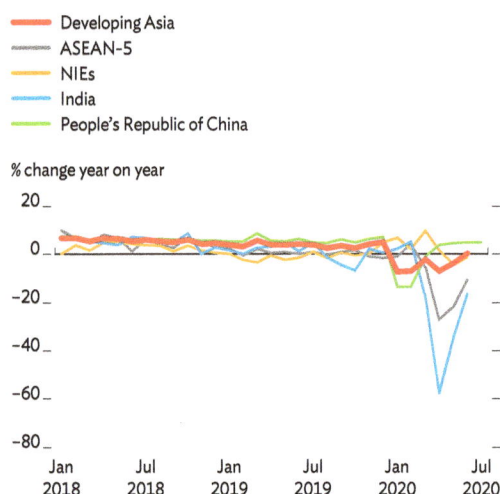

ASEAN-5 = Association of Southeast Asian Nations members Indonesia, Malaysia, the Philippines, Thailand, and Viet Nam, NIEs = newly industrialized economies of the Republic of Korea; Singapore; and Taipei,China.

Note: PRC data is combined for the months of January and February.

Sources: CEIC Data Company, National Bureau of Statistics (both accessed 10 August 2020); ADB estimates.

Table 1.1.1 Markit purchasing managers' index, selected economies

... and recovery is evident in purchasing managers' indexes.

	Manufacturing purchasing managers' index, seasonally adjusted																	
	2019												2020					
Economy	Q1			Q2			Q3			Q4			Q1			Q2			Q3
PRC	48.3	49.9	50.8	50.2	50.2	49.4	49.9	50.4	51.4	51.7	51.8	51.5	51.1	40.3	50.1	49.4	50.7	51.2	52.8	53.1
India	53.9	54.3	52.6	51.8	52.7	52.1	52.5	51.4	51.4	50.6	51.2	52.7	55.3	54.5	51.8	27.4	30.8	47.2	46.0	52.0
Indonesia	49.9	50.1	51.2	50.4	51.6	50.6	49.6	49.0	49.1	47.7	48.2	49.5	49.3	51.9	45.3	27.5	28.6	39.1	46.9	50.8
Malaysia	50.9	50.6	50.2	52.4	51.8	50.8	50.6	50.4	50.9	52.3	52.5	53.0	51.8	51.5	51.4	34.3	48.6	54.0	53.0	52.3
Philippines	52.3	51.9	51.5	50.9	51.2	51.3	52.1	51.9	51.8	52.1	51.4	51.7	52.1	52.3	39.7	31.6	40.1	49.7	48.4	47.3
Republic of Korea	48.3	47.2	48.8	50.2	48.4	47.5	47.3	49.0	48.0	48.4	49.4	50.1	49.8	48.7	44.2	41.6	41.3	43.4	46.9	48.5
Taipei,China	47.5	46.3	49.0	48.2	48.4	45.5	48.1	47.9	50.0	49.8	49.8	50.8	51.8	49.9	50.4	42.2	41.9	46.2	50.6	52.2
Thailand	50.2	49.9	50.3	51.0	50.7	50.6	50.3	50.0	50.6	50.0	49.3	50.1	49.9	49.5	46.7	36.8	41.6	43.5	45.9	49.7
Viet Nam	51.9	51.2	51.9	52.5	52.0	52.5	52.6	51.4	50.5	50.0	51.0	50.8	50.6	49.0	41.9	32.7	42.7	51.1	47.6	45.7
	Services purchasing managers' index, seasonally adjusted																	
PRC	53.6	51.1	54.4	54.5	52.7	52.0	51.6	52.1	51.3	51.1	53.5	52.5	51.8	26.5	43.0	44.4	55.0	58.4	54.1	54.0
India	52.2	52.5	52.0	51.0	50.2	49.6	53.8	52.4	48.7	49.2	52.7	53.3	55.5	57.5	49.3	5.4	12.6	33.7	34.2	41.8

PRC = People's Republic of China, Q = quarter.

Notes: For Malaysia, the series is adjusted by adding 3 points because historical experience suggests that values above 47 are consistent with expansion. Pink to red indicates contraction (<50), and white to green indicates expansion (>50).

Sources: CEIC Data Company (accessed 7 September 2020); ADB estimates.

Figure 1.1.9 Inflation in developing Asia

Headline and food price inflation fell, while core inflation remained stable except in Central and South Asia.

— East Asia
— Central Asia
— Southeast Asia
— South Asia
— Developing Asia

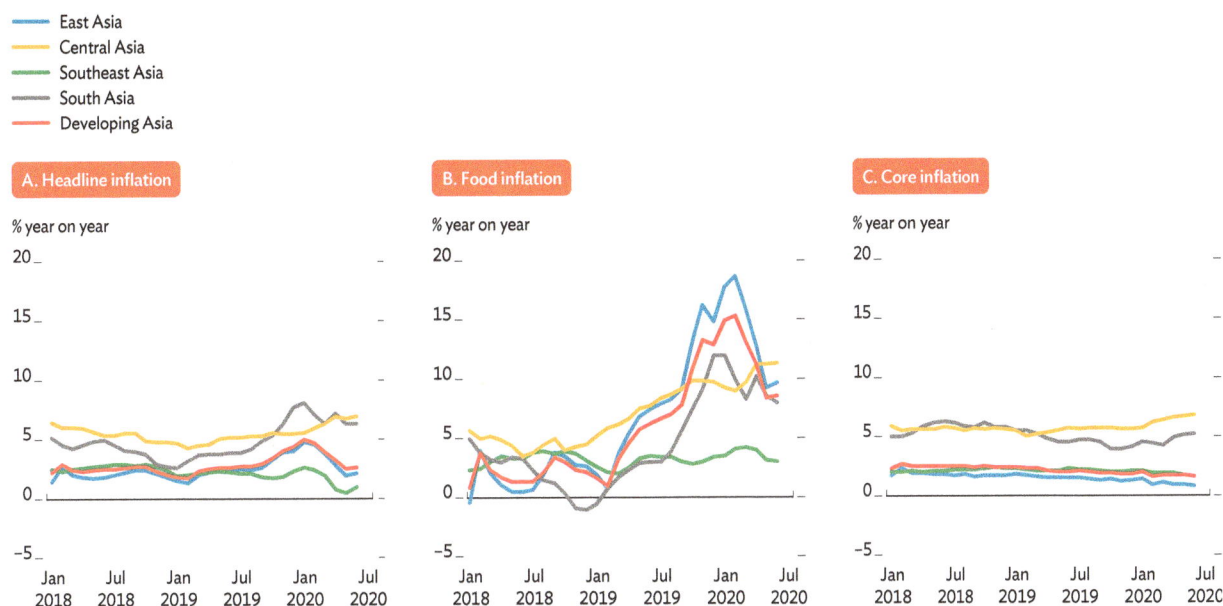

A. Headline inflation

B. Food inflation

C. Core inflation

Note: The Pacific is excluded because data are not available.
Sources: CEIC Data Company (accessed 28 August 2020); ADB estimates.

1.1.1 After a historic plunge, trade shows signs of revival

World trade declined sharply in first half of 2020 in tandem with the collapse in global economic activity and the introduction of extensive restrictions on travel and transport (Figure 1.1.10). Global trade was down by close to 20% year on year in April and May. The collapse was even bigger for trade in the major advanced economies as their aggregate exports fell by 27% year on year in April. Since then, trade has shown signs of recovering.

Developing Asia's trade also shrank but by less than elsewhere because demand for health-care supplies and electronics helped support regional exports of manufactures. Countering the broad aggregate decline in manufacturing exports in many economies in the region, upticks for some product categories seem to reflect rising demand for goods related to COVID-19 (Figure 1.1.11). Specifically, medical, pharmaceutical, and chemical products from Hong Kong, China; the PRC; and Singapore bucked the trend in Q2 2020 as external demand rose. Growing demand for digital devices and infrastructure—possibly linked to demand for devices to support work from home and online education (Box 1.1.1)—boosted exports of electrical, electronic, and optical equipment from Hong Kong, China; the PRC; Singapore; and Taipei,China.

Figure 1.1.10 World trade

Trade collapsed and then bottomed out, with Asia's trade falling by less than global trade.

— World
— G3
— Developing Asia

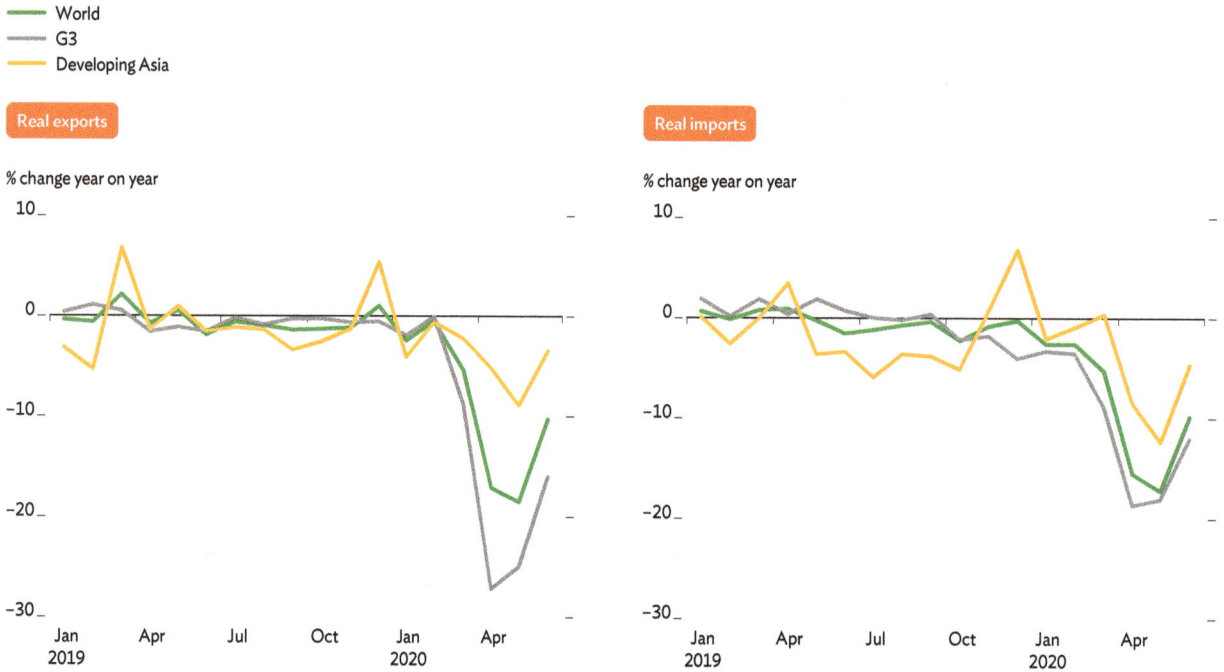

Real exports

Real imports

Developing Asia = weighted average of Hong Kong, China; India; Indonesia; Malaysia; Pakistan; the People's Republic of China; the Philippines; the Republic of Korea; Singapore; Taipei,China; Thailand; and Viet Nam, G3 = weighted average of the United States, Japan, and the euro area.

Source: CPB Netherlands Bureau for Economic Policy Analysis. Available: https://www.cpb.nl/en/worldtrademonitor (accessed 26 August 2020).

Figure 1.1.11 Growth in exports of health and electronics products, selected economies in developing Asia

There have been upticks in exports of health equipment and electronics from some economies.

■ Q4 2019
■ Q1 2020
■ Q2 2020

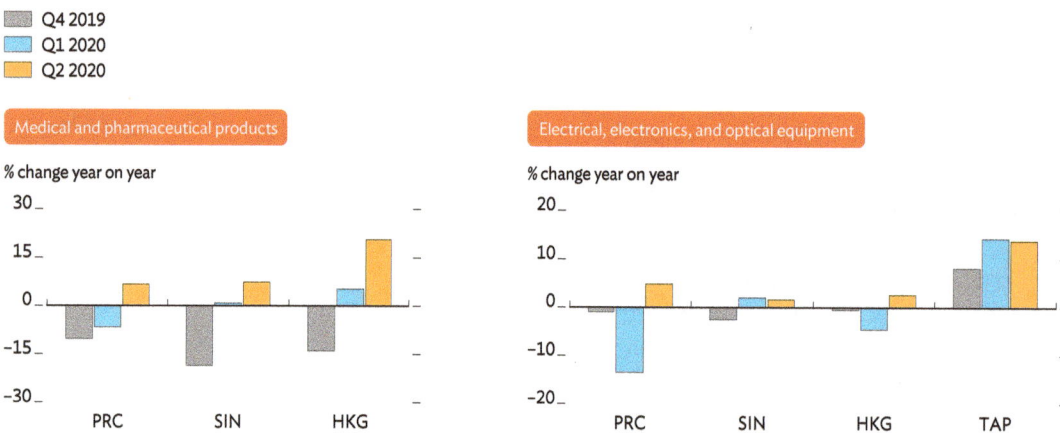

Medical and pharmaceutical products

Electrical, electronics, and optical equipment

HKG = Hong Kong, China, PRC = People's Republic of China, SIN = Singapore, TAP = Taipei,China, Q = quarter.

Notes: Medical, pharmaceutical, and chemical products refer to Standard International Trade Classification Rev. 3 Division codes 51, 52, and 54 but excludes rubber gloves (Code 848) and medical instruments and equipment (Code 872) for lack of data. Electrical, electronics, and optical equipment refer to Codes 75, 76, 77, and 87.

Sources: ADB estimates using data from CEIC Data Company and Haver Analytics (accessed 30 August 2020).

Box 1.1.1 COVID-19 and digitalization in Asia—the case of education and finance

The COVID-19 pandemic is felt in many areas as households and businesses adjusted to new and often stringent mobility restrictions and containment measures. This has created incentives to further digitalize many activities, a process already under way in many areas but accelerated by COVID-19, notably in education and finance.

To contain the outbreaks, more than 180 governments around the world have mandated temporary school closure, affecting some 85% of the world's student population.[a] In India, for example, countrywide closure has affected more than 320 million students, including 143 million primary students and 133 million secondary students.[b]

Along with the severe stress it imposes on education systems, the COVID-19 pandemic provides an opportunity to develop alternative learning modes. Some countries have invested in remote learning using various media, including television, radio, mobile phones, and the internet. Governments have built nationwide platforms to provide electronic learning resources to students at all levels. The appendix table on page 39 summarizes the digital programs being implemented in developing Asia.

As the first economy hit by COVID-19, the PRC made strides in providing a large share of its students with digital learning opportunities. On 10 February, CETV4 launched a television program called "Taking the Same Class," which invited nearly 100 celebrated schoolteachers to broadcast their courses live, the curriculum ranging from elementary school to junior and senior high school. On 17 February, the Ministry of Education launched the National Online Cloud Classroom (http://ykt.eduyun.cn/), a free online learning platform for primary and secondary school students studying at home during the COVID-19 outbreak.[c]

Many Asian countries want to increase the use of digital education, but stark inequality in access to communication technology poses a persistent challenge to remote learning. Two billion people in Asia, or 46% of the population, remain offline.[d] While the internet has reached most people in some economies like Brunei Darussalam, Malaysia, and Singapore, more than 70% of people in Cambodia, Indonesia, the Lao People's Democratic Republic, and Myanmar remain offline and so cannot fully participate in the digital economy.[e] Poor or nonexistent internet connections and a lack of computers or other internet devices are common pitfalls for students in poor households and threaten to further widen education gaps.

The United Nations Children's Fund (UNICEF) estimates that access to remote learning during school closure is beyond the reach of 80 million school children in East Asia and the Pacific, 147 million in South Asia, and 25 million in Eastern Europe and Central Asia.[f] Especially for these children, investment to address the digital divide offers substantial benefits to education and significant knock-on benefits to the rest of the economy.

Similarly, changes induced by COVID-19 in everyday life—such as social distancing, mobility restrictions, and the risk of infection from using coins and bills—have made financial technology (fintech) an attractive option for accessing financial services, dramatically accelerating a digital transformation already under way. Daily downloads of mobile finance applications are estimated to have increased since February 2020 by 24%–32%, translating to an average daily increase of 5.2 million–6.3 million in 74 countries.[g] From December 2019 and March 2020, the use of finance apps increased substantially in several countries, notably by 55% in Japan, 35% in the Republic of Korea, and about 20% in the PRC and the US, and in several European countries as well.[h]

Government policies helped speed up the digital transformation in finance. In response to advice from the World Health Organization to use payments methods that avoid physical contact, several central banks have actively promoted fintech. Mobile payments in particular have been adopted to facilitate government transfers to households and small businesses. In the PRC, for instance, many local governments use mobile payment platforms like Alipay and WeChat Pay to distribute free digital coupons to stimulate domestic consumption.[i] Fintech faces several challenges, however, including risks from cyberattacks, money laundering, and threats to data privacy.

Even as the spread of COVID-19 boosts digitalization, particularly education and finance, the challenge remains to ensure that it is effective and inclusive. To fully exploit the advantages that digitalization offers, both during the crisis and into the recovery and beyond, it will be imperative for policy makers in the region to ensure that the necessary infrastructure and protections are put in place.

[a] Data from the World Bank. https://www.worldbank.org/en/topic/edutech#1.

[b] Data from the United Nations Educational, Scientific, and Cultural Organization. https://en.unesco.org/covid19/educationresponse/.

[c] Ministry of Education. http://en.moe.gov.cn/news/press_releases/202003/t20200302_426337.html.

continued next page

Box 1.1.1 *Continued*

d   The figure comes from https://www.internetworldstats.com/stats3.htm.

e   IMF 2018.

f   United Nations Children's Fund. https://www.unicef.org/press-releases/covid-19-least-third-worlds-schoolchildren-unable-access-remote-learning-during.

g   Fu and Mishra 2020.

h   Rudden, J. 2020. Global growth in finance app usage during COVID-19. https://www.statista.com/statistics/1116563/fintech-apps-growth-usage-covid19.

i   South China Morning Post. https://www.scmp.com/tech/e-commerce/article/3077525/local-governments-china-issue-free-digital-coupons-stimulate.

References:

BRAC. 2020. *A Rapid Assessment: Impact of COVID-19 on Education in Bangladesh*. http://www.brac.net/program/wp-content/uploads/2020/07/Rapid-assessment-impact-of-COVID-19-education-in-Bangladesh.pdf.

Fu, J. and M. Mishra. 2020. The Global Impact of COVID-19 on Fintech Adoption. *Swiss Finance Institute Research Paper Series* No. 20-38. https://ssrn.com/abstract=3588453.

International Monetary Fund. 2018. Chart of the Week: The Digital Divide in Asia. *IMF Blog*. https://blogs.imf.org/2018/09/25/chart-of-the-week-the-digital-divide-in-asia-2/.

This box was written by Bihong Huang of the Economic Research and Regional Cooperation Department, ADB, Manila.

Tourism-dependent economies in the region have been hit hard by the global collapse in travel. Travel restrictions and precautionary behavior significantly dampened tourism, causing substantial losses for hospitality and transportation businesses. Tourist arrivals fell dramatically by 90%–100% across most economies (Figure 1.1.12A).

Figure 1.1.12 Tourism collapse and sluggish recovery

Tourism activity has collapsed, and recovery will be slow as tourists defer travel plans.

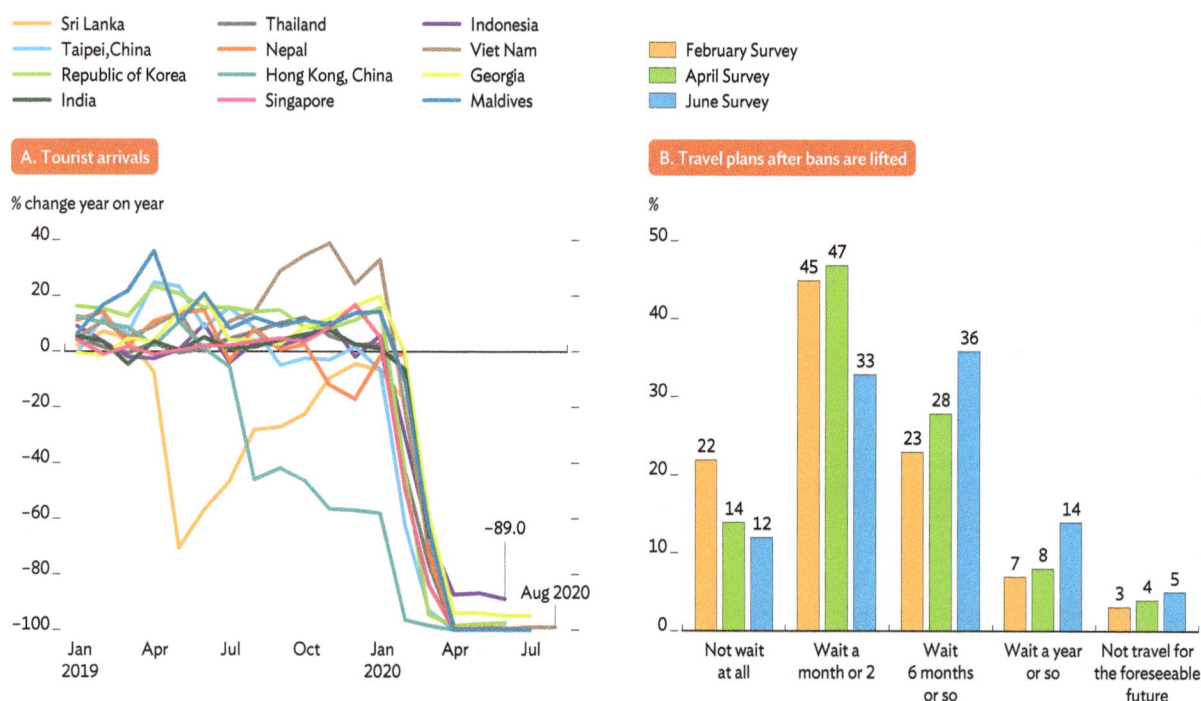

Legend:
— Sri Lanka   — Thailand   — Indonesia
— Taipei,China   — Nepal   — Viet Nam
— Republic of Korea   — Hong Kong, China   — Georgia
— India   — Singapore   — Maldives

February Survey
April Survey
June Survey

A. Tourist arrivals

B. Travel plans after bans are lifted

Sources: **Figure A**: CEIC Data Company; Ministry of Tourism. Republic of Maldives. https://www.tourism.gov.mv/statistics/monthly-updates/; Republic of Palau National Government. https://www.palaugov.pw/visitor-arrivals/; Vanuatu National Statistics Office. https://vnso.gov.vu/index.php/new-releases/monthly-news/tourism-news#latest-tourism-news; Fiji Bureau of Statistics. https://www.statsfiji.gov.fj/index.php/statistics/tourism-and-migration-statistics/visitor-arrivals-statistics; Georgian National Tourism Administration. https://gnta.ge/statistics/; NagaCorp Ltd. https://www.nagacorp.com/eng/ir/tourism.php; Census and Statistics Department. Government of the Hong Kong SAR. https://www.censtatd.gov.hk/hkstat/sub/sp130.jsp?productCode=D5600551; Tourism Tracker. Asia and Pacific Edition. Issue 4. 19 June 2020. International Monetary Fund. https://www.imf.org/~/media/Files/Countries/ResRep/pis-region/tourism-tracker/june-2020-tourism-tracker.ashx?la=en. **Figure B**: International Air Transportation Association. https://www.iata.org/en/ (all accessed 31 August 2020).

A full recovery in tourism is unlikely to come soon. Over half of respondents in a survey conducted in June by the International Air Transport Association said that they would wait for 6 months to a year or more before traveling, even after travel restrictions are lifted (Figure 1.1.12B).

Similarly, a number of economies in Asia have been adversely affected by declining remittance inflow, an income source that is traditionally a stabilizing mechanism but now appears to have been significantly weakened by the global scope of COVID-19. Plunging global economic activity and lower oil demand and prices have caused wage cuts and lost employment for migrant workers in advanced and oil-exporting economies, disrupting remittance flow to developing Asia (Box 1.1.2).

Box 1.1.2   The COVID-19 impact on remittances in developing Asia

Remittances, an important income source in many economies in developing Asia, have declined sharply under COVID-19. Remittances to low- and middle-income countries are projected to fall this year by almost 20% from 2019, according to the World Bank (2020). This is a significant loss of crucial financing for vulnerable households dependent on these transfers.

Remittance inflows quickly stagnated in the month immediately after COVID-19 lockdowns were imposed in major industrial economies (box figure 1). Most developing member countries with available data reported sharp declines in remittances from the previous year. In particular, the Kyrgyz Republic reported a 61% drop in remittances in April 2020 and the Philippines a 19% decline in May 2020—both record declines, reflecting the impact of the crisis on the large migrant populations from these countries. In addition, collapsing oil prices have severely weakened oil-exporting economies, which have large concentrations of migrant workers from many countries in developing Asia. However, data show remittances gradually recovering in line with nascent economic recovery. Economies with available data in Central and South Asia show positive growth in remittances as of June 2020, but it is too early to tell if recovery is durable or simply a transitory response to dire economic situations in some recipient economies.

The sharp decline in remittances may have wide-ranging macroeconomic consequences (box figure 2). In contrast with a 2.7% decline in remittance flow to economies in Asia and the Pacific during the GFC, the expected double-digit decline this year will be unprecedented in scale.

1 Remittance growth during the COVID-19 outbreak, selected economies

Remittances dropped immediately after lockdowns were imposed in response to the COVID-19 pandemic...

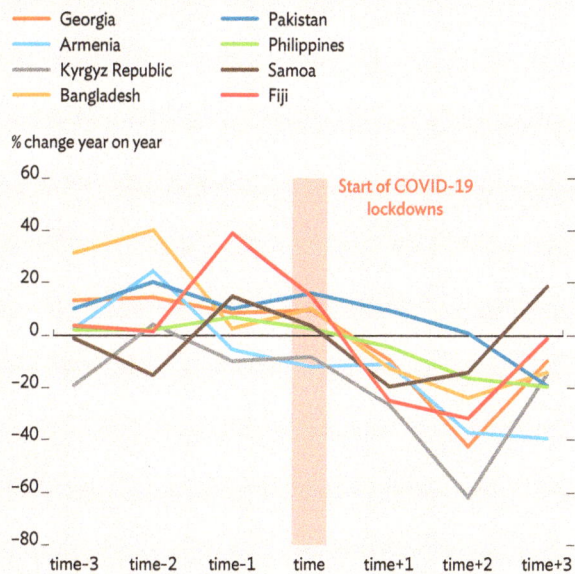

— Georgia
— Armenia
— Kyrgyz Republic
— Bangladesh
— Pakistan
— Philippines
— Samoa
— Fiji

% change year on year

Start of COVID-19 lockdowns

Note: The COVID-19 outbreaks started gathering steam started in February 2020. In the figures, *time* is the start month, and numbers indicate the number of months before or after it.
Sources: Central banks; CEIC Data Company (accessed 31 August 2020).

Takenaka et al. (2020) shows how economic fallout from the COVID-19 pandemic and consequent containment measures permanently threatens the jobs and livelihoods of over 91 million international migrants from the region.

continued next page

Box 1.1.2 *Continued*

Remittances to Asia and the Pacific are expected to drop by $31.4 billion–$54.3 billion in 2020, or by 11.5%–19.8% from 2018, the most recent year with a firm estimate. For individual economies in the region, remittance declines from the 2018 baseline range from a manageable 5.2% for Malaysia, the least affected, to a massive 28.7% plunge for Nepal, the worst affected. The next four worst-affected economies are Tajikistan, where remittances are on track to fall by 27.9%, Bangladesh by 27.8%, Pakistan by 26.8%, and the Kyrgyz Republic by 25.2%. Most economies in Central Asia are forecast to suffer remittance declines exceeding 21%, in Southeast Asia exceeding 15%, and in Pacific economies by about 13%.

Economies where remittances are higher either as a share of GDP or per capita, or where more households are dependent on remittances, are more likely to be affected. For instance, the Philippines is projected to suffer a slightly smaller percent decline in remittances, at 20.2%, than Indonesia, at 21.4%, but the macroeconomic impact on the Philippines is likely to be greater because remittances are 10% of GDP (vs. 1.1% of GDP in Indonesia), and because 8% of Philippine households depend on remittances while only 3% of Indonesian households do (Takenaka et al. 2020).

This pandemic highlights how vulnerable migrant workers and their families are to global economic shocks. A sudden stop in remittance flows to developing Asia, in particular to the Pacific and Central Asia, could push more remittance-dependent households into poverty. Aggressive policies may be needed to soften the impact in developing Asia and enable migrant workers and recipient households to recover.

References:

Takenaka, A., J. Villafuerte, R. Gaspar, and B. Narayanan. 2020. COVID-19 Impact on International Migration, Remittances, and Recipient Households in Developing Asia. *ADB Briefs* No. 148. Asian Development Bank.

Jha, S. and C. Vargas-Silva. 2009. The Global Crisis and the Impact on Remittances to Developing Asia. *ADB Economics Working Paper Series* No. 185. Asian Development Bank.

World Bank. 2020. *World Bank Predicts Sharpest Decline of Remittances in Recent History*. Press release. 22 April.

2 Remittances lost to Asia and the Pacific under the worst-case scenario

...and this may herald record declines in remittances to Asia.

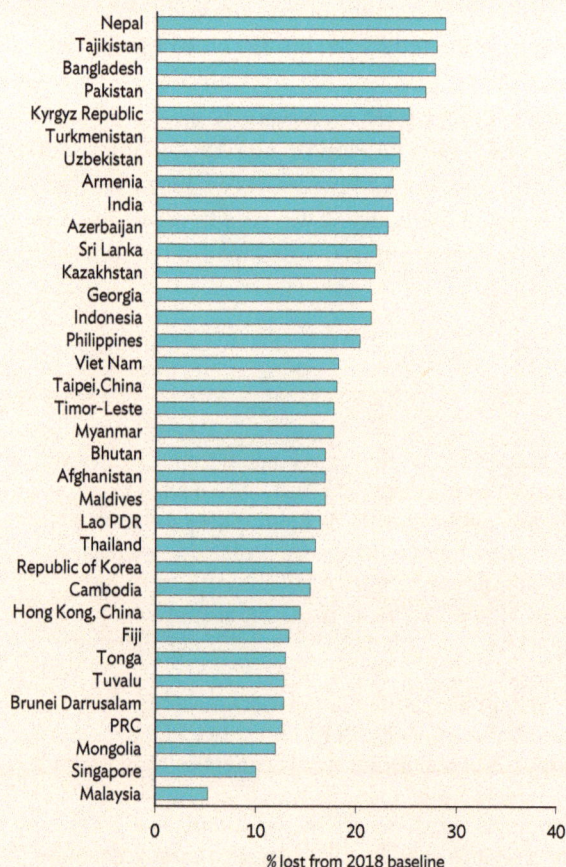

Lao PDR = Lao People's Democratic Republic, PRC = People's Republic of China.
Note: The worst-case scenario is the expected decline in remittance receipts from baseline remittances in 2018 if economies take about a year to get their domestic outbreaks under control and restore normal economic activity.
Source: Takenaka et al. (2020).

This box was written by Matteo Lanzafame, Irfan Qureshi, Emmanuel Alano, and Michael Timbang of the Economic Research and Regional Cooperation Department, ADB, Manila.

1.1.2 After a nosedive, financial conditions improve

Financial conditions have improved since a turbulent March, when negative sentiment in response to the global spread of COVID-19 weighed on financial markets, but risk appetite in the region has not fully recovered (Figure 1.1.13). Major Asian stock indexes collectively retreated in March, when India's Bombay Stock Exchange (SENSEX) tumbled by 22.7%, followed by a 17.7% decline in markets in major economies in the Association of Southeast Asian Nations (ASEAN-5: Indonesia, Malaysia, the Philippines, Thailand and Viet Nam), an 11.6% decline in newly industrialized economies (NIEs: Hong Kong, China; the Republic of Korea; Singapore; and Taipei,China) and a 7.4% decline in the PRC's Shanghai Stock Exchange. By 23 March, major Asian equity markets had incurred a cumulative loss of 28.2% since 2 January, the first trading day of 2020. Meanwhile, the average JP Morgan Emerging Markets Bond Index stripped spread for four ASEAN economies and the PRC—a proxy for risk premium in bond markets—tripled from 123 basis points on 2 January to 364 points on 23 March (Figure 1.1.14).

Boosted by the introduction of stimulus packages and measures to address the health crisis, financial markets have gradually stabilized since late March. By 28 August, major Asian equity markets had rallied, with the SENSEX gaining 39.6%, the Shanghai Stock Exchange in the PRC 24.5%, the NIES 16.7%, and the ASEAN-5 15.2% since April. In the same period, the average bond yield spread narrowed by 136 basis points. Nevertheless, risk sentiment has not fully recovered to pre-pandemic levels in equity or bond markets. Between 2 January and 28 August, major Asian stock indexes were down 4.8% on average, and the average bond yield spread was still up by 47 basis points.

Foreign portfolio investment outflows began in late February and peaked in mid-March (Figure 1.1.15). Outflows from major Asian equity markets peaked at $19.1 billion during the week of 13 March, and outflows from bond markets peaked at $8.4 billion during the week of 20 March. As financial markets stabilized in late March, portfolio outflows slowed. Portfolio investment started to return to Asia in May, boosted by relatively effective containment of the pandemic in the region, the relaxation of lockdowns in many countries, and higher returns on assets in emerging Asia. From May to August, average weekly portfolio investment in major Asian equity markets reached $930 million, with weekly equity inflows peaking at $8.3 billion during the week of 5 June. Portfolio flows into selected Asian bond markets also recovered, aggregating from June to August at $1.7 billion.

Figure 1.1.13 Equity index, selected economies

Since a nadir in March, financial conditions have improved, fueling rallies in major stock markets in Asia...

- India
- People's Republic of China
- NIEs
- ASEAN-5
- United States

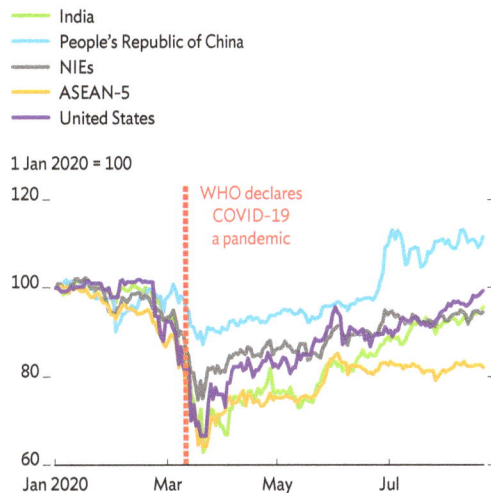

ASEAN-5 = Association of Southeast Asian Nation members Indonesia, Malaysia, the Philippines, Thailand, and Viet Nam, NIEs = newly industrialized economies of Hong Kong, China; the Republic of Korea; Singapore; and Taipei,China, WHO = World Health Organization.
Note: The World Health Organization declared COVID-19 a pandemic on 11 March.
Sources: CEIC Data Company; Bloomberg (both accessed 31 August 2020).

Figure 1.1.14 JP Morgan Emerging Market Bond Index stripped spreads, selected Asian economies

...and recovery in bond markets, though risk premiums remain higher than before COVID-19.

- People's Republic of China
- Indonesia
- Malaysia
- Philippines
- Viet Nam

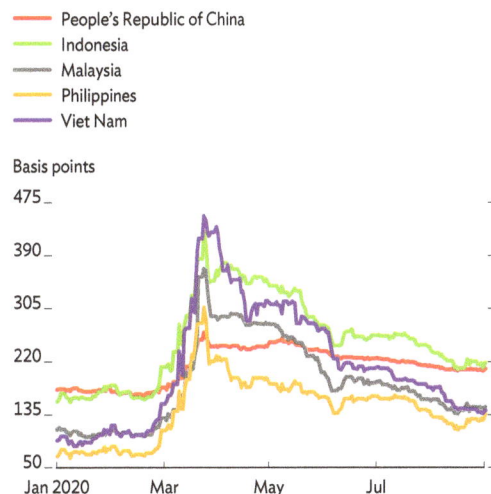

Source: Bloomberg (accessed 31 August 2020).

Figure 1.1.15 Foreign portfolio investment

After substantial outflow in March, foreign portfolio investment returned to Asia.

■ Equity
■ Debt

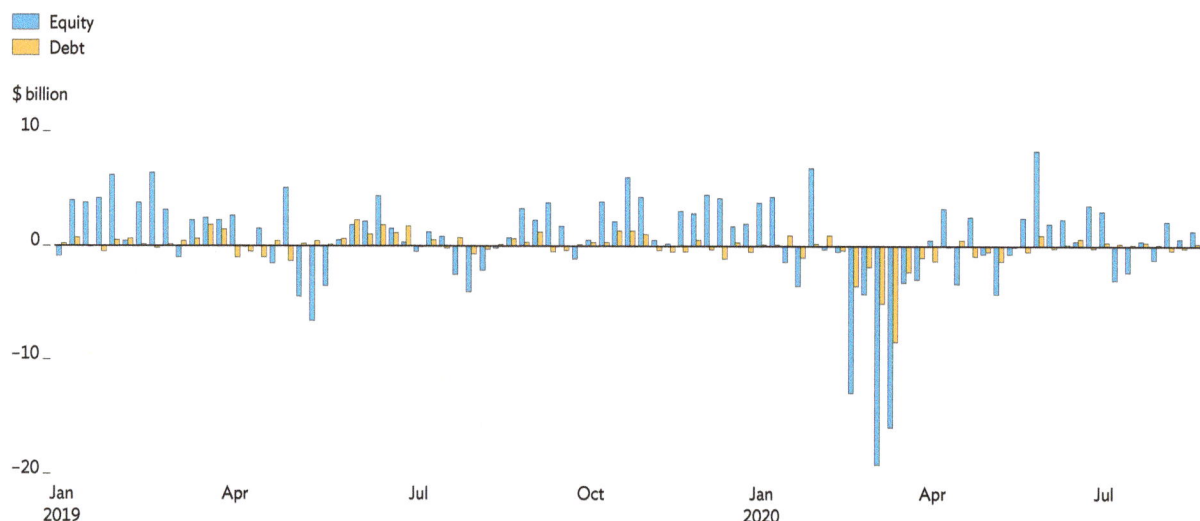

Notes: Equity flow data include India; Indonesia; Pakistan; the People's Republic of China; the Philippines; the Republic of Korea; Sri Lanka; Taipei,China; Thailand; and Viet Nam. Debt flow data include only India, Indonesia, and Thailand.
Source: Institute of International Finance Capital flow tracker database (accessed 31 August 2020).

Movements in exchange rates reflected the broad pattern observed in financial conditions and capital flows. Most Asian currencies weakened against the US dollar in Q1 2020, when investment sentiment soured and safe-haven demand for the US dollar rose under the pandemic (Figure 1.1.16). During market turmoil in March, most Asian currencies weakened against the US dollar, with the Indonesian rupiah suffering the sharpest depreciation in the region, by 9.1%, followed by the Indian rupee, which fell by 3.8%. In the same period, the currencies of Bangladesh, the Philippines, and Viet Nam remained relatively stable against the US dollar.

Buoyed by liquidity injections, effective containment measures, and robust fundamentals, Asian currencies stabilized and gained ground against the US dollar from May. From May to August, almost all major Asian currencies strengthened against the dollar, led by the Sri Lankan rupee with a 4.4% gain and the Philippine peso, up 3.9%.

Financial conditions improved with the help of accommodative monetary policies. From April to August, most regional central banks further cut policy rates to ease liquidity constraints (Figure 1.1.17). Sri Lanka lowered its policy rate three times by a total of 175 basis points to 4.50%, the lowest since 2003. In two rate cuts each, the Philippines lowered its policy rates by 100 basis points, Malaysia by 75 points, and Indonesia by 50 points. After raising its policy rate to 12.00% in March, Kazakhstan cut it twice, in April and July, by a total of 300 basis points.

Figure 1.1.16 Exchange rates

After depreciating in Q1, most Asian currencies have strengthened since May.

- Q1 2020
- April–August

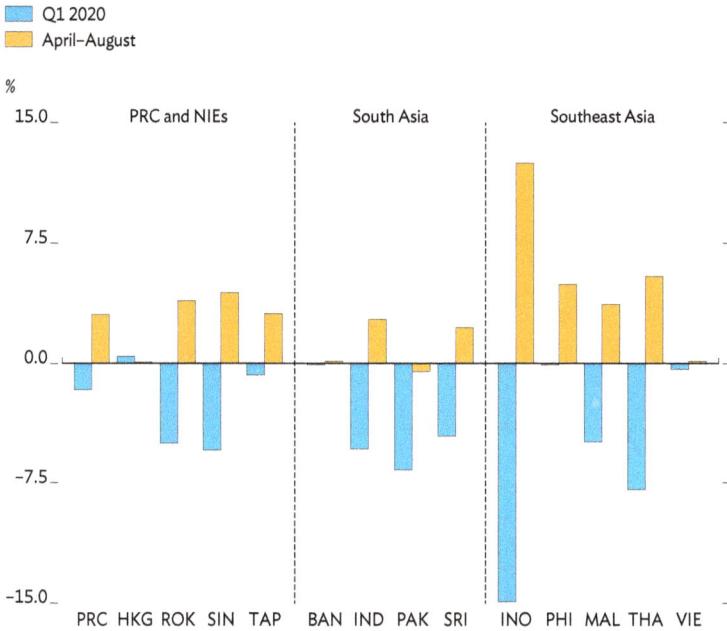

BAN = Bangladesh, HKG = Hong Kong, China, IND = India, INO = Indonesia, MAL = Malaysia, NIEs = newly industrialized economies, PAK = Pakistan, PHI = Philippines, PRC = People's Republic of China, Q = quarter, ROK = Republic of Korea, SIN = Singapore, SRI = Sri Lanka, TAP = Taipei,China, THA = Thailand, VIE = Viet Nam.

Note: Exchange rates are against the US dollar, with positive values indicating local currency appreciation.

Source: CEIC Data Company (accessed 31 Aug 2020).

Figure 1.1.17 Policy rates

Regional central banks eased monetary policy.

- 1 January 2020
- 31 March 2020
- 31 August 2020

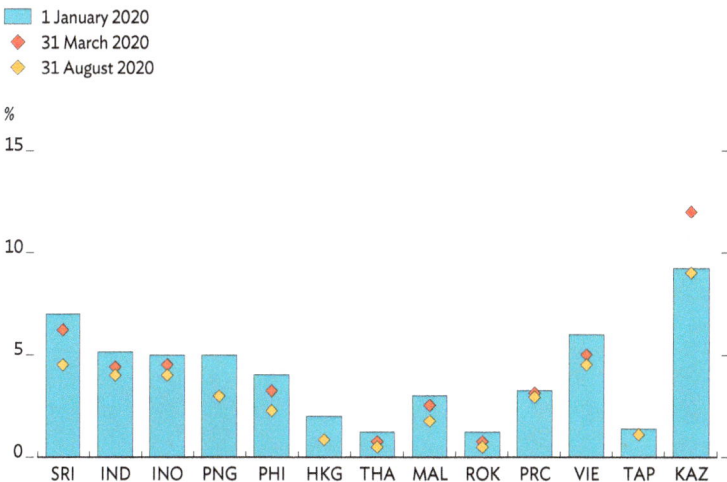

HKG = Hong Kong, China, IND = India, INO = Indonesia, KAZ = Kazakhstan, MAL = Malaysia, PHI = Philippines, PNG = Papua New Guinea, PRC = People's Republic of China, ROK = Republic of Korea, SRI = Sri Lanka, TAP = Taipei,China, THA = Thailand, VIE = Viet Nam.

Source: Bloomberg (accessed 31 August 2020).

Most regional central banks reduced policy rates at least once from April to August. Accommodative global and regional monetary conditions have also contributed to relative financial stability in Asia.

Despite abundant liquidity in global and domestic markets, financing conditions for micro, small, and medium-sized enterprises (MSMEs) remain tight in developing Asia. According to an ADB survey of four ASEAN economies, more than one-third of MSMEs are short of working capital and report having either no cash on hand or just enough to run the business for only 1 month (Shinozaki, forthcoming). As obtaining credit from formal financial services remained challenging for most MSMEs, more than one-third of them relied on informal sources such as personal savings or loans from family and friends. MSMEs responded to deteriorating financial conditions in various ways. Across the four economies, 52.6% of them tried to defer loan repayments, 40.8% reported delayed tax payment, 33.4% reduced employee salaries, and 31.1% laid off staff. MSME financing problems raise broader concerns about the debt-servicing capacity and the sustainability of businesses run by vulnerable groups in developing Asia, who generally lack adequate financial services.

Other problems may arise from rising debt burdens. Public and private demand is rising for funds with which to soften the impact of the pandemic, further pushing up debt. According to the Global Debt Monitor of the Institute of International Finance, debt in emerging Asia rose from the equivalent of 260% of GDP in Q1 2019 to 280% in Q1 2020 (Institute of International Finance, 2020). The negative impact of COVID-19 on economic fundamentals in the public and private sectors thus raises concerns about the sustainability of higher debt levels. With worsening fundamentals—and especially if the pandemic persists—nonperforming loans are likely to rise further and may weaken financial stability in the region, even triggering renewed capital outflow (Park and Shin, 2020). This would severely hinder economic recovery.

1.1.3 Asian governments respond with economic support policies

In response to the pandemic-induced economic downturn, governments in the region have pledged a wide array of compensating policies. The value of declared support packages amounts to $3.6 trillion, about 15% of combined GDP in developing Asia (Figure 1.1.18). This compares with $15.3 trillion, or about 32% of GDP, in the advanced economies. Roughly half of the value of the packages in Asia provides direct income or revenue support through government transfers, loan cancellations, tax cuts, or forbearances.

Figure 1.1.18 Policy packages in developing Asia

A wide array of policies have been pledged to soften the impact of the crisis and aid recovery.

- Government support to income/revenue
- Credit creation
- Liquidity support
- Direct long-term lending
- Equity support

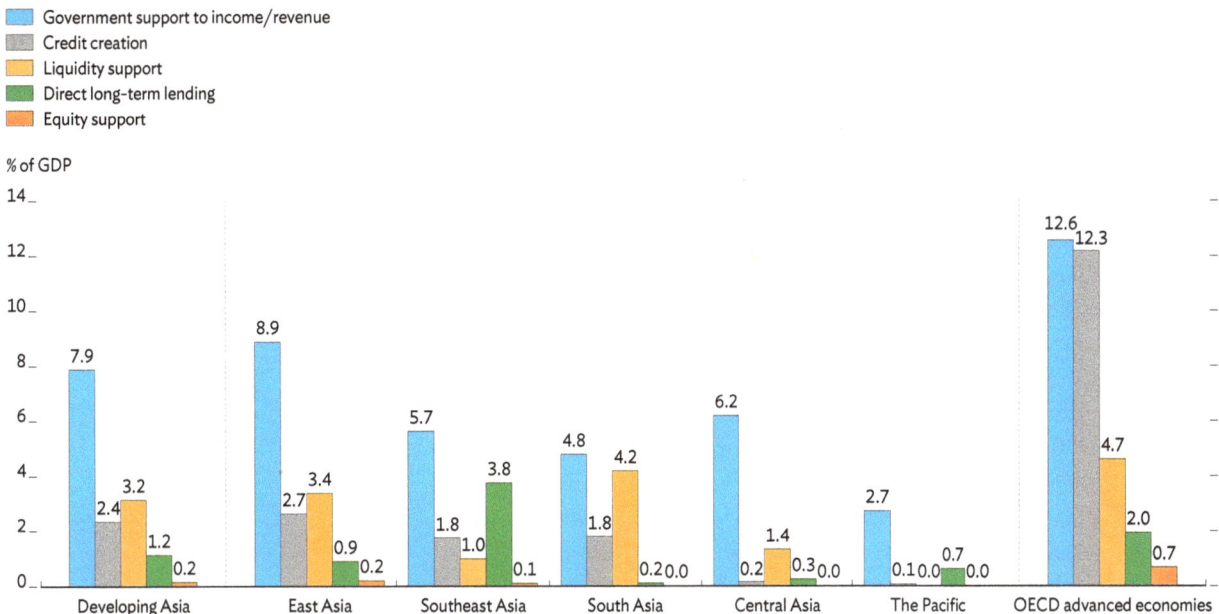

% of GDP

OECD = Organisation for Economic Co-operation and Development, GDP = gross domestic product.
Notes: The OECD advanced economies are Australia, Austria, Belgium, Canada, Denmark, Finland, France, Germany, Ireland, Italy, Japan, Luxembourg, the Netherlands, New Zealand, Norway, Portugal, Spain, Sweden, Switzerland, the United Kingdom, and the United States. Kiribati, Niue, and Turkmenistan are excluded from the sample due to lack of data. Data as of 24 August 2020.
Sources: Compiled from the ADB COVID-19 Policy Database. https://covid19policy.adb.org/ (accessed 8 September 2020); World Bank World Development Indicators; National Statistics Taipei,China; Ministry of Finance and Economic Management of the Cook Islands.

About a quarter bolsters credit creation via government loans to the financial sector, interest rate changes, or loan guarantees. The rest provides liquidity through government or central bank loans to the private sector, and provides direct long-term lending or equity support.

While advanced economies deliver a large proportion of their policy support through credit creation instruments, these measures play a smaller role in developing Asia—which might reflect the different stages of financial development in the latter. Some differences also exist across subregions. Whereas East Asia pledges about 16% of GDP for policy schemes, the Pacific allocates only 3.5%. Further, Central Asia and the Pacific stand out in that direct income support accounts for more than 75% of the total, while in East and South Asia liquidity support also plays an important role.

Cross-country analysis suggests that per capita GDP is strongly associated with the overall size of policy packages and with the value of income-support measures per capita (Felipe et al. forthcoming). Other positive correlations are observed with the expected decline in the growth rate, number of COVID-19 cases and deaths per 100,000 population, the share of wage and salaried workers in total employment, and the share of the population at least 65 years old.

1.2 Outlook: Partial recovery after contraction in 2020

Despite large commitments to pandemic-relief policy packages, the world economy is still expected to contract sharply this year before recovering next year. Tough containment measures taken as COVID-19 spread globally in March were followed by sharp GDP contraction, as slumps in investment and consumer spending dragged down economic activity around the world. The major advanced economies are forecast to contract deeply this year, having fallen into recession in the first half (Annex on page 42). Combined GDP in the US, euro area, and Japan is projected to fall by 6.2% in 2020 before expanding by 4.4% next year (Table 1.2.1). The US is now forecast to contract by 5.3% in 2020, rather than grow by 0.4% as expected in April; output in the euro area is projected to plunge by 8.0% rather than decline by 1.0%; and Japan's GDP will fall by 5.4% rather than by 1.5%, as projected earlier. Forecasts for 2021 are heavily corrected upward in line with the expectation that the major advanced economies will recover from their 2020 slump, with GDP growth rebounding by 4.0% in the US, 6.0% in euro area, and 2.0% in Japan.

Table 1.2.1 Baseline assumptions on the international economy

The major industrial economies will contract sharply this year.

	2020			2021		
	ADO	ADOS	ADO Update	ADO	ADOS	ADO Update
GDP growth (%)						
Major industrial economies	−0.3	−5.8	**−6.2**	1.8	4.1	**4.4**
United States	0.4	−5.3	−5.3	2.1	3.8	4.0
Euro area	−1.0	−7.0	−8.0	1.6	5.5	6.0
Japan	−1.5	−5.0	−5.4	0.9	2.0	2.0
Brent crude spot prices (average, $ per barrel)	35.00	35.00	42.50	55.00	45.00	50.00

... = unavailable, ADO = Asian Development Outlook, ADOS = ADO Supplement, GDP = gross domestic product.
Note: Average growth rates are weighted by gross national income, Atlas method.
Source: ADB estimates.

A similar growth trend is expected in developing Asia, where the outlook worsened regionwide following the COVID-19 outbreak (Table 1.2.2). The assumption underlying the baseline forecast is that countries' outbreaks are contained within the second half of 2020, enabling the authorities to loosen their containment measures and allow economic activity to resume in earnest.

Table 1.2.2 GDP growth rate, % per year

Economy/subregion	2019	2020			2021		
		April ADO 2020	June ADOS	September Update	April ADO 2020	June ADOS	September Update
Central Asia	**4.9**	**2.8**	**–0.5**	**–2.1**	**4.2**	**4.2**	**3.9**
Armenia	7.6	2.2	–3.5	–4.0	4.5	3.5	3.5
Azerbaijan	2.2	0.5	–0.1	–4.3	1.5	1.2	1.2
Georgia	5.1	0.0	–5.0	–5.0	4.5	5.0	4.5
Kazakhstan	4.5	1.8	–1.2	–3.2	3.6	3.4	2.8
Kyrgyz Republic	4.5	4.0	–5.0	–10.0	4.5	4.0	4.0
Tajikistan	7.5	5.5	–3.6	–0.5	5.0	7.0	6.0
Turkmenistan	6.3	6.0	3.2	3.2	5.8	5.8	5.8
Uzbekistan	5.6	4.7	1.5	0.5	5.8	6.5	6.5
East Asia	**5.4**	**2.0**	**1.3**	**1.3**	**6.5**	**6.8**	**7.0**
Hong Kong, China	–1.2	–3.3	–6.5	–6.5	3.5	5.1	5.1
Mongolia	5.1	2.1	–1.9	–2.6	4.6	4.7	5.1
People's Republic of China	6.1	2.3	1.8	1.8	7.3	7.4	7.7
Republic of Korea	2.0	1.3	–1.0	–1.0	2.3	3.5	3.3
Taipei,China	2.7	1.8	0.8	0.8	2.5	3.5	3.5
South Asia	**4.3**	**4.1**	**–3.0**	**–6.8**	**6.0**	**4.9**	**7.1**
Afghanistan	3.0	3.0	–4.5	–5.0	4.0	3.0	1.5
Bangladesh	8.2	7.8	4.5	5.2	8.0	7.5	6.8
Bhutan	4.4	5.2	2.4	2.4	5.8	1.7	1.7
India	4.2	4.0	–4.0	–9.0	6.2	5.0	8.0
Maldives	5.9	–3.0	–11.3	–20.5	7.5	13.7	10.5
Nepal	7.0	5.3	2.3	2.3	6.4	3.1	1.5
Pakistan	1.9	2.6	–0.4	–0.4	3.2	2.0	2.0
Sri Lanka	2.3	2.2	–6.1	–5.5	3.5	4.1	4.1
Southeast Asia	**4.4**	**1.0**	**–2.7**	**–3.8**	**4.7**	**5.2**	**5.5**
Brunei Darussalam	3.9	2.0	1.4	1.4	3.0	3.0	3.0
Cambodia	7.1	2.3	–5.5	–4.0	5.7	5.9	5.9
Indonesia	5.0	2.5	–1.0	–1.0	5.0	5.3	5.3
Lao People's Democratic Republic	5.0	3.5	–0.5	–2.5	6.0	4.5	4.5
Malaysia	4.3	0.5	–4.0	–5.0	5.5	6.5	6.5
Myanmar	6.8	4.2	1.8	1.8	6.8	6.0	6.0
Philippines	6.0	2.0	–3.8	–7.3	6.5	6.5	6.5
Singapore	0.7	0.2	–6.0	–6.2	2.0	3.2	4.5
Thailand	2.4	–4.8	–6.5	–8.0	2.5	3.5	4.5
Timor-Leste	3.4	–2.0	–3.7	–6.3	4.0	4.0	3.3
Viet Nam	7.0	4.8	4.1	1.8	6.8	6.8	6.3
The Pacific	**3.5**	**–0.3**	**–4.3**	**–6.1**	**2.7**	**1.6**	**1.3**
Cook Islands	5.3	–2.2	–9.0	–7.0	1.0	–15.4	–15.4
Federated States of Micronesia	1.2	1.6	–2.0	–5.4	3.0	–1.5	–1.9
Fiji	–1.3	–4.9	–15.0	–19.8	3.0	–0.7	1.0
Kiribati	2.4	1.6	0.6	0.6	1.8	1.8	1.8
Marshall Islands	3.8	2.5	–5.5	–5.5	3.7	–1.4	–1.4
Nauru	1.0	0.4	–1.7	–1.7	1.1	0.8	0.5
Niue	...	...	...	...	...	...	...
Palau	–1.8	–4.5	–9.5	–9.5	1.2	–12.8	–12.8
Papua New Guinea	5.0	0.8	–1.5	–2.9	2.8	2.9	2.5
Samoa	3.5	–3.0	–5.0	–5.0	0.8	–2.0	–9.7
Solomon Islands	1.2	1.5	–6.0	–6.0	2.7	2.5	1.0
Tonga	0.7	0.0	–3.0	–3.0	2.5	–4.0	–8.0
Tuvalu	4.1	2.7	2.0	2.0	3.2	2.5	2.5
Vanuatu	2.9	–1.0	–9.8	–9.8	2.5	2.0	1.0
Developing Asia	**5.1**	**2.2**	**0.1**	**–0.7**	**6.2**	**6.2**	**6.8**
Developing Asia excluding the NIEs	**5.6**	**2.4**	**0.4**	**–0.5**	**6.7**	**6.6**	**7.2**

... = unavailable, *ADOS = ADO Supplement*, GDP = gross domestic product, NIEs = newly industrialized economies (Hong Kong, China; the Republic of Korea; Singapore; and Taipei,China).

Source: *Asian Development Outlook* database.

Containment in this context does not mean full elimination of COVID-19 in a country—rather it means that countries flatten the curve sufficiently to allow easing of restrictions so that their economies can reopen, and the countries learn to live with COVID-19. Even under these assumptions, regional output is expected to contract, for the first time since the early 1960s, by 0.7% in 2020. This is a downward revision of 2.9 percentage points relative to the April 2020 *Asian Development Outlook* report, and 0.8 percentage points relative to the June 2020 *ADO Supplement* (Figure 1.0.1A). Regional growth is expected to rebound to 6.8% next year. Despite the rebound in growth next year, regional GDP next year will be smaller than envisioned before the pandemic (Figure 1.2.1). This means recovery regionwide will not be V-shaped—which implies a quick return to the precrisis trend—but L-shaped or "swoosh"-shaped; see Sheiner and Yilla (2020) for a taxonomy of recovery shapes. It will take some time for developing Asia's economy to return to its pre-pandemic trajectory.

ADB simulations show that, without the COVID-19 pandemic, the number of poor in developing Asia would have continued to decline in line with experience over the past 2 decades. Thus, the number of people in poverty, defined as living on no more than $1.90 per day, would have declined to 114 million by the end of 2020. Using $3.20 as the poverty line, the number would have fallen to 734 million. COVID-19 reversed this trend. Growth forecasts in this report mean that the estimated number of poor in the region will likely rise instead to 192 million by the end of 2020 using the $1.90 poverty line, or to 896 million using the $3.20 poverty line. Depending on the poverty definition, this means an additional 78 million or 162 million poor, reversing poverty reduction achieved over the past 3–4 years.

The path and speed of economic recovery in regional economies will depend on many different factors, the most important of which is ability to control and contain the pandemic.

The PRC contracted sharply in Q1 during the peak of its outbreak, but quick containment and strong monetary and fiscal policy support helped the economy rebound. Growth resumed in Q2, and further modest acceleration is expected in the second half of the year. GDP growth is now forecast at 1.8% in 2020, revised down from 2.3% projected in *ADO 2020* in April. Although constrained by weak fiscal revenue, fiscal policy will continue to support growth, especially through infrastructure investment. Consumption will likely recover gradually as discretionary spending remains depressed. Investment will be the main driver of growth in 2020, with infrastructure investment expected to remain strong for the

Figure 1.2.1 Projected recovery path in developing Asia

The recovery will be gradual, and GDP will not return to its pre-COVID-19 trend in 2021.

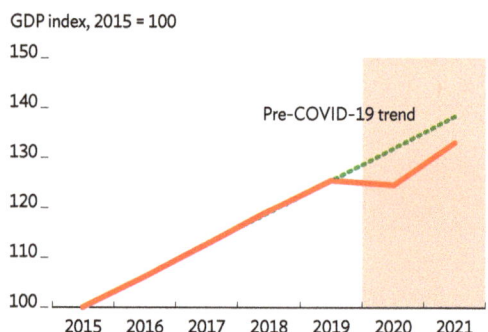

GDP = gross domestic product.
Source: *Asian Development Outlook* database.

remainder of the year, supported by local government special bond issues. Consumption is expected to recover in 2021 and help fuel a projected 7.7% rebound, 0.4 percentage points faster than envisaged in April. Monetary policy is expected to stay largely accommodative, though concern over financial stability may prevent significant further easing.

In India, the COVID-19 outbreak accelerated from April, the beginning of fiscal year 2020 (FY2020), for dramatically different economic prospects. GDP growth forecast by *ADO 2020* in April at 4.0% in FY2020 is now revised to 9.0% contraction. The lockdown has stalled the economy, and the continuing outbreak looks likely to prevent economic activity from resuming fully in the remaining 3 quarters of FY2020. With local lockdowns and consumers made risk-averse by the pandemic, private consumption is likely to suffer and precautionary savings to rise despite negative real interest rates. Investment will contract as investors are deterred by heightened risk and uncertainty, and industrial production and services will not fare well. Economic activity may resume in early FY2021, rebounding by 8.0%

Trajectories for economic recovery in 2021 similarly vary across subregions. The 2020 growth forecast for East Asia is lowered from *ADO 2020*, following contraction in the first half of the year. However, recovery in 2021 is now expected to be more robust. The growth forecast for the dominantly weighted PRC dictates the projected recovery path for the subregion. Most other subregional economies contracted in Q1, mainly from the impact of COVID-19. However, accommodative policies moderated some of the pandemic's impact in Taipei,China, providing a floor for mild economic expansion by 0.8% in the first half. In the whole subregion, GDP growth is forecast to slow from 5.4% in 2019 to 1.3% in 2020 and then recover to 7.0% in 2021. Only in the PRC and Taipei,China is growth expected to remain positive in 2020, with contraction expected in Hong Kong, China; Mongolia; and the Republic of Korea. All economies in the subregion are forecast to return to growth in 2021.

In Southeast Asia, the COVID-19 pandemic is causing a severe downturn. The subregion, forecast in April to grow by 1.0% in 2020, is now expected to contract by 3.8% before bouncing back by 5.5% next year. Major economies in the subregion slumped in Q2 2020 under stringent travel restrictions and quarantines, with double-digit declines in Malaysia, the Philippines, Singapore, and Thailand. Growth forecasts are downgraded from *ADO 2020* for all 10 economies, with only 3 of them—Brunei Darussalam, Myanmar, and Viet Nam—remaining in positive territory. Most governments aggressively loosened fiscal and monetary policies to cushion broad declines in consumption, investment, and trade as the COVID-19 pandemic worsened.

With all economies vulnerable to another wave of COVID-19 in the absence of effective vaccines, growth could slow even further if cases continue to soar as they have recently in Indonesia and the Philippines.

South Asia's 2020 GDP forecast is revised down sharply from 4.1% growth foreseen in April to 6.8% contraction as the pandemic spreads widely and containment measures are maintained. The worsening subregional forecast is mainly determined by a large revision to the forecast for India, its weighting in South Asia nearly as dominant as that of the PRC in East Asia. Bangladesh, Bhutan, and Nepal managed to grow in their recently completed fiscal years because COVID-19 affected only their tail end. Maldives plunged into a double-digit contraction in 2020 as tourism collapsed. Assuming the pandemic is contained before the end of the year, South Asia is forecast to grow by 7.1% in 2021, revised up from 6.0% in *ADO 2020*.

The COVID-19 pandemic has similarly undermined subregional growth prospects for Central Asia in 2020, with the outlook for all countries looking grimmer than in April. A difference in this subregion is that the gloom extends into 2021 with diminished growth expectations for half of the economies in the subregion—including Kazakhstan, by far the largest. GDP projections for Central Asia are adjusted down from 2.8% growth to 2.1% contraction in 2020 and from 4.2% growth to 3.9% growth in 2021. The pandemic has inflicted severe damage to every economy in the subregion in 2020, hydrocarbon exporters and importers alike. The impact is heaviest in the Kyrgyz Republic. GDP having shrunk by 6.1% in the first 7 months of 2020, with the worst yet to come, the projection for the whole year is downgraded from 4.0% growth in April to 10.0% contraction. In Turkmenistan, even though no COVID-19 cases have been reported, the growth forecast for this year is slashed from 6.0% in April to 3.2%. The negative impact of containment policies is expected to take its toll within this year, allowing for an upward revision to the forecast for 2021.

In the Pacific, the forecast for subregional GDP contraction in 2020 is deepened. This reflects deteriorating prospects for most economies under the pandemic but particularly for the two largest: Papua New Guinea and Fiji. After a downward revision of 5.8 percentage points from April, the Pacific is forecast to contract by 6.1% in 2020. The tourism industry is essentially closed and not expected to recover until at least Q1 2021. For Fiji and other economies heavily dependent on tourism, this means contractions in 2020 forecast in or near double digits. Although Fiji aims to establish a *bula* bubble (named using a Fijian greeting) to promote travel to and from Australia and New Zealand, the return of tourists will still be determined primarily by how the pandemic evolves (Box 1.2.1).

Box 1.2.1 Establishing travel bubbles to promote tourism

The COVID-19 pandemic and subsequent containment measures have hit tourism particularly hard, and governments are currently looking into various options to help it survive. One strategy is to establish so-called travel bubbles or green corridors with other countries. Travel bubbles are agreements by their signatories to open their borders to each other's nationals. They may cover only business travel or include leisure travel. They typically include detailed health protocols that need to be followed when crossing borders.

The first travel bubble in Asia and the Pacific was established between the PRC and the Republic of Korea on 1 May 2020. The agreement is limited to business travelers, who need to be invited by a company in the other country. Travelers need to monitor their health for 2 weeks and get tested for the virus within 72 hours before departure. Upon entry into the other country, travelers are tested again and quarantined for up to 2 days. The two countries are currently discussing an expansion of this program. In June, travel bubbles for business travelers were introduced between the PRC and Singapore and between Japan and Viet Nam. In August, Malaysia and Singapore finalized an agreement that allows citizens of both countries with a valid work pass to cross the border for work, provided they spend at least 90 days in their country of employment.

The travel bubbles currently operating follow a similar pattern. In most cases, the trip must be strictly for business, and testing occurs prior to departure and again on arrival. The length of quarantine is then typically shorter. Based on the emerging examples, economic incentives and trust between partners are the necessary conditions for establishing travel bubbles or green corridors. Economic considerations can extend to the importance of the partner as a tourism market. Trust is needed to ensure effective control and management of COVID-19.

Travel bubbles hold potential to restart tourism and thereby provide an important lifeline for the industry. The following paragraphs analyze the potential of travel bubbles to close the gap left by international tourists. Simulations assume that economies in the region set up a travel bubble with the largest partner: Fiji with Australia, for example, and Thailand with the PRC. For simplicity, the number of bilateral travelers is assumed to reach pre-crisis levels in 2018 within the travel bubble and that all other previously outbound tourists would vacation at home.

The results of this scenario analysis are shown in the box figure. For each economy, the bars indicate the surplus in green or deficit in red when tourism is reopened to the preferred partner.

For example, in 2018 Thailand reported to the United Nations World Tourism Organization having 11.6 million outbound tourists and 36.8 million foreign visitors. The deficit between outbound and inbound tourists, defined as a ratio of inbound tourists, is thus 68%. Assuming that Thailand entered into a travel bubble with the PRC and using 2018 data, 0.83 million Thais would travel to PRC and 10.65 million residents of the PRC would travel to Thailand. At the same time, the PRC and Thailand are assumed to enter into other bilateral travel bubbles, which reduces the potential of domestic tourism. For Thailand, preferred partner travel arrangements would improve its tourism deficit from 68% to 46%.

Bilateral travel bubbles would help most economies that depend heavily on tourism from a single market. For example, the gap for Fiji would drop from 84% to 44% if it entered into a bilateral agreement with Australia. While these are significant improvements, they still leave large deficits. In addition, it is unlikely that bilateral tourism would quickly reach pre-crisis levels. As they do in domestic tourism, social distancing and other containment measures would constrain supply. Further, traveling in bubbles often requires multiple testing, the cost of which will deter some people from traveling abroad.

The scenarios in the box figure were based only on tourism flows. However, tourism depends crucially on the pandemic situation at both the origin and the destination. Travel bubbles can usually be agreed only once both economies are well beyond their peak of new infections. Indeed, the recent reemergence of COVID-19 outbreaks in the region has led several governments to adopt a more cautious approach, with Sri Lanka delaying plans to reopen to tourists and Indonesia, Malaysia, and Thailand likely to follow suit. Another determinant of a successful travel bubble is testing capacity and pandemic preparedness in case of resurgent infection. As of August 2020, only a few country pairs enjoyed pandemic situations and preparedness sufficient to allow travel bubbles to be established.

Once the pandemic situation improves, we may see additional efforts to establish travel bubbles. They should be carefully prepared. Current travel bubbles feature exacting test protocols and require well-coordinated cross-border collaboration for seamless contact tracing. Data sharing needs to be subject to appropriate policies on privacy. Finally, it is important to remember that travel bubbles are only the second-best option. If the pandemic allows, less-discriminatory regimes would be preferred and travel bubbles removed.

continued next page

Box 1.2.1 *Continued*

Scenario analysis of a tourism bubble with the largest partner in terms of the number of tourists

Across Asia and the Pacific, bilateral travel agreements have the potential to revive tourism in many economies.

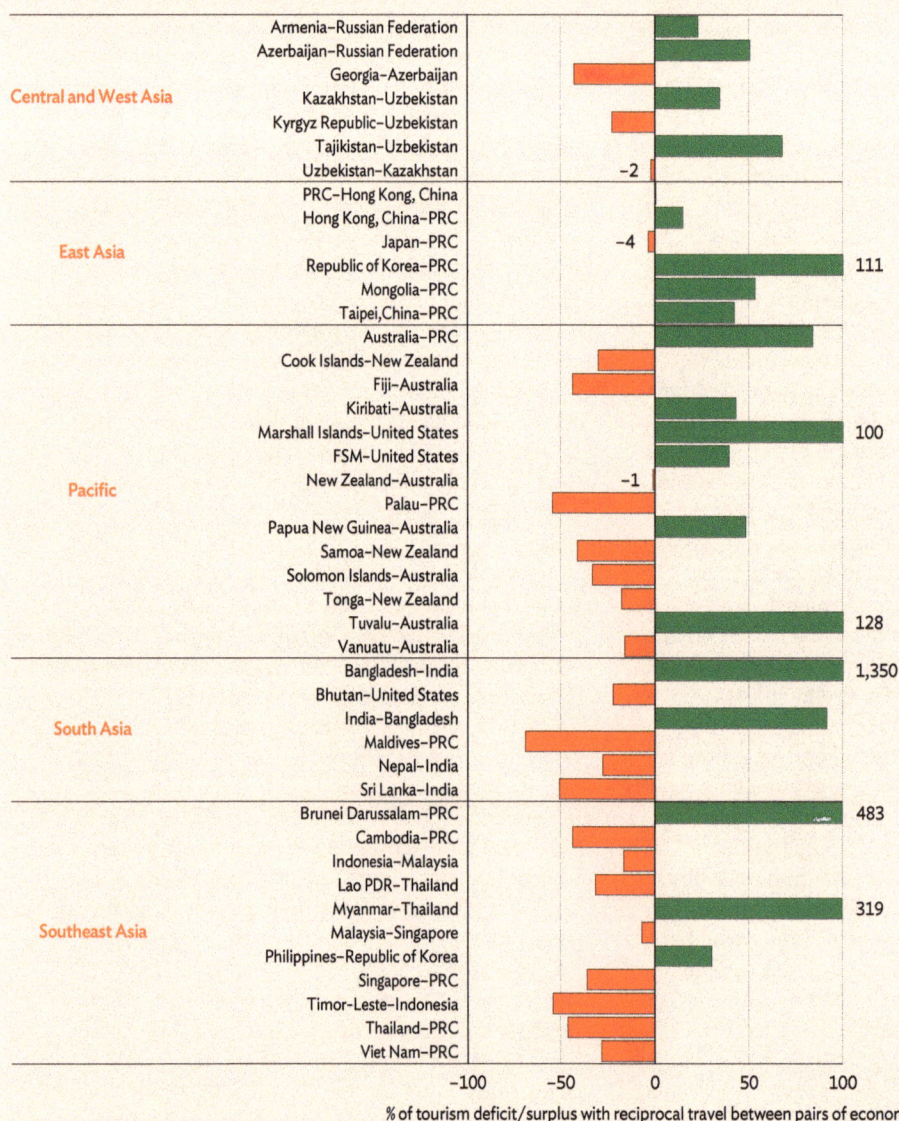

% of tourism deficit/surplus with reciprocal travel between pairs of economies

FSM = Federated States of Micronesia, Lao PDR = Lao People's Democratic Republic, PRC = People's Republic of China.

Notes: Using 2018 data, we assumed that domestic tourists who would otherwise leave the economy will stay at home in this scenario. We then got the difference between international tourist arrivals and the sum of inbound tourists from the economy's preferred partner and its own domestic tourists. We then divided this figure by the total number of international tourist arrivals to get this ratio.

Green bars indicate by how much the combined domestic tourists from an economy and its preferred partner would surpass the number of international tourists. Some economies and their preferred partner—including Bangladesh, Brunei Darussalam, the Marshall Islands, the Republic of Korea, Tuvalu, and Myanmar—have values that surpass 100%, which suggests that their combined tourists would more than double their 2018 international tourist arrivals. Economies with red bars indicate a gap in arrivals, even with mobilization of domestic tourists and arrivals from their preferred partner.

Arrival data from 2017 was used for the Marshall Islands, Tonga, and Tuvalu; 2016 for the FSM; and 2014 for Bangladesh. No arrivals data were available for Afghanistan, Pakistan, Turkmenistan, or Tuvalu for any year.

Source: Asian Development Bank calculations based on the United Nations World Tourism Organization statistical database (accessed 13 June 2020).

Reference:

ADB. 2020. Reviving Tourism Amid the COVID-19 Pandemic. *ADB Briefs*. Asian Development Bank. https://www.adb.org/publications/reviving-tourism-amid-covid-19-pandemic.

This box was written by Matthias Helble of the Economic Research and Regional Cooperation Department, ADB, Manila.

In Papua New Guinea and other economies dependent on commodity trade, quarantine requirements on shipments have disrupted transport and trade. In addition, construction on large infrastructure projects has been hampered by the travel restrictions. Prospects for recovery in 2021 depend largely on how quickly and safely trade and travel restrictions can be lifted. As in Central Asia but more so, the forecast for subregional growth in 2021 is lowered, from 2.7% to 1.3%.

1.2.1 Inflation eases and the current account balance stabilizes

Regional inflation is expected to ease and remain benign to the forecast horizon. The inflation forecast for 2020 is adjusted down from 3.2% in *ADO 2020* to 2.9% as the slowdown in demand is expected to outweigh supply-side disruptions (Figure 1.2.2). While growth is expected to pick up next year, output in the region will remain below its pre-pandemic trend and below potential output, as considerable slack remains in the labor market and in the economy more generally. Relatively low and stable international oil prices will contribute to the disinflationary trend, such that inflation is forecast to ease further to 2.3% in 2021, as forecast in *ADO 2020.*

Changes in inflation forecasts for developing Asia are not uniform, particularly for 2020. Reflecting different inflationary dynamics under the pandemic, some economies see downward price adjustments as lower demand more than compensates for higher cost pressures from supply disruption, while other economies see the opposite.

The outlook in East Asia is dominated by price dynamics in the PRC where slow recovery in consumer demand is the primary reason the inflation forecast for 2020 is revised down from 3.6% projected in April to 3.0%. Although higher food prices in the PRC drove inflation to average 3.9% in the first half of 2020, pork prices should normalize by the end of 2020 and allow inflation to ease further to 1.8% in 2021. Subregional inflation remained subdued in the first half of 2020. As forecast in April, inflation will remain high but stable in Mongolia and elsewhere subdued by weak demand.

Following GDP contraction in Southeast Asia, the 2020 inflation forecast is revised down from 1.9% in *ADO 2020* to 1.0% in 2020. Within the subregion, forecast revisions are mixed, revised down for Indonesia, Malaysia, Myanmar, Singapore, Thailand, and Timor-Leste but revised up for Brunei Darussalam, the Lao People's Democratic Republic, and the Philippines as domestic food prices rise. In sum, subregional inflation is seen muted in the forecast horizon.

Figure 1.2.2 Inflation in developing Asia

Depressed demand and low oil prices see the regional inflation forecast for 2020 revised down.

- ■ East Asia
- ■ Southeast Asia
- ■ South Asia
- ■ Central Asia
- ■ The Pacific

Percentage points

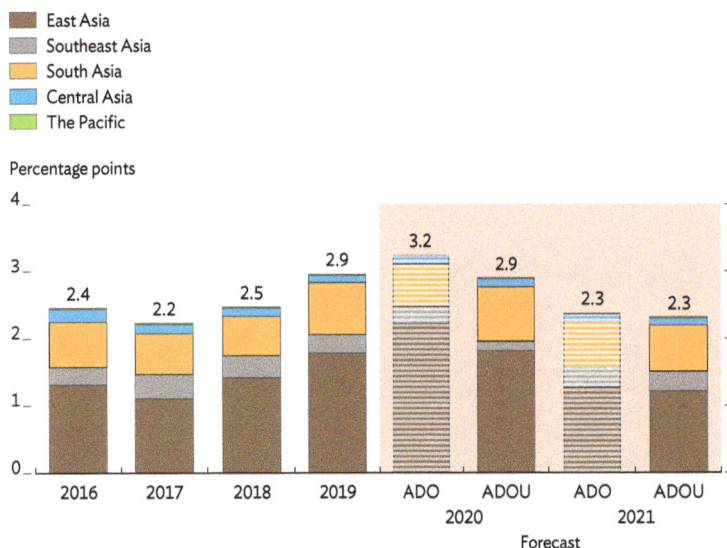

Source: *Asian Development Outlook* database.

The subregional inflation forecast for South Asia is revised up on rising pressures on food prices from supply chain disruption. An upward revision to India's inflation forecast for FY2020 (ending 30 March 2021) reflects supply disruption from the pandemic that exceeds expectations. The forecast for FY2021 is adjusted up only slightly from 3.8% to 4.0% on a forecast revival of economic activity and demand. Upward revisions are made elsewhere in the region, except in Pakistan and Sri Lanka.

Upward revisions to inflation forecasts for Central Asia reflect mainly lockdown-related supply-side constraints and other restrictive policy measures, but also currency depreciation in some countries. Projections for 2020 inflation are raised for Azerbaijan, Georgia, Kazakhstan, the Kyrgyz Republic, and Tajikistan as supply-side constraints outweigh demand contraction. In addition to the upward revision for 2020, inflation in 2021 is now forecast higher, revised from 6.3% in *ADO 2020* to 6.6%.

In the Pacific, average inflation is forecast at 2.8% in 2020, slightly revised up from April. Price pressures will remain benign across most of the Pacific with soft international commodity prices and subdued demand under declining economic activity. Only for the Federated States of Micronesia, Solomon Islands, and Vanuatu are inflation projections revised substantially upward, reflecting supply disruption following Cyclone Harold. Consistent with more downbeat economic growth prospects in 2021, the subregional inflation forecast for next year is corrected downward from 3.8% to 3.1%.

Figure 1.2.3 Current account balance in developing Asia

Current accounts will remain stable for the region, though Central Asia and the Pacific will see their current account balances deteriorate.

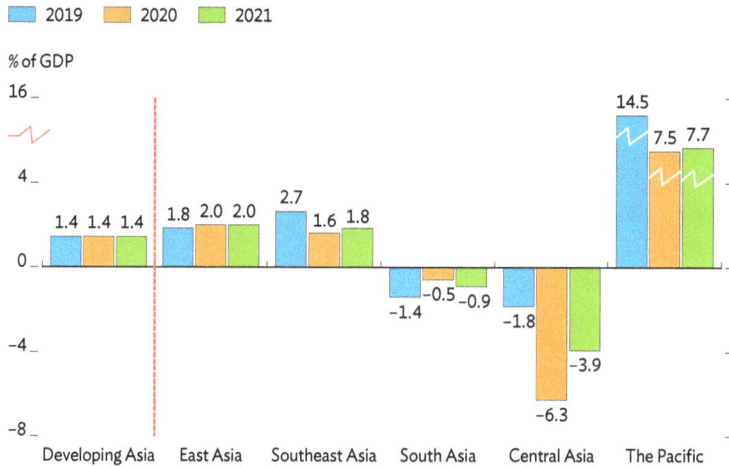

Source: *Asian Development Outlook* database.

Developing Asia's current account is projected to remain stable to the forecast horizon (Figure 1.2.3). The region's current account surplus will be unchanged from 2019 at 1.4% this year and next. By subregion, surpluses are projected to show little change from earlier projections in East Asia, in line with the dynamics of the PRC. The current account is expected to decline in Southeast Asia this year on the back of contraction in exports, collapse in tourism and supply chain disruptions. It will edge up next year as the expected recovery in the PRC improves the outlook for some exports, notably industrial metals, from Indonesia. South Asia's current account deficit is forecast to shrink as imports plummet more than exports because of a sharp contraction in domestic demand in India due to prolonged containment measures and sluggish domestic demand elsewhere in the subregion, before widening as recovery takes hold. Central Asia's current account deficit will widen this year as a significant fall in exports of commodities from the largest economies outstrips a decline in imports then shrink again next year. In the Pacific, the large subregional surplus will narrow sharply as tourism receipts collapse and foreign exchange earnings grind to a halt due to weak exports and remittances before edging up marginally next year as recovery takes hold.

1.3 Risks: Looming threats in an unsettled new normal

The outlook for developing Asia is subject to several significant risks. The prospect of a prolonged pandemic, in the form of extended or multiple COVID-19 waves, casts the largest shadow as it can result in extended containment measures. Such restrictions would damage the global economy directly and indirectly by undermining confidence and lowering expectations. Box 1.3.1 quantifies the potential impact of a prolonged pandemic. The analysis shows that renewed outbreaks and containment measures in the second half of this year would harm economies by disrupting both supply and demand. The main impact would be domestic but with some global spillover through trade and financial channels. Growth in 2020 would bear the brunt, but effects would linger and losses persist into 2021.

Box 1.3.1 Quantifying the impact of an extended pandemic

A recent spate of outbreaks around the world has raised the specter of a prolonged pandemic. New COVID-19 cases are still high or rising in some countries that are still in their first wave, while other countries are seeing second or third waves emerge. These trends in new cases spark some fear that governments would have to reimpose in the coming months containment measures similar to those imposed in April and May.

What would such a scenario imply for the global economy? We shed some light on this question with a modified version of the Global Projection Model (GPM++),[a] a multiregional general equilibrium model that features Asian economies in three separate blocks—one for the PRC, one for India, and an "emerging Asia" block containing several other ADB developing member countries. In contrast to the *Update's* baseline forecast which assumes containment of countries' outbreaks and a gradual renormalization of activity in the second half of 2020, we simulate the growth implications of a prolonged outbreak necessitating a return to more stringent containment measures. The scenario assumes that continued or renewed outbreaks require the reimposition of containment measures in many places, particularly those with high or rising cases as of the end of August. This includes the US, Europe, India, the "emerging Asia" block, and other places in Latin America and Eastern Europe. Notably, we do not include in the simulation a containment shock on the PRC because the number of cases there has remained flat (Figure 1.1.2B). We assume that containment will be implemented in a more targeted way that does not excessively limit mobility and activity. As a result, the economic impact of these renewed lockdowns is assumed to be less than in Q2 2020.

Specifically, we consider persistent or renewed outbreaks causing another quarter of GDP contraction in the second half of 2020 in several places around the world, followed by somewhat less vibrant recovery in the subsequent quarter. In the US, euro area, Japan, India, emerging Asian economies, and elsewhere, lockdown shocks drag down both demand and supply, reducing GDP growth by about half the magnitude of its fall in Q2, followed by much weaker recovery afterwards. In addition, we consider the implications of a possible substantial financial shock to the global economy as high unemployment and business closures stress the financial sector. In this scenario, tighter bank lending in the US reaches the peak recorded in Q4 2008 during the global financial crisis.

Our simulations show that, although individual countries' renewed lockdowns affect their domestic economy the most, effects spill over to other economies through trade and financial channels.

continued next page

Box 1.3.1 *Continued*

Economic implications of more lockdowns: Deviations from the baseline forecasts

Renewed lockdown would send the world into deeper contraction, depressing prices even further.

A. Gross domestic product

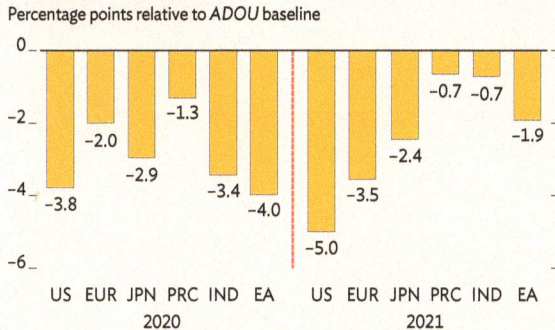

Percentage points relative to *ADOU* baseline

B. Inflation

Percentage points relative to *ADOU* baseline

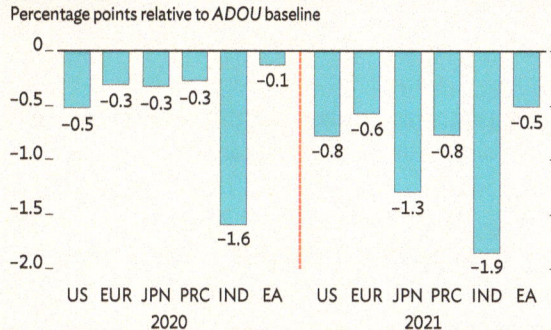

ADOU = ADO Update, EA = emerging Asia (Hong Kong, China; Indonesia; Malaysia; the Philippines; the Republic of Korea; Singapore; Taipei,China; Thailand; and Viet Nam), EUR = euro area, IND = India, JPN = Japan, PRC = People's Republic of China, US = United States.
Note: Data for India are in fiscal years that end on 31 March of the next year.
Source: ADB estimates using the Global Projection Model.

The blow to GDP would be felt around the globe, Asia included. A renewed lockdown in the US, for example, could shave the 2020 growth rate by 0.4 percentage points in the PRC and India, and by 0.5 points in other emerging Asian economies, with negative effects lingering into 2021. Another lockdown in the euro area would worsen Asia's prospects in 2021. Growth could be reduced in the PRC by another 0.3 percentage points, in India by 0.1 points, and in other emerging Asia economies by 0.4 points. In total, the combined lockdown shocks would lower 2020 growth relative to the *ADO Update* baseline by an additional 1.3 percentage points in the PRC, 3.4 points in India, and 4.0 points in the emerging Asia block. Further losses occur in 2021, by 0.7 percentage points in the PRC and India and by 1.9 points in other emerging Asia (box figure A).

A prolonged pandemic and renewed lockdowns would depress international oil prices by $7.80/barrel in 2020 and $14.70/barrel in 2021, relative to the *ADO Update* baseline. Weaker domestic demand and lower international oil prices would reduce inflation globally, particularly in 2021 (box figure B). Note that inflation in India would appear lower in FY2020 with a fall in prices in Q1 2021, which is Q4 of fiscal year 2020 in India.[b]

[a]   https://igpmn.org/#/about
[b]   In India, FY2020 includes Q1 of 2021, when the major effect of the negative shock to the global economy is already affecting prices.

This box was written by Arief Ramayandi and Dennis Sorino of the Economic Research and Regional Cooperation Department, ADB, Manila.

Debt and financial vulnerabilities would be exacerbated by a prolonged pandemic and could further stifle recovery. Lower corporate earnings and higher unemployment would make debt payments more difficult for firms and households alike, worsening the risk of bank losses as nonperforming loans proliferate. While the risk of a crisis is greater for heavily indebted emerging economies, evidence suggests that negative spillover would likely be global (Park and Shin 2020). An additional threat to financial stability may come from squeezed US dollar liquidity.

Since the global financial crisis of 2008–2009, high-income Asian economies have increased their US dollar lending to developing Asian economies. A period of financial distress caused by elevated US dollar funding costs might force them to curtail lending, heightening financial vulnerability in the region (Park et al. 2020).

Another concern is worsening geopolitical tensions, most notably persistent US–PRC friction over trade and technology. Although US and PRC trade representatives reaffirmed in late August their plan to fulfill obligations under the "phase one trade deal" signed in January, the combined effects of depressed consumption, falling oil prices, and African swine flu in the PRC suppressed its US imports in the year to July to just 48% of deal targets to that month. A phase two agreement to tackle cyber theft and state subsidies in exchange for more tariff rollbacks now looks less likely, and many tariffs imposed before the phase one deal remain in place. Meanwhile, tensions over technology have increased. An order effective from 1 April 2020 prohibits US companies from dealing with several foreign entities, including Shenzhen-based Huawei, over national security concerns. Relations were further roiled by a new set of executive orders signed on 6 August that ban the use of the PRC-owned technology platforms WeChat and TikTok by US entities and individuals. Few signs of compromise have so far emerged from either side, and bilateral tensions are likely to persist beyond the US presidential election.

One upside risk to the outlook is quicker virus containment than assumed in the baseline. The development and deployment of an effective vaccine sooner than expected—or breakthroughs in COVID-19 treatment—would allow faster economic recovery in developing Asia and beyond. However, this scenario is tempered by a risk of "vaccine nationalism," which could disrupt its distribution and raise international tensions.

The COVID-19 pandemic has the potential to leave in its wake long-lasting economic and social impacts. The acceleration of digitalization may generate innovations and new efficiencies but the "digital divide" in terms of technology access in many economies may worsen inequality (Box 1.1.1). The pandemic has also intensified the challenges that confront cities as they deal with the health crisis and plan their future development (Box 1.3.2). Finally, the crisis highlights to individuals and policy makers the importance of wellness— as discussed in the theme chapter of this report.

Box 1.3.2 Cities and the challenge of COVID-19

COVID-19 has hit cities hard. With over 90% of cases occurring in urban areas (United Nations 2020), city residents have borne the brunt of the pandemic and the harshest measures to contain it. Within cities, the urban poor have suffered the most. The risk of exposure to COVID-19 is greatest for those living in high-density environments such as informal settlements and slums, which house 3 of every 10 urban residents in developing Asia.

Even before COVID-19, cities in developing Asia faced a number of challenges. The pandemic has intensified them, and they often aggravate the health crisis in turn.

One challenge is inadequate urban and social infrastructure. Most cities in developing Asia have inadequate urban services and deficits in basic urban infrastructure for transportation, energy, water supply and sanitation, and managing wastewater and solid waste. Social infrastructure is often insufficient as well, unable to provide adequate health care and education, maintain public and community facilities, and ensure affordable housing. Living in overcrowded, unsafe, and unhealthy conditions defeats residents' efforts to comply with social distancing and hygiene demands, so the pandemic is aggravated.

Another challenge is underdeveloped, fragmented, and inefficient infrastructure for information and communication technology (ICT). Despite high internet and mobile phone penetration in Asia, cities often lack integrated ICT systems, and access to ICT is very unequal. Inefficient ICT complicates efforts to address the health crisis by hindering information sharing, contact tracing, and other measures to contain viral outbreaks.

Because COVID-19 has been concentrated primarily in urban areas, cities have borne the brunt of the strict lockdowns imposed in the first few months of the pandemic. The result has been an urban economic crisis at both the macro and micro level.

Urban areas are home to half of the world's population and generate some 80% of global economic activity (World Bank 2020), so any collapse in urban economic activity upends macroeconomic performance nationally. At the micro level, the costs are highest for the most vulnerable segments of society: low-income households whose members often work in retail and other services and therefore cannot work from home, and smaller enterprises with little access to finance to tide them over to better times.

Local governments with sorely strained finances are challenged to ramp up their planning and management in real time. On the front lines of the crisis, they have had to respond quickly to emergencies that sometimes overwhelmed their capacity. City revenues have dropped sharply with declines in both tax collection and fiscal transfers, even as costs mounted for local responses to the COVID-19 crisis.

The primary challenge in the near term is to maintain and improve urban infrastructure and services and to ensure equitable access. Transportation is notable among the services that must adapt to physical distancing needs, as must the management of public, commercial, and industrial spaces—especially with some public spaces repurposed for emergency response. As cities navigate the immediate crisis and set their sights on recovery, it is important that they prioritize investments able to build resilience and inclusion over the long term. This will help them better weather future shocks and stresses.

References:

United Nations. 2020. https://data.unicef.org/resources/how-covid-19-is-changing-the-world-a-statistical-perspective/.

World Bank. 2020. https://www.worldbank.org/en/topic/urbandevelopment/overview.

This box was written by Hong Soo Lee, Lindy Lois Gamolo, and Aldrin Plaza of the Sustainable Development and Climate Change Department, ADB, Manila.

References

Chen, L., D. Raitzer, R. Hasan, R. Lavado, and O. Velarde. Forthcoming. Letting Loose Without Letting Up: Cross Country Evidence on Controlling COVID-19. *ADB Working Paper.*

Felipe, J., S. Fullwiler, D. F. Bajaro, A. Yusoph, S. A. Askin, and M. A. Cruz. Forthcoming. An Analysis of the Worldwide Response to the COVID-19 pandemic: What and How Much? *ADB Working Paper.*

Institute of International Finance. 2020. Sharp Spike in Debt Ratios. *Global Debt Monitor,* 16 July. https://www.iif.com/Portals/0/Files/content/Research/ Global%20Debt%20Monitor_July2020.pdf.

Park, C. Y., P. Rosenkranz, and M. C. Tayag. 2020. COVID-19 Exposes Asian Banks' Vulnerability to US Dollar Funding. *ADB Policy Brief* No. 146. https://www.adb.org/sites/ default/files/publication/616091/covid-19-asian-banks- vulnerability-us-dollar-funding.pdf.

Park, C. Y. and K. Shin. 2020. The Impact of Nonperforming Loans on Cross-Border Bank Lending: Implications for Emerging Market Economies. *ADB Policy Brief* No. 136. https://www.adb.org/sites/default/files/ publication/609481/adb-brief-136-nonperforming-loans- cross-border-lending.pdf.

Sheiner, L. and K. Yilla. 2020. The ABCs of the post-COVID economic recovery. The Hutchins Center Explains. https://www.brookings.edu/blog/up-front/2020/05/04/ the-abcs-of-the-post-covid-economic-recovery/.

Shinozaki, S. Forthcoming. Impact of COVID-19 on Micro, Small, and Medium-sized Enterprises in Developing Asia. *Asia SME Monitor 2020.* Special chapter.

Appendix table
Digital education programs in developing Asia

Country	Program	Description	Platform	Link
Bangladesh	My School at My Home	Bangladesh Television broadcasts educational television lessons for students in grades 6–10 daily from 9.00 a.m. to 12:30 p.m. The lessons can be accessed as well by the Bangladesh Television YouTube channel.	TV and web	https://hao.360.com/?hj=llq2c
Bangladesh	Digital content	This platform contains interactive multimedia content to teach Bengali, English, mathematics, science, and other core subjects in alignment with the primary curriculum (1–5 class), prepared by National Curriculum and Textbook Board.	Web	http://digitalcontent.ictd.gov.bd/index.php/site/index
Bangladesh	E-books	Initiated by the National Curriculum and Textbook Board and the Access to Information Program of the Prime Minister's Office, the platform collects e-books for all primary and secondary textbooks.	Web	http://www.ebook.gov.bd/
Cambodia	MoEYS	Video lessons are streamed on Facebook by the Ministry of Education for various grade levels and on various subjects.	Web	https://www.facebook.com/pg/moeys.gov.kh/videos/?ref=page_internal
People's Republic of China	Taking the Same Class	Live broadcast lessons through Chinese Network Education Television 4 covers the curriculum content of elementary school and junior and senior high school.	TV	http://www.centv.cn/cetv4/index.html
People's Republic of China	National online cloud classroom	This platform provides free teaching and learning resources to primary and secondary school students.	Web	http://www.eduyun.cn/
Fiji	FEMIS, live version	An official education management system that provides information and resources to schools, teachers, and students.	Web	http://www.femis.gov.fj/?fbclid=IwAR1TC7hWXfmtovNkKJLrPiaGVGuVBXAnE8hP0PXf14AbJjBO2JAIIWM6m0U
Fiji	RF One and RF Two radio channels	A set of planned supplementary programs are delivered through the Schools Broadcasting Unit and Fiji Broadcasting Corporation	Radio	
India	National Repository of Open Educational Resources	The portal provides a host of resources for students and teachers in multiple languages including books, interactive modules, and videos. Content is mapped to the curriculum for classes 1–12 and includes aligned resources for teachers.	Web	https://nroer.gov.in/
India	DIKSHA	The DIKSHA platform offers teachers, students, and parents engaging learning materials relevant to the prescribed school curriculum, including video lessons, worksheets, textbooks, and assessments. The app can be used offline.	Web	https://diksha.gov.in/
India	Swayam	A platform that facilitates the hosting of all the courses taught in classrooms from class 9 to postgraduate. Subjects align with the curriculum and include engineering including robotics, humanities, social sciences, law, and management.	Web	https://swayam.gov.in/

continued next page

Appendix table: *Continued*

Country	Program	Description	Platform	Link
India	National Digital Library of India	An official online library that provides academic content by subject area for different levels of education, including lifelong learning.	Web	https://ndl.iitkgp.ac.in/
Indonesia	TV Edukasi	An Indonesian television station that offers channel 1 for students and channel 2 for teachers. It is managed by Pustekkom, a semiautonomous body under the direction of the Ministry of Education.	TV and web	https://tve.kemdikbud.go.id/
Indonesia	Rumah Belajar	A platform that provides learning content and a learning management system for the digital classroom, as well as other resources that enable its users to interact and communicate online and organize distance learning activities.	Web	https://belajar.kemdikbud.go.id/
Indonesia	SPADA	This e-learning platform is for students in tertiary education.	Web	https://spada.kemdikbud.go.id/
Kiribati	School e-resources	Domestic electronic resources are provided by the Ministry of Education to students in grades 1–13.	Web	https://www.moe.gov.ki/?fbclid=IwAR34Aj4q_Nr9NzM3AfJPumCnCdz-2NB0P7Fs786Eek4lrmDNE5MtTJ17CY0#h.p_ID_64
Malaysia	EduwebTV	This online learning platform of its Ministry of Education hosts content on demand for students from pre-kindergarten to secondary school, as well as digital textbooks.	Web and TV	http://eduwebtv.moe.edu.my/
Malaysia	TV Okey	This free-to-air television channel is used to air educational programs for students during COVID-19 school closure.	Web and TV	https://okey.rtm.gov.my/
Malaysia	Digital Educational Learning Initiative Malaysia	This online learning platform, launched by the Ministry of Education on 15 June 2020, offers all the applications and services required by teachers and students in the Malaysian school system.	Web	https://sites.google.com/moe.edu.my/login/login
Maldives	Filaa	This educational platform, developed by the Government of Maldives, provides online learning materials to students and supports teachers.	Web	https://filaa.moe.gov.mv/
Maldives	YesTV	Public Service Media provides classes for grade 10 and 11 students to prepare for upcoming examinations.	TV	
Mongolia	ESIS Edu	Public education television is organized by the Ministry of Education, Culture, Science, and Sports, and a website hosts e-content for students from pre-kindergarten to grade 12, as well as textbooks.	Web and TV	http://econtent.edu.mn/
Nepal	Learning portal	This online platform offers educational resources to students.	Web	https://learning.cehrd.edu.np/
Nepal	Radio Jingle	The Ministry of Education, Science, and Technology, in collaboration with the United Nations Educational, Scientific, and Cultural Organization (UNESCO), introduced radio learning programs for children under lockdown.	Audio	
Pakistan	Open courseware	This portal of the Virtual University of Pakistan offers a repository of course materials organized by subject area.	Web	https://ocw.vu.edu.pk/

continued next page

Appendix table: *Continued*

Country	Program	Description	Platform	Link
Pakistan	Sindh school monitoring system	This system allows more effective and transparent monitoring of staff, students, and school infrastructure.	Web	http://www.sindheducation.gov.pk/pages.jsp?page=sindhschoolmonitoringsystem
Philippines	DepEd Commons	This online platform for public school teachers supports distance learning to continue the delivery of basic education.	Web	https://commons.deped.gov.ph/
Republic of Korea	Korea Educational Broadcasting System	Complementing public education in the Republic of Korea, this broadcast system supports the broadcasting of educational television program across the country.	Web, TV, and radio	https://www.ebs.co.kr/main
Republic of Korea	Onschool	This portal provides learning materials to students and teachers from kindergarten to grade 12.	Web	http://onschool.edunet.net/onSchool/listBoardForm.do?board_seq=6#none
Samoa	2AP radio station	Radio lessons on various subjects are broadcasted on 2AP radio station.	Radio	
Samoa	LA OSO O AOAOGA FOU	This TV program broadcasts relevant content for early childhood education and primary school.	TV	https://mesc.gov.ws/aoaoga-mo-fanau/
Solomon Islands	Solomon Islands iResource	This online platform offers educational resources for primary and secondary students	Web	http://www.iresource.gov.sb/
Solomon Islands	SIBC radio	Broadcast radio lessons have been produced by the Ministry of Education and Human Resources Development since the end of April.	Radio	
Sri Lanka	Channel Eye and Nethra TV	State-run TV channels broadcast educational content during school closure.	TV	http://www.channeleye.lk/rupavahini-tv-schedule
	E-thaksalava	The national e-learning portal offers materials to facilitate learning from home for grades 1–12.	Web	http://www.e-thaksalawa.moe.gov.lk/
Thailand	Digital Learning Centre	An online learning platform developed by the Office of Private Education Commission provides education via internet connections to the general public and all elementary and secondary students nationwide during the pandemic.	Web	https://www.opec.go.th/
Timor-Leste	Timor-Leste Learning passport	This e-learning portal contains various resources that facilitate distance learning.	Web	https://timorleste.learningpassport.unicef.org/?fbclid=IwAR1Sab9ALbc5fyqyQ7JDv3uAeoAcv2RJv5dLFYkyhOvrrFY1D6H8L3AZLnU
Vanuatu	Moodle	The Ministry of Education launched this platform to facilitate continuity in learning during school closure.	Web	https://www.viewpx.org/e-learning-with-moodle/
Viet Nam	E-learning	This official platform for distance learning offers learning resources from pre-primary to secondary school, divided by subject area.	Web	http://taphuan.moet.edu.vn/
Viet Nam	National and local TV channels	Local and national television stations broadcast lessons to ensure continuity in learning for students in grades 1–12.	TV and web	https://moet.gov.vn/tintuc/Pages/lich-hoc-truc-tuyen.aspx
	Taphuan	This platform of the Ministry of Education contains resources for distance learning.	Web	http://taphuan.moet.edu.vn/

Sources: World Bank. https://www.worldbank.org/en/topic/edutech/brief/how-countries-are-using-edtech-to-support-remote-learning-during-the-covid-19-pandemic; United Nations Educational, Scientific, and Cultural Organization. https://en.unesco.org/covid19/educationresponse/nationalresponses#ASIA%20&%20THE%20PACIFIC; various country education websites.

Annex: Global economy plunges as pandemic rages

The external environment continues to suffer from the effects of the pandemic. This Update envisages the advanced economies of the United States, the euro area, and Japan contracting more sharply in 2020 than projected in Asian Development Outlook 2020 (ADO 2020) as the pandemic and measures to contain it continue to suppress consumption, investment, trade, and travel. GDP in the second quarter showed unprecedented deep contractions in the major advanced economies. In aggregate, they are expected to contract by 6.2% in 2020 before growth resumes at 4.4% in 2021 (Table A1.1).

Table A1.1 Baseline assumptions on the international economy

	2019	2020			2021		
	Actual	April ADO 2020	June ADOS	September Update	April ADO 2020	June ADOS	September Update
GDP growth (%)							
Major industrial economies[a]	1.7	−0.3	−5.8	−6.2	1.8	4.1	4.4
United States	2.2	0.4	−5.3	−5.3	2.1	3.8	4.0
Euro area	1.3	−1.0	−7.0	−8.0	1.6	5.5	6.0
Japan	0.7	−1.5	−5.0	−5.4	0.9	2.0	2.0
Prices and inflation							
Brent crude spot prices (average, $/barrel)	64.03	35.00	35.00	42.50	55.00	45.00	50.00
Consumer price index inflation (major industrial economies' average, %)	1.4	1.4	0.9	0.7	1.7	1.6	1.4
Interest rates							
United States federal funds rate (average, %)	2.2	0.4	...	0.4	0.1	...	0.1
European Central Bank refinancing rate (average, %)	0.0	0.0	...	0.0	0.0	...	0.0
Bank of Japan overnight call rate (average, %)	−0.1	−0.1	...	−0.1	−0.1	...	−0.1
$ Libor[b] (%)	2.2	0.4	...	0.4	0.1	...	0.1

... = unavailable, ADO = Asian Development Outlook, ADOS = ADO Supplement, GDP = gross domestic product.

[a] Average growth rates are weighted by gross national income, Atlas method.

[b] Average London interbank offered rate quotations on 1-month loans.

Sources: US Department of Commerce, Bureau of Economic Analysis, http://www.bea.gov; Eurostat, http://ec.europa.eu/eurostat; Economic and Social Research Institute of Japan, http://www.esri.cao.go.jp; Consensus Forecasts; Bloomberg; CEIC Data Company; Haver Analytics; World Bank, Global Commodity Markets, http://www.worldbank.org; ADB estimates.

This annex was written by Matteo Lanzafame, Nedelyn Magtibay-Ramos, Madhavi Pundit, Pilipinas Quising, Arief Ramayandi, Dennis Sorino, and Priscille Villanueva of the Economic Research and Regional Cooperation Department, ADB, Manila, and Michael Timbang, consultant, Economic Research and Regional Cooperation Department, ADB, Manila.

Recent developments in the major advanced economies

United States

The US economy fell into a technical recession in the first half of 2020 as the pandemic continued to weigh on economic activity. After a 5.0% drop in the first quarter (Q1) in seasonally adjusted annualized terms (as assumed for all quarterly growth rates in this annex unless otherwise noted), the economy contracted by 31.7% in Q2 (Figure A1.1). This is the most severe quarterly contraction in the US since World War II, and almost four times as large as the deepest contraction during the global financial crisis of 2008–2009. Private consumption was the largest factor in GDP contraction, plunging by 34.1%, and investment dropped even more steeply, by 46.2%. Government spending provided some relief to the economy, growing by 2.8% thanks to the execution in the US of the Coronavirus Aid, Relief, and Economy Security Act. Net exports made a slight positive contribution as a decline in imports outpaced that of exports. Trade suffered widespread decreases in both goods (particularly capital goods) and services, mainly in travel and transport.

Measures taken to contain the COVID-19 outbreak crippled both consumption and investment. As mobility became tightly restricted and employment nosedived, consumer confidence and spending withered and retail sales dropped by 12.7% month on month in April. Demand for services fell by 43.1% in Q2, almost across the board. As demand dropped notably for clothing and gasoline from stay-at-home consumers, sales of nondurable goods also fell sharply, by 14.9%. The manufacturing purchasing managers' index (PMI) dipped from March to May below the 50 threshold that signals future growth or contraction. This reflected slumping investment as purchases of equipment and structures tumbled and inventory dropped in tandem with falling retail trade.

Indicators are somewhat mixed, but more recent data suggest conditions turning a corner as pandemic containment measures were eased in mid-June. The consumer confidence index started to recover in June but remained well below levels predating COVID-19 (Figure A1.2). Consumption started to recover somewhat as the retail sales index improved in May by 17.3% month on month to reach 145.2 in July, its highest gain since the global financial crisis of 2008–2009. Production and employment indicators also suggest that a partial recovery is under way. Industrial production has crept up, and the PMI has stayed in expansionary territory since June.

Figure A1.1 Demand-side contributions to growth, United States

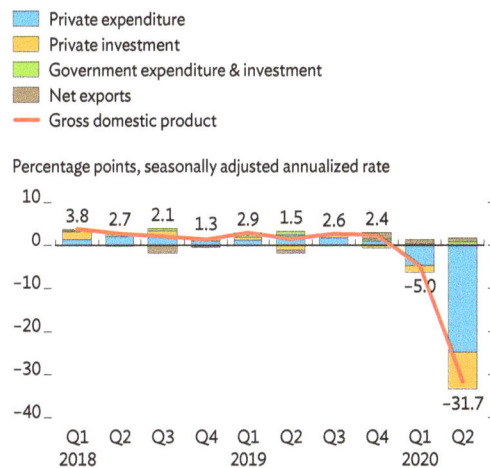

Q = quarter.
Sources: US Department of Commerce. Bureau of Economic Analysis. http://www.bea.gov; Haver Analytics (both accessed 31 August 2020).

Figure A1.2 Business activity and consumer confidence indicators, United States

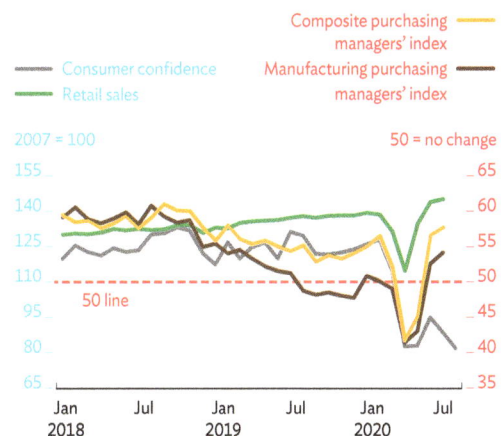

Note: A purchasing managers' index reading <50 signals deterioration, >50 improvement.
Source: Haver Analytics (accessed 31 August 2020).

The labor market is showing some improvement after unemployment surged more than 10 percentage points to 14.7% in April, but employment is still far from making up for jobs lost in March and April. Unemployment was still elevated at 10.2% in July but suggesting gradual improvement from the pandemic blow (Figure A1.3).

With the sharp drop in demand, headline inflation slowed in March to 1.5% and further to 0.1% in May before rallying to 0.6% in June and 1.0% in July (Figure A1.4). Core inflation also softened, to 1.2% in May and June and up by 1.6% in July after hovering above 2.0% until March 2020. The US Federal Reserve is seen continuing its accommodative polices going forward to support the economy. The Fed funds rate, the main conduit for policy, has been held near zero since mid-March, and the Fed has committed to keeping it there as long as necessary. The Fed has also committed to further increasing its holdings of Treasury and agency mortgage-backed securities to sustain smooth market function and foster the effective transmission of monetary policy.

The path forward will rely on policy actions taken at all levels of government to provide relief and support recovery. With continued commitment from the government and the Fed to support the economy, recovery is expected in the second half of 2020, with the growth rate consolidating in Q3 and accelerating in Q4. Strong growth should continue into 2021 and normalize in the second half, but with GDP still below its level before COVID-19 to the end of 2021. On an annual basis, GDP is forecast to contract by 5.3% in 2020 and grow by 4.0% in 2021. Inflation will remain muted at 0.9% in 2020 before doubling to 1.8% in 2021. Risks to the outlook remain heavily on the downside as the number of COVID-19 cases in the US continues to rise. Worsening outbreak dynamics expose the economy to the risk of having to return to more stringent containment measures, which would again impede economic activity.

Figure A1.3 Unemployment rate, United States

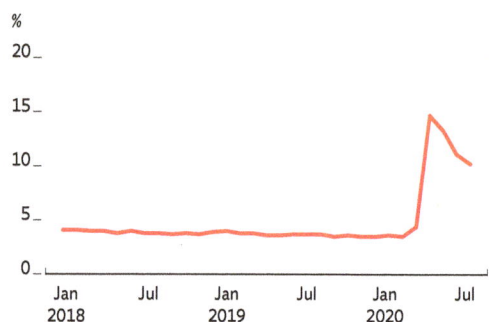

Source: Haver Analytics (accessed 31 August 2020).

Figure A1.4 Inflation and the US Federal Reserve rate, United States

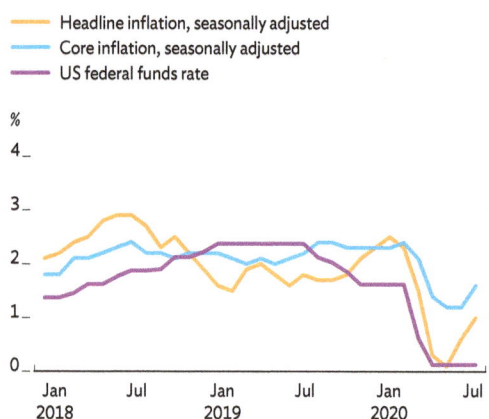

Source: Haver Analytics (accessed 31 August 2020).

Euro area

Following 0.2% growth in the last quarter of 2019, GDP in the euro area plunged by 14.1% in Q1 2020, undermined by the first COVID-19 outbreaks in March. Domestic and external demand were both severely hit by strict lockdown measures adopted by governments to contain the pandemic. Amid sinking consumer confidence, falling employment, and gloomy prospects, private consumption expenditure contracted by 16.8% in Q1, and fixed investment fell by 19.2%. Government spending also declined, by 2.8%. Similarly, exports and imports plunged as global trade tumbled, causing net exports to subtract 1.9 percentage points from growth. Consistent with the regionwide contraction, GDP dropped in France by 21.5%, in Germany by 7.8%, in Italy by 20.1%, and in Spain by 19.3%.

As more countries struggled to reduce infection rates, and as lockdowns paralyzed economic activity, GDP further plummeted by 39.4% in Q2—the worst contraction since records began in 1995 (Figure A1.5). Growth suffered from both the collapse in global trade and a steep decline in domestic demand. Recession in Q2 was felt across all major euro area economies, with contraction by 44.8% in France, 33.5% in Germany, 42.2% in Italy, and 55.8% in Spain.

Leading indicators suggest the euro area economy may have bottomed out in Q2 and started to gain traction at the beginning of Q3. The manufacturing PMI inched up from 47.4 in June to 51.1 in July, reaching positive territory following the unwinding of containment measures in early May. The composite PMI recovered from 48.5 in June to 54.8 in July, its strongest reading since June 2018 (Figure A1.6). The services PMI climbed from 48.3 in June to 55.1 in July as output and new orders returned to growth, and as business sentiment strengthened in expectation of further reopening. The economic sentiment indicator improved from 75.8 in June to 82.3 in July, reflecting recovering confidence in the service sector, notably retail, which returned to positive growth month on month in May, at 17.8%. Growth in industrial production turned positive the same month, reaching 12.4% month on month. However, the labor market deteriorated slightly as the unemployment rate inched up from 7.7% in May to 7.8% in June.

Given the magnitude of the first-half decline, the COVID-19 pandemic is set to hammer the euro area economy this year. Private consumption is expected to contract by 9.0% as uncertainty inhibits household spending—especially on travel and recreational services—even as containment measures are lifted. Investment is likely to take a double-digit hit as firms are constrained by supply, demand, and financial factors. External trade is expected to fall by 13.0%. The consolidated fiscal deficit is forecast to rise to equal 8.5% of GDP in light of the expansionary stance adopted in response to the outbreak. Assuming that the easing of lockdowns is sustained, the economy will recover in the second half of the year, buoyed by accommodative policy and alleviated uncertainty. The euro area is forecast to shrink by 8.0% in 2020 and then grow by 6.0% in 2021.

Headline inflation increased marginally from 0.3% year on year in June to 0.4% in July, while core inflation rose from 1.1% to 1.3% (Figure A1.7). Consumer price inflation averaged 0.6% from January to July, undershooting the European Central Bank target of just below 2.0%. The central bank left interest rates unchanged at record lows in July and maintained its emergency quantitative easing program at €1.35 trillion. As price pressures remain weak in the region in light of rising unemployment, subdued economic activity, and low oil prices, inflation is forecast to average 0.5% in 2020 and 1.2% in 2021.

Figure A1.5 Demand-side contributions to growth, euro area

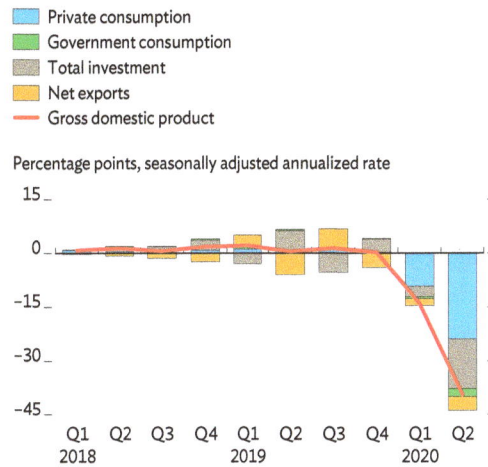

- Private consumption
- Government consumption
- Total investment
- Net exports
- Gross domestic product

Percentage points, seasonally adjusted annualized rate

Q = quarter.
Source: Haver Analytics (accessed 8 September 2020).

Figure A1.6 Economic sentiment and purchasing managers' indexes, euro area

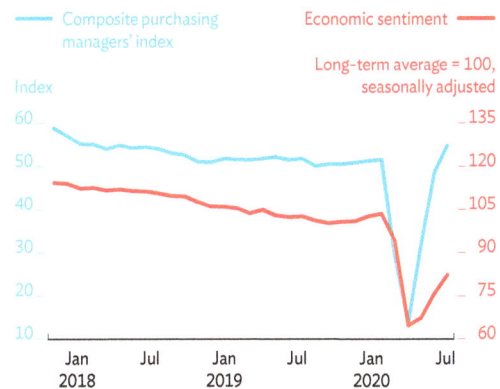

— Composite purchasing managers' index
— Economic sentiment

Long-term average = 100, seasonally adjusted

Sources: CEIC Data Company; Haver Analytics (both accessed 2 August 2020).

The euro area outlook is highly uncertain, with risks tilted to the downside. A second wave of COVID-19 infections could require a return to stringent containment measures, and some countries could see fragile banks and debt sustainability severely tested. Several policy measures have been rolled out to mitigate these risks. To keep liquidity shortages from snowballing into a solvency crises, the central bank announced its Pandemic Emergency Purchase Programme in mid-March and, on 30 April, lowered rates on long-term liquidity auctions. On 9 April, euro area ministers approved an emergency package worth €540 billion to help countries through the European Stability Mechanism, companies through the European Investment Bank, and workers through the newly established scheme called Support to Mitigate Unemployment Risks in an Emergency. In July, European Union leaders agreed on a recovery package worth €750 billion in grants and low-interest loans to member states toward mitigating fallout from the pandemic.

Figure A1.7 Headline and core inflation, euro area

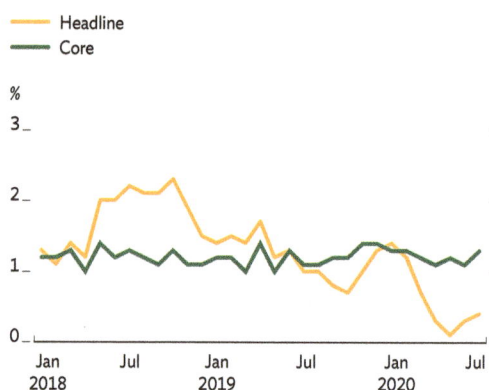

Source: Haver Analytics (accessed 2 August 2020).

Japan

The economy fell into a recession as the effects of the COVID-19 pandemic in early 2020 exacerbated a slowdown that started in 2019. The slowdown was a consequence of natural disasters, a consumption tax hike in October and a long-running trade conflict between the US and the People's Republic of China (PRC). The economy showed signs of recovery at year end but slowed again significantly in March with the onset of the pandemic. Restrictions under a state of emergency from early April until 25 May severely curbed economic activity in the period.

GDP shrank 27.8% seasonally adjusted annualized rate in Q2, marking the third consecutive quarterly contraction after the tax hike, and surpassing the 17.8% decline in Q1 2009 in the wake of the global financial crisis. Consumer spending plunged by 28.9% and exports by 56.0% amid devastated global activity and demand. Investment declined by a relatively less severe 4.1%, while government spending recorded an underwhelming 1.0% drop (Figure A1.8).

Production slumped by 16.8% quarter on quarter in Q2, in line with the deep downturn. But early signs of recovery emerged in industrial activity with a 2.0% rise month on month in June.

Other monthly indicators also suggest that Japan may be past the worst, and that economic activity, particularly consumption, is underway aided by government stimulus programs. With non-essential businesses reopening and consumers returning to stores, retail sales surged by 13.1% in June back to pre-pandemic levels. Consumer confidence also ticked up, though still falling short of readings in March.

Figure A1.8 Demand-side contributions to growth, Japan

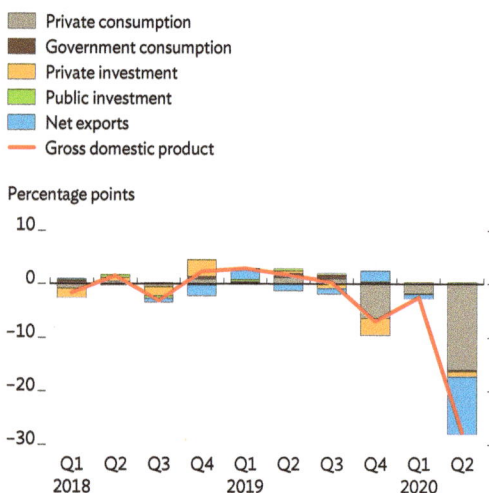

Q = quarter.
Source: Economics and Social Research Institute, Cabinet Office, Government of Japan. http://www.esri.cao.go.jp (accessed 17 August 2020).

The unemployment rate edged down from a 36-month high of 2.9% in May to 2.8% in June, which suggests a possible rebound in labor income and therefore consumption. However, a sharp recovery of expenditure on services, as indicated by a spike in the services PMI from May to June stalled subsequently, partly reflecting a response to a second wave of restrictions.

Meanwhile, capital spending is sluggish. Although manufacturing PMI climbed from 40.1 to a five-month high of 45.2 in July, it remains in contractionary territory, well under the threshold value of 50 (Figure A1.9). The Tankan survey of large manufacturers reported sentiment on current business conditions in Q2 falling further below the 0 threshold to –34.0, and core machinery orders declined by 7.6% in June, additional indications that any recovery in investment may lag. On a positive note, business sentiment among workers with jobs sensitive to economic trends, as reflected in the Cabinet Office's Economy Watchers Survey, recorded the biggest monthly increase ever in June, after restrictions were eased.

A slump in global demand in response to the pandemic took a toll on Japan's major export categories: automobiles, machinery, and other durable goods. July's trade data showed a 18.0% year on year drop in exports. But it marked an improvement from the 25.8% fall in June, on the back of a recovery in the PRC which if continued will support a rebound in Q3. Imports fell by 21.2% in the same month, reflecting weak demand and declining oil prices (Figure A1.10).

Despite downward pressure, annual headline inflation ticked up to 0.4%% in July from 0.1% in June. Core consumer inflation, which excludes energy and fresh food, is maintained at 0.3%. At its latest meeting, the Bank of Japan left monetary policy unchanged—the short-term policy rate at –0.1% and the 10-year yield on Japanese government bonds capped at about zero—and continued to provide financial support to businesses through its recently expanded programs.

The outlook for growth in Japan is downbeat and rife with uncertainty, with risks looming large. The economy will shrink in 2020 by 5.4%. If the pandemic is contained, 2021 could see recovery by 2.0%. The government announced significant fiscal policy stimulus, estimated at over 40% of GDP, to support businesses and employment. This comes in addition to accommodative monetary policies, which will soften the downturn.

While a rebound in consumer spending is key to recovery in the near term, a major uncertainty is the resurgence of COVID-19 sweeping through many urban centers, bringing a renewed state of emergency in some prefectures.

Figure A1.9 Consumption and business indicators, Japan

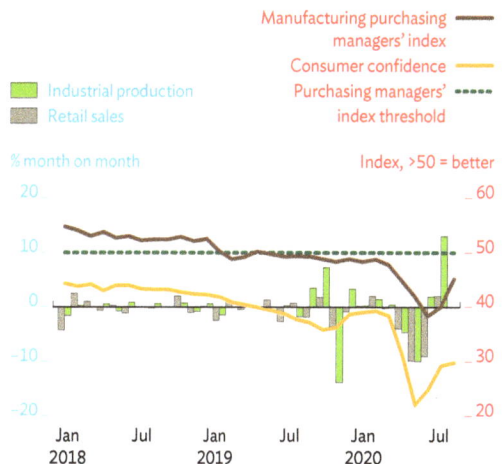

Notes: A purchasing managers' index reading <50 signals deterioration, >50 improvement. A consumer confidence reading >50 signals better conditions.
Source: CEIC data company (accessed 20 August 2020).

Figure A1.10 Trade indicators, Japan

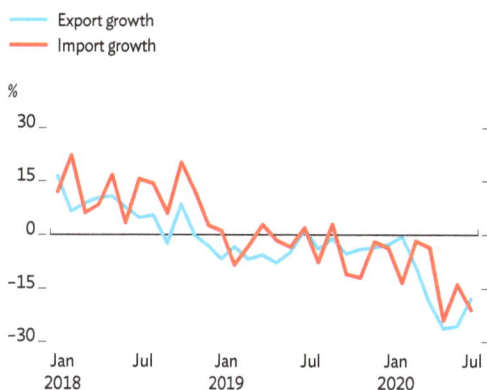

Source: CEIC Data Company (accessed 20 August 2020).

Although blanket business closure has not been imposed, restrictions will weigh heavily on sentiment and domestic spending for consumers and businesses alike, as might changes in the political landscape. Curbs on domestic travel and the postponement of the Tokyo 2020 Olympic Games until next year will continue to thwart tourism. While economic recovery in the PRC, a major trade partner, could boost Japanese exports, the risk of a prolonged slowdown in the external sector remains with another wave of infections in other large economies, including the US.

Recent developments and outlook in nearby economies

Australia

A prolonged drought and lockdown measures caused economic growth to contract by 1.2% in Q1 2020. Consumption declined by 1.6% and fixed investment by 3.0%, dragging down growth. Public consumption expenditure, meanwhile, expanded by 7.2% as the government fast-tracked infrastructure spending to revitalize the economy. As imports of goods and services contracted by 22.6% and exports by 13.4%, net exports contributed 1.9 percentage points to GDP growth (Figure A1.11).

The lockdown from March until the lifting of restrictions in June was reflected in most leading indicators. Consumer sentiment declined below the 100-point threshold dividing optimism and pessimism, falling to a low of 75.6 in April before partly recovering to 87.9 in July. Similar troughs appeared in March–April in retail sales growth, business confidence, and the Australian Industry Group's performance of manufacturing index, followed by partial recoveries. The seasonally adjusted unemployment rate climbed to 7.4% in June, the highest in almost 22 years.

Inflation plunged from 2.3% in Q1 to 0.5% deflation in Q2, far below the 2%–3% target set by the Reserve Bank of Australia. The central bank board decided at its 4 August 2020 meeting, to keep the cash interest rate at 0.25% as part of a comprehensive and coordinated package of fiscal and monetary policies to lower funding costs and support the supply of credit to the economy, which includes a 3-year government bond yield target of about 0.25% and a term funding facility for the banking system to boost lending to businesses.

These supportive fiscal and monetary policies promise to help mitigate the effects of the pandemic, but recovery will depend on how soon economic activity can normalize—an open question given the risk of recurrent waves of COVID-19 infection. Melbourne was placed under lockdown again in

Figure A1.11 Demand-side growth, Australia

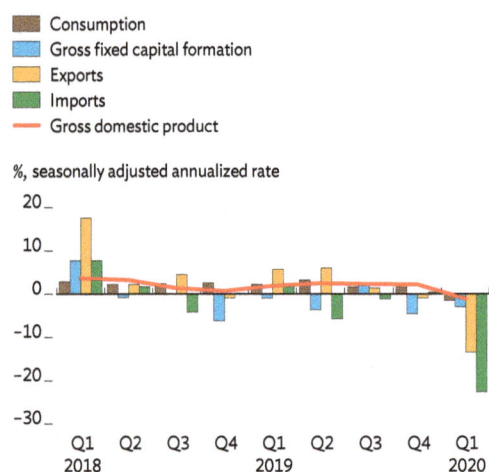

- Consumption
- Gross fixed capital formation
- Exports
- Imports
- Gross domestic product

%, seasonally adjusted annualized rate

Q = quarter.
Source: CEIC Data Company (accessed 11 August 2020).

early July, which tightened on 2 August to a stricter stage 4 lockdown. A state of disaster was declared for the whole state of Victoria, which was placed from 5 August under stage 3 restrictions. These developments could disrupt supply chains well beyond Victoria, the location of the biggest container port in the country. The August 2020 Consensus Forecast was for GDP to contract by 4.0% in 2020 and expand by 2.8% in 2021.

New Zealand

The economy contracted by 5.0% in Q1 2020 as strict coronavirus containment measures curbed domestic demand and the pandemic battered the global economy. Private consumption declined by 1.0% while government consumption was unchanged but fixed investment dropped by 11.6%. Net exports contributed 5.5 percentage points to growth as a 20.7% decline in imports greatly outpaced a 8.2% decline in exports (Figure A1.12).

The lockdown from 25 March severely undermined private consumption, consumer and business confidence, and manufacturing. Some indicators rebounded after restrictions were eased in May. Change in retail sales quarter on quarter reversed 14.4% growth in Q4 2019 with 8.8% contraction in Q1 2020. Consumer confidence waned and became pessimistic in Q2, dropping below the threshold of 100 to 97.2. Business confidence wallowed in pessimistic territory, plunging to –66.6 in April, the lowest in 29 years, but improving to –42.4 in August. The seasonally adjusted performance manufacturing index dropped to 26.0 in April, its lowest reading ever, which signaled extreme contraction in manufacturing. However, the index jumped above the threshold of 50 in June to 56.2, signifying future growth in manufacturing. The seasonally adjusted unemployment rate improved to 4.0% in Q2. Inflation slowed from 2.5% in Q1 to 1.5% in Q2, staying within the Reserve Bank of New Zealand target range of 1%–3%, despite a rise in food inflation.

The government is supporting the economy by ramping up fiscal stimulus as the central bank eases its monetary stance. On 12 August, the Monetary Policy Committee decided to keep the official cash rate at 0.25% and to increase funding of the Large-Scale Asset Purchase program up to $100 billion, designed to keep interest rates low in the short term. The government announced in May that its 2020 budget included an additional allotment of $50.0 billion for COVID-19 response and recovery on top of $12.1 billion for the economic recovery package announced on 17 March. To further sustain economic recovery, the government announced on 5 July that it would extend to the end of 2020 an interest-free loan program for small businesses.

Figure A1.12 Demand-side growth, New Zealand

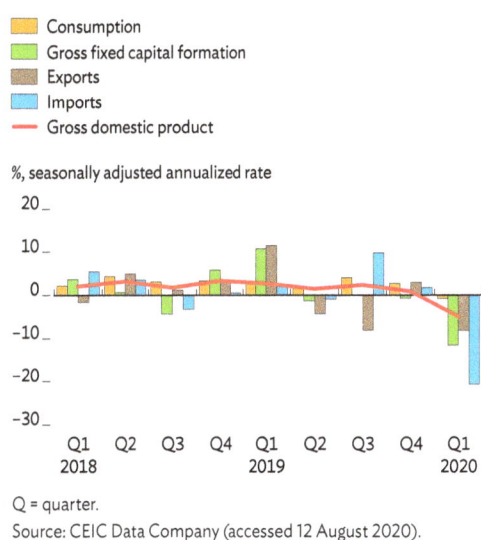

Consumption
Gross fixed capital formation
Exports
Imports
Gross domestic product

%, seasonally adjusted annualized rate

Q = quarter.
Source: CEIC Data Company (accessed 12 August 2020).

The spread of COVID-19 was restrained in the country and lockdown measures lifted relatively quickly in early June. However, the lockdown resumed on 12 August due to a community coronavirus outbreak after more than 100 days without any local transmission. Tourism is still down because of international travel restrictions, with accommodation, hospitality, and retail the services hardest hit. The August 2020 Consensus Forecast was for GDP to contract by 5.9% in 2020 and expand by 4.8% in 2021.

Russian Federation

A decline in exports caused GDP growth to decelerate from 2.1% in Q4 2019 to 1.6% in Q1 2020. Consumption grew by 2.8% and gross capital formation by 2.6%, while exports dropped by 3.4% as the pandemic weakened external demand, forcing net exports down by 20.5% (Figure A1.13).

Economic indicators in Q2 indicate acute economic tightening with the enforcement of strict lockdown measures and the slowdown in global demand. Retail trade turnover plunged by 20.6% in April and continued to contract until June. Unemployment climbed from 4.5% in January to an 8-year high of 6.3% in June. Industrial production contracted by 6.6% year on year in April and 9.6% in May. The Markit manufacturing PMI dived below the 50-point threshold indicating contraction to 31.3 in April before improving to 49.4 in June. The services PMI was in April an abysmal 12.2 but recovered to 47.8 in June. Inflation climbed from a low of 2.3% in February to 3.4% in July.

On 24 July 2020, the Bank of Russia decided to reduce the key rate by 25 basis points to 4.25% per annum to support lending, particularly to the most vulnerable segments of the economy. The government has laid out measures intended to alleviate the effects of the COVID-19 pandemic, and the current fiscal stimulus will raise the share of spending on household income—including public sector salaries, pensions, and other social benefits—in the consolidated budget to about 60% in 2020.

The economy is forecast to recover gradually as restrictions are lifted step by step. Business recovery is still moderate and uneven across industries and regions. A downturn in domestic demand that reflects lower investment and deteriorating consumer demand is expected to persist to the end of this year, while low global oil prices and disrupted supply chains likely batter exports. The August 2020 Consensus Forecast was for GDP to contract by 5.1% in 2020 and expand by 3.4% in 2021.

Figure A1.13 Demand-side growth, Russian Federation

- Consumption
- Gross capital formation
- Exports
- Imports
- Gross domestic product

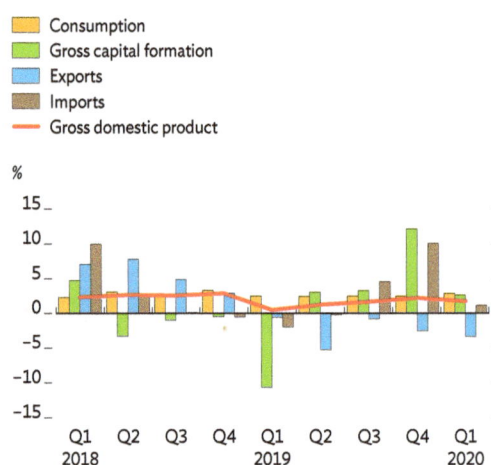

Source: CEIC Data Company (accessed 12 August 2020).

Oil prices

The price of Brent crude oil gyrated wildly in the first 7 months of 2020 (Figure A1.14). After starting the year at close to $70/barrel, the price collapsed to a near-2-decade low of $17/barrel on 21 April. Since then, it has partly recovered, rising above $40/barrel in June as governments began to lift quarantine measures and as global oil supply fell with successful production cuts coordinated by the Organization of the Petroleum Exporting Countries and others (OPEC+). Oil prices have remained above $42/barrel since mid-July. The Brent crude average in the year to 31 August was $41.64/barrel.

The International Energy Agency (IEA) reported in July that global oil supply had fallen to a 9-year low of 86.9 million barrels/day (mbd) in June as a result of high compliance with the OPEC+ output deal and steep declines from other producers, led by the US and Canada. With a compliance rate of 107% in June, OPEC crude oil production fell to 22.3 mbd, the lowest since November 1991. However, in August, OPEC+ started to taper its output cuts. Outside of the OPEC+ group, the US Energy Information Administration expects average US crude oil production to fall to 11.3 mbd in 2020, or 7.7% below the 2019 average of 12.2 mbd, and then fall further to 11.1 mbd in 2021, or 9.4% lower than the 2019 benchmark. If the OPEC+ cuts survive as agreed and output from other major producers declines as well, the IEA forecasts global oil supply to plunge by a record 7.1 mbd in 2020 before staging a partial recovery by 1.6 mbd in 2021.

Turning to global oil demand, the IEA, in August expects the recovery in the second half of 2020 to be more gradual than previously projected. Average demand in the year will thus contract by 8.1 mbd in 2020 before rising by 6.0 mbd in 2021. It is noteworthy that, even if global oil demand recovers as expected in 2021, it will still be 2.9 mbd below demand in 2019 as the aviation industry continues to grapple with weak demand.

Expectations of a V-shaped recovery in global oil demand have diminished, and the consensus is now for a much flatter recovery as market sentiment is dampened by current expectations for a slower global recovery and concerns about COVID-19 resurgence. The expected return of previously withheld production from OPEC+ and North America is tempering any upward pressure on the oil prices from a decline in US crude oil inventories, higher crude oil imports to the PRC, a weaker US dollar, and reported promising results from vaccine clinical trials. Oil price volatility has diminished of late, and global oil prices appear to have settled at around $44/barrel. In sum, the Brent crude oil price is forecast to increase slowly in the last 5 months of this year to average $42.50/barrel in 2020 (Figure A1.15). As economic activity normalizes and the oil market rebalances, Brent crude is forecast to average $50/barrel in 2021.

Figure A1.14 Brent crude spot prices

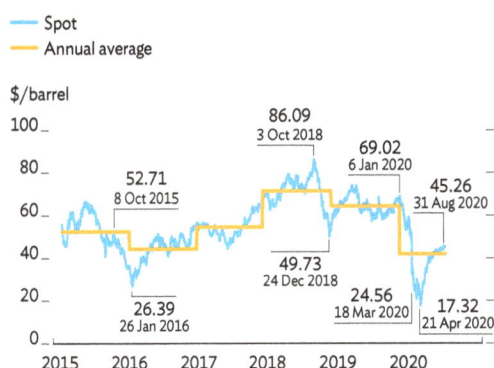

Source: Bloomberg (accessed 31 August 2020).

Figure A1.15 Oil price forecast

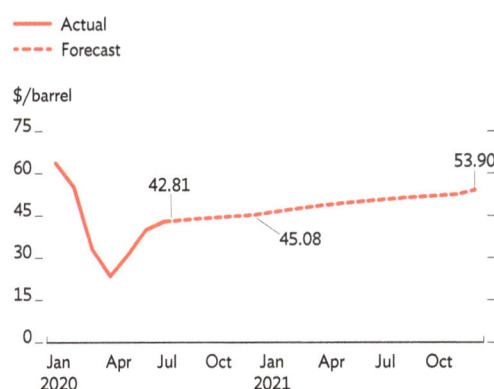

Sources: Bloomberg (accessed 31 August 2020); ADB estimates.

2

WELLNESS IN WORRYING TIMES

Wellness in worrying times

Wellness is vital for post-pandemic recovery in developing Asia. Coronavirus Disease 2019 (COVID-19) removes any doubt that wellness—or the deliberate pursuit of activities that bring holistic health, happiness, and well-being—is essential to all, not just an indulgence for those who can afford it. Public health, both physical and mental, has taken a beating during this pandemic. In Asia, as elsewhere, wellness can revive the human body, mind, and spirit, which are the first steps toward rebuilding the economy and society.

Wellness is a large and growing part of the Asian economy. Even before COVID-19, Asians demanded more wellness as their incomes rose, chronic lifestyle diseases became more prevalent, and the population aged. A result has been a rapidly growing wellness economy, comprising industries that enable consumers to incorporate wellness activities into their daily lives. The wellness economy provides 11% of output in Asian countries, having grown annually by 10% in recent years. COVID-19 is likely to further boost demand in the coming years and support a strong recovery.

Asian wellness traditions can serve both well-being and the economy. Although modern wellness industries originated in Western countries, Asia has a wealth of wellness traditions. Those traditions are productive assets for the wellness economy. At the same time, tapping these traditions can promote mental and physical health in the lives of Asians. As such, the present is the opportune time for Asia to rediscover its wellness roots.

Wellness polices should be comprehensive and target all Asians. Government efforts to boost physical and mental well-being fall into four policy domains: create a healthy urban environment, enable and support physical activity, encourage healthy diets, and enhance wellness in the workplace. Because healthy aging begins in childhood, a lifelong wellness policy framework such as Japan's 100-Year Life Program should complement the four policy domains. And, because the poor have fewer opportunities for wellness activities, governments must invest in wellness infrastructure that benefits them.

This chapter was written by Donghyun Park, Matthias Helble, Madhavi Pundit, Pilipinas Quising, Irfan Qureshi, and Shu Tian. It draws on the background papers listed at the end of the chapter. Strategic advice was provided by Gerry Bodeker, Katherine Johnston, and Ophelia Yeung. Other contributions are listed in the Acknowledgments section.

2.1 A pandemic brings wellness to the fore

Coronavirus Disease 2019 (COVID-19) highlights the importance of both physical and mental health. Medical evidence indicates that individuals with underlying physical health conditions such as obesity, asthma, or diabetes face a much higher risk of severe infection, as do the elderly. Meanwhile, isolation, fear, uncertainty, and economic hardship triggered by the pandemic are causing psychological stress and anxiety around the world. A United Nations report released in May 2020 warns that pandemic-induced mental distress may trigger a global mental health crisis. This bolsters the case for individuals to take action to strengthen their own physical and mental health by pursuing wellness activities.

Developing Asia is relatively easy to nudge in this direction. Demand for wellness was growing across the region even before the pandemic as populations aged and in response to the rising incidence of chronic lifestyle diseases. While the idea of wellness has grown in popularity, people may not understand exactly what it means. How does wellness differ from happiness and well-being?

2.1.1 Wellness defined

Wellness was an unfamiliar concept just a decade ago, but in the past few years it has spread all around the world. Consumer interest in all things related to wellness is accelerating, and wellness has become a selling point for many products and services—from food and vitamins to real estate and vacation packages, and from gym memberships and health care plans to meditation apps and DNA testing kits. The global wellness economy was worth an estimated $4.5 trillion in 2018 alone (GWI 2018a, 2019). That consumers in developing Asia are increasingly interested in wellness is evident in the proliferation across the region of fitness centers, spas, and tai chi and yoga classes.

Wellness is a modern word with ancient roots. It has emerged only recently as an industry but has existed for thousands of years as a concept and practice. The key tenets of wellness, which promote health care that is both preventive and holistic, can be traced back to ancient civilizations spanning East to West. Ayurveda—an ancient health care system described more than 2,000 years ago in sacred Hindu texts—strives to create harmony of body, mind, and spirit (Guha undated). Traditional Chinese medicine, another of the world's oldest systems of medicine, is influenced by Buddhist and Taoist philosophies and includes in the concept of health the individual's harmonious relationships with the family, community, and environment (Hafner undated). The ancient Greek physician Hippocrates was the first member of the medical profession recorded as emphasizing disease prevention. His wellness concept is captured in the modern Hippocratic Oath: "I will prevent disease wherever I can, for prevention is preferable to cure (Tyson 2001)."

Around the world, the popular understanding and usage of the word wellness may vary according to cultural, historical, and linguistic differences. In Europe, for example, wellness is often associated with spas, health resorts, seawater-based thalassotherapy, and other types of alternative treatments offered at such facilities. Many Europeans use the term well-being to mean holistic health. In Asia, many ancient spiritual traditions, healing modalities, and life philosophies—including yoga, ayurveda, traditional Chinese medicine, tai chi, reiki (energy healing), meditation, herbal medicines, and ikigai (Japanese "reason for being")—are deeply ingrained in culture and daily life. However, these activities may not be associated in Asia with wellness, as they are in the West. For example, the Chinese concept closest to wellness is *yangsheng*, which means "looking after one's health" or "keeping fit," but the word wellness is generally translated into Chinese as a synonym of "health."

As the popularity of wellness practices has grown in recent years, diverse understanding and usage of the term wellness have gradually converged on a universal definition, one closely related to and complementary with health. Since 1948, the World Health Organization has defined health as "a state of complete physical, mental and social well-being and not merely the absence of disease or infirmity" (WHO 1948). This definition is significant for going beyond the physical state of simply being free of disease, emphasizing a holistic approach that includes social and mental dimensions.

However closely related they may be, wellness and health are distinct concepts, as evident in a comparison of the medical and wellness paradigms (Figure 2.1.1). The medical paradigm is reactive and seeks to help individuals recover from poor health to neutral health. In contrast, the wellness paradigm is proactive and seeks to lift individuals from neutral health to optimal health.

Figure 2.1.1 Medical paradigm versus wellness paradigm

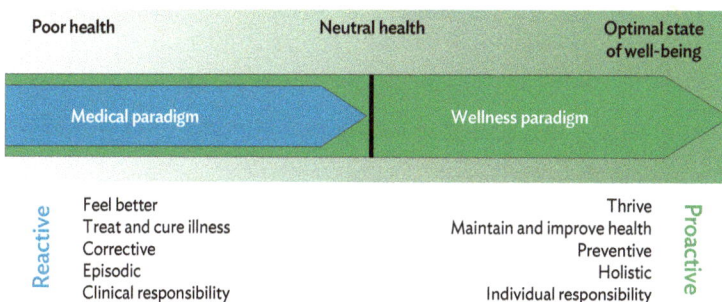

Source: Global Wellness Institute.

While the two paradigms overlap in preventive health care, much of medical care treats and cures illness, while wellness focuses on behavior—most iconically exercising, eating healthy food, and perhaps meditating—that allow one to achieve better health.

In contrast with related concepts such as happiness and well-being, which are subjective conditions, wellness is to a process through which one actively makes choices that bring optimal health. Following the definition from the Global Wellness Institute, wellness can best be understood as "the active pursuit of activities, choices, and lifestyles that lead to a state of holistic health" (GWI 2018a). It extends beyond physical health and incorporates many different dimensions: mental/intellectual, emotional, spiritual, social, and environmental. Figure 2.1.2 summarizes the similarities and differences between wellness on the one hand and well-being and happiness on the other. Figure 2.1.3 illustrates the multidimensional nature of wellness.

Figure 2.1.2 Wellness versus well-being and happiness

Wellness	Well-being and happiness
Both are multidimensional, dynamic, subjective, and personal yet subject to historical and cultural differences and contexts	
• Relates to intention, action, and activities. • Has a prominent physical dimension. • Is associated by consumers with healthy lifestyles, choices, and market offerings. • Is commonly used in the context of business and private industry, such as the wellness industry. • Is a useful concept for measuring industry size and discussing business opportunities in the wellness economy.	• Are perceptions of states of being. • Have prominent mental and emotional dimensions. • Are associated by community members with feelings of satisfaction and a sense of fulfillment. • Are commonly used in the context of government and policy, such as a well-being budget. • Are useful for measuring the welfare of individual residents, such as with the Global Happiness Index, and organizing policies and interventions.

Source: Global Wellness Institute.

Popular understanding of the word wellness may vary around the world in line with cultural, historical, and linguistic differences. While usage of the term may differ, common threads stand out in the definition of wellness. They can be summarized as follows:

- **Wellness is multidimensional.** It incorporates physical, mental, emotional, social, and other aspects of an individual.
- **Wellness is holistic.** Each dimension influences the other dimensions of wellness, and they must work in harmony.
- **Wellness changes along a continuum over time.** It is not a static state or an end point, but is experienced as a continuum along which an individual attempts to move toward an optimal sense of health and well-being.

Figure 2.1.3 Different dimensions of wellness

Source: Yeung and Johnston 2020a.

- **Wellness is both individual and environmental.** It depends upon individual choices, behavior, and lifestyle but is also significantly influenced by the physical, social, and cultural environment in which people live.
- **Wellness entails personal responsibility.** It requires individuals to be aware and proactively make choices that enable better health and well-being.

2.1.2 COVID-19 and wellness

COVID-19 is a once-in-a-century shock to global health and the world economy, unprecedented in living memory. It underscores the importance of physical and mental wellness in a number of ways. Most notably, medical evidence indicates that unfit and unhealthy individuals are significantly more vulnerable to the disease. Keeping fit and healthy through regular exercise and other physical activity boosts immunity against infectious diseases. Social isolation during lockdowns and community quarantines can impair people's sense of mental well-being. Activities such as deep breathing exercises or meditation can help them regain their mental balance (Mayo Clinic 2020, Harvard Health Publishing 2020). Other activities such as eating healthier food and practicing yoga can enhance both physical and mental well-being. Demand for wellness has been growing across the region, and heightened awareness of the benefits of being and staying well against the backdrop of a pandemic will likely give further impetus to the pursuit of wellness activities.

Importance of physical health

Living under COVID-19 restrictions highlights the importance of being physically fit and healthy, which helps prevent infection. In addition, physical fitness mitigates mental health issues stirred by worry and stress. Therefore, in addition to taking preventive measures such as wearing a face mask, washing hands frequently, social distancing, and self-isolating, individuals need to safeguard their overall physical health through physical wellness activities.

The evidence to date shows that people with underlying medical conditions such as cardiovascular disease, diabetes, chronic respiratory disease, and cancer face a higher risk of severe illness from COVID-19 (WHO 2020a, Huang et al. 2020, Wang et al. 2020, Yang et al. 2020, Liang et al. 2020). Obesity is identified as another major risk factor (CDC 2020). In many cases, these conditions are caused by harmful behavior—smoking, excessive drinking, and overeating—and can be prevented by lifestyle changes such as starting a proper diet and regular physical activity.

Community lockdowns and quarantines implemented to contain COVID-19 discourage physical activity and impose greater reliance on processed and canned food, which may increase the risk of metabolic disease (Jiménez-Pavón, Carbonell-Baeza, and Lavie 2020, Narici et al. 2020). A study of children and adolescents aged 6–17 years in five schools in the People's Republic of China revealed a substantial decrease in physical activity and an increase in internet screen time during the COVID-19 pandemic, causing obesity and eye disease (Xiang, Zhang, and Kuwahara 2020). Studies have long linked reduced physical activity and prolonged sedentary behavior to poor physical and mental health (Korczak, Madigan, and Colasanto 2017, Haapala, Vaisto, and Lintu 2017, WHO 2010). Equally well established are the beneficial effects on health from regular physical activity (Pedersen and Saltin 2015, Powell, Paluch, and Blair 2011).

Wellness activities like getting good nutrition and adequate sleep, exercising regularly, and meditating play important roles in preventing COVID-19 infection and recovering from it. Potentially long-lasting scars from the disease strengthen the case for wellness practices during recovery (Mintz 2020, Parshley 2020, Wu et al. 2020). COVID-19 survivors need healthy nutrition, good care, and engagement in wellness activities to recover fully and put their lives back on track.

Mental health in a pandemic

The COVID-19 pandemic is, first and foremost, a physical health crisis arising from a virus, but it has the potential to evolve into a mental health crisis as well. In fact, various surveys and studies already document significant negative psychological consequences from COVID-19 around the world. A survey of 28 countries showed COVID-19 dominating the concerns of global citizens (Figure 2.1.4). The pandemic's response score was the highest recorded since the survey started 10 years ago, which suggests that COVID-19 has become a uniquely dominant global concern. In opinion polls conducted in individual countries including Canada, the United Kingdom, and the US, respondents reported their mental health suffering from worries and stress over COVID-19 (Angus Reid Institute 2020, Office for National Statistics 2020, National Public Radio 2020, Morning Consult 2020).

More broadly, COVID-19 is a startling global crisis that is hammering both public health and the economy. From the perspective of individual mental well-being, health fears concerning infection, death, and the loss of family members may be compounded by stress over economic hardship from lost or endangered jobs and income (Haushofer and Fehr 2014).

Figure 2.1.4 Top five global concerns

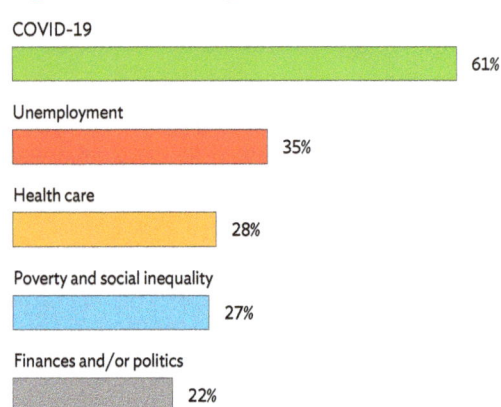

COVID-19 — 61%
Unemployment — 35%
Health care — 28%
Poverty and social inequality — 27%
Finances and/or politics — 22%

COVID-19 = Coronavirus Disease 2019.
Note: Research conducted in April 2020 among adults aged 16–64 in 28 participating countries.
Source: Atkinson, Skinner, and Gebrekal 2020.

Online surveys revealed anxiety to be the most common mental health symptom, often so intense that impairs sleep (Xiao et al. 2020, Rossi et al. 2020, Liu et al. 2020). Some contributory factors were poor physical health (Wang et al. 2020), forced responses to the pandemic in daily life (Rossi et al. 2020), misinformation and high exposure to social media (Zandifar and Badrfam 2020, Gao et al. 2020), and quarantine or social isolation (Rossi et al. 2020, Zandifar and Badrfam 2020). Many hospital staff, including frontline medical personnel, face mental health issues (Kang et al. 2020, Tan et al. 2020, Xiao et al. 2020, Zhang et al. 2020). Reasons cited include overly long work hours, risk of infection, lack of personal protective equipment, loneliness, physical exhaustion, and separation from families.

Individuals have many options for maintaining mental health during and beyond the pandemic: sustaining healthy everyday habits such as eating well, exercising regularly, and keeping in touch, if only online, with family and friends. Specialized wellness practices such as meditation, tai chi, and yoga can also benefit mental health (Bodeker et al. 2020).

2.1.3 Wellness and sustainable development

Even before COVID-19, demand for wellness in developing Asia had been on the rise in response to structural factors: higher incomes, the emergence of a large middle class, increased urbanization, and a rise in chronic lifestyle conditions referred to as noncommunicable diseases or NCDs (Box 2.1.1). Decades of rapid economic growth have left many Asians much richer than their forebears. Consequently, they are more aware of the benefits of healthier lifestyles as, most starkly, hunger for more calories gives way to a quest for better, more balanced nutrition. The rise of NCDs such as heart disease, stroke, diabetes, and cancer in the region is encouraging Asians to exercise more, eat better, and seek healthier life choices. In addition, Asia's population is aging. Older populations are more subject to chronic disease, as well as to loneliness and mental health issues. Asia's worsening pollution presents yet another clear and present danger to health. Heightened awareness of the importance of wellness during the COVID-19 pandemic will thus reinforce Asia's growing demand for wellness.

Wellness can contribute to sustainable development and improve the mental and physical health of the poor. As the active pursuit of well-being, wellness aligns with the United Nations Sustainable Development Goals, in particular the third goal: Ensure healthy lives and promote well-being for all at all ages. A focus on wellness promises to bring a more balanced and holistic view of development than does measuring its progress simply as increased income per capita.

In principle, many wellness activities such as physical exercise are available to all. In practice, though, the poor are disadvantaged by their relative lack of money or time to devote to wellness, of access to health facilities, and of ready knowledge of nutritious food. These gaps can be narrowed by public investment in wellness infrastructure in poor neighborhoods such as community recreation centers and green parks, as well as in health education campaigns.

Box 2.1.1 The rise of chronic lifestyle disease in developing Asia

Sustained economic growth in developing Asia has brought rapid urbanization and expansion of the middle class. The resulting lifestyle changes have contributed to the rise of noncommunicable diseases (NCDs) in the region. Such negative side effects of economic success encourage Asians to pursue healthier lifestyles that can improve their well-being.

A landmark in the growth of the middle class, September 2018 was the tipping point at which more than half of the global population, or 3.8 billion people, were now middle class or rich. Most of the new entrants to the middle class live in developing Asia (Kharas and Hamel 2018). Middle class consumers drive global economic growth with their large numbers and discretionary spending, not least to enhance the quality of life or search for fulfillment and happiness through good health, education, travel, entertainment, and experiences. The wellness economy has benefited from this growing consumer base.

A parallel development is rapid urbanization. In 2018, fully 55% of the global population lived in urban areas—a share that will reach 68% by 2050. Much of this growth will come in large developing countries such as India, Indonesia, and the People's Republic of China (United Nations 2018).

The twin phenomena of a growing middle class and urbanization have upended traditional lifestyles and aspirations pertaining to living arrangements, eating habits, physical activities, work, families, communities, values, tastes, and much more. This modern lifestyle has many unhealthy aspects, though, such as automobile dependency, excessive consumption of processed foods, sedentary lives, stress, loneliness and social isolation, and heightened exposure to pollutants. These changes are risk factors for chronic disease and therefore spur demand for wellness.

Most chronic lifestyle and environmental diseases are classified as NCDs, which, with improved control of infectious disease, have become leading causes of death, collectively responsible for 71% of them worldwide (Kharas 2017). More than three-quarters of NCD-related deaths globally occur in low- and middle-income countries (WHO 2018b). According to the World Health Organization, properly addressing these risk factors could prevent at least 80% of heart disease, stroke, and Type 2 diabetes, as well as 40% of cancer cases (WHO 2005). Consumers are becoming aware that they can reduce risk through physical activity, healthy diets, moderated use of tobacco and alcohol, stress-avoidance, and healthier lifestyles overall.

References:

Kharas, H. 2017. The Unprecedented Expansion of the Global Middle Class: An Update. *Brookings Global Economy & Development Working Paper 100.* Brookings Institution. February. https://www.brookings.edu/wp-content/uploads/2017/02/global_20170228_global-middle-class.pdf.

Kharas, H. and K. Hamel. 2018. *A Global Tipping Point: Half the World Is Now Middle Class or Wealthier.* Brookings Institution. 27 September. https://www.brookings.edu/blog/future-development/2018/09/27/a-global-tipping-point-half-the-world-is-now-middle-class-or-wealthier/.

United Nations. 2018. *World Urbanization Prospects: The 2018 Revision—Key Facts.* https://esa.un.org/unpd/wup/Publications/Files/WUP2018-KeyFacts.pdf.

WHO. 2005. *Preventing Chronic Diseases: A Vital Investment—Misunderstanding #4.* World Health Organization. https://www.who.int/chp/chronic_disease_report/part1/en/index11.html.

——. 2018b. *Fact Sheet: Noncommunicable Diseases.* World Health Organization. 1 June. http://www.who.int/en/news-room/fact-sheets/detail/noncommunicable-diseases.

Source: Yeung, O. and K. Johnston. 2020a. *Global Wellness Industry and Its Implications for Asia's Development.* ADB.

2.2 Contours of wellness in Asia

This section takes stock of the current state of wellness in developing Asia. An index constructed specifically to measure wellness ranked the region a little below the world average, with significant variation across regional economies. Further analysis to estimate the size of the wellness economy showed that wellness and related industries have been expanding rapidly in many Asian countries, increasing the segment's share of total output and making it an increasingly important driver of the regional economy.

2.2.1 Quantifying wellness: cross-country comparison

Gross domestic product (GDP) per capita has been used historically as the de facto measure of a country's success and well-being. While GDP captures material well-being, it often does not provide a comprehensive measure of wellness (e.g., Dowrick and Quiggin 1994). More recently, a clamor has arisen to use more holistic measures of well-being (Stiglitz, Sen, and Fitoussi 2009). One such measure is the Wellness Index, which follows the Global Wellness Institute definition of wellness with four pillars or dimensions: physical, intellectual, environmental, and social (Ahmad and Qureshi 2020).

The Wellness Index uses readily available, public data to create a cross-country ranking of wellness. The aim is to fill an important gap by estimating relative wellness across countries and measuring average individual wellness (Box 2.2.1). The index provides policy makers in particular with an important gauge of how effectively public interventions may have improved wellness in a country.

Figure 2.2.1 shows the global distribution of the Wellness Index, revealing large differences across countries and regions. Europe, North America, Australia, and New Zealand emerge as the top performers, and Latin America performs consistently well. Asia and Africa exhibit marked variance in wellness scores.

On average, developing Asia's wellness performance is close to the global average but typically falls below that of members of the Organisation for Economic Co-operation and Development (OECD) and of Latin America and the Caribbean (Figure 2.2.2). Evenly spread Asian rankings show the Republic of Korea and Singapore on top and Pakistan and Afghanistan at the bottom end.

Box 2.2.1 Wellness Index

The Wellness Index adopts a bottom-up approach, defining wellness at the individual level, which distinguishes it from other aggregate measures of national well-being. The index is broadly based on the Global Wellness Initiative definition of individual wellness, founded on four pillars: physical, intellectual (mental), environmental, and social. Physical wellness captures a nation's ability to meet the health needs of its populace, intellectual wellness measures access to education and its quality, social wellness considers the social environment, and environmental wellness addresses environmental health.

Because wellness is not directly observable, the index applies strict criteria to identify indicators to use as proxies for the four pillars. A selected indicator must be recent, reliable, and replicable, while keeping imputation to a minimum.

To guide data collection, the index focuses on 25 core countries of interest and uses an indicator only if applicable in at least 20 of them within the past 5 years. If an indicator is missing from a core country, time trend imputations are used to fill the gap. If this is not possible, limited cross-indicator imputations are used. This data collection strategy yields 20 indicators across 153 economies to create a global index of wellness. The box figure lists the indicators used to create the index.

Principal component analysis (PCA), a dimensionality reduction technique, is used to collate the data for each pillar. While the pillars of wellness are themselves unobservable, PCA allows ordinal ranking across economies by exploiting variance in related indicators. For instance, while physical wellness is unobservable, the Wellness Index uses variance in mortality rates and disease burden to rank countries by their average level of physical wellness, as countries with lower values in these indicators can be reasonably judged to have greater physical wellness.

Scores from pillar-level PCA are normalized and then averaged to create the index. The index thus connects macro-level development indicators with the national level of wellness. From a policy perspective, improved life expectancy, for example, can be expected to improve the wellness ranking.

Indicators for each pillar of wellness

Physical

1. Life expectancy at birth
2. Maternal mortality rate
3. Under-5 child mortality rate
4. Prevalence of undernourishment
5. Disability-adjust life years lost to noncommunicable diseases
6. Disability-adjust life years lost to communicable diseases

Intellectual

1. Adult literacy rate
2. Mean years of schooling
3. Harmonized test scores

Environmental

1. Mortality rate attributed to household and ambient air pollution, standardized by age
2. Mean annual exposure to air pollutant particles no larger than 2.5 micrometers, in micrograms per cubic meter
3. Total protected area
4. Average nitrogen dioxide level
5. Degree to which the ground in the most populous city is impervious to water

Social

1. Gender parity index, literacy rate of youth aged 15–24
2. Gini index as estimated by the World Bank
3. Female-to-male ratio of labor force participation rate (%)
4. World Bank estimate of control of corruption
5. World Bank estimate of the rule of law
6. Social class equality in terms of civil liberty
7. Social group equality in terms of civil liberty
8. Power distribution by social group

Source: Ahmad and Qureshi 2020.

The index can therefore be used to prioritize areas for wellness policy.

Source: Ahmad, H. and I. Qureshi. 2020. *Cross-Country Comparison of Wellness: An Empirical Assessment*. ADB.

Significant variation across subregions shows no single subregion consistently outperforming the others. East Asia ranks highest on physical wellness, Central Asia on intellectual wellness, and the Pacific on environmental and social wellness (Figure 2.2.3).

Figure 2.2.1 Wellness Index coverage and scores

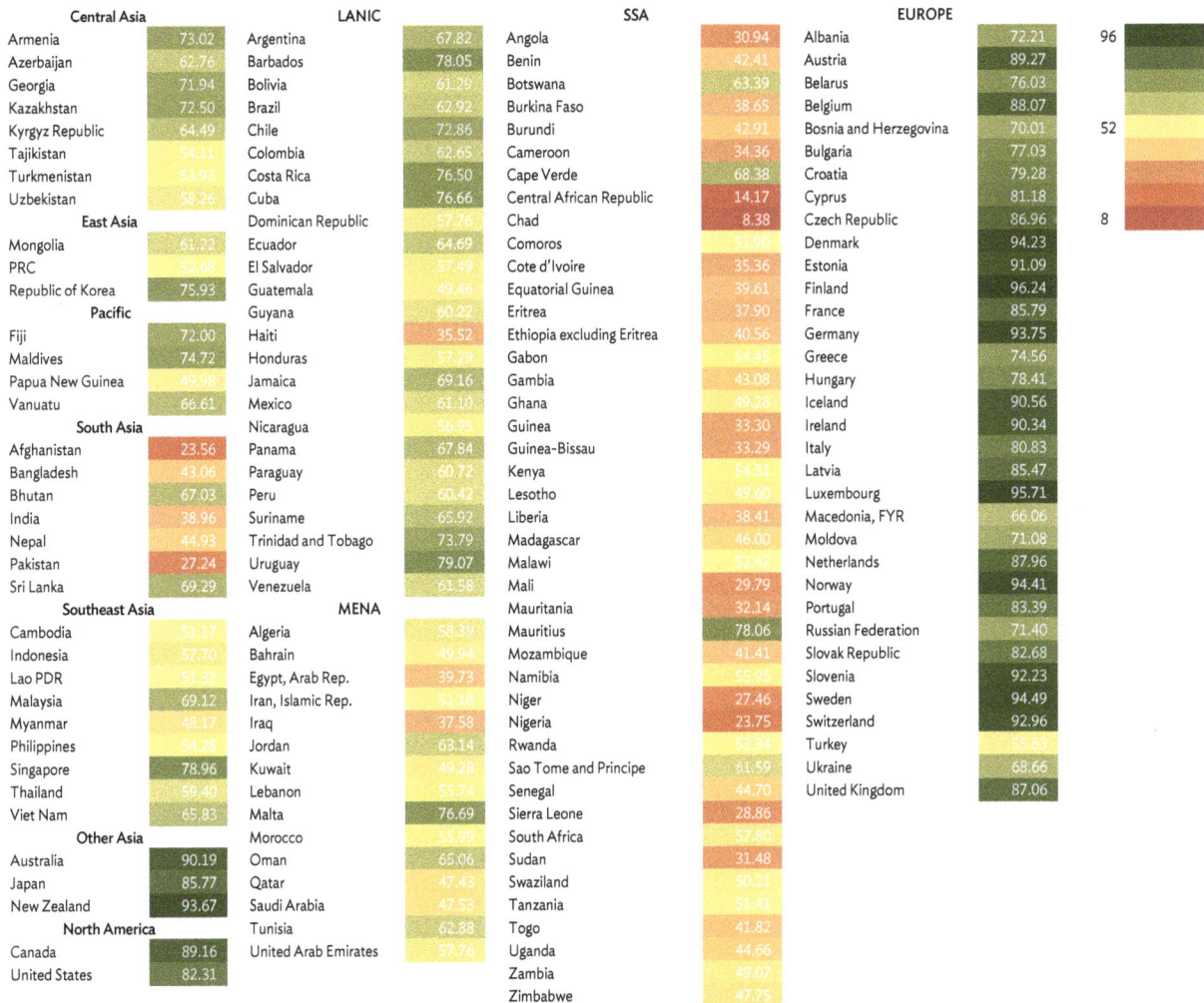

Central Asia		LANIC		SSA		EUROPE		
Armenia	73.02	Argentina	67.82	Angola	30.94	Albania	72.21	96
Azerbaijan	62.76	Barbados	78.05	Benin	42.41	Austria	89.27	
Georgia	71.94	Bolivia	61.29	Botswana	63.39	Belarus	76.03	
Kazakhstan	72.50	Brazil	62.92	Burkina Faso	38.65	Belgium	88.07	
Kyrgyz Republic	64.49	Chile	72.86	Burundi	42.91	Bosnia and Herzegovina	70.01	52
Tajikistan	54.11	Colombia	62.65	Cameroon	34.36	Bulgaria	77.03	
Turkmenistan	53.93	Costa Rica	76.50	Cape Verde	68.38	Croatia	79.28	
Uzbekistan	58.26	Cuba	76.66	Central African Republic	14.17	Cyprus	81.18	
East Asia		Dominican Republic	57.76	Chad	8.38	Czech Republic	86.96	8
Mongolia	61.22	Ecuador	64.69	Comoros	51.98	Denmark	94.23	
PRC	52.68	El Salvador	57.49	Cote d'Ivoire	35.36	Estonia	91.09	
Republic of Korea	75.93	Guatemala	49.46	Equatorial Guinea	39.61	Finland	96.24	
Pacific		Guyana	60.22	Eritrea	37.90	France	85.79	
Fiji	72.00	Haiti	35.52	Ethiopia excluding Eritrea	40.56	Germany	93.75	
Maldives	74.72	Honduras	57.29	Gabon	54.45	Greece	74.56	
Papua New Guinea	49.98	Jamaica	69.16	Gambia	43.08	Hungary	78.41	
Vanuatu	66.61	Mexico	61.10	Ghana	49.28	Iceland	90.56	
South Asia		Nicaragua	56.95	Guinea	33.30	Ireland	90.34	
Afghanistan	23.56	Panama	67.84	Guinea-Bissau	33.29	Italy	80.83	
Bangladesh	43.06	Paraguay	60.72	Kenya	54.31	Latvia	85.47	
Bhutan	67.03	Peru	60.42	Lesotho	49.60	Luxembourg	95.71	
India	38.96	Suriname	65.92	Liberia	38.41	Macedonia, FYR	66.06	
Nepal	44.93	Trinidad and Tobago	73.79	Madagascar	46.00	Moldova	71.08	
Pakistan	27.24	Uruguay	79.07	Malawi	52.42	Netherlands	87.96	
Sri Lanka	69.29	Venezuela	61.58	Mali	29.79	Norway	94.41	
Southeast Asia		**MENA**		Mauritania	32.14	Portugal	83.39	
Cambodia	51.17	Algeria	58.39	Mauritius	78.06	Russian Federation	71.40	
Indonesia	57.70	Bahrain	49.94	Mozambique	41.41	Slovak Republic	82.68	
Lao PDR	51.37	Egypt, Arab Rep.	39.73	Namibia	55.95	Slovenia	92.23	
Malaysia	69.12	Iran, Islamic Rep.	51.18	Niger	27.46	Sweden	94.49	
Myanmar	48.17	Iraq	37.58	Nigeria	23.75	Switzerland	92.96	
Philippines	54.28	Jordan	63.14	Rwanda	53.34	Turkey	55.63	
Singapore	78.96	Kuwait	49.28	Sao Tome and Principe	61.59	Ukraine	68.66	
Thailand	59.40	Lebanon	55.74	Senegal	44.70	United Kingdom	87.06	
Viet Nam	65.83	Malta	76.69	Sierra Leone	28.86			
Other Asia		Morocco	55.63	South Africa	57.80			
Australia	90.19	Oman	65.06	Sudan	31.48			
Japan	85.77	Qatar	47.43	Swaziland	50.21			
New Zealand	93.67	Saudi Arabia	47.53	Tanzania	51.43			
North America		Tunisia	62.88	Togo	41.82			
Canada	89.16	United Arab Emirates	57.76	Uganda	44.66			
United States	82.31			Zambia	49.07			
				Zimbabwe	47.75			

FYR = former Yugoslav republic, LANIC = Latin America and the Caribbean, Lao PDR = Lao People's Democratic Republic, MENA = Middle East and North Africa, PRC = People's Republic of China, SSA = Sub-Saharan Africa.

Source: Ahmad and Qureshi 2020.

Figure 2.2.2 Average wellness by pillar across regions

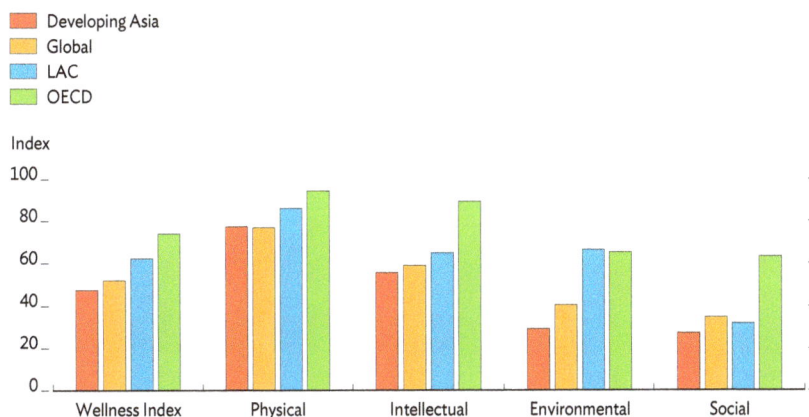

Legend:
- Developing Asia
- Global
- LAC
- OECD

Index (y-axis: 0, 20, 40, 60, 80, 100)

Categories (x-axis): Wellness Index, Physical, Intellectual, Environmental, Social

LAC = Latin America and the Caribbean, OECD = Organisation for Economic Co-operation and Development.

Note: Regional scores reflect national scores weighted by population.

Source: Ahmad and Qureshi 2020.

Figure 2.2.3 Wellness and pillar averages across subregions in developing Asia

Central Asia
East Asia
Pacific
South Asia
Southeast Asia

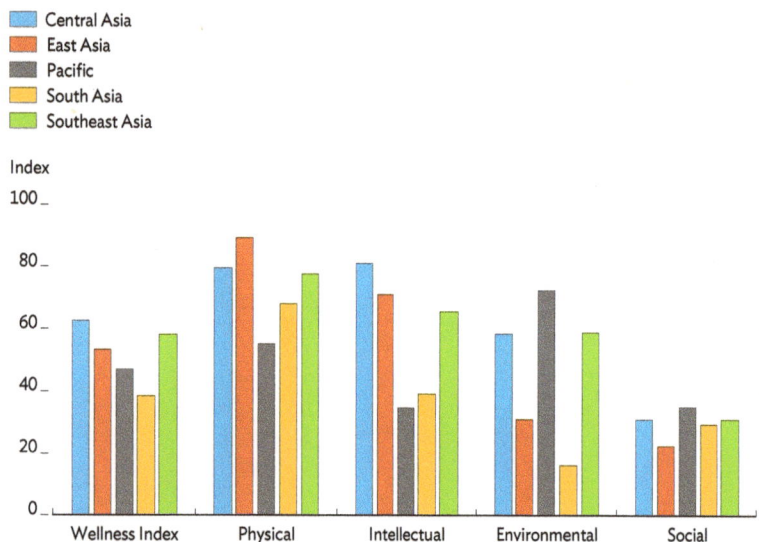

Note: Subregions scores reflect national scores weighted by population.
Source: Ahmad and Qureshi 2020.

The distribution of wellness scores versus GDP per capita by purchasing power parity suggests a close link between the two (Figure 2.2.4). A strong positive relationship exists, as countries with higher GDP tend to score better on wellness, both globally and within developing Asia. This result is intuitive and may justify or at least explain the historical use of GDP per capita as a measure of a nation's well-being. Countries with higher GDP per capita would intuitively have more resources to spend on their residents, better allowing them to meet wellness needs. However, wide dispersion in the data suggests that the relationship, while intuitive, is not straightforward. Observations appearing below the fitted line in Figure 2.2.4 indicate economies where wellness lags that of other economies with similar economic output per capita.

The Wellness Index presented here provides a global measure of relative wellness. In a way similar to how GDP per capita provides an easy-to-use measure of material well-being, the Wellness Index provides policy makers with an easy-to-use measure of national wellness in less material terms. Other indexes related to wellness exist but lack some of the features of the Wellness Index (Table 2.2.1). When used in conjunction with GDP, the Wellness Index provides a holistic view of wellness in a country. The indicators can be tracked over time, enabling policy makers in the future to assess how a shock such as the COVID-19 pandemic has affected wellness in the region and in individual economies.

Figure 2.2.4 Gross domestic product and wellness

● Asian economy   ----- Linear fit

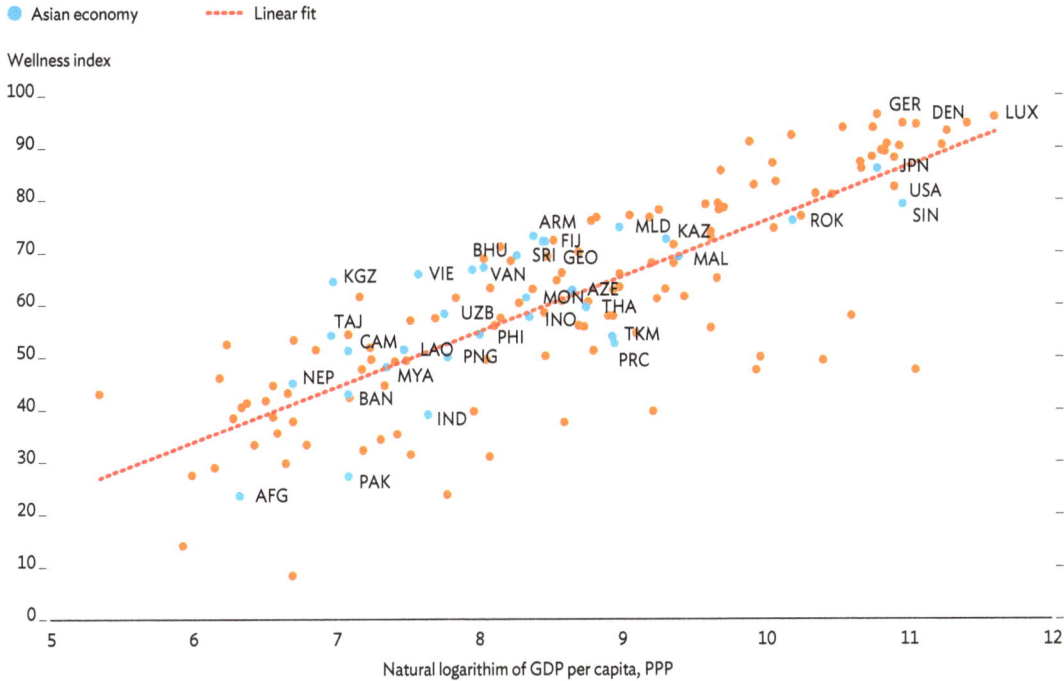

AFG = Afghanistan, ARM = Armenia, AZE = Azerbaijan, BAN = Bangladesh, BHU = Bhutan, CAM = Cambodia, GER = Germany, DEN = Denmark, FIJ = Fiji, GDP = gross domestic product, GEO = Georgia, IND = India, INO = Indonesia, JPN = Japan, KAZ = Kazakhstan, KGZ = Kyrgyz Republic, LAO = Lao People's Democratic Republic, LUX = Luxembourg, MAL = Malaysia, MLD = Maldives, MON = Mongolia, MYA = Myanmar, NEP = Nepal, PAK = Pakistan, PHI = Philippines, PNG = Papua New Guinea, PPP = purchasing power parity, PRC = People's Republic of China, ROK = Republic of Korea, SIN = Singapore, SRI = Sri Lanka, TAJ = Tajikistan, THA = Thailand, TKM = Turkmenistan, USA = United States of America, UZB = Uzbekistan, VAN = Vanuatu, VIE = Viet Nam.

Source: Ahmad and Qureshi 2020.

Table 2.2.1 Summary and pillar evaluation of other indexes that touch on wellness

Name	Methodology	Physical	Intellectual	Environmental	Social	Independent of growth
Human Development Index	Composite indicator created using GNP, life expectancy, and rates of literacy and school enrollment	🟡	🟡	🔴	🔴	🔴
OECD Better Life Index	11 sub-indicators capturing different dimensions of wellness	🟡	🟡	🟡	🔴	🔴
Indigo Wellness Index	Based primarily on physical health data and consumer spending	🟢	🔴	🔴	🔴	🔴
Social Progress Index	Composite of 51 measures of social progress, divided into three categories: basic human needs, foundations of well-being, and opportunity	🟢	🟡	🟡	🟢	🟢
Happy Planet Index	Combines four components to measure the efficient use of environmental resources	🟡	🔴	🟡	🟡	🟢
Inclusive Green Growth Index	Composite indicator created to measure inclusion, growth, and environmental sustainability	🟡	🟡	🟡	🟡	🔴

🟢 = yes, 🔴 = no, 🟡 = partly, GDP = gross domestic product, OECD = Organisation for Economic Co-operation and Development.

Source: Ahmad and Qureshi 2020.

2.2.2 The global wellness economy

The wellness economy can be defined as industries that enable consumers to incorporate wellness activities and lifestyles into their daily lives. Aggregating the economic size of these industries, the Global Wellness Institute estimated the global wellness economy at $4.5 trillion in 2018, or 5.5% of global economic output (Yeung and Johnston 2020). Global health expenditures, by comparison, were $7.4 trillion in 2016. The wellness economy grew from $3.4 trillion in 2013 to $4.2 trillion in 2017, or by about 5% or more annually in nominal terms. The wellness economy is thus a substantial and fast-growing segment of the global economy.

Figure 2.2.5 displays 10 sectors closely associated with the global wellness economy. In Asia and the Pacific—defined as developing Asia plus Australia, Japan, and New Zealand— economic output related to physical activity was valued in 2018 at $240.4 billion, wellness tourism at $136.7 billion, wellness real estate at $46.8 billion, thermal and mineral springs at $31.6 billion, spas at $26.5 billion, and workplace wellness at $9.3 billion. Wellness industries in the region are not only large, but they are growing rapidly, with wellness tourism, for example, expanding by an annual average of 10.9% from 2015 to 2017. Data for the remaining four wellness industries are unavailable disaggregated by country and region, precluding any estimation of national and regional wellness economies (Yeung and Johnston 2020a).

Figure 2.2.5 The global wellness economy, 2018

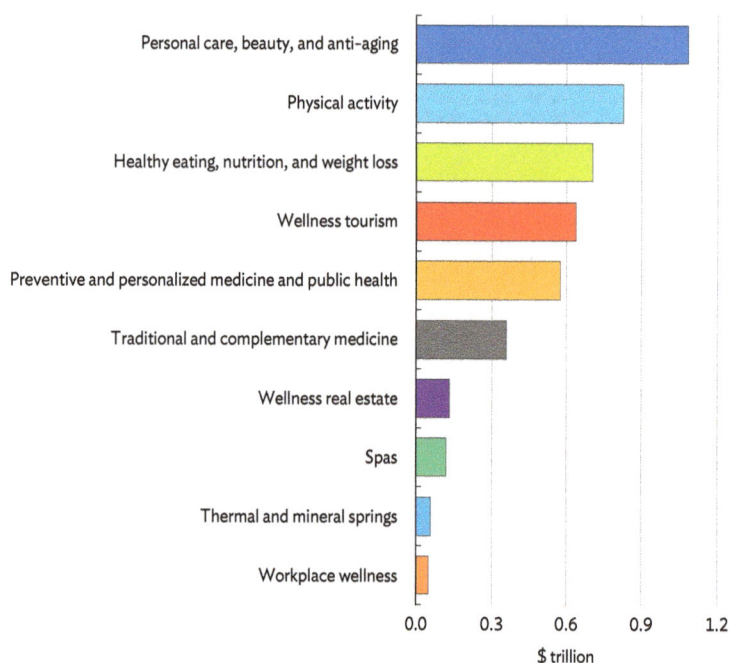

Source: Yeung and Johnston 2020a.

Box 2.2.2 Wellness industries as defined by the Global Wellness Institute

All 10 sectors in the wellness economy contribute to the pursuit of activities that promote physical and mental well-being. They are defined as follows:

(i) **Personal care, beauty, and anti-aging.** Consumer expenditure on beauty and salon services excluding spas; skin-, hair-, and nail-care services and products; cosmetics, toiletries, and other personal care products; dermatology; prescription pharmaceuticals for skin care; and products and services that specifically address age-related health and appearance issues, such as cosmetics and cosmeceuticals for skin, face, or body care, hair care and growth, and pharmaceuticals and supplements that treat age-related health conditions.

(ii) **Physical activity.** Consumer spending associated with deliberate physical activities performed during leisure and recreation, including three recreational activity segments (sports and active recreation, fitness, and mindful movement) and three enabling segments (technology, equipment and supplies, clothing and apparel).

(iii) **Healthy eating, nutrition, and weight loss.** Consumer expenditure on vitamins and supplements, fortified or functional foods and nutraceuticals, natural and organic foods, health foods, sports nutrition, nutrition and dietary services, and products and services for weight loss and management.

(iv) **Wellness tourism.** All spending by wellness tourists—primary and secondary, international and domestic—including on lodging, food and beverages, activities and excursions, shopping, and in-country transportation.

(v) **Preventive and personalized medicine and public health.** Spending on medical services that focus on treating people who are well, preventing disease, or detecting risk factors: notably routine physical exams, diagnostic and screening tests, and genetic testing. Includes personalized health uses of sophisticated information and data for individual patients, such as health analysis, diagnostics, and genetic, molecular, and environmental screening; personalized disease management services; and health information technology such as electronic health records, telemedicine, and remote patient monitoring to provide tailored approaches for preventing disease, diagnosing and managing risk factors, or managing and treating conditions.

(vi) **Traditional and complementary medicine.** Expenditure on diverse medical, health care, holistic, and mentally or spiritually based systems, services, and products that are not generally considered to be part of conventional medicine or the dominant health care system, such as homeopathy, naturopathy, chiropractics, traditional Chinese medicine, ayurveda, energy healing, and herbal and other traditional remedies and supplements. The nomenclature for this sector is evolving alongside growing consumer adoption of traditional, indigenous, complementary, alternative, and integrative medical practices outside of the conventional Western medical system.

(vii) **Wellness real estate.** Expenditure on the construction of residential, commercial, and institutional properties for offices, hospitality, mixed- and multi-family use, medicine, and leisure that deliberately incorporate wellness elements in their design, materials, and execution, as well as in their amenities, services, and programming.

(viii) **Spa economy.** Includes revenue earned by spas and the related cluster of businesses that support and enable spas through targeted education, consulting, capital investment, and associations, as well as spa-related media and events.

(ix) **Thermal and mineral springs.** Encompasses the revenue of businesses associated with the wellness, recreational, and therapeutic uses of water with special properties, including thermal water, mineral water, and seawater.

(x) **Workplace wellness.** Includes expenditure by employers on programs, services, activities, and equipment aiming to improve their employees' health and wellness by raising awareness, providing education, and offering incentives that address specific health risk factors and behavior—lack of exercise, poor eating habits, stress, obesity, and smoking—and encourage employees to adopt healthier lifestyles.

Source: Yeung, O. and K. Johnston. 2020a. *Global Wellness Industry and Its Implications for Asia's Development.* ADB.

2.2.3 Size of the wellness economy based on national accounts

The wellness economy can be measured using a country's system of national accounts. Applying the method laid out in Box 2.2.3 to nine Asian Development Bank developing member countries—Fiji, Kazakhstan, Malaysia, Mongolia, the Philippines, the People's Republic of China (PRC), Sri Lanka, Thailand, and Viet Nam—reveals the region's wellness economy to be large and growing. As noted above, data limitations prevent the Global Wellness Institute from estimating the size of the wellness economy at the national or regional level (Yeung and Johnston 2020a).

Box 2.2.3 Estimating the wellness economy using national accounts

While wellness can refer to activities for which no money changes hands, the reality is that many wellness activities are economic transactions. As such, they can be tracked through the system of national accounts to estimate a country's wellness economy. This method is useful in that it shows the direction in which a country is headed in terms of its production of wellness goods and services and how important they have become to the economy overall.

The first step in estimating a country's wellness economy is to identify which industrial codes in the United Nations' International Standard Industrial Classification of All Economic Activities (ISIC) pertain to wellness goods and services. As much as possible, the selected codes must include the different definitions and aspects of wellness discussed in past literature (e.g., Dunn 1959, WHO 2006, Roscoe 2009, Global Wellness Institute 2018). These codes broadly capture a variety of wellness goods and services in various industries: activities tied to human health, residential care, social work, tourism, amusement, recreation, sports, creativity, arts, entertainment, culture, and personal care; the construction of wellness-related structures such as health and sports facilities; and the manufacture and retail trade of wellness goods such as pharmaceutical, beauty, and sports products.

The second step is to extract the gross value added (GVA) from national accounts corresponding to the chosen ISIC codes using national supply–use or input–output tables. These tables, generally aggregated by sector and product, should be disaggregated where necessary to capture only the GVA attributable to wellness industries. Depending on the availability and quality of data for each country, national accounts can be disaggregated in several ways, using data from a country's national statistics office, individual firms, or economically similar countries.

The steps above give only the GVA generated directly by industries producing wellness goods and services. However, measuring the whole wellness economy must include GVA attributable to related industries: electricity and other inputs used in the production of wellness goods and services, for example, and the value added in the production of capital products needed to enable and support the production of wellness goods and services. These factors can be included by employing the methodology provided by de los Santos and Lumba (2020), which decomposes the final-use vector from an input–output table into value-added contributions made by different sectors of the economy (delos Santos and Lumba 2020).

References:

de los Santos, C. and A. J. Lumba. 2020. The Core of the Digital Economy: A Proposed Framework. Unpublished.

Dunn, H. 1959. High-level wellness for man and society. *American Journal of Public Health* 49(6).

Global Wellness Institute. 2018. *Global Wellness Economy Monitor 2018.* https://globalwellnessinstitute.org/industry-research/2018-global-wellness-economy-monitor/.

Roscoe, L. J. 2009. Wellness: A Review of Theory and Measurement for Counselors. *Journal of Counselling and Development* 87(2).

World Health Organization. 2006. *Health Promotion Glossary Update.* Geneva.

Source: Consing, R. M. III, M. J. Barsabal, J. T. Alvarez, and M. J. Mariasingham. 2020. *Using the System of National Accounts to Estimate a Country's Wellness Economy.* ADB.

Figure 2.2.6 Wellness economies, % of total GVA

- 🟩 Contribution from wellness industries
- 🟧 Contribution from support industries

% of total GVA

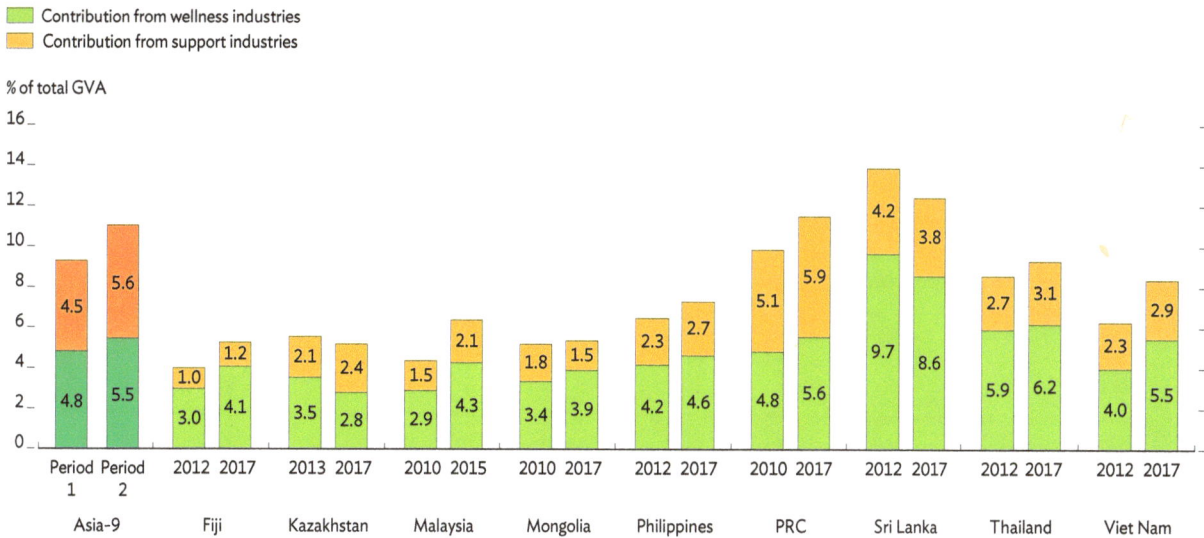

Asia-9 = aggregate of the nine countries in the figure, GVA = gross value added, PRC = People's Republic of China.

Notes: The two comparison years vary to accommodate data limitations, but taking the Asia-9 figures together as a proxy for developing Asia gives an idea of how big the region's wellness economy has become. This is done by summing the GVA attributable to wellness in all countries and dividing it by the sum of their total GVA in each year.

Source: Consing et al. 2020.

Figure 2.2.6 shows the size of the wellness economy in each country at two different times, separated by about 5 years within the past decade, as a percentage of each country's gross value added (GVA). Green bars show the contribution of wellness industries, and orange bars the contribution of industries supporting the wellness economy—for instance GVA from electricity consumed as an intermediate input by a firm in the wellness industry, such as a gym. Summing these two bars gives the estimated size of the wellness economy in each country during that year.

The wellness economy share of total GVA is generally increasing. That the share fell in Kazakhstan and Sri Lanka does not indicate that the wellness economy shrank in absolute terms in either country, only that it grew more slowly than the rest of the economy. The PRC shows relatively large orange support bars in both years, indicating that its wellness industries are relatively developed and sophisticated, with multiple industries contributing to their production and dependent on them for business.

The rising importance of the wellness economy in the larger national economy reflects how much wellness economies have grown in real terms. Table 2.2.2 shows the average annual growth rate for each country's wellness economy GVA after adjusting for inflation, using 2010 as the base year.

Table 2.2.2 Real average annual growth rate of wellness economies

Country	Average annual growth rate (%)
Fiji	10.2
Kazakhstan	1.2
Malaysia	13.2
Mongolia	9.3
Philippines	8.6
People's Republic of China	10.5
Sri Lanka	1.3
Thailand	5.2
Viet Nam	11.8

Source: Consing et al. 2020.

As shown, the wellness economy grew in each country between the sample years, even after adjusting for inflation. Several—Fiji, Malaysia, the PRC, and Viet Nam—experienced average annual growth rates exceeding 10%. If sustained for 7 years, such growth at least doubles each country's wellness economy in that period. Other countries with rapidly growing wellness economies are Mongolia, with associated GVA rising by 9.3%, and the Philippines, by 8.6%. Growth in the wellness economy generally outpaces overall economic growth in the countries sampled.

Treating these nine economies as a proxy for developing Asia informs two other key insights. One relates to the sector's contribution to the overall economy, with the wellness economy likely accounting for over 11% of total GVA in the region and growing by an average of about 9.9% annually in recent years, weighed by each country's total GVA. The other pertains to the contribution of wellness to employment. Using an established procedure for input–output analysis (Miller and Blair 2009) yields the finding that, in recent years, about 13.7% of employment in developing Asia can be traced to the wellness economy.

2.3 Holistic pathway to physical wellness

COVID-19 underscores the importance of physical wellness. Proper diet, regular physical activity, and other lifestyle changes prevent medical conditions such as cardiovascular disease, diabetes, and obesity, which have been shown to worsen vulnerability to infection. As workplaces in the region become increasingly unwell and impose a heavy toll on the health of Asian workers, they need effective ways to promote physical health. Physical activity such as regular physical exercise is perhaps the most important contributor to physical health, highlighting the importance of community planning and infrastructure such as public parks. As poor nutrition increasingly poses a risk to the physical health of Asians, policies must be adopted to guide the public toward better diets, safeguard public health, and minimize the eventual burden on the public health care system.

2.3.1 Physical inactivity—a worsening threat to public health in developing Asia

Physical activity, defined in Box 2.3.1, is intrinsic to wellness. As advocated by physicians and public health authorities around the world, regular and adequate physical activity is vital to our health in all aspects: muscular and cardiorespiratory fitness; bone and functional health; energy, balance, and weight control; and lower risk of depression and a number of chronic diseases such as hypertension, coronary heart disease, stroke, diabetes, and various types of cancer. Yet, recent decades have seen an alarming trend of declining physical activity in countries around the world. Recent data indicate that as many as 31% of adults may be physically inactive (Guthold et al. 2018, Hallal et al. 2012). Research across countries—including in Asia—associates low or declining physical activity with high or rising national incomes, and it shows women and girls generally less active than men and boys.

These trends are occurring at a time when we need physical activity more than ever to mitigate the rise of chronic disease and the impacts of aging populations. *The Lancet* has described worsening physical inactivity as a "pandemic, with far-reaching health, economic, environmental, and social consequences" (Kohl et al. 2012). Obesity, which is linked to physical inactivity, has nearly tripled worldwide since 1975, with 39% of adults now overweight (WHO 2018).

Box 2.3.1 Definition of physical activity

The World Health Organization defines physical activity as "any bodily movement produced by skeletal muscles that requires energy expenditure—including activities undertaken while working, playing, carrying out household chores, traveling, and engaging in recreational pursuit" (Yeung and Johnston 2020c). It adds that maintaining good health requires children and adolescents to engage daily in 60 minutes of moderately to vigorously intense physical activity, and adults weekly in 150 minutes of moderately intense physical activity or 75 minutes of vigorous physical activity. The benefits of physical activity are varied, widely proven, and well-known: preventing chronic disease, reducing stress, managing weight, strengthening functional mobility, improving sleep, alleviating depression, and improving cognitive function. To receive these benefits, engagement in physical activity needs to be regular, consistent, and sustained—not intermittent, only during holidays, or only when we want to lose weight or can find the time.

Physical activities can be broadly divided into natural movement and recreational physical activity.

Natural movement encompasses the physical activities that are essential to our daily lives, by category transportation (walking and cycling), occupation (work that requires manual labor), and domestic (household chores and gardening). From time immemorial, such activities have been the core of human physical activity. Unfortunately, as discussed below, natural movement is now on the decline around the world, increasingly at odds with modern lifestyles and built environments.

Many people engage in optional and intentional movement as a hobby or to fill leisure time. Recreational physical activity includes going to a gym, playing sports, taking a walk, cycling for fun, dancing, and, in the case of children, playing on a playground. As natural movement declines, recreational physical activity becomes essential for a growing number of people to stay fit and healthy.

Source: Yeung, O. and K. Johnston. 2020c. *The Physical Activity Economy in Asia: Market Size, Participation, Barriers, and Options to Increase Movement.* ADB.

Physical inactivity and obesity are key lifestyle risk factors that directly contribute to the rise of chronic or noncommunicable diseases—heart disease, stroke, cancer, diabetes, and chronic lung disease—which collectively cause 71% of deaths worldwide every year (WHO 2018). The global economic burden of physical inactivity was estimated at $67.5 billion in 2013, comprising $53.8 billion in direct health care costs and $13.7 billion in productivity losses (Ding et al. 2016).

Current state of physical inactivity in Asia

The most recent country data on physical activity, compiled by *The Lancet*, show 27.5% of the global adult population performing insufficient physical activity, if defined as not meeting the World Health Organization standards described above.[1] As shown in Table 2.3.1, the degree of physical inactivity varies widely across Asia.

In general, inactivity is lower than the global average in developing Asia. By subregion, it is lower than the global average in all subregions except South Asia. Disparity in inactivity rates between men and women is generally less stark in East and Southeast Asia than in other subregions across developing Asia. Asian countries with the largest inactive populations are, in descending order, the Philippines, Malaysia, Singapore, Japan, the Republic of Korea (ROK), India, and

Pakistan, as well as a number of Pacific nations such as the Marshall Islands, Nauru, Palau, Kiribati, and the Federated States of Micronesia. Asian countries with the lowest rates of inactivity are, in descending order, Cambodia, Myanmar, Nepal, the Kyrgyz Republic, and the PRC, and in the Pacific, Niue, Vanuatu, Samoa, and Papua New Guinea. Countries with the least disparity in inactivity between men and women are, in descending order, Armenia, Cambodia, Georgia, Mongolia, Vanuatu, Indonesia, Niue, Kazakhstan, Nepal, Japan, the PRC, and Singapore. In many economies across the region, women are far more inactive than men: in desending order, Palau, Bangladesh, Tuvalu, India, the Philippines, Pakistan, Tajikistan, the Cook Islands, Tonga, Sri Lanka, and Timor-Leste.

Table 2.3.1 Physical inactivity in developing Asia and Japan, 2016

Subregion/economy	Population with insufficient physical activity (%)	Men (%)	Women (%)
Central Asia	**22.1**	**17.7**	**26.1**
Armenia	22.6	23.3	22.1
Georgia	18.0	17.3	18.6
Kazakhstan	27.5	26.1	28.7
Kyrgyz Republic	13.9	10.9	16.7
Tajikistan	29.3	19.9	38.7
Uzbekistan	19.1	13.3	24.4
East Asia	**14.8**	**16.5**	**13.2**
Mongolia	18.6	17.8	19.4
People's Republic of China	14.1	16.0	12.2
Republic of Korea	35.4	29.5	41.0
Southeast Asia	**25.5**	**22.8**	**28.1**
Brunei Darussalam	27.3	21.2	33.9
Cambodia	10.5	9.8	11.1
Indonesia	22.6	23.5	21.7
Lao People's Democratic Republic	16.3	11.7	20.6
Malaysia	38.8	34.6	42.8
Myanmar	10.7	8.1	13.1
Philippines	39.7	30.1	49.1
Singapore	36.5	34.3	38.6
Thailand	24.6	21.8	27.2
Timor-Leste	17.8	10.3	25.5
Viet Nam	25.4	19.9	30.6

continued next page

Table 2.3.1 *Continued*

Subregion/economy	Population with insufficient physical activity (%)	Men (%)	Women (%)
South Asia	**33.0**	**23.7**	**42.8**
Bangladesh	27.8	16.1	39.5
Bhutan	23.0	17.7	29.5
India	34.0	24.7	43.9
Maldives	30.3	25.8	34.8
Nepal	13.4	12.0	14.6
Pakistan	33.7	24.4	43.3
Sri Lanka	28.9	20.2	36.7
The Pacific	**15.7**	**11.9**	**19.6**
Cook Islands	18.5	9.8	27.2
Federated States of Micronesia	36.6	32.9	40.5
Fiji	17.4	10.8	24.1
Kiribati	40.4	34.5	45.8
Marshall Islands	43.5	37.0	50.0
Nauru	42.1	34.9	49.4
Niue	6.9	7.8	6.0
Palau	40.9	28.3	53.5
Papua New Guinea	14.8	11.4	18.2
Samoa	12.6	8.2	17.2
Solomon Islands	18.2	13.3	23.2
Tonga	17.4	8.5	25.9
Tuvalu	27.3	17.5	37.2
Vanuatu	8.0	7.2	8.8
Developing Asia	**24.8**	**20.7**	**28.9**
Japan	35.5	33.8	37.0
Global average	**27.5**	**23.4**	**31.7**

Note: Regional averages are weighted by population.

Sources: Yeung and Johnston 2020c; Guthold et al. 2018; ADB estimates using data from UN Department of Economics and Social Affairs, World Population Prospects Rev. 2019. https://population.un.org/wpp/; Pacific Data Hub. https://pacificdata.org/.

There is no question that modern lifestyles and livelihoods require much less physical exertion than those of previous generations of farmers, fishers, herders, traders, and industrial workers. In all aspects, daily lives have become more sedentary. Across Asia, urbanization, technological developments, and growing numbers of office jobs have drawn more people into sedentary pursuits. For the growing middle class, and for people in general who live in middle- and high-income countries, household chores such as cooking and cleaning have been greatly eased by modern appliances and industrialized food production. Meanwhile, the digital revolution has enabled us to shop, socialize, and consume news and entertainment without leaving our homes or even our sofas.

The trend is equally alarming for youth. Studies have found a long-term decline in cardiovascular fitness among children and adolescents, especially in upper- and middle-income countries (Tomkinson, Lang, and Tremblay 2019, Tomkinson et al. 2012, Macfarlane and Tomkinson 2007). In many countries, fewer children walk or bike to school (Uddin et al. 2019, Lu et al. 2014). With urbanization, the spontaneous and unsupervised outdoor play of past generations of Asian children has given way to fewer opportunities for outdoor physical activity. As with adults, teens now have less motivation to be active, glued as they are to their mobile devices for social media, games, and other entertainment.

What is the physical activity economy?

Physical activity generates significant economic activity, both in Asia and around the world. As leisure-time fitness, exercise, and active recreation become more popular, these pursuits will increasingly become important items in private household spending. Government spending also plays a substantial role in supporting physical activity. Both private and public expenditure play major roles in the physical activity economy (Box 2.3.2).

The physical activity market is defined as consumer spending associated with intentional physical activities performed during leisure and recreation, with the core being the services that allow consumers to participate in three categories of recreational physical activities: sports and active recreation, fitness, and mindful movement. The market includes three support segments that enable and facilitate consumer participation in these activities: technology, equipment and supplies, and apparel and footwear.

To estimate the size of the global physical activity market, this chapter focuses on private spending on recreational physical activity (GWI 2019). This is mainly for lack of clear data on public spending, spanning as it does all levels of government and multiple agencies, but it is worth noting that private spending is the best gauge for rising consumer interest in intentional recreational physical activities and related services.

Asia's physical activity economy

Asia has one of the largest and most diverse physical activity markets in the world, estimated at $240.4 billion in 2018.[2] The physical activity market in the region is large, diverse, and dynamic. It accounts for 29% of the $828.2 billion global economy for physical activity and is the second-largest regional market in the world for physical activity, after North America (Figure 2.3.1). Within the Asian physical activity market, $115.4 billion, or 48%, is direct consumer expenditure on a variety of recreational physical activities, primarily sports and active recreation, fitness, and mindful movement.

Box 2.3.2 Public and private expenditure on physical activity

- **Private expenditure** goes primarily to intentional recreational physical activities, which individuals and families increasingly choose to pursue in their leisure time. These expenditures include fees to join a gym, take a fitness or yoga class, join a recreational sports team or club, swim laps at a pool, run a marathon, and so on. Individuals also spend money on special clothes and shoes, fitness equipment, sporting goods, and technology devices and services that support their participation in recreational physical activities—and may also support walking or biking as transportation, which are natural movement physical activities.

- **Public expenditure**, often by local governments, supports both natural movement and recreational physical activities primarily through infrastructure investment and spending on youth and education. In most countries, governments support recreational physical activities and sports in a variety of ways: building and maintaining public sports fields, swimming pools, tennis courts, and running paths and trails, as well as funding youth and community sports leagues and training programs. A smaller number of governments build and/or subsidize community fitness centers and gyms. Governments fund physical education classes in schools, which expose children early to a variety of sports and physical activities and help instill lifelong healthy habits. Public expenditure is also critical to facilitating natural movement physical activity, especially through urban planning and public transport investments that create infrastructure appropriate for people who walk and ride bicycles as they commute to work or go about their daily activities.

Source: Yeung, O. and K. Johnston. 2020c. *The Physical Activity Economy in Asia: Market Size, Participation, Barriers, and Options to Increase Movement*. ADB.

Expenditure on physical activity

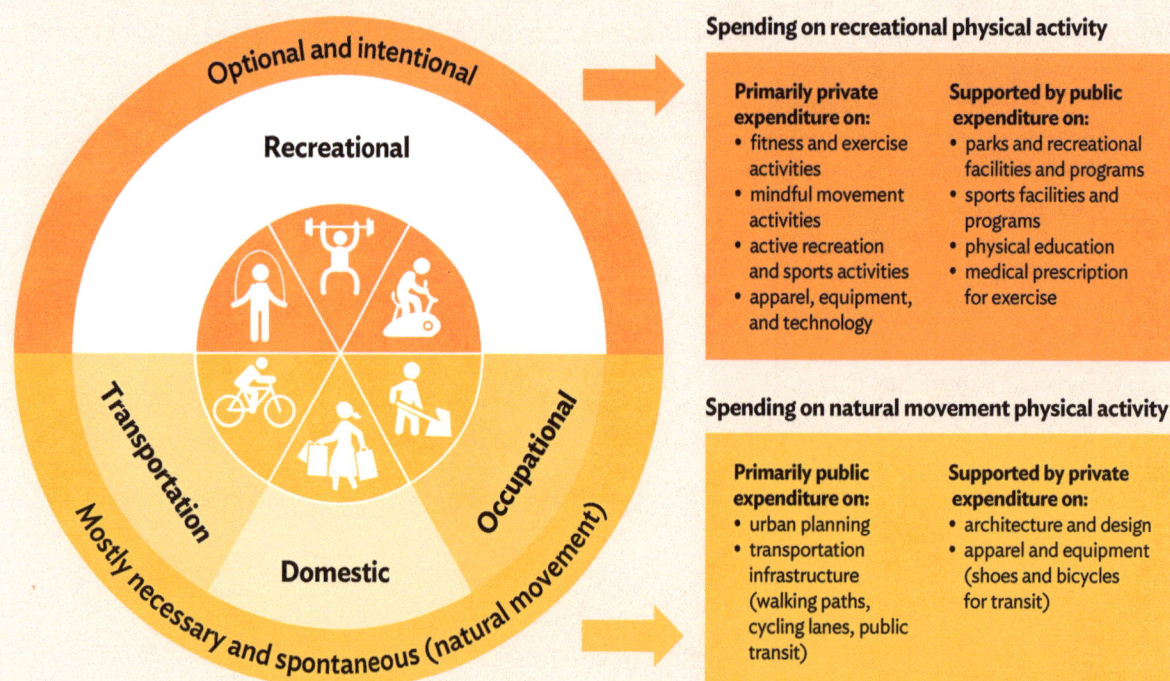

Source: Yeung and Johnston 2020c.

Figure 2.3.1 Physical activity economy by region, 2018

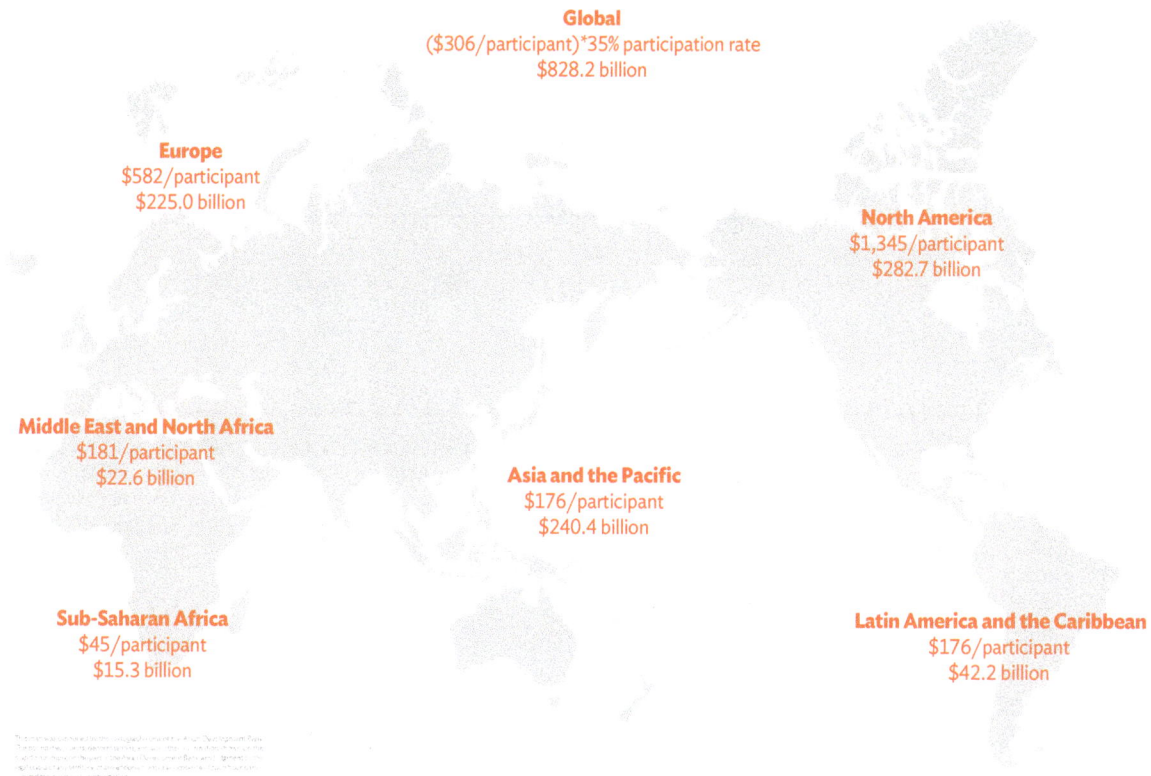

Global
($306/participant)*35% participation rate
$828.2 billion

Europe
$582/participant
$225.0 billion

North America
$1,345/participant
$282.7 billion

Middle East and North Africa
$181/participant
$22.6 billion

Asia and the Pacific
$176/participant
$240.4 billion

Sub-Saharan Africa
$45/participant
$15.3 billion

Latin America and the Caribbean
$176/participant
$42.2 billion

Note: Physical activity spending per participant is total expenditure on physical activity divided by the number of people who participate in recreational physical activities regularly, at least monthly. Regional groupings follow those of the Global Wellness Institute.

Source: Yeung and Johnston 2020c.

The remaining $125.0 billion, or 52%, is expenditure on a variety of enabling and supporting supplies: primarily clothing and footwear but also fitness equipment, sporting goods, and fitness- and exercise-supporting technologies.

Annual physical activity spending averages $176 per participant in Asia and the Pacific: $85 spent on participating in recreational physical activities and $92 spent on associated apparel, footwear, equipment, sporting goods, and technology devices and services (Table 2.3.2). Expenditure per participant in Asia is considerably lower than the global average of $306. In Asia's most developed economies and largest metropolitan areas, middle- and upper-income consumers have access to a well-developed industry of fitness and sporting facilities: gyms and health clubs, sporting clubs, swimming pools, and yoga and dance studios. In these places, participants' spending is higher because average incomes are higher and also because there is a wider variety of fitness and recreational physical activities that people can pay for.

Table 2.3.2 Physical activity economy in Asia and the Pacific, 2018

Item	Participation rate (%)	Market size ($ billion)	Average spending per participant
Recreational physical activities	**33.2**	**116.6**	**85**
Sports and active recreation	30.4	83.0	66
Fitness	1.1	22.7	494
Mindful movement	4.5	10.9	58
Enabling segments		**125.5**	**92**
Apparel and footwear		87.5	8
Equipment and supplies		27.6	20
Technology		10.8	64
Total physical activity economy in Asia and the Pacific		**240.4**	**176**

Notes: The participation rate is the share of the total population that engages in one or more of the three physical activity categories regularly, at least once a month. Market size is consumer expenditure on classes, memberships, entry fees, trainers, and related services and methods of participation. Physical activity spending per participant is total expenditure on physical activity divided by the number of people who participate regularly, at least once a month. Numbers may not sum precisely because of rounding or segment overlap. Asia and the Pacific in the table follows the Global Wellness Institute definition.
Source: Yeung and Johnston 2020c.

However, for most people in Asia, the private market and infrastructure for fitness and sports are not well developed. In these places, people who engage in recreational physical activity spend little or nothing to do so using public facilities: playing soccer in a local league or with friends, going for a run outside, or doing tai chi in a city park. For this reason, average spending per participant can vary widely across Asia, ranging from $622 in the ROK, $495 in Japan, and $460 in Singapore to $66 in India, $55 in the Philippines, and $29 in Indonesia and Viet Nam (Table 2.3.3).

Not surprisingly, the largest physical activity markets in the region are in the PRC and Japan, which rank second and third globally after the US. The top three markets in Asia—the PRC, Japan, and the ROK—account for nearly three-quarters of all physical activity spending in the region. It is noteworthy that, in several Asian markets—Bangladesh, Cambodia, India, Myanmar, Pakistan, Sri Lanka, and Thailand—spending on enabling supplies is larger than spending on recreational physical activity participation. In other markets—Australia, New Zealand, the ROK and Singapore—the opposite is the case. These differences largely reflect how much people spend on apparel and shoes in these economies.

Buoyed by economic growth, the rising purchasing power of the middle class, and a growing interest in healthy and active lifestyles, Asia's physical activity economy is growing quickly and becoming increasingly competitive. Asia will have the world's fastest-growing regional economy for physical activity spending over the next 5 years—with an average annual growth rate of 9.2%, compared with 6.6% globally—and will overtake North America as the largest region by expenditure in 2023.

Table 2.3.3 Top 20 physical activity markets in Asia and the Pacific, 2018

	Recreational physical activity		Enabling supplies ($ billion)	Total physical activity market ($ billion)	Rank in 2018	Spending per participant ($)
	Participation rate (%)	Market size ($ billion)				
People's Republic of China	48.6	53.56	56.89	109.35	1	158.88
Japan	69.6	20.79	23.16	43.89	2	495.49
Republic of Korea	73.7	14.25	9.32	23.46	3	622.04
Australia	84.1	11.45	5.37	16.73	4	803.06
India	15.0	3.51	10.02	13.39	5	66.00
Taipei,China	84.0	3.69	4.08	7.73	6	388.48
Hong Kong, China	58.2	1.40	2.72	4.11	7	951.39
New Zealand	83.8	1.72	1.32	3.03	8	760.37
Thailand	27.8	0.74	2.16	2.89	9	150.26
Indonesia	34.2	1.30	1.34	2.61	10	28.60
Malaysia	41.1	0.75	1.29	2.04	11	154.99
Pakistan	13.2	0.28	1.68	1.95	12	73.23
Philippines	32.7	0.68	1.23	1.90	13	54.54
Bangladesh	25.2	0.22	1.58	1.79	14	42.70
Singapore	64.9	1.08	0.67	1.73	15	460.07
Viet Nam	35.7	0.47	0.54	1.00	16	28.90
Sri Lanka	19.2	0.16	0.44	0.60	17	149.31
Macau, China	51.1	0.16	0.32	0.47	18	1,456.61
Myanmar	21.3	0.07	0.40	0.47	19	40.59
Cambodia	21.4	0.06	0.15	0.21	20	59.11

Notes: The participation rate is the share of the total population that engages in one or more of the three physical activity categories regularly, at least once a month. Market size is consumer expenditure on classes, memberships, entry fees, trainers, and related services and methods of participation.
Physical activity spending per participant is total expenditure on physical activity divided by the number of people who participate regularly, at least once a month. Numbers may not sum precisely because of rounding or segment overlap.
Sources: Yeung and Johnston 2020c; UN World Population Prospects 2019. https://population.un.org/wpp/ (accessed 3 July 2020); authors' calculations.

Over 40% of the global increase in the physical activity market will be in Asia and the Pacific, and India and the PRC together are projected to account for nearly one-third of market growth. In Asia's higher-income countries and major cities, consumers keenly follow the latest fitness and recreational trends and offerings, while the region's vibrant private sector innovates, imports, improvises, and adapts to meet rising demand. Across the region, rising concern about obesity and chronic disease, and awareness of their link to inactivity, will continue to push governments, nonprofits, medical systems, employers, and consumers to pay more attention to physical activity.

Low correlation between spending and participation

Higher spending on physical activity does not necessarily correspond, however, to higher participation. The percentage of the population that participates in recreational physical activity in Asia and the Pacific is estimated at 33.2%, just below the global average of 35.5%.[3] The region thus has a lower participation rate than Latin America and the Caribbean despite its spending per participant being quite a bit higher (Figure 2.3.2). The participation rate in Asia and the Pacific is only slightly higher than in Sub-Saharan Africa, despite spending per participant being more than seven times higher.

Figure 2.3.2 Recreational physical activity participation rate by region, 2018

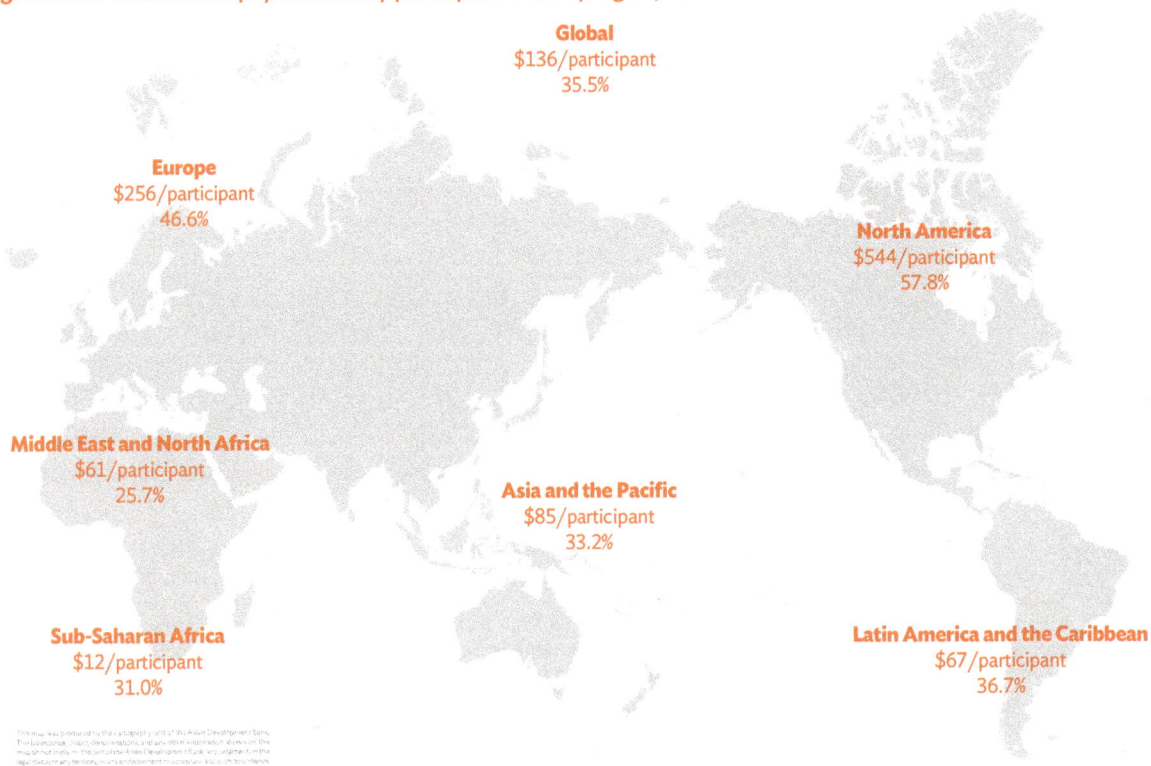

Global
$136/participant
35.5%

Europe
$256/participant
46.6%

North America
$544/participant
57.8%

Middle East and North Africa
$61/participant
25.7%

Asia and the Pacific
$85/participant
33.2%

Sub-Saharan Africa
$12/participant
31.0%

Latin America and the Caribbean
$67/participant
36.7%

Note: Regional groupings follow those of the Global Wellness Institute.
Source: Yeung and Johnston 2020c.

Across Asia and the Pacific, participation in recreational physical activity varies widely, from a high of 84% in Australia and Taipei,China to a low of 13%–15% in India and Pakistan (Table 2.3.4). Importantly, many people in Asia conduct their leisure-time physical activity in public places that require little or no spending. In lower-income countries, people participate in sports and other recreational activities in a variety of public and free venues: public parks and plazas, free sporting facilities such as neighborhood basketball courts or ball fields, vacant lots, streets, and at home.

Table 2.3.4 Recreational physical activity participation rates in Asia and the Pacific, 2018

Economy	Participation rate (%)	Rank	Economy	Participation rate (%)	Rank
Australia	84.1	1	Viet Nam	35.7	14
Taipei,China	84.0	2	Indonesia	34.2	15
New Zealand	83.8	3	Philippines	32.7	16
Mongolia	75.0	4	Thailand	27.8	17
Republic of Korea	73.7	5	Timor-Leste	26.3	18
Japan	69.6	6	Bangladesh	25.2	19
Singapore	64.9	7	Cambodia	21.4	20
Hong Kong, China	58.2	8	Myanmar	21.3	21
Macau, China	51.1	9	Nepal	20.0	22
People's Republic of China	48.6	10	Sri Lanka	19.2	23
Papua New Guinea	46.4	11	India	15.0	24
Malaysia	41.1	12	Pakistan	13.2	25
Lao People's Democratic Republic	39.8	13			

Note: The participation rate is the share of the total population that participates in one or more of the three physical activity categories regularly, at least monthly.
Source: Yeung and Johnston 2020c.

Because private fitness and recreation businesses, facilities, and infrastructure are less developed, out-of-pocket spending tends to be low, even zero.

Free individual and group exercise in public outdoor gyms, plaza dancing, and tai chi in parks are very popular in the PRC, especially among seniors. "Plaza dancing" (*guangchang wu*) has become a major exercise phenomenon, practiced by an estimated 100 million women (and some men), most of them middle-aged or older, in public squares, parks, parking lots, and other public venues. The physical inactivity rates discussed above do not necessarily correlate with recreational physical activity rates. For example, in poorer countries, individuals may engage in a lot of physical activity, such as farm work or other physical labor, but have little time or resources for recreational physical activity.

Even in higher-income markets, many people pay nothing to participate in sports and other recreational physical activities. National survey data show that 67% of adult participants in Japan, 25% in the ROK, and 41% in Australia spend no money to participate in these activities, yet participation rates in all three countries are quite high (Japan Sports Agency 2017, ROK Ministry of Culture, Sports, and Tourism 2017, Australian Sports Commission Clearinghouse for Sport and Physical Activity 2019).

Complementing well-developed private sector fitness markets, the governments in all three of them have invested in widespread, publicly subsidized fitness and sports facilities and infrastructure, which allow their populations to participate with very low out-of-pocket expenditure.

2.3.2 Increasingly unwell Asian workplace

Because Asians spend a large part of their life working, their physical and mental well-being at the workplace is vital to wellness overall. Workplace safety or its absence greatly affects the physical well-being of many workers. Every day, over 1.9 billion people in Asia go to work (ILO 2018). In a lifetime, the average person spends at least 90,000 hours working (Pryce-Jones 2010). Yet the health and wellness of Asian workers is far from optimal. The issues vary across countries and industries, from the office worker who is perpetually exhausted by working 14-hour days to the small business employee who receives no benefits or sick leave, the manufacturing worker who is allowed no break and is forced to work overtime, and the miner who toils in life-threatening conditions.

In 2017, an estimated 2.8 million people worldwide died from occupational injuries or work-related diseases, with Asia accounting for over two-thirds of the total (ILO 2019). The most vulnerable workers are typically the poorest and the least informed, trained, and protected: women, children, disabled workers, migrant workers, and ethnic minorities. Not only do these injuries, diseases, and resulting fatalities bring immense suffering to workers and their families, they impose massive economic losses on businesses, communities, and the larger economy. Among the estimated 1.8 million occupational fatalities in Asia, the biggest killers were work-related circulatory and cardiovascular diseases and stroke at 31%, work-related cancers at 24%, work-related respiratory diseases at 21%, and occupational injuries at 15% (Hämäläinen et al. 2017).

Size and coverage of Asia's workplace wellness sector

The workplace wellness market covers employer expenditure on programs, services, activities, and equipment deployed to improve their employees' health and wellness (GWI 2018). These efforts typically seek to raise awareness, provide education, and offer incentives that encourage employees to adopt healthier lifestyles. Workplace wellness programs target a wide range of employee behavior—lack of exercise, poor eating habits, smoking, and lack of sleep—and risk factors such as chronic illness, obesity, addiction, depression, and stress.

Programs can encompass a variety of services, products, and platforms: health screening, diagnostic testing, in-house amenities or subsidized memberships for fitness clubs and exercise classes, healthy food offerings in company cafeterias, wearable fitness trackers, incentives for participation in wellness activities, and health fairs, educational programming, and counseling services for wellness. While some companies may design and administer their own wellness programs, a sizable industry of third-party service providers has emerged to administer these programs for companies. In addition, many private insurance companies administer wellness programs for the companies whose employees they insure.

The workplace wellness market in Asia was estimated at $9.3 billion in 2017, almost a fifth of $47.5 billion in workplace wellness expenditures worldwide. Market size varies widely from country to country (Table 2.3.5). Asia's workplace wellness expenditures grew by 5.1% annually from 2015 to 2017 (GWI 2018). This indicates that worker wellness is gaining some attention in Asia, motivated by growing concerns about managing health care costs, boosting productivity and competitiveness, and improving employee morale, recruitment, and retention. A recent survey of office-based companies in the Asia and the Pacific found that 60% of those surveyed already had some type of workplace wellness program or intended to start one in the near future (CBRE Group 2017).

Current workplace wellness expenditure in Asia is low, as it is globally, when viewed from the perspective of employee coverage. The 97.8 million workers in Asia estimated to benefit from some form of workplace wellness program are only 5.2% of all employed workers in the region. This compares poorly with an estimated 9.8% of workers globally who benefit from workplace wellness programs (GWI 2018). Across Asia, workplace wellness is still not a widespread concept, benefiting only a small slice of workers— mostly those who work for multinational corporations and in such knowledge-intensive areas as finance, investment, consulting, information technology, high-tech, higher education, and creative industries, or more inclusively those living in the region's wealthiest countries and cities.

As workplace wellness programs and spending expand in Asia, daunting work-related wellness challenges continue to grow. A 2018 workplace survey in Australia; Hong Kong, China; Malaysia; the PRC; and Thailand found that 51% of employees suffered from at least one kind of work-related stress, 83% had at least one musculoskeletal condition, and health-related productivity loss ranged from 48 to 78 days per year (AIA Vitality 2019). Evidence shows more than 67% of workers in India, Indonesia, the Philippines, and the PRC felt that their work environment caused body pain, and more than 60% said their work environment caused head pain—human suffering that also translates into significant productivity loss (GSK Consumer Healthcare 2017).

Table 2.3.5 Top 20 workplace wellness markets in Asia and the Pacific, 2017

Economy	Number of workers covered (million)	Share of all employment (%)	Expenditure ($ million)
Japan	21.4	32.8	3,915.2
Republic of Korea	8.3	31.2	1,524.8
Australia	5.9	47.7	1,112.1
Taipei,China	3.5	30.6	634.6
People's Republic of China	33.1	4.3	496.7
Indonesia	2.5	2.1	222.6
Hong Kong, China	1.2	31.5	220.4
New Zealand	1.2	45.6	212.5
Singapore	1.0	27.8	186.5
India	9.2	2.6	184.2
Thailand	1.6	4.1	130.5
Viet Nam	1.5	2.7	119.9
Philippines	1.4	3.5	115.9
Malaysia	0.6	3.9	47.7
Bangladesh	2.0	3.3	40.6
Pakistan	1.8	2.9	36.3
Macau, China	0.1	31.5	20.1
Myanmar	0.9	1.0	18.3
Sri Lanka	0.2	2.7	17.6
Brunei Darussalam	0.1	26.8	7.5

Sources: Yeung and Johnston 2020b; CEIC Data Company Ltd.; ILOSTAT. https://ilostat.ilo.org/data/country-profiles/ (both accessed 2 July 2020); authors' calculations.

Workplace wellness concerns vary widely across countries and economic conditions. In wealthier countries, issues typically revolve around preventable chronic disease, mitigating stress, improving work–life balance, enhancing engagement, and improving workplace culture and management structure. In lower-income countries, a large share of the workforce suffers dire and often life-threatening exploitation and workplace threats to safety and health in jobs that lack employment security and fail to pay a living wage—challenges beyond the purview of typical workplace wellness programs.

Current workplace wellness practices

Most Asian countries provide only limited coverage of workplace wellness, excluding most workers, especially those in contingent, part-time, or informal employment. Further, the participation rate is low even among those who are offered wellness benefits, and no conclusive evidence exists about how effective programs are. This suggests a need to improve workplace wellness programs, which often suffer from a siloed and reactive approach that aims to fix problems only after they arise rather than prevent them. They tend to overemphasize health problems outside the workplace, rather than problems caused by or otherwise in the workplace, such as physical dangers, rampant stress, and overwork.

To be effective, a workplace wellness framework must be holistic and focus first on wellness challenges that arise within the workplace. At a minimum, employers must ensure physically safe working conditions and healthy environments. Adhering to existing standards and regulations and applying safe and healthy practices should be the baseline for every employer.

However, basic physical health and safety are not enough to meet the demands of the new economic era. Employers need to go further, proactively infusing health- and wellness-enhancing features into physical work environments to encourage motivated, happy, and productive workers. In this context, employers can promote healthy behavior at work through various measures. Ergonomic workstations, standing desks, and cafeterias with healthy food options are some examples. Cultivating a healthy work culture by, for example, recognizing and mitigating overwork and stress—and by supporting healthy habits outside work, such as by providing subsidized gym membership—also contribute significantly to workplace wellness. Finally, employers should pay serious attention to and promote a better work–life balance to ensure the physical and mental well-being of their workers.[4]

2.3.3 Promoting wellness through infrastructure and planning

The built environment affects people's ability to pursue physical wellness activities. Some cities are pedestrian and bicycle friendly, for example, while others not. More broadly, wellness real estate incorporates human health and wellness as a central concept in urban planning, real estate, and infrastructure development. Wellness real estate was a $134 billion industry in 2017, with Asia and the Pacific accounting for $47 billion (Table 2.3.6).[5]

Compared with the broader construction and real estate industries in Asia, wellness real estate is a nascent development. Asian consumers are only recently beginning to recognize that the built environment has a major impact on healthy lifestyles, health outcomes, and longevity. The recent rise of wellness lifestyle real estate—the building of homes with wellness features and elements—can be traced to consumer interest in extending wellness experiences from their vacation destinations and leisure activities into their homes and everyday life. In major Asian cities, demand for these types of homes or vacation properties reflects as well environmental concerns and intensifying stress.

Public investment can contribute significantly to wellness-focused built environments. Governments can invest, for example, in infrastructure that encourages physical activity, such as pedestrian sidewalks, paths and trails, and public parks.

Key features of wellness-focused built environments include design and infrastructure that encourage physical activity by building sidewalks, paths and trails, parks, and other options for "active transit" (getting around using muscle power); healthy eating through community gardens, farmers' markets, and edible landscaping; social connections through public spaces and plazas, controlled housing density and setbacks, mixed-use zoning, and community events and programming; and mental and emotional wellness through green space, biophilic design, and public art. Such planning approaches serve multiple purposes, creating neighborhoods and communities that are healthier for residents by enhancing their quality of life, happiness, and well-being.

Wellness infrastructure can engender social capital and trust, which contributes to well-being and happiness. A new but growing body of evidence is demonstrating that the built environment has an enormous effect on relationships and civic life within communities. Many urban planning approaches in recent decades have perversely reinforced individual and societal patterns toward loneliness, isolation, segregation, and distrust. Wellness-focused design and infrastructure emphasizes parks, plazas, and other social and community spaces as critical to creating a healthy living environment for individuals. Investment in the design, upkeep, and equitable distribution of such civic assets and public spaces further engenders trust in public institutions and people, encouraging civic engagement and pride.

Table 2.3.6 Top 15 wellness real estate markets in Asia and the Pacific, 2017

Market	Size ($ million)
People's Republic of China	19,939.6
Australia	9,471.4
India	6,088.3
Republic of Korea	4,194.8
Japan	2,246.4
Malaysia	917.1
Singapore	818.7
New Zealand	802.6
Taipei,China	652.0
Indonesia	570.6
Viet Nam	482.4
Hong Kong, China	297.7
Thailand	248.2
Philippines	35.0
Macau, China	16.6

Note: The 2018 Global Wellness Institute report *Build Well to Live Well* defines wellness real estate as the construction of residential and commercial and/or institutional properties that incorporate intentional wellness elements into their design, materials, and building as well as in their amenities, services, and/or programming.

Source: Yeung and Johnston 2020a.

2.3.4 Double burden of malnutrition in Asia: undernutrition and obesity

Recognition is growing of the importance of good nutrition to physical and mental health and to sustainable development. Undernutrition, particularly early in life, is associated with worsened risk of infection, stunted cognition and educational achievement, and, consequently, reduced economic productivity (Hickson and Julian 2018, Madjdian et al. 2018).

Two-thirds of the 49.5 million children around the world under 5 years of age who are diagnosed as wasted, or abnormally low weight for their height, live in Asia. Over half of pregnant women in South Asia, meanwhile, are anemic, meaning they suffer iron deficieny (Harding et al. 2018, FAO et al. 2019). Annual economic losses from low weight, poor childhood growth, and micronutrient deficiency in Asia equal an average 11% of GDP (UNICEF 2019).

At the same time, the prevalence of obesity and diet-related chronic disease are increasing rapidly in tandem with rising living standards and greater food availability.

Poor nutrition caused by unhealthy diets is also associated with an increased risk of being overweight or obese and contracting diabetes, cardiovascular disease, and some cancers, notably of the colon, pancreas, and breast (Grosso et al. 2017, Jannasch et al. 2017, Schwingshackl et al. 2017). Diets high in fruits, vegetables, whole grains, legumes, seeds, nuts, fish, and dairy—and low in processed meat, sweets, and salty foods— have been shown to reduce the risk of chronic lifestyle disease (Maghsoudi et al. 2016, Ndanuko et al. 2016, Guasch-Ferré et al. 2019, Schwingshackl et al. 2019).

Asians eat more these days but not necessarily better. Overweight and obese conditions are on the rise in Asia and the Pacific (Figure 2.3.3), generating significant economic costs. The annual burden of direct medical costs has been estimated equal to 0.78% of GDP (Helble and Francisco 2018). Diets in Asia and the Pacific have changed rapidly with improved living standards, modernization, and globalization. Consumption of fruits and vegetables remains low in many countries, however, while consumption of refined staple carbohydrates, such as white rice, dominates many diets. Consumption of highly processed foods has risen dramatically over the past 20 years (Baker and Friel 2016, Sievert et al. 2019b).

Countering malnutrition should be a regional priority because it imposes significant personal, social, and economic costs in Asia and the Pacific. While diets have become in most countries more diverse and sufficient in calories, challenges remain in countries with very low incomes. As caloric intake improves, the region faces the emerging challenge of unhealthy diets as the consumption of fat, sugar, and highly processed food rises. Population segments at high risk of poor dietary intake include young children during weaning, women and girls, households with low incomes, and rural landless households.

Food environments are improving across the region as calorie availability per capita rises (Figure 2.3.4). In all but 8 of the 34 ADB developing member countries for which data are available, supply now exceeds 2,500 calories per capita per day, a widely used benchmark for calorie sufficiency.[6] Food prices are fairly stable, but high prices for nutritious foods contribute to both undernutrition and unhealthy diets. Despite improved standards, food safety remains a challenge across the region, particularly in informal settings. Higher incomes, urbanization, and globalization are changing diets by affecting food availability, marketing, and retail.

Figure 2.3.3 Prevalence of overweight and obese children aged 5–9 years, %

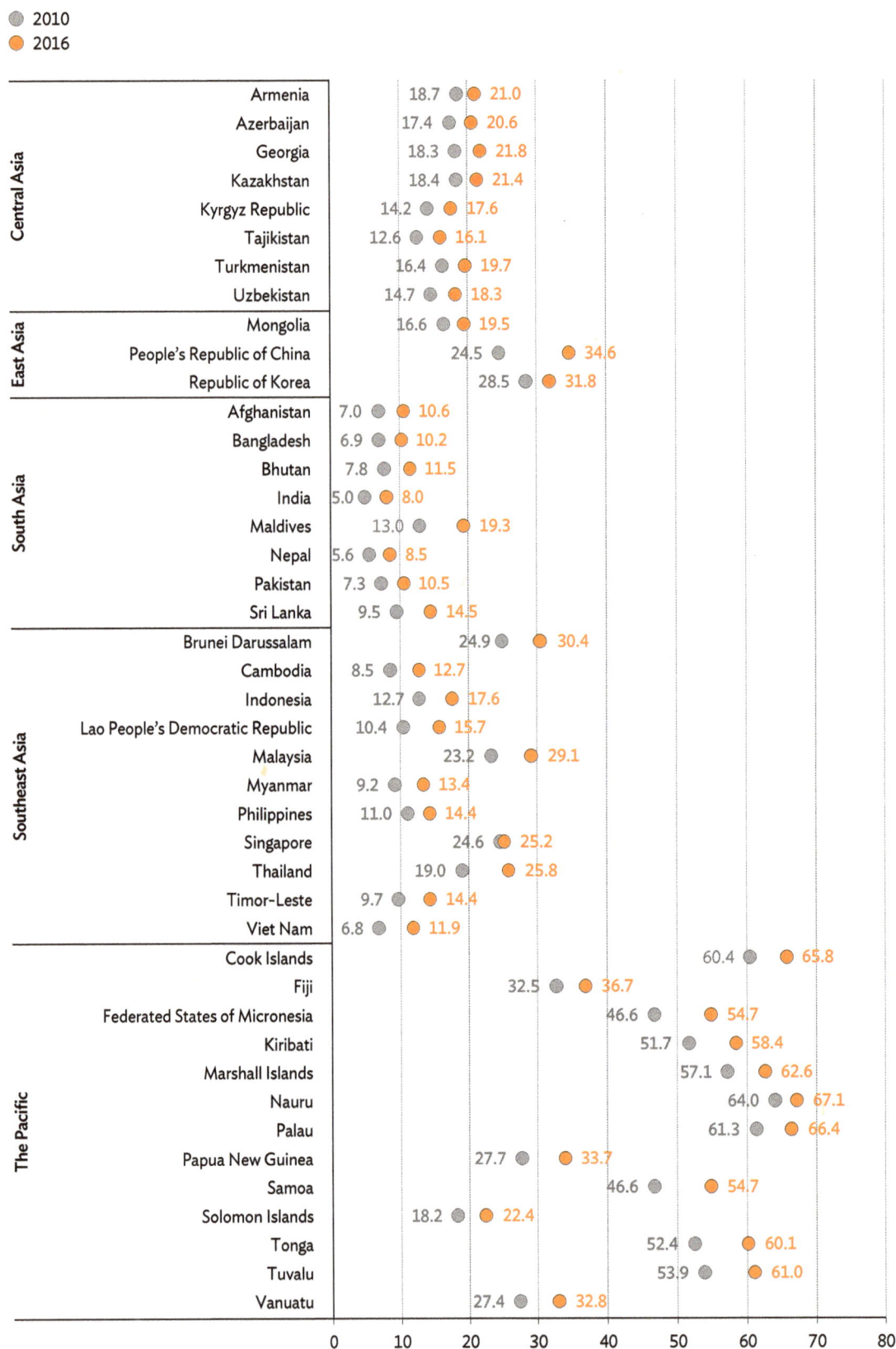

○ 2010
● 2016

		2010	2016
Central Asia	Armenia	18.7	21.0
	Azerbaijan	17.4	20.6
	Georgia	18.3	21.8
	Kazakhstan	18.4	21.4
	Kyrgyz Republic	14.2	17.6
	Tajikistan	12.6	16.1
	Turkmenistan	16.4	19.7
	Uzbekistan	14.7	18.3
East Asia	Mongolia	16.6	19.5
	People's Republic of China	24.5	34.6
	Republic of Korea	28.5	31.8
South Asia	Afghanistan	7.0	10.6
	Bangladesh	6.9	10.2
	Bhutan	7.8	11.5
	India	5.0	8.0
	Maldives	13.0	19.3
	Nepal	5.6	8.5
	Pakistan	7.3	10.5
	Sri Lanka	9.5	14.5
Southeast Asia	Brunei Darussalam	24.9	30.4
	Cambodia	8.5	12.7
	Indonesia	12.7	17.6
	Lao People's Democratic Republic	10.4	15.7
	Malaysia	23.2	29.1
	Myanmar	9.2	13.4
	Philippines	11.0	14.4
	Singapore	24.6	25.2
	Thailand	19.0	25.8
	Timor-Leste	9.7	14.4
	Viet Nam	6.8	11.9
The Pacific	Cook Islands	60.4	65.8
	Fiji	32.5	36.7
	Federated States of Micronesia	46.6	54.7
	Kiribati	51.7	58.4
	Marshall Islands	57.1	62.6
	Nauru	64.0	67.1
	Palau	61.3	66.4
	Papua New Guinea	27.7	33.7
	Samoa	46.6	54.7
	Solomon Islands	18.2	22.4
	Tonga	52.4	60.1
	Tuvalu	53.9	61.0
	Vanuatu	27.4	32.8

Source: Thow, Farrell, Helble, and Rachmi 2020.

While urbanization can improve access to a variety of foods, urban residents tend to eat out more and consume more processed food. Food has become less expensive and more readily available, mitigating food insecurity and malnutrition but encouraging unhealthy eating with too much intake of calories, sugar, salt, and fat. Trade liberalization has made food supply chains more resilient, enabling year-round access to all kinds of food, seasonal or not, but can also worsens markets' vulnerability to global price shocks and perversely make unhealthy processed food more available and affordable.

Figure 2.3.4 Calorie availability by subregion and economy, 2000 and 2017

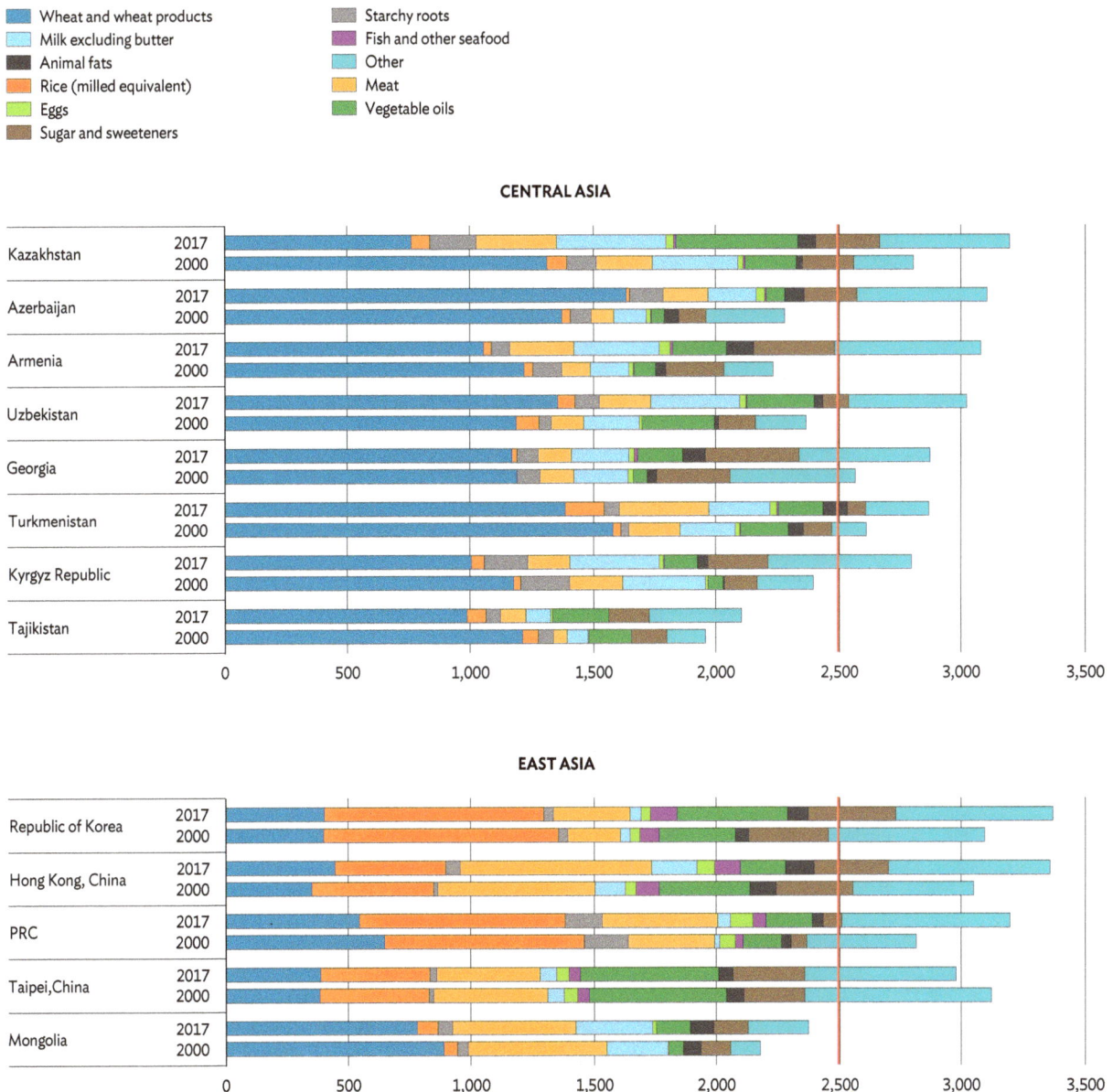

- Wheat and wheat products
- Milk excluding butter
- Animal fats
- Rice (milled equivalent)
- Eggs
- Sugar and sweeteners
- Starchy roots
- Fish and other seafood
- Other
- Meat
- Vegetable oils

CENTRAL ASIA

EAST ASIA

continued next page

Figure 2.3.4 *Continued*

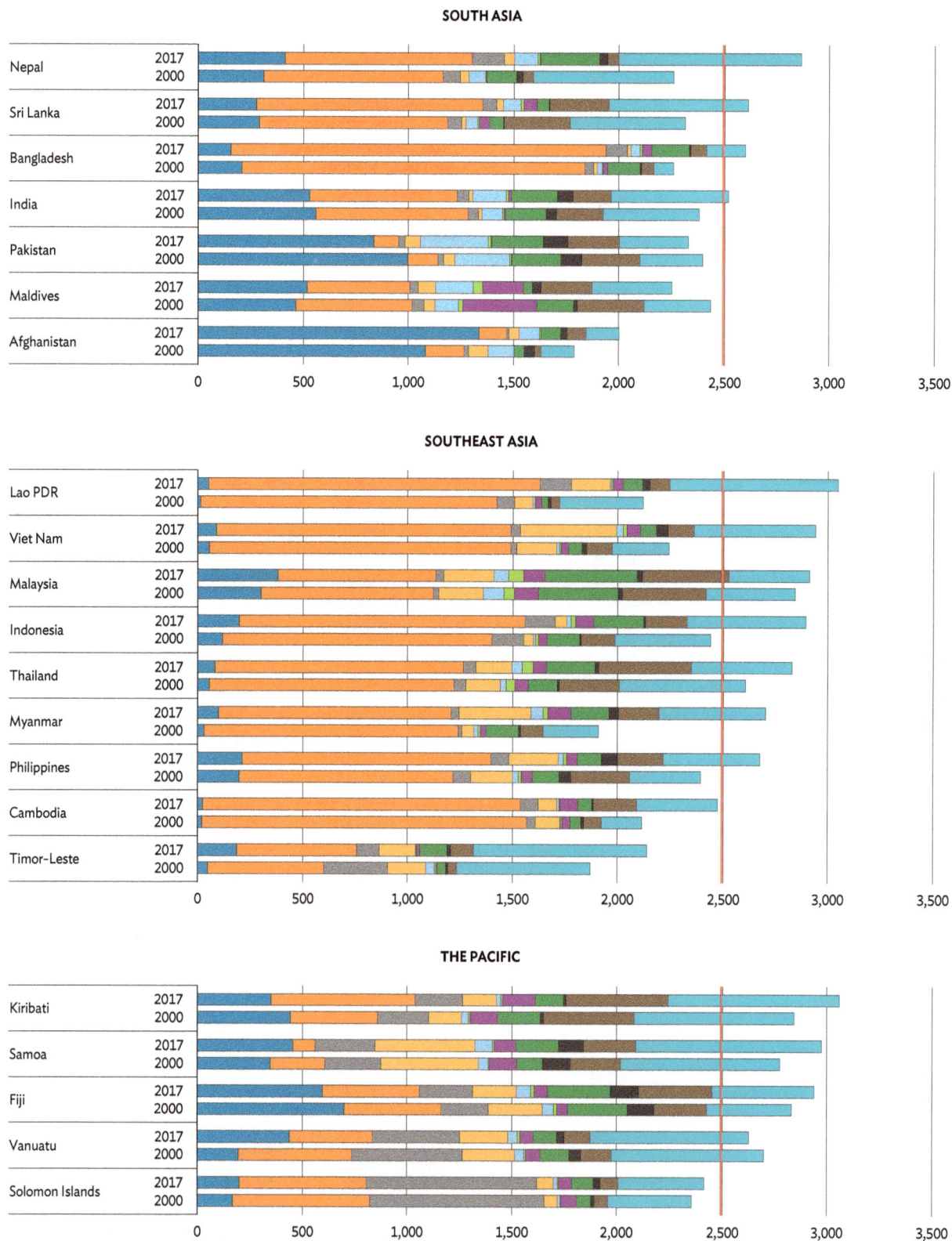

SOUTH ASIA

SOUTHEAST ASIA

THE PACIFIC

Lao PDR = Lao People's Democratic Republic, PRC = People's Republic of China.
Note: The economies included are those in the region for which 2017 FAO Food Balance Sheet data are available.
Source: Thow, Farrell, Helble, and Rachmi 2020.

In line with these changes in diet and the food environment, the prevalence of undernutrition has been reduced, but, in common with world trends, evidence exists in the region of a worsening double burden of malnutrition at every level: household, community, and nation. Undernutrition remains pervasive, and obesity rates are increasing in all countries. Obesity has risen across the region in all income groups but especially lower income (Helble and Sato 2018). Higher obesity rates translate into higher risk of developing diabetes and a number of cancers, imposing substantial costs to human well-being, family budgets, and health care systems. Further, high prevalence childhood obesity predicts further increases in obesity rates. Finally, all forms of malnutrition hamper educational attainment and productivity.

Policies that favor the supply of healthy food and encourage demand for it, such as taxes on sugary drinks and public education on nutrition, can guide consumers toward better diets and minimize the burden on the public health care system. Efforts to improve policy should integrate nutrition interventions to prevent undernutrition and obesity and diet-related lifestyle diseases, promote nutrition-sensitive social welfare, and strengthen agriculture and supply chains to promote healthy foods, sound food environment policies, and innovation.

2.4 Leveraging Asian traditions for mental wellness

Being physically fit is only half of the well-being and happiness equation. The other is mental wellness. A state of holistic health requires sound mind as well as sound body. While the boundary between physical and mental health is sometimes blurred—as exhaustion from overwork, for instance, harms both body and mind—it is nevertheless conceptually useful to distinguish the two. This section explores the activities, choices, and lifestyles that Asians may pursue to achieve mental well-being. Both individual and community approaches exist to reduce the burden of mental illness and promote mental well-being throughout the wellness lifespan. Prioritizing the mental health of Asians has become urgent in view of the region's rapidly aging population. Fortunately, Asia can draw on an abundance of wellness traditions. The region also has a growing wellness tourism industry, which can greatly benefit the mental health of Asians.

2.4.1 The road to mental wellbeing

COVID-19 is a physical health crisis but it can also sow the seeds of a mental health crisis. Further, the pandemic is not only an alarming public health crisis but also a severe economic crisis. Large segments of the population are in psychological distress around the world (Figure 2.4.1).[7] Surveys conducted by Ipsos in 27 countries showed COVID-19 dominating the concerns of people worldwide, with the COVID-19 score in April the highest recorded since the survey started 10 years ago and still groundbreakingly high in June (Gebrekal 2020). In opinion polls conducted in several individual countries, including Canada, the United Kingdom, and the US, respondents report their mental health harmed by worries and stress over COVID-19 (Angus Reid 2020, Office for National Statistics of the United Kingdom 2020, National Public Radio 2020, and Morning Consult 2020). With the pandemic fueling people's anxiety worldwide, health concerns are the immediate cause of the distress. Many people are afraid of being infected, losing their lives, or losing loved ones to the pandemic. Lockdowns, community quarantines, and stay-at-home restrictions have cut individuals off from friends, colleagues, and relatives. Confinement in the small space of one's home and a sense of isolation from society weigh on mental health.

Figure 2.4.1 Prevalence of mental distress in the population during COVID-19

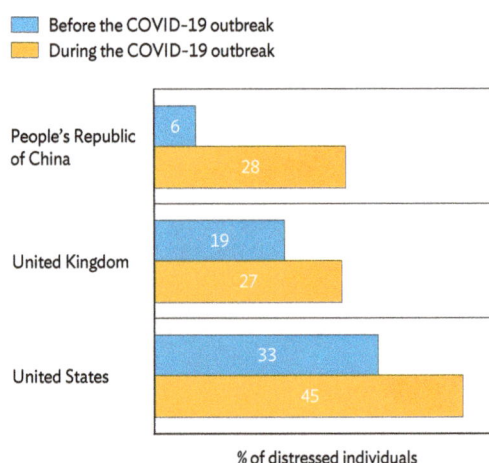

- Before the COVID-19 outbreak
- During the COVID-19 outbreak

People's Republic of China: 6 (before), 28 (during)
United Kingdom: 19 (before), 27 (during)
United States: 33 (before), 45 (during)

% of distressed individuals

Sources: Panchal et al. 2020; Pierce et al. 2020; Shi et al. 2020; United Nations 2020.

Stress, anxiety and fears about personal health, and social separation and loneliness are compounded by economic hardship. The mental health of all population groups, including children who cannot go to school or socialize with their friends during lockdowns, has been adversely affected by COVID-19 (Figure 2.4.2).

Defining mental wellness

The process of maintaining mental wellness is viewed as lifelong and entails developing the skills and knowledge to make conscious and intentional choices toward living a healthy, purposeful, and fulfilling life. This lifelong process enables individuals to realize their potential, cope with daily stresses, work productively and contribute meaningfully to their family, community, and society (Bodeker et al. 2018).

The following are the various constructs underlying mental health and well-being that societies must begin to consider:

Emotional well-being. This refers to the experience of positive feelings, such as happiness, and the perception that one's life overall provides satisfaction (Diener et al. 1999, Magyar and Keyes 2019).

Psychological well-being. This relates to the different modalities of positive functioning wherein individuals realize their potential in terms of autonomy and personal growth. Those with high emotional well-being feel good about life, while those with high psychological well-being or social well-being are resilient and function well in their daily routine (Patel et al. 2018, Magyar and Keyes 2019).

Resilience and balance. Good mental health includes resilience, which is the capability to adapt extraordinarily well in the face of significant adversity or risk, rather than simply cope with the normal stresses of life (Christmas and Khanlou 2019, Tusaie et al. 2007, WHO 2016). A more recent definition of well-being calls it "the balance point between an individual's resource pool and the challenges faced" (Hanc, McAndrew, and Ucci 2018).

Optimal functioning, or flourishing. This is now also a common approach in well-being research, as pioneered by positive psychology founder Marten E. Seligman. The optimal perspective aligns the definition of wellness to endeavors that strive to capture the complex nature of human flourishing—that is, through positive emotion, engagement, relationships, meaning, and accomplishment rather than just preventing or ameliorating mental illness (Seligman, Parks, and Steen 2004; Hanc, McAndrew, and Ucci 2018).

Figure 2.4.2 Parents' reports of children's difficulties during COVID-19 confinement

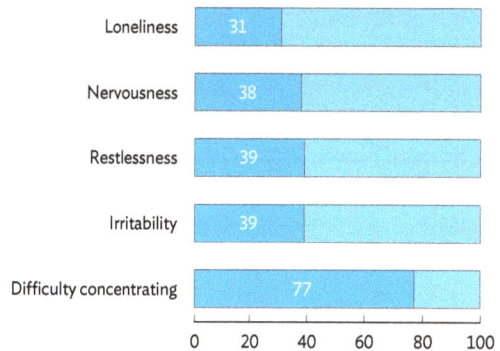

Source: United Nations 2020.

The Lancet Commission defines mental wellness as "an asset or resource that enables positive states of wellbeing and provides the capability for people to achieve their full potential" (Patel et al. 2018). The challenge of demarcating the differences between mental wellness and disorder is such that an individual may struggle with symptoms of mental disorder but still be able to maintain a degree of mental health in terms of their expectations of life satisfaction, flourishing, and achieving their potential. The association between mental health and disorder is not linear, though they may seem to exist on a continuum.

The United Nations' *World Happiness Report 2017* identifies four social foundations of well-being: social support, the freedom to make life choices, generosity, and the absence of corruption in government and business. Among the many findings cited, two key social variables—social support and volunteering or generosity—are consistently associated with better self-reported health status.

Rising concern about mental unwellness in Asia

Poor mental health is the third-largest contributor to years lost to disability, after lower-back pain and headache. Across Asia and the Pacific, a growing percentage of the adult population experiences a diagnosable mental illness in any given year: from 4% reported in Singapore to 20% in Australia, New Zealand, Thailand, and Viet Nam. Prevalence rates have also increased in India, Japan, Malaysia, the PRC, and the ROK (Yates 2018).

Data from the World Health Organization and the Organisation for Economic Co-operation and Development identify the five leading mental health problems in Asia and the Pacific to be depression, anxiety, post-traumatic stress disorder, suicidal behavior, and substance abuse (Bodeker 2020b). Few of these conditions are adequately addressed in the region.

The past few years have seen efforts in Asia and the Pacific to raise the profile of mental health, establish legal and policy frameworks for more comprehensive and coordinated disease management, expand investment in infrastructure and human resources, and reduce the stigma attached to poor mental health. This is partly in response to the heavy economic toll exacted by mental illness. Without factoring in suicide, mental health issues are projected to reduce output in India and the PRC by more than $9 trillion each from 2016 to 2030 (Gietel-Basten 2018).

Lower-middle-income countries such as India, Indonesia, Pakistan, the Philippines, and Viet Nam face many challenges, including insufficient medical treatment, meager health-care budgets typically at less than 1% of GDP, lack of capacity to spend funds effectively, dilapidated facilities, and critically low numbers of mental health professionals. India and Indonesia, for example, have only about 0.3 psychiatrists per 100,000 population (WHO 2020b).

The PRC has about 2.2 psychiatrists per 100,000 people.
Li (2017) estimates that 92% of an estimated 173 million people in
the PRC who suffer mental disorders go without appropriate care.

Common goals across the region include deinstitutionalization
and changing the focus of mental health management from
secondary care to integrated community-based care with
multidisciplinary inputs. Yet, while global models of mental
health prioritize the individual, more family-oriented cultures
prevail in Asia and the Pacific. This family orientation to mental
health may, on the one hand, complicate moves to expand
community-based services and access to professional care,
especially if a lack of funding obliges families to accommodate
patients. On the other hand, it opens new opportunities for
preventive and supportive care that align better with a shift
toward patient-centered and integrated mental health care.
This holds strong potential for strengthening mental wellness
pathways and alleviating anxiety and depression, which are
the leading causes of mental health problems in Asia and their
economic burden in the region.

Overview of mental wellness modalities

Wellness modalities are a range of activities and programs that
have positive effects on mental well-being. This section provides
a general introduction to a few mental wellness modalities,
including both healthy everyday routines such as eating well
and exercising regularly, and more specialized activities such as
dance and meditation.

Good nutrition is vital to mental wellness. The International
Society for Nutritional Psychiatry underscores the importance
of a traditional whole-food diet with lots of vegetables, fruits,
seafood, whole grains, lean meat, nuts, and legumes, while
avoiding processed foods. Such a diet is more likely to provide
the nutrients that afford resistance to mental disorders.

The gut–brain axis has emerged in recent studies—reported
most notably in a collection of articles published by *Nature*
in 2017—as a key pathway for modulating behavior. Bidirectional
signaling reportedly exists between the gastrointestinal tract
and the brain, often involving gut microbiota, that are vital
to regulating satiety and hunger, as well as inflammation.
Disruption of the gut–brain axis has been found in a diverse
range of diseases, including Parkinson's disease and irritable
bowel syndrome. Research has additionally associated gut
disorders, known as functional gastrointestinal disorders,
with both depression and anxiety (Pinto-Sanchez et al. 2017).
A substantial body of research is now examining the benefit
of nutrient supplementation in people with mental disorders
(Firth et al. 2019).

Exercise is another important component of mental wellness. In addition to the well-documented effects of exercise on longevity and the quality of life, the scientific literature shows an emerging body of evidence that exercise benefits mental well-being (Lear et al. 2017). One such study demonstrated how exercise can serve as a secondary treatment for patients with major depressive disorder (Trivedi et al. 2011). Exercise in general brought significant improvement to patients in the study, though a higher-dose exercise program was found more effective. A succeeding study found the response of a patient to an initial exercise session, particularly a high-intensity one, to be a reliable predictor of treatment outcome for depression (Suterwala et al. 2016). Such knowledge can help clinicians predict the treatment response to exercise in depression and thus enable them to match patients with the right exercise treatment (Suterwala et al. 2016).

Some studies document a positive effect on mental health of two well-known Asian exercise modalities, yoga and tai chi. A survey of yoga research concludes that yoga has a positive effect on health in the workplace, particularly in reducing stress (Valencia et al. 2019). Many studies have found significant beneficial effects from yoga on stress, anxiety, fatigue, and depression, with improved well-being and vigor. Several studies also found less depression after extended yoga practice over a couple of months. In all studies, yoga was found to have improved sleep efficiency and quality, with more sleep time and fewer awakenings.

Military veterans with post-traumatic stress symptoms took part in a four-session introduction to tai chi in Boston. In addition to reporting high satisfaction with the program, participants reported feeling very engaged during the sessions and found that tai chi helped them manage such distressing symptoms as intrusive thoughts, difficulty in concentration, and physiological arousal (Niles et al. 2016). A map of 107 systematic reviews of tai chi published in 2016 identified a number of areas with evidence of potentially effective treatment. In addition to positive effects on physical health, tai chi improved cognitive performance and mitigated depression (Koch et al. 2014).

Apart from eating well and exercising regularly, other specialized activities such as dance and meditation can also help build a sound mind (Box 2.4.1).

2.4.2 Asia's wealth of wellness traditions

Asians have a plethora of richly developed wellness traditions to draw upon in their quest for mental and physical well-being. For quite some time, in their rush toward economic growth and modernization, Asians neglected and overlooked these valuable assets to some extent. In recent years, though, in line with rising affluence and demand for well-being, Asians have begun to rediscover their wellness roots.

Box 2.4.1 Dance and meditation as specialized mental wellness activities

Two specialized activities that contribute to better mental health are dance and meditation.

Dance. The diverse cultures of Asia boast many traditional dances influenced by the region's various religions, rituals, and mythical stories, and dancing remains popular in modern-day Asia. In the People's Republic of China (PRC), an estimated 100 million people or more, primarily older women, pour into public squares and parks daily to engage in a variety of dances, from tangos and waltzes to traditional Chinese dance (NDTV 2018). The country's 2016 national fitness plan identified square dancing as a team sport to be vigorously developed. Square dancing eventually became an official event in the PRC National Games in 2017, along with traditional sports such as athletics and swimming.

A quarter of a century of research has underscored the benefits of dance and dance movement therapy on generalized mental well-being (Koch et al. 2014) and brain development in adults and children (Brown and Parsons 2008, Karpati et al. 2015); on mood stabilization in adolescents (Anderson et al. 2014); and in reducing depression and anxiety across different ages (Bräuninger 2012). In short, dance has been shown to combine many different factors that help improve the competence needed in everyday life (Ritter and Lowe 1996).

A *New England Journal of Medicine* study examined physical and cognitive activities associated with reduced risk of developing Alzheimer's disease. It associated cognitive activities such as reading, playing board games, and playing musical instruments with lower risk of dementia. Of 11 physical activities, dancing was the only physical one associated with a lower risk of dementia (Verghese et al. 2003). Further, such mental health conditions as anxiety and depression have been reduced through participation in dance and dance movement therapy.

Meditation. Meditation is exercise for the brain and has been shown to help maintain mental health and improve memory and empathy, among other benefits. A meta-analysis in the *Journal of the American Medical Association* identified almost 19,000 studies on different forms of meditation. Four decades of studies highlight how meditation enhances immunity, reduces depression and anxiety, improves academic performance, slows age-related cognitive decline, boosts happiness and the quality of life, and helps manage and reduce trauma.

Brain changes associated with the practice of meditation include enhanced neural plasticity and increased grey and white matter development. Recent studies of transcendental meditation found reduced anxiety (Tomljenović, Begić, and Maštrović 2016) and post-traumatic stress (Rees et al. 2014) and improved mental health in caregivers (Nidich et al. 2015).

A study of survivors of the devastating earthquake and tsunami in Japan in 2011 found improvements in both mental and physical symptoms in patients who had been instructed in transcendental meditation (Yoshimura et al. 2015).

With benefits ranging from enhanced mental well-being to a reduction of deeply traumatic stress, and from changes in brain structure and functioning to changes in gene expression and reduced age-related decline, meditation stands as a primary pathway for lifelong enhancement of physical and mental wellness.

References:
Anderson, A. N., H. Kennedy, P. DeWitt, E. Anderson, and M. Z. Wamboldt. 2014. Dance movement therapy impacts mood states of adolescents in a psychiatric hospital. *Arts in Psychotherapy* 41(3).

Bräuninger, I. 2012. The Efficacy of Dance Movement Therapy Group on Improvement of Quality of Life: A Randomized Controlled Trial. *The Arts in Psychotherapy* 39(4).

Brown, S. and L. M. Parsons. 2008. The neuroscience of dance. *Scientific American* 299(1).

Karpati, F. J., C. Giacosa, N. E. Foster, V. B. Penhune, and K. L. Hyde. 2015. Dance and the brain: A review. *Annals of the New York Academy of Sciences* 1337(1).

Koch, S., T. Kunz, S. Lykou, and R. Cruz. 2014. Effects of dance movement therapy and dance on health-related psychological outcomes: A metaanalysis. *The Arts in Psychotherapy* 41(1).

NDTV. 2018. China's 'Dancing Aunties' Take Over Public Places in Jitterbug Craze. https://www.ndtv.com/offbeat/chinas-dancing-aunties-take-over-public-places-in-jitterbug-craze-1927165.

Nidich, S., R. J. Nidich, J. Salerno, B. Hadfield, and C. Elder. 2015. Stress Reduction with the Transcendental Meditation Program in Caregivers: A Pilot Study. *International Archives of Nursing and Health Care* 1(2).

Rees, B., F. Travis, D. Shapiro, and R. Chant. 2014. Significant Reductions in Posttraumatic Stress Symptoms in Congolese Refugees Within 10 days of Transcendental Meditation Practice. *Journal of Traumatic Stress* 27.

Ritter, M. and K. G. Lowe. 1996. The effectiveness of dance/movement therapy. *The Arts in Psychotherapy* 23(3).

Tomljenović, H., D. Begić, and Z. Maštrović. 2016. Changes in trait brainwave power and coherence, state and trait anxiety after three-month transcendental meditation (TM) practice. *Psychiatria Danubina* 28(1).

Verghese, J., R. B. Lipton, M. J. Katz, et al. Leisure activities and the risk of dementia in the elderly. *The New England Journal of Medicine* 348(25). doi:10.1056/NEJMoa022252.

Yoshimura, M., E. Kurokawa, T. Noda, Y. Tanaka, K. Hineno, Y. Kawai, and M. Dillbeck. 2015. Disaster Relief for the Japanese Earthquake–Tsunami of 2011: Stress Reduction through the Transcendental Meditation Technique. *Psychological Reports* 117(1). doi:10.2466/02.13.PR0.117c11z6.

Source: Bodeker, G. 2020b. *Mental Wellness in Asia.* ADB.

Asian governments are similarly placing higher priority on wellness traditions. In 2014, for example, the Government of India set up a new ministry of ayush—combining ayurveda, yoga and naturopathy, unani, siddha, and homeopathy— to promote the development of traditional medicine. Yet, the region needs to do much more to capitalize on its traditions that enhance well-being and thereby reduce the burden of poor health on governments, national economies, and society. Ideally, this can be done in a manner that is evidence-based but still culturally relevant, providing to people economical ways to independently manage their health.

Asia is home to two major systems of traditional health knowledge: traditional Chinese medicine and Indian ayurveda. Both systems are grounded on principles of living healthily and well throughout the human lifespan. Lifestyle is given primary emphasis over medicine in the classical texts. East Asia and Viet Nam are strongly influenced by traditional Chinese health knowledge, especially the knowledge in the classic texts *Sun Simiao's Encyclopaedia of Medicine* and *Huangdi Neijing*. The health traditions of South Asia and most of Southeast Asia are grounded in ayurvedic theory and practice, which have as their core text *Charaka Samhita of Ayurveda*.

The guiding principle underlying these Asian traditions of wellness is that understanding people's different metabolic styles should be the basis for developing personalized preventive health and wellness routines. Also of primary importance in Asian wellness theory and practice is an individualized and balanced approach to nutrition based on body type and traditional food culture. Integrative exercise is also prioritized along with stress reducing and integrative breathing and meditative practice. A regular connection with nature is seen as a balancing influence on overall well-being.

Many practices from Asian wellness traditions have become widely popular in the West, generating a sizeable global economy around yoga, tai chi, Asian massage, and Asian herbal supplements, among other traditions. This has spurred a surge in research into the health benefits of Asian health and wellness practices. Scientific journals now exist for studies on Chinese medicine, Japanese medicine (*kampo*), Korean medicine, ayurvedic medicine, and so on. This has generated a large body of evidence not only on the medicines from Asian health traditions but also on their lifestyle practices and preventive strategies, such as integrative exercise programs like yoga and tai chi and the untapped potential of Asia's vast diversity of martial arts practices (Table 2.4.1). By and large, the evidence indicates that Asia's wellness traditions can significantly contribute to physical and mental well-being (Bodeker 2020a).

Table 2.4.1 Selective list of Asian martial arts

Taekwondo	Republic of Korea
Iaido and judo	Japan
Sinmoo hapkido	Japan
Clinch fighting, Chinese style	PRC
Wing chun	PRC
Kuntao-silat	Indonesia, Malaysia, the Philippines, and Singapore
Chen taijiquan	PRC
Ryukyu kenpo	Japan
Baguazhang	PRC
Kodokan judo	Japan
Muso shinden-ryu iaido	Japan
Goju-ryu karate	Japan
Zheng-style taijiquan	PRC
Ryukyu kobudo shinkokai	Japan
Mantis boxing	PRC
Arnis, also called kali, eskrima, or escrima	Philippines
Jujutsu and judo	Japan, Brazil
Niten ichi-ryu and shinto-ryu	Japan
Ving tsun double knives	Hong Kong, China
Bajiquan	PRC
Goshin jutsu and washin-ryu	Japan
Taiji spear	PRC
Kalarippayattu	South India
Thang-ta	Northeast India

PRC = People's Republic of China.
Source: Bodeker 2020a.

The World Health Organization and national health administrations now recognize that lifestyle changes are the only effective way to reverse the rise of chronic lifestyle diseases. With the evidence base that has been built in support of Asian wellness traditions—that is, their efficacy in lowering noncommunicable disease risk, reducing stress and mental health issues, and enhancing longevity and the quality of life—Asia now has an opportunity to integrate its own cultural traditions into national and regional health guidelines. Apart from fostering Asia's own cultural heritage, this development can reduce costs in national health systems and open up economic opportunities for wellness tourism and create new possibilities for entrepreneurship. However, fostering Asia's rich wellness traditions must not come at the expense of environmental degradation, for instance encroachment on wildlife.

Asia's dietary traditions

Asian diets feature a diversity of vegetables and fruit, including many plant foods that are beneficial to health. Many food preparation methods use microorganisms, now understood as critical to healthy digestion and physical function.

A growing body of evidence indicates that chronic disease increases when people start to lose touch with ancestral food traditions. This has awakened interest in traditional and indigenous food cultures in Asia, which are important not only for their own sake, but for the legacy of food knowledge they can confer on future generations. A concern is a lack of documentation of many of these traditions.

Asian diets are known for incorporating medicinal ingredients. One can find *reishi* mushrooms in Japanese cuisine, *goji* berries in Chinese menus, and turmeric and other potent medicinal species in Indian recipes. Malaysia has its *ulam*, a unique and pharmacologically potent medicinal herbal salad (Table 2.4.2). Indonesia meanwhile has its *jamu* herbal beverages, which are based on nature's most powerful anti-inflammatory agent, turmeric, and a powerful digestive agent, ginger.

Research has shown that lower calorie intake and higher amounts of plant-based nutrients and antioxidants—common features of traditional diets—help prevent the development of such chronic conditions as obesity, diabetes, heart disease, cancer, and rheumatism.

Table 2.4.2 Some components of Malaysia's ulam salad and their health properties

Jantung pisang (banana blossom)	An edible flower from the banana plant, its common name literally translates as "banana heart." The tender inner core is usually served lightly blanched or in kerabu, a fragrant, tangy, and spicy local salad. The flower has antimicrobial properties.
Temulawak (Java ginger, *Curcuma zanthorrhiza*)	Traditionally consumed as an herbal remedy, it can be eaten fresh for a sourish, bitter taste. *Curcuma zanthorrhiza* is used as a medicinal plant. The rhizome contains 5 milliliters of an ethereal oil per kilogram that primarily consists of sesquiterpenes, as well as curcumin and starch. *Curcuma zanthorrhiza* is used for dyspepsia and as a spice. Some hold it to be an effective deterrent and pesticide for mushroom mites.
Selom (Java waterdropwort, *Oenanthe javanica*)	Selom is prized by ulam lovers for its delicate lemony taste. Its tender stems and leaf stalks are used fresh as salad, to garnish steamed rice and other dishes, or boiled and chopped as greens. It is high in beta-carotene, ascorbic acid, iron, and protein and extremely high in vitamin E, with medium levels of riboflavin and calcium. Chlorophyll-rich leaves have antigenotoxic and antioxidative properties.
Kerdas (*Pithecellobium bubalinum*)	A thin layer of skin covers the light green seed inside. The fruit emanates a strong smell and is eaten as an appetizer. It is described as having cooling properties and is used to manage fever in Indonesia.
Ulam raja (*Cosmos caudatus*)	Called "king of ulam," it has a grassy taste accentuated by a subtle peppery tinge. It is consumed to enhance blood circulation, and studies have shown it to protect bones and counter diabetes.

Source: Bodeker 2020a.

Traditional medicine in Asia: a need for greater integration

More than half of the Asian population reportedly uses traditional medicine on a regular basis. Usage is higher in rural areas than urban. By income and educational attainment, usage shows a bimodal curve, high at both extremities but lower in the middle. The richer and more educated set typically takes traditional medicine to promote health and prevent disease—that is, for wellness.

Asia has always shown widespread acceptance of traditional medicine at the community level. Such practices have also gained formal recognition over the decades. In 1956, Viet Nam became the first country in Asia to formally incorporate traditional medicine into its national health-care system. The PRC did the same in 1958 and India in 1970. However, instead of offering an integrated model of care, the systems ran on two parallel tracks—modern and traditional—and choosing between them was left largely to the consumer. To fully leverage Asia's rich tradition of traditional medicine, Asian countries must strive to integrate modern and traditional medicine and maximize synergies between the two.

Some developments have already occurred in this direction. In the PRC, for instance, early collaborative research on traditional medicines for fever, or febrifuges, identified the plant *Artemisia annua*, which can be used to manage hot–cold fevers such as those caused by malaria, and thus facilitated the identification of the sesquiterpene lactone artemisinin. This paved the way for the development of an entire new class of antimalarial drugs and the awarding of the 2015 Nobel Prize for Medicine to Tu Youyou, a professor in the Yunan Institute of Pharmacy and the Shangdong Institute of Parasitology.

2.4.3 Population aging and wellness in Asia

As people grow older, their cognitive and other mental faculties tend to deteriorate, albeit with wide variation among individuals. The worst conditions, such as Alzheimer's disease, severely impair mental faculties. At the same time, physical capability also tends to deteriorate. Asia's aging population therefore makes the need for healthy aging all the more urgent.

The share of developing Asia's population aged 65 or older is projected to rise from 6% in 2010 to 9% in 2020 and 18% in 2050. Figure 2.4.3 shows the distribution of various age groups by gender from 1990 to 2020 and United Nations projections to 2050. The figure illustrates a striking demographic shift from a typical pyramid shape to a structure that is more top heavy as the population ages. In 2010, only 1 person in 16 living in developing Asia was over 65 years old. In 2050, it could be 1 in 6.

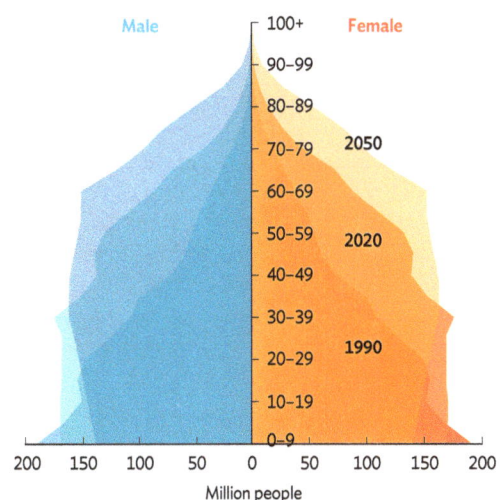

Figure 2.4.3 Population distribution, developing Asia

Source: UN World Population Prospects 2019. https://population.un.org/wpp/ (accessed 15 January 2020).

Population aging and demand for wellness: empirical evidence

Both mental and physical health deteriorate with age, but people are not powerless to mitigate the negative effects of aging on their mental and physical health. Indeed, by choosing activities and lifestyles that are conducive to well-being, people can age in a healthier way. Some individuals age better than others by taking care of their mind and body. As more and more Asians join the ranks of the elderly, demand for wellness products and services can be expected to grow. Recent Asian Development Bank research provides empirical evidence for a positive relationship between population aging and demand for wellness (Box 2.4.2).

Box 2.4.2 Empirical analysis of the link between aging and wellness: data and methodology

Cross-country regression analysis described below empirically tested whether two population variables with regard to aging—share of the population 65 and older and life expectancy—significantly affected three wellness industries: hot springs, spas, and wellness tourism. To evaluate the factors that drive the development of the wellness industry across countries, we used cross-sectional regression with the following specification:

$$Y_i = \beta_0 + \sum_{j=1}^{k} \beta_i X_{ij} + \epsilon_i,$$

where k is a set of explanatory variables X_j that includes GDP growth rate, log GDP per capita, log financial consumption expenditure per capita, life expectancy at birth, urbanization ratio as a percentage of the total population, the ratio of people 65 and older to the total population, and socioeconomic conditions in each country i. In the analysis, 1-year lags of the explanatory variables were used to explain the development of wellness industry in the sample countries. All dependent variables were log transformed in the analysis.

The Global Wellness Institute served as the primary data source for the dependent variables in this study. It has conducted country-level research to define and quantify five segments of the wellness economy: wellness real estate, workplace wellness, wellness tourism, spas, and thermal and mineral springs. For the other five sectors, it drew upon secondary sources to produce a global aggregate figure.

In our analysis, the number and revenue of hot springs, spas, and wellness tourist arrivals were selected as proxies for the wellness industry. The sample included 124 global economies in 2017.

Data on the GDP growth rate, GDP per capita, financial consumption expenditure per capita, urban population as a percentage of the total population, and life expectancy at birth were collected from the World Bank's World Development Indicators. The ratio of people 65 and older to the total population was from the United Nations Population Division. Political risk rating on socioeconomic conditions was collected from the PRS Group's International Country Risk Guide. The socioeconomic variable was an assessment of the socioeconomic pressures at work in society that could constrain government action or fuel social dissatisfaction. The risk rating score had three subcomponents: unemployment, consumer confidence, and poverty.

The study found that a 1% increase in population aged 65 and older increased the number of hot spring establishments by 20% and raised their revenue by 29%. The evidence also supported a significant positive link between life expectancy on the one hand and spas and wellness tourism on the other. While more research needs to be done on the aging–wellness nexus, the research suggests that, as populations grow older, they demand more wellness to safeguard mental and physical health.

Source: Bodeker, G., M. Pundit, S. Tian, and P. Quising. 2020. *Aging and Wellness in Asia.* ADB.

Pathways to living a long and healthy life

Longevity is a blessing that is multiplied many times over if it comes with sound body and mind. Many of the diseases suffered by older people result from dietary factors, some of which start operating in infancy. Traditional Asian diets have much to offer toward reducing the risk of lifestyle diseases and are culturally more acceptable than the widely recommended Mediterranean diet. Policies on food, agriculture, and trade—originally devised to ensure food quantity rather than quality—must remove incentives to produce less healthy foods. They must instead create incentives to produce diverse and nutritious foods using sustainable practices, generating healthy food environments supported by nutrition education, especially in schools.

Exercise is one health-promoting approach that has excellent potential to support aging populations. The health benefits of exercise for older people include reduced risk of coronary and cardiac disease, diabetes, obesity, and some cancers such as colorectal cancer, as well as reduced risk of falls (Sims et al. 2006). In addition to reducing the risk of many health conditions and chronic diseases, exercise can improve the quality of life through improved mental heath, with reduced depression and better moods, and improved physical performance in terms of balance, strength, mobility, and function.

Tai chi is an excellent form of exercise for older people and has been shown to improve strength, balance, and cardiovascular performance. Dance is another especially beneficial form of exercise for older people. Dance promotes social exchange and is a form of movement that communicates, thus activating communication areas of the brain. It has shown benefits by reducing the symptoms of both Parkinson's and Alzheimer's disease. Social support, especially friendship and meaningful social interaction, are vital to ensuring mental well-being later in life. The Japanese philosophy of *ikigai* highlights the essence of a purposeful life with good nutrition, regular movement, solid social networks, and a positive outlook anchored on a smile—all contributing to optimal aging into later years.

Aging at home is desirable only if the home meets the special needs of the elderly. Desirable goals with respect to aging in place include optimizing function through improved home design, caregiving, and reducing isolation with social network and support and the help of technology. Enabling elders to live at home rather than enter a care institution or be hospitalized reduces the economic burden of a growing population of frail elderly and provides humane options for those who are vulnerable.

Age-friendly environments outside of the home include immediate surroundings and urban characteristics further from home, such as walkability, supportive neighborhoods that build a sense of community, green spaces, and designs for healing environments such as hospitals.

Through its Global Age-Friendly Cities Project, the World Health Organization offers direction and guidelines for planning toward keeping the elderly active in their home environments.

The impact of retirement on wellness is ambiguous. On the negative side, people often suffer psychologically if they can no longer view themselves as productive contributors to society. On the positive side, retirement can be an opportunity to restart life with more freedom and time to build relationships and engage in health-improving activities. In the end, what matters for old-age wellness is to stay mentally and physically active and fit during retirement by eating well and exercising regularly, and by engaging in intellectually stimulating activities. Social engagement and participation in leisure activities positively affect life satisfaction in retirement, especially by alleviating depression in the oldest members of society, 75 and older (Hajek et al. 2017).

2.4.4 Global rise of wellness tourism

People typically vacation to take a break from exhausting work routines and recharge mind and body. Almost all tourism is rest and relaxation and thus benefits mental wellness. Prior to COVID-19, tourism was one of the largest and fastest-growing industries worldwide. According to the World Travel and Tourism Council, the direct, indirect, and induced impact of travel and tourism provided 10.3% of global GDP in 2019 and 330 million jobs, or 1 job in 10 around the world. The industry grew by 3.5% in 2019, outpacing global economic growth of 2.5%. Indeed, it outpaced global growth for 9 consecutive years.

The tourism industry has been hit hard by COVID-19 with suspended flights, closed hotels, and travel restrictions almost everywhere. Indeed, tourism is one of the industries that has been most severely affected by the pandemic. According to the United Nations World Tourism Organization, arrivals fell by 98% in May 2020 and by 56% in the first 5 months of 2020 (UNWTO 2020). Depending on when travel restrictions are relaxed, international tourism may drop by 58%–78% in the whole year.

The wellness tourism industry around the world

Wellness tourism is travel associated with the pursuit of maintaining or enhancing one's personal well-being. The Global Wellness Institute estimates that wellness tourism was a $639 billion global market in 2017, growing more than twice as quickly as tourism overall. In 2013, the institute unveiled the inaugural edition of the *Global Wellness Tourism Economy* report—a landmark study on the emerging wellness tourism industry, which has since accelerated around the world.

Wellness tourism is a fast-growing tourism segment that expanded annually from 2015 to 2017 by 6.5%, or more than twice the growth rate of tourism overall. Travelers made 830 million wellness trips in 2017, which is 139 million more than in 2015. Growth has been driven by an expanding global middle class, growing consumer desire to adopt a wellness lifestyle, rising interest in experiential travel, and more affordable flights and other travel arrangements. Across regions, Europe remains the destination for the largest number of wellness trips, with North America leading in wellness tourism expenditure (Figure 2.4.4). Asia has made the most gains in the number of wellness trips and expenditure as strong economies and an expanding middle class stimulated demand. For developing Asia, covering 42 member economies of the ADB, wellness trips in 2017 totaled 209 million amounting to $100 billion.

The wellness tourism market has two broad types of travelers: primary wellness travelers, who are motivated by wellness to take a trip or choose their destination based on its wellness offerings, such as someone visiting a wellness resort or participating in a yoga retreat, and secondary wellness travelers, who seek to maintain wellness or engage in wellness activities during any kind of travel, by visiting a gym, getting a massage, or prioritizing healthy food while traveling.

Figure 2.4.4 Wellness tourism by region, 2017

Europe
$210.8 billion expenditure
292 million trips

North America
$241.7 billion expenditure
204 million trips

Middle East and North Africa
$10.7 billion expenditure
11 million trips

Asia and the Pacific
$136.7 billion expenditure
258 million trips

Sub-Saharan Africa
$4.8 billion expenditure
7 million trips

Latin America and the Caribbean
$34.8 billion expenditure
59 million trips

Notes: Number of wellness tourism trips and expenditure, inbound and domestic. Regional groupings follow those of the Global Wellness Institute.
Source: Global Wellness Institute 2018a.

The bulk of wellness tourism is attributed to secondary wellness travelers, who in 2017 accounted for 89% of trips and 86% of spending. In 2015–2017, secondary wellness tourism grew by 10% annually, more quickly than primary wellness tourism, at 8%.

Domestic wellness travel dwarfs international wellness travel, but international wellness trips have been growing more quickly. Globally, domestic travel accounts for 82% of total wellness tourism trips and 65% of expenditure. International wellness trips are proportionally a larger share of expenditure because average spending is much higher on international trips. International wellness tourism trips expanded at a faster pace in 2015–2017, by 12% annually, as domestic wellness tourism trips expanded by 9%.

The wellness tourism industry in Asia

The market for wellness tourism in the Asia and the Pacific was estimated at $137 billion in 2017, comprising 257.6 million inbound and domestic wellness tourism trips. Expenditures by wellness tourists include lodging, food and beverages, activities and excursions, shopping, in-country transportation, and other services. Some of the spending items were wellness-related, such as getting a massage, attending a meditation retreat, or staying at a wellness hotel, while others were generic, such as hiring a local car.

Altogether, Asia and the Pacific accounted for 21.4% of global wellness tourism expenditure and 31.0% of all wellness tourism trips in 2017. Asia's largest wellness tourism markets are, in descending order, the PRC, Japan, India, Thailand, the ROK, Indonesia, Malaysia, Viet Nam, and the Philippines (Table 2.4.3). The Asian Development Bank estimates that the rising wellness tourism industry directly employs 10.1 million workers in the region.

Not only is wellness tourism a sizable and high-growth market, it is higher-yield than tourism in general. Wellness tourists—whether international or domestic—spend more than the average tourist. In 2017, inbound international wellness tourists in Asia and the Pacific spent on average $1,741 per trip, 33% more than the typical international tourist. The premium for domestic wellness tourists was even higher, with average spending of $268 per trip, or 120% more than the typical domestic tourist. This is because wellness travelers are typically affluent, educated, well-traveled, and willing to seek out new and novel experiences.

In recent years, wellness tourism has experienced rapid growth in Asia and the Pacific as more stressed-out people look to travel for respite and rejuvenation. To meet the growing sophistication of Asian travelers, wellness travel offerings have expanded tremendously in breadth and depth, moving far beyond typical offerings such as detox, weight loss, spa treatments in a gazebo, and yoga on the beach.

Table 2.4.3 Top 20 wellness tourism markets in Asia and the Pacific, 2017

	Number of Trips (thousands)			Expenditure ($ million)
	Inbound	**Domestic**	**Total**	
People's Republic of China	7,724.3	62,442.2	70,166.5	31,705.9
Japan	1,585.5	38,900.0	40,485.5	22,466.1
India	4,542.4	51,426.3	55,968.6	16,299.7
Thailand	5,691.9	6,764.1	12,456.0	12,018.4
Australia	876.2	9,122.1	9,998.3	10,520.9
Republic of Korea	1,709.8	17,908.6	19,618.3	7,186.6
Indonesia	5,183.5	3,151.7	8,335.2	6,928.5
Malaysia	3,331.7	4,956.1	8,287.8	5,019.2
Viet Nam	3,149.5	6,465.8	9,615.3	4,001.1
New Zealand	341.0	2,736.5	3,077.5	3,036.0
Philippines	1,552.2	1,169.0	2,721.2	2,592.5
Taipei,China	675.4	3,235.7	3,911.1	2,477.5
Hong Kong, China	1,723.9	360.5	2,084.5	2,439.5
Cambodia	1,741.5	656.1	2,397.6	1,853.7
Singapore	777.7	125.8	903.5	1,159.7
Maldives	483.2	103.8	587.0	938.4
Macau, China	174.9	36.7	211.6	770.9
Sri Lanka	416.8	220.5	637.3	720.2
Fiji	583.5	125.6	709.1	708.5
Nepal	759.2	433.3	1,192.5	611.0

Notes: Including both primary and secondary wellness trips. Expenditure data combine both international inbound and domestic wellness tourism spending.
Source: Yeung and Johnston 2020a.

Across Asian destinations, there has been a tremendous increase in demand for all types of wellness modalities and experiences, from hot springs bathing to sound therapy, from tai chi to reiki, and from meditation to spiritual guidance. With the worsening of air pollution across major cities in India, the PRC, and other Asian countries, some travelers are even traveling in search of healthier air, planning "lung-cleansing" and "smog-escape" wellness trips.

More than 20 countries in Asia and the Pacific now promote wellness on their national tourism websites. Governments in many of these countries actively support the development of wellness tourism products, especially around thermal springs. Some countries promote other wellness assets, such as beauty and traditional bathhouses in the ROK; healthy eating in Viet Nam; meditation, ayurveda, and yoga in Sri Lanka and India; and spirituality, meditation, and healing in Nepal and Bhutan.

Several countries, including Bhutan, India, Malaysia, the Philippines, the PRC, and Sri Lanka, provide economic incentives to companies investing in wellness-related programs. Through its Market Development Assistance Scheme, India, for example, supports new and redeveloped projects in wellness tourism.

Gearing for post-COVID recovery

Before COVID-19, wellness tourism was an important driver of tourism, which was in turn an important driver of economic growth and employment. But wellness and other forms of tourism were hit hard by the pandemic. After it subsides, wellness tourism may offer a faster path to recovery than other segments.

Wellness tourism emphasizes healthy living, well-being, and the preservation of nature and cultural heritage even as it attracts some of the highest-spending tourists. As a segment that emphasizes sustainability and can be considered a model for other tourism segments, wellness tourism offers a possible fast-track to recovery after the virus. Destinations with established strategies will be best positioned to leverage and further develop their wellness tourism segments, benefiting their entire economies and maximizing sustainability. Sri Lanka and Thailand are two Asian countries with concrete strategies (Box 2.4.3).

Box 2.4.3 Wellness tourism strategies in Sri Lanka and Thailand

Sri Lanka and Thailand both successfully flattened their COVID-19 curves and began reopening more than most other countries thanks to coordinated, whole-of-government strategies to prevent the spread of the virus. Having benefited from the flattening, the travel and tourism industry is helping to restore both countries' economies. Wellness tourism has been a centerpiece of an industry that is a significant part of the economy in both countries, thanks in part to successfully implemented strategies in each country.

In Sri Lanka, the government has implemented strategies to promote wellness and medical tourism, including economic incentives and simplified project approval procedures for companies investing in wellness-related developments. The country's National Export Strategy, 2018–2022 supports wellness tourism by coordinating the development of traditional and modern health and medical tourism, establishing a quality assurance system for wellness and traditional health systems, and providing an information system for the Sri Lankan health tourism sector and its target markets.

In Thailand, the Tourism Authority launched a health and wellness marketing strategy in 2014 in cooperation with Thai Airways International, Asia Web Direct, and more than 30 providers of health, beauty, and spa treatments. The strategy's digital marketing initiative for health and wellness was aimed at women in Asia and the Pacific. Under the slogan "Find Your Fabulous," the campaign helped promote over 150 packages of wellness and beauty treatments, spa packages, and hotel stays throughout the country. The Global Wellness Institute estimated that Thailand earned in 2017 about $12 billion from wellness tourism from 12.5 million wellness-related arrivals, thus ranking the country 13th globally as a wellness tourism destination.

Source: Wayne, R. 2020. *Analysis of the Global and Asian Wellness Tourism Sector.* ADB.

2.5 Wellness for happiness and inclusion

Healthier individuals tend to be happier, and wellness activities by their very nature can be sources of happiness. This seems to be true not only conceptually but empirically. The flourishing of wellness industries is highly correlated with greater happiness across many countries, as this section reports. Besides promoting happiness, the wellness economy may also generate more inclusive growth and development by providing greater employment and entrepreneurial opportunities for small local businesses, especially those run by women.

2.5.1 Asia's low subjective happiness

Interest in happiness has grown since Richard Easterlin showed that income growth may not always correlate with higher self-reported happiness (Easterlin 1974). The economics of happiness has been one of the fastest-growing fields in economics over the past few decades, particularly in the most recent one (Clark 2018, Clark et al. 2018, Frey 2020). Complementing the explosion of academic research on happiness, interest in happiness is growing among policy makers worldwide. Happiness is gradually becoming viewed as a new and important measure of people's well-being and a potential policy target that can complement traditional income measures (Global Happiness Council 2018).

"Happiness" is often used to mean subjective well-being according to a range of individual self-assessments and moods. Among various measures of happiness, the primary distinction is made between cognitive life evaluations and affective well-being (e.g., Helliwell and Wang 2012, Kahneman et al. 1999). Eudaimonic measures, linked to having a sense of meaning or purpose in life, are sometimes collected in surveys.

In cognitive life evaluations, the questions revolve around how satisfied people are with their lives overall, how happy they are generally, or how they position their life on a life ladder. For example, the survey question for life satisfaction in the Gallup World Poll asks, "All things considered, how satisfied are you with your life as a whole these days? Use a 0 to 10 scale, where 0 is dissatisfied and 10 is satisfied." In other surveys, the answer might be on 1–5 or 1–4 point scales. As this sort of question was first designed by Hadley Cantril (Cantril 1965), the life ladder score is commonly called a Cantril ladder or Cantril's self-anchoring striving scale.

Happiness in Asia

Happiness is becoming a higher priority for policy makers around the world, including in developing Asia. In the United Kingdom, the Office of National Statistics has randomly sampled residents on happiness since 2012 and used the data to guide policy. Bhutan is probably the best-known global example of a wellness-oriented government thanks to its gross national happiness index. The PRC, meanwhile, laid out in 1992 "people's happiness" (*xingfu gan*) as one of its strategic national goals. At the subnational level, the Seoul metropolitan government in the ROK has identified sustainable development and happiness as its main aims.

Figure 2.5.1 ranks happiness scores in 30 economies in developing Asia.[8] Two important findings emerge from the data, as detailed below.

Figure 2.5.1 Ranking of happiness in developing Asia

Happiness score

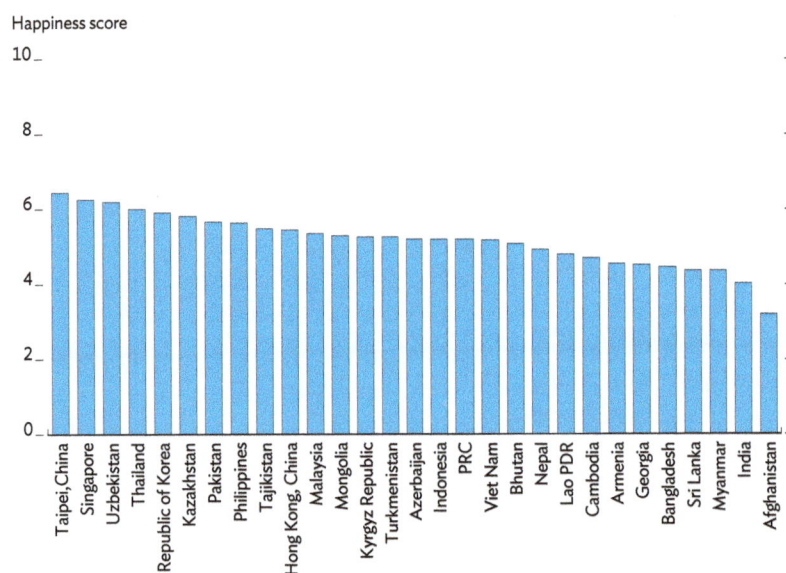

Lao PDR = Lao People's Democratic Republic, PRC = People's Republic of China.
Source: Wang 2020.

2.5.2 The wellness economy and happiness

The development of wellness industries can be expected to play an important role in the pursuit of a better quality of life by promoting happiness, either directly or indirectly, through known determinants of happiness: personal income, employment, health, consumption, and leisure time (e.g., Di Tella et al. 2001, 2003, Helliwell and Wang 2012, Helliwell et al. 2019).

Many wellness segments such as recreational physical activities, worksite wellness programs, and spa therapy have been linked with better health outcomes. Studies show that going on retreats brings significant and sustained improvements, for up to 6 weeks, along several dimensions of health and well-being (Cohen et al. 2017, Gilbert et al. 2014). Spa therapy significantly reduces both absenteeism and hospitalization (Klick and Stratmann 2008), while yoga practice has been shown to promote significant improvements in exercise capacity and health-related quality of life (Desveaux et al. 2015).

There has been less research on the direct correlation between wellness and happiness, with most studies exploring the impact of health activities (Zhang and Chen 2019). Results have been consistent, however, with physical activity in particular seen to contribute significantly to happiness in adolescents and adults around the world (Lathia et al. 2017, Richards et al. 2015, Wang et al. 2012, Min et al. 2017, Norris et al. 1992, Straatmann et al. 2016, Maher et al. 2016). Box 2.5.1 presents an empirical analysis of the link between wellness activities and happiness.

The results suggest a positive relationship overall between indicators of wellness industries and happiness (box table). This directly associates wellness with happiness, in addition to other contributing determinants of happiness such as health. The findings are stronger for workplace wellness, wellness real estate, and recreational physical activity.

The results found that a 1% increase in workplace wellness spending per capita lifted national happiness by 0.0015 units on a scale of 1 to 10 (Wang 2020). By extrapolation, if workplace wellness spending per capita doubled from the world average of $10.83 to $21.66, happiness would increase by 0.15 units.

Understanding of the wellness–happiness nexus would benefit from more rigorous analysis in the future, when more detailed wellness data become available. One caveat in the empirical analysis is that it covers only some wellness activities on the market. Analysis nevertheless yields some preliminary evidence of a positive association between wellness activities and happiness.

2.5.3 Wellness and inclusive growth

In addition to promoting happiness, the wellness economy can promote inclusive growth in developing Asia. As seen above, developing Asia has a large wellness economy that has expanded rapidly in recent years as demand for mental and physical health increased in tandem with Asian's growing affluence. As a result, wellness industries have become a major engine of economic growth and job creation. Wellness tourism expenditure in the region, for example, grew by 11% annually in 2015–2017 to $136.7 billion. The industry directly employed 3.74 million in India, 1.78 million in the PRC, and 530,000 in Thailand (GWI 2018b).

Box 2.5.1 Empirical analysis: data, methodology, and results

Because the Global Wellness Institute has data available for only six wellness segments—hot springs, spas, wellness tourism, workplace wellness, wellness real estate, and recreational physical activity—it is not feasible to empirically examine the correlation between overall wellness development and national happiness. We thus used the data available for the six wellness sectors to perform a preliminary empirical analysis of the relation between wellness segments and national happiness.

The global sample was 146 countries with data on both happiness and the six wellness segments—only 29 of them in developing Asia, making it more practical to perform empirical analysis on the global sample. The study used national data on the six segments from 2017, gathered by the Global Wellness Institute.

Per capita values for each sector were calculated to compare the relative size of each wellness segment across countries. The coefficient of correlation with happiness ranged from 0.46 for log per capita hot spring revenue to 0.81 for log per capita workplace

wellness spending by employers. The correlation between log per capita expenditure on physical activities and happiness was 0.80, the second highest among the six wellness segments.

A preliminary empirical analysis of the relationship between wellness industry and happiness was conducted using the following OLS model:

$$Happiness = \beta_0 + \beta_1 x + \beta_2 lngdp + \varepsilon,$$

where *Happiness* denoted national happiness scores averaged over 2016–2018; x denoted the log value of each of the six wellness segments; *lngdp* represented the natural log of GDP per capita in 2017, purchasing power parity adjusted in 2011 dollars; and ε was the error term. The regression controlled for GDP because it was an important determinant of happiness. The coefficient β_1 captured the relationship between the wellness segment and happiness.

Source: Wang. S. 2020. *Wellness for Happiness in Developing Asia.* ADB.

Wellness and happiness in the world: Regression results

	(1)	(2)	(3)	(4)	(5)	(6)	(7)	(8)	(9)	(10)	(11)	(12)	(13)
Log per capita hot spring revenue	0.07 (0.06)	0.01 (0.05)											
Log per capita spa revenue			0.19*** (0.05)	0.04 (0.05)									
Log per capita wellness tourism expenditure					0.16*** (0.05)	0.03 (0.05)							
Log per capita workplace wellness spending by employers							0.27*** (0.04)	0.15* (0.06)					
Log per capita wellness real estate construction value									0.40*** (0.06)	0.22** (0.07)			
Log per capita expenditure on recreational physical activity											0.43*** (0.08)	0.30⁺ (0.15)	
Log GDP per capita		0.56*** (0.10)		0.52*** (0.10)		0.51*** (0.11)		0.31* (0.14)		0.44*** (0.11)		0.20 (0.19)	0.56*** (0.10)
Region dummies	Yes	Yes	Yes	Yes	Yes	Yes	Yes	Yes	Yes	Yes	Yes	Yes	Yes
Number	146	146	146	146	146	146	146	146	146	146	146	146	146
Adjusted R-squared	0.579	0.695	0.627	0.696	0.637	0.697	0.697	0.710	0.658	0.715	0.706	0.707	0.697

Note: Robust standard errors in parentheses, ⁺ p<0.10, * p<0.05, ** p<0.01, *** p<0.001.
Source: Wang 2020.

The rise of the wellness economy can support small and female-operated businesses in the region, as many wellness segments are service-oriented and dominated by locally owned enterprises. Such businesses typically include those providing lodging and tour guide services, restaurants, retail shops, spas, yoga studios, and makers of local products and crafts. Wellness consumers increasingly favor organic, locally sourced, and sustainable products, as well as experiences that are authentic and come with unique and compelling stories. Consumers are often willing to pay a premium for these offerings, which can include local and traditional culinary experiences, healing modalities, herbal and traditional remedies, natural skincare and personal care products, native textiles, crafts, and the performing arts. Rising demand for these types of wellness products helps stimulate entrepreneurship and encourages micro and small enterprises, helping them to leverage local heritage and make good use of indigenous materials to create products and experiences that can further attract wellness consumers.

Small businesses can play a critical role in promoting physical activity in their own communities. Many of today's big branded and franchised fitness chains started out as small, independent studios. Small gyms and yoga and dance studios can be launched with relatively modest investments and be viable while still small, which means they can be tailored to local needs and price points. Whereas large, multinational branded chains tend to cluster in first-tier and higher-density urban areas, independent entrepreneurs—many of whom began as instructors or personal trainers—often launch new businesses in their own communities. Indeed, small business dominates the fitness industry in lower-income countries, second-tier cities in middle-income countries, and suburban and lower-density areas in higher-income countries. Beyond fitness, independent, unbranded businesses and local proprietors are especially dominant in industry segments such as yoga and Pilates studios, martial arts centers, dance studios, and local sports leagues and clubs.

Most wellness consumers are women, and many wellness-related occupations are traditionally female-dominated: massage therapist, complementary medicine practitioner, traditional healer, and tourism and retail worker. Growth in the wellness industry thus supports job creation for women across Asia. The Global Wellness Institute estimates that spa facilities employed more than 900,000 people in Asia and the Pacific in 2017, including over 500,000 spa therapists and 90,000 spa managers and directors, most of them women (Yeung and Johnston 2020d). Spa employment is projected to increase to 1.2 million in 2022, which means the region will need an additional 160,000 trained therapists and 30,000 experienced managers and directors in the spa industry alone within the next several years. Female workers will benefit from this growth.

Looking more specifically at employment in Asia, women are the majority in occupational categories related to personal services and personal care across a number of countries: 73% in the Lao People's Democratic Republic, 84% in Mongolia, 53% in Myanmar, 57% in the Philippines, and 69% in Thailand. In these same countries, women fill only 38%–47% of jobs across all occupations (Yeung and Johnston 2020d).[9]

Moreover, traditional wellness knowledge of, for instance, healing modalities and herbal remedies, is often transmitted matrilineally, passing from grandmother to mother to daughter. The rise of the wellness industry creates economic and entrepreneurship opportunities for women in many communities at all income levels while strengthening the preservation of cultural heritage and indigenous knowledge.

However, an ongoing challenge arises from the perception that many wellness jobs require mainly skills traditionally considered to be female: hands-on caring, healing, serving, food production, gardening, and craft making. Consequently, many occupations in the wellness industry remain undervalued in society, paying wages below average. Worse, wellness occupations sometimes face stigma, such as when the public conflates massage therapists with sex workers, discouraging women from pursuing careers in these fields. The dominance of female workers in the wellness industry may also worsen the risk of worker exploitation and abuse. Governments that seek to promote and support the development of the wellness industry therefore need to be mindful of the role, condition, and needs of female workers in it.

2.6 Policies for physical and mental wellness

Government policies to promote wellness benefit individuals, the economy, and society at large. Wellness makes people happier and more productive, and wellness industries are a growing part of the economy. Yet wellness is poorly understood by governments, which have not incorporated it into policy making as an overarching framework or explicit priority. Nevertheless, wellness brings an important perspective to policy making that is complementary to public health, health policy, and the emerging field of happiness.

Wellness-related policies must be geared toward improving the health and well-being of the whole population. This naturally highlights the role of public investment in projects geared toward improving physical and mental health, which benefit everyone. Landscaping and maintaining a green public park in a crowded city, for example, provide a place of rest and relaxation for all the city's residents.

Further, government intervention can especially benefit poorer Asians, who are often disadvantaged in access to wellness facilities. In contrast with richer Asians, who can and do spend their own money on wellness activities, poorer Asians get most of their physical exercise and other wellness activities at free facilities such as neighborhood parks or basketball courts. Asian governments would thus do well to pay special attention to the needs of the poor by investing in sports and physical recreation infrastructure, facilities, and programs, for example, and in other activities that the public can access at very little or no cost.

Wellness policies are measures that nudge people to proactively make healthy choices and live healthy lifestyles, as well as create living environments that support and encourage healthy behavior and lifestyles. These policies ideally run through four cross-cutting domains and follow a lifespan approach, as explained in the next two sections.

2.6.1 Four cross-cutting wellness policy domains

Wellness policies generally cover four cross-cutting policy domains. First, Asian governments can adopt measures geared to help create a healthy built environment, such as by prioritizing walkability and physical movement in urban and regional planning. Second, they can enable and support physical activity by funding public infrastructure, facilities, and programs for recreational physical activities. Third, policy makers can encourage healthy eating by improving consumer awareness of nutrition and diet. Finally, they can enhance wellness in the workplace by ensuring a safe and healthy physical work environment. Taken together, policies from the four cross-cutting domains can promote the mental and physical wellness of Asians.

Creating a healthy built environment

The modern-day built environment—both urban and suburban—is often described as obesogenic, with many factors interacting and conspiring against a physically active lifestyle and encouraging sedentary behavior. The built environment also influences social interactions, mental wellness, and even levels of civic engagement.

Several policy areas offer opportunities to counter and reverse the unwellness that is embedded in many of today's living environments. Policy interventions on infrastructure and the built environment can have some of the widest-ranging impacts because they affect the entire population of a neighborhood or community. They also provide opportunities to target disadvantaged or marginalized neighborhoods and population groups.

Four specific priority areas for creating a healthy built environment are to (i) prioritize walkability and physical movement in urban and regional planning, (ii) create green spaces and natural sanctuaries for urban residents, (iii) protect people from harmful indoor environments and materials, and (iv) support wellness real estate and make healthy homes affordable and accessible. Table 2.6.1 shows sample policies specifically to prioritize walkability and physical movement.

Two other aspects of the living environment also have important impacts on population health and well-being:

(i)   **Modern sanitation.** Globally, 2 billion people lack access to basic sanitation services (WHO 2019). Investment in sanitation infrastructure such as modern toilets, sewage systems, and wastewater treatment plants directly improves health in underdeveloped communities around the world.

(ii)   **Pollution and environment.** Pollution of the air, water, and soil has a large and growing impact on human health. Environmental policies that reduce pollution offer direct benefits for people's physical and mental well-being.

Table 2.6.1 Creating a healthy built environment by prioritizing walkability and physical movement in urban and regional planning

Planning and prioritization	• Craft active transit (by muscle power) and public transport master plans that proactively address how a neighborhood, city, or region will deploy resources to prioritize walkability and bikeability in all infrastructure projects.
Public investment	A. Plan, design, and invest in infrastructure that emphasize walkability and bikeability: 　1. **Complete streets.** Ensure that street infrastructure enables safe, convenient, comfortable walking, biking, and public transport, as well as personal vehicle use, with wide sidewalks, accessible crosswalks, pedestrian signals, separated bike lanes, special bus lanes, median refuge islands, curb extensions, and narrow vehicle lanes. 　2. **Connectivity.** Remember that walkability is affected by connectivity in streets, grid networks, and block length, as well as by how pedestrian and biking infrastructure connect to each other and to public transport, workplaces, parks, and other key destinations. 　3. **Streetscape design.** Design and place amenities like trees, street lighting, benches, wayfinding signage, public art, street-level storefronts, and bike parking to promote walking and improve real and perceived safety. 　4. **Public investment in multi-use trails.** 　5. **Public support or funding for bike-sharing programs.** 　6. **Parking design and policies.** Remember that the quality, quantity, and location of parking can affect walkability. 　7. **Traffic calming.** Adopt slower speed limits on selected thoroughfares for pedestrians and cyclists. B. Prioritize and fund infrastructure and building projects located near public transport and walking and cycling routes. C. Invest in public transport that encourages active transit, because most such trips begin and end with walking or cycling.
Regulation	A. Ensure that zoning, building codes, and land-use regulations encourage high density and mixed-use development because they encourage walking and biking by allowing people to live closer to work and commercial areas. B. Designate car-free zones, especially in city centers. C. Use congestion pricing to reduce traffic.
Tax and fiscal incentives	A. Offer incentives to people who commute by active transit or public transport. B. Reward developers that include walkability and bikeability in their projects.

Source: Johnston, Yeung, and Bodeker 2020.

Supporting physical activity

Physical activity is essential to good health, yet over 27% of adults worldwide do not get enough of it. As shown in section 3 above, rates of inactivity vary across developing Asia, from over one-third of the population currently inactive in India, Pakistan, the Philippines, the Republic of Korea, and Singapore to only 15%–16% in most of East Asia and the Pacific. People can be physically active through natural movement—for transportation, work, or domestic chores—or through recreational activities in leisure time. As natural movement is on the decline around the world, increasingly discouraged by our modern lifestyles and built environments, recreational physical activities are becoming more essential for people to stay healthy.

When people in Asia are asked why they do not participate in recreational physical activity, the most often cited reasons are lack of time, energy, or interest or else physical or health impairment. For children, the most important barriers are lack of time, interest, or access to facilities (GWI 2019). Governments can play an important role in enabling, encouraging, and widening participation in recreational physical activity through four broad priorities: (i) invest in public infrastructure and facilities, (ii) prioritize government investments in disadvantaged areas and target groups at risk, (iii) engage the medical community to prescribe exercise, and (iv) help children and youth to build lifelong healthy habits through school and youth sports. Government initiatives that prioritize walkability and active transit in the built environment, as elaborated in the previous section, are also critical for encouraging more physical activity in natural movement.

Encouraging healthy eating

Developing Asia has experienced a major nutrition transition over the past few decades, shifting from food insufficiency and undernutrition to a rise in poor eating patterns and overconsumption of unhealthy foods, notably the increased consumption of foods that are overly processed, prepared outside the home, and from animal sources; larger portion sizes; and higher use of oils and sweeteners. The spread of modern, industrialized farming and of commercial food production, marketing, and distribution—often supported and encouraged by government policy—is linked to the spread of unhealthy, nutrition-poor, highly processed Western diets across Asia. These unhealthy eating patterns contribute to the rise of obesity and chronic disease in Asia and worldwide. A study of the global burden of disease found poor diet to be a factor in one out of five deaths around the world (Lancet 2019).

Today's health and wellness challenges related to food and nutrition encompass a host of concerns, from poor nutrition, processed foods, and obesity to food insecurity, food equity, food safety, and so-called urban food deserts, where access to affordable and nutritious food is limited. While individuals are responsible for the foods they purchase and consume, poor choices are encouraged and facilitated by unhealthy food environments, unhealthy ingredients and additives, easy and cheap access to nutritionally poor meals, and a lack of awareness about healthy food groups. Government policies have a major influence on all these factors, which means that they can promote healthy eating (Mozaffarian et al. 2018, Institute of Medicine and National Research Council 2009, Gorski and Roberto 2015).

The five specific priority areas for encouraging healthy eating are (i) improving consumer awareness of nutrition and diet, (ii) creating economic incentives for healthy eating choices, (iii) creating healthier food environments and expanding access for high-risk groups, (iv) strengthening industry standards and regulations on ingredients and marketing, and (v) treating food as good medicine in patient care. Table 2.6.2 shows sample policies specifically to improve consumer awareness of healthy diets.

Table 2.6.2 Encouraging healthy eating by improving consumer awareness of nutrition and diet

Public awareness and education	A. Establish national dietary guidelines and ensure that they are up to date, reflect the latest scientific evidence on healthy eating, and are culturally sensitive and adaptable.
	B. Conduct public awareness and educational campaigns on nutritional guidelines and healthy eating practices, especially targeting children, the disadvantaged, and other populations at risk.
	C. Add food and nutrition education to the public school curricula, along with cooking skills.
	D. Develop community-based cooking and nutrition programs, especially targeting populations and communities at high risk.
Regulation	A. Establish food labeling standards and guidelines for packaged foods and beverages, either mandatory or voluntary, that include:
	1. clear and consistent labeling of ingredients, additives, sizes, nutrition, and recommended daily intake;
	2. front-of-package labels, warnings, symbols, or color-coding to alert consumers to unhealthy ingredients or additives, or to highlight healthy choices;
	3. regulated usage of labels or claims on food packaging, such as "healthy," "natural," "low fat," "low sugar," to ensure that they are used consistently and do not make false claims.
	B. Establish labeling standards and guidelines for restaurant menus, either mandatory or voluntary, that provide, for example, calorie information, and develop special labels for healthier options.

Source: Johnston, Yeung, and Bodeker 2020.

Enhancing wellness in the workplace

Workers in Asia are plagued by unwellness: rising chronic disease; workplace illness, injuries, and death; financial insecurity; rampant stress and burnout; and widespread employee disengagement. Some of these issues are closely intertwined with globalization, technological change, new business models, and shifting relationships between workers and employers as the economy evolves, in particular with the rise in the gig economy of short-term contract work. Within this evolving landscape, governments can help to protect and enhance workers' well-being through policies and regulation, as well as by leading and promoting best practices as an employer of a large government workforce.

Five broad policy priorities for enhancing wellness in the workplace are to (i) ensure a safe and healthy physical work environment; (ii) protect workers from hostile work environments, overwork, and other triggers of emotional and mental distress; (iii) provide living wages, unemployment benefits, and paid family and sick leave; (iv) make government a leader and best-practice employer in terms of workplace wellness; and (v) establish legal structures that enable and support community-enhancing "benefit corporations" and environmental, social, and governance reporting. In sum, government policy should protect workers from physical and mental harm, encourage employers to create a work environment that is conducive to wellness, and promote better work–life balance for all workers.

2.6.2 A lifespan approach to wellness policy making

Healthy aging needs to begin in childhood, within an overarching lifespan framework such as Japan's 100-Year Life Program (Box 2.6.1). Preventive interventions in the first 1,000 days of life can have lifelong effects, requiring support from appropriate policies. Authorities should start in the early years and consider incorporating wellness as part of the formal education system, from school curricula to the learning and social environment for students. Further along the lifespan, a range of policies can support healthy aging: lifelong learning, reskilling, personal growth and transformation, and, for seniors, safe and wellness-enabling homes and appropriate nutrition.

Box 2.6.1 Japan's 100-Year Life Program

Between a "healthy lifespan" and an "average lifespan" in Japan is a gap of about 10 years—a decade of poor health. The healthy lifespan for men rose from 71.19 years in 2013 to 72.14 years in 2016 and for women from 74.21 to 74.79 years, as estimated by the Ministry of Health in March 2018. Meanwhile, the average lifespan for Japanese men lengthened from 80.21 years in 2013 to 80.98 years in 2016, and for Japanese women from 86.61 to 87.14 years. Thus, because of lengthening healthy lifespans, life expectancy after one's healthy years shortened by 0.18 years for men and by 0.05 years for women.

Japanese spend most of their lifelong medical expenses in the 10-year period after the end of their healthy lifespan. This places considerable strain and—despite a slightly shortening gap—a growing burden on the health-care system and the national budget, especially as average lifespan increases in Japan (Maruyama forthcoming).

To address this challenge, Japan has introduced its 100-Year Life Program, which aims to promote wellness and a healthy long life. Traditionally, planners have considered life in three stages: education, employment, and retirement. The program aims to shift the paradigm toward a multistage life, with support provided at every stage. The new approach allows individuals to acquire new skills and knowledge to help them as they progress through their envisioned century-long lifespan.

Japan established the Council for Designing 100-Year Life Society to formulate a grand policy framework for the government to implement. The goals of the council are to significantly improve pay for long-term care workers, dramatically expand recurrent education to enhance mid-career employment prospects, and lay the groundwork for raising elderly employment rates.

Council priorities are to ensure that educational opportunities are open to all people, reduce the cost burden of education, and promote education for adults who want to resume learning regardless of their age. Higher education must be reformed to this end, as the conventional liberal arts courses for young students that are currently offered at universities may not be sufficient to meet the needs of the whole of Japanese society.

Another council priority is to loosen and diversify corporate hiring practices beyond the current practice of hiring new graduates just once a year, by introducing various employment formats for the elderly. Such changes are considered key to securing capable human resources, as companies cannot secure the necessary talent simply by employing new graduates in one sweep.

Finally, the council prioritizes reforming the current social security system, which emphasizes benefits for the elderly based on the three traditional life stages: youth and students, adults and workers, and the retired elderly. The existing elderly-centered system must eventually morph into a social security system that benefits all cohorts of the population equally.

Reference:

Maruyama, T. Forthcoming. Enriching the Lives of Seniors in Japan—Ikigai Healthy Ageing Policy. In C. Goh, G. Bodeker, and K. Kariippanon, eds. *Healthy Ageing in Asia*. Taylor & Francis.

Source: Johnston, K., O. Yeung, and G. Bodeker. 2020. *Policy Options to Promote Wellness in Asia*. ADB.

An adaptive lifetime framework for wellness policy would clearly be optimal, as individuals face different wellness needs at different stages in their lives. The World Health Organization takes a lifespan approach to understanding the risk factors and determinants of mental health, explicitly recognizing that mental health priorities depend on age.

Along with the crosscutting wellness policies discussed above, lifelong wellness measures can help Asians navigate the uncertain, stressful COVID-19 world toward a better new normal after COVID-19. COVID-19 is a wake-up call to the world to place a higher priority on wellness. The current pandemic is a startling global health and economic crisis that has spread a great deal of fear and anxiety everywhere. Never before have health and well-being declined so rapidly and synchronously for so many people around the world. Pursuing universal health care and strengthening primary health care would amplify the benefits of wellness for all Asians.

Wellness is never more important than in difficult times like these. Families and friends, communities, businesses, and governments all shape people's lives and determine whether they have access to wellness. Some of the suffering from COVID-19 can be lessened if societies are able to strengthen their wellness foundations. These difficult times show where future priorities belong, and where wellness can offer a roadmap for healing and growth.

Endnotes

1   The study included data on physical activity across four key domains—for work, in the household (paid or unpaid), for transport to get to and from places on foot or by bicycle, and leisure time sports and active recreation. The data were collected through random sampling with sample sizes of at least 200 representative of a national or defined subnational population (Guthold et al. 2018).

2   For developing Asia, covering 42 member economies of the Asian Development Bank (ADB), the total physical activity economy is estimated at $177.7 billion, with expenditure per participant estimated at $138.26.

3   Average participation rate for developing Asia covering 42 developing member economies of ADB is 31.6%.

4   A culture of overwork and burnout seems to be particularly rampant in East Asia. Death by overwork is definitely a thing in East Asia, called *karoshi* in Japan, *guolaosi* in the PRC, and *gwarosa* in the ROK. A 2016 Japanese paper on *karoshi* found that working more than 60 hours per week significantly increased the risk of *karoshi* in males, while the threshold for females was about 45 hours. Because Japanese women tend to bear more of the home burden, adding housework to overly long work hours imposes on women a serious risk of *karoshi*.

5   Data on the wellness real estate market presented here encompass both residential projects, referred to as wellness lifestyle real estate, and commercial and institutional projects (office, hospitality, mixed- or multi-family, medical, and leisure developments) that have wellness components. As it is impossible to separate out the residential and nonresidential components in commercial and institutional projects, the Global Wellness Institute estimates wellness real estate in aggregate.

6   Because it is the typical caloric intake for an adult male, 2,500 calories is generally used to approximate aggregate calorie sufficiency with respect to national food availability. Food availability data indicate food supply but may underestimate the availability of processed food, particularly imported processed food, which contributes significantly to fat, salt, and sugar intake. Conversely, availability is likely to be higher than actual consumption considering loss and wastage at the point of consumption. Generally, food balance sheets are constructed for products derived from primary crops up to the first stage of processing and to the second or third stage for livestock and fish products. http://www.fao.org/economic/ess/fbs/ess-fbs02/en/ (accessed 6 April 2020).

7   In the United Kingdom, the prevalence of clinically significant mental distress rose from 18.9% of the population in 2018–2019 to 27.3% in April 2020, which was 1 month into

the lockdown there (Pierce 2020). In the US, an April 2020 poll conducted by KFF found 45% of adults reporting that their mental health had been compromised by worry and stress over the virus; a similar poll in 2018 found 32.5% of adults reporting that they felt worried, nervous, or anxious either daily, weekly, or monthly (Panchal et al. 2020). In the PRC, a survey in late February and March 2020 revealed 27.9% of respondents reporting depression, 31.6% anxiety, 29.2% insomnia, and 24.4% acute stress (Shi et al. 2020). The prevalence of these mental health symptoms during the pandemic was higher than before the outbreak, when rates of moderate-to-severe depression were 6.0%, moderate-to-severe anxiety 5.3%, and insomnia 15.0%.

8   National averages of happiness were obtained from chapter 2 of the *World Happiness Report 2019*, which is based mainly on the Gallup surveys from 2016 to 2018 (Helliwell et al. 2019).

9   These figures are estimates by the authors, combining two ISCO-08 occupational categories: *51-Personal service workers* (including travel guides, cooks, waiters, hairdressers, beauticians, housekeeping supervisors, etc.) and *53-Personal care workers* (including personal care workers in health services, and childcare workers and teachers' aides). Data are for 2017 and 2018.

Background papers

Ahmad, H. and I. Qureshi. 2020. *Cross-Country Comparison of Wellness: An Empirical Assessment*. ADB.

Bodeker, G. 2020a. *Asian Traditions of Wellness*. ADB.

——. 2020b. *Mental Wellness in Asia*. ADB.

Bodeker, G., M. Pundit, S. Tian, and P. Quising. 2020. *Aging and Wellness in Asia*. ADB.

Park, D. and P. Quising. 2020. *Why does Wellness Matter so much in the Age of COVID-19? A Selective Literature Review*. ADB.

Thow, A. M., P. Farrell, M. Helble, and C. N. Rachmi. 2020. *Eating in Developing Asia: Trends, Consequences and Policies*. ADB.

Wang. S. 2020. *Wellness for Happiness in Developing Asia*. ADB.

Wayne, S. 2020. *Analysis of the Global and Asian Wellness Tourism Sector*. ADB.

Yeung, O. and K. Johnston. 2020a. *Global Wellness Industry and Its Implications for Asia's Development*. ADB.

——. 2020b. *Improving Workplace Wellness in Asia: A Business Case, Approaches, and Successful Practices*. ADB.

——. 2020c. *The Physical Activity Economy in Asia: Market Size, Participation, Barriers, and Options to Increase Movement*. ADB.

Johnston, K., O. Yeung, and G. Bodeker. 2020. *Policy Options to Promote Wellness in Asia*. ADB.

Background notes

Consing, R. M. III, M. J. Barsabal, J. T. Alvarez, and M. J. Mariasingham. 2020. *Using the System of National Accounts to Estimate a Country's Wellness Economy*. ADB.

Park, D. and P. Quising. 2020a. *COVID-19 and Mental Health*. ADB.

———. 2020b. *COVID-19 and Physical Health*. ADB.

Pundit, M. 2020. *Gender and Wellness*. ADB.

Yeung, O. and K. Johnston. 2020d. *Women and Small Business in the Wellness Economy*. ADB.

All background papers and notes are available at https://www.adb.org/documents/asian-development-outlook-2020-update-background-papers.

References

AIA Vitality. 2019. *Healthiest Workplace Survey 2018*. https://healthiest workplace.aia.com/regional/eng/ (accessed 12 November 2019).

Anderson, A. N., H. Kennedy, P. DeWitt, E. Anderson, and M. Z. Wamboldt. 2014. Dance Movement Therapy Impacts Mood States of Adolescents in a Psychiatric Hospital. *Arts in Psychotherapy* 41(3).

Angus Reid Institute. 2020. *Worry, Gratitude & Boredom: As COVID-19 Affects Mental, Financial Health, Who Fares Better; Who is Worse?* http://angusreid.org/covid19-mental-health/.

Atkinson, S., G. Skinner, and T. Gebrekal. 2020. *Coronavirus Dominates Global Worries*. https://www.ipsos.com/en/coronavirus-dominates-global-worries.

Australian Sports Commission Clearinghouse for Sport and Physical Activity. 2019. *AusPlay National Data Tables—July 2018 to June 2019 data*. https://www.clearinghouseforsport.gov.au/research/smi/ausplay/results/national.

Baker, P. and S. Friel. 2016. Food Systems Transformations, Ultra-processed Food Markets and the Nutrition Transition in Asia. *Globalization and Health* 12(1).

Bodeker, G. (ed.) et al. 2018. *White Paper on Mental Wellness: Pathways, Evidence and Horizons*. Global Wellness Institute.

Bräuninger, I. 2012. The Efficacy of Dance Movement Therapy Group on Improvement of Quality of Life: A Randomized Controlled Trial. *The Arts in Psychotherapy* 39(4).

Brown, S. and L. M. Parsons. 2008. The Neuroscience of Dance. *Scientific American* 299(1).

Cantril, H. 1965. *The Pattern of Human Concerns*. New Brunswick, New Jersey: Rutgers University Press.

CBRE Group. 2017. *Workplace Wellness Gains Traction in Asia Pacific*. https://www.cbre.com.au/about/media-center/workplace-wellness-gains-traction-in-asia-pacific0.

Centers for Disease Control and Prevention (CDC). 2020. *Groups at Higher Risk of Severe Illness*. https://www.cdc.gov/coronavirus/2019-ncov/need-extra-precautions/groups-at-higher-risk.html.

Christmas, C. M. and N. Khanlou. 2019. Defining Youth Resilience: a Scoping Review. *International Journal of Mental Health and Addiction* 17.

Clark, A. E. 2018. Four Decades of the Economics of Happiness: Where Next? *The Review of Income and Wealth* 64(2).

Clark, A. E., S. Flèche, R. Layard, N. Powdthavee, and G. Ward. 2018. *The Origins of Happiness: The Science of Well-being Over the Life Course.* Princeton University Press.

Cohen, M., F. Elliott, L. Oates, A. Schembri, and N. Mantri. 2017. Do Wellness Tourists Get Well? An Observational Study of Multiple Dimensions of Health and Well-being after a Week-long Retreat. *Journal of Alternative and Complementary Medicine* 23(2).

de los Santos, C. and A. J. Lumba. 2020. The Core of the Digital Economy: A Proposed Framework. Unpublished.

Desveaux, L., A. Lee, R. Goldstein, and D. Brooks. 2015. Yoga in the Management of Chronic Disease: A Systematic Review and Meta-analysis. *Medical Care* 53(7).

Di Tella, R., R. MacCulloch, and A. J. Oswald. 2001. Preferences over inflation and unemployment: Evidence from surveys of happiness. *American Economic Review* 91(1).

———. 2003. The Macroeconomics of Happiness. *The Review of Economics and Statistics* 85(4).

Diener, E., E. M. Suh, R. E. Lucas, and H. L. Smith. 1999. Subjective Well-being: Three decades of progress. *Psychological Bulletin* 125(2). http://dx.doi.org/10.1037/0033-2909.125.2.276.

Ding, D., K. Lawson, T. Kolbe-Alexander, E. Finkelstein, P. Katzmarzyk, W. van Mechlen, and M. Pratt. 2016. The Economic Burden of Physical Inactivity: A Global Analysis of Major Non-communicable Diseases. *The Lancet* 388(10051). https://doi.org/10.1016/S0140-6736(16)30383-X.

Dowrick, S. and J. Quiggin. 1994. International Comparisons of Living Standards and Tastes: A Revealed-Preference Analysis. *American Economic Review* 84(1).

Dunn, H. 1959. High-level Wellness for Man and Society. *American Journal of Public Health* 49(6).

Easterlin, R. 1974. Does economic growth improve the human lot? Some Empirical Evidence. In P. A. David and M. W. Reder, eds. *Nations and Households in Economic Growth.* Academic Press.

FAO, IFAD, UNICEF, WFP, and WHO. 2019. *The State of Food Insecurity in the World: Safeguarding against economic slowdowns and downturns.* FAO.

Firth, J., S. B. Teasdale, K. Allott, D. Siskind, W. Marx, J. Cotter, N. Veronese, F. Schuch, L. Smith, M. Solmi, A. F. Carvalho, D. Vancampfort, M. Berk, B. Stubbs, and J. Sarris. 2019. The Efficacy and Safety of Nutrient Supplements in the Treatment of Mental Disorders: A Meta-review of Meta-analyses of Randomized Controlled Trials. *World Psychiatry* 18(3). https://doi.org/10.1002/wps.20672.

Frey, B. S. 2020. What are the Opportunities for Future Happiness Research? *International Review of Economics* 67.

Gao, J., P. Zheng, Y. Jia, H. Chen, Y. Mao, S. Chen, Y. Wang, H. Fu, and J. Da. 2020. Mental Health Problems and Social Media Exposure during COVID-19 Outbreak. *PLoS ONE* 15(4): e0231924. https://doi.org/10.1371/journal.pone.0231924.

Gebrekal, T. 2020. *What Worries the World: 13 of the 27 Surveyed Nations Cited COVID-19 as the Top Concern.* https://www.ipsos.com/en/what-worries-world-july-2020.

Gietel-Basten, S. 2018. *The Population Problem in Pacific Asia.* New York, NY: Oxford University Press (International Policy Exchange Series).

Gilbert, A., E. Epel, R. Tanzi, R. Rearden, S. Schilf, and E. Puterman. 2014. A Randomized Trial Comparing a Brief Meditation Retreat to a Vacation: Effects on Daily Well-being. *Journal of Alternative and Complementary Medicine* 20(5).

Global Happiness Council. 2018. *Global Happiness Policy Report 2018.* New York: Sustainable Development Solutions Network.

Global Wellness Institute. 2018a. *Global Wellness Economy Monitor 2018.* https://globalwellnessinstitute.org/industry-research/2018-global-wellness-economy-monitor/.

——. 2018b. *Build Well to Live Well: Wellness Lifestyle Real Estate and Communities.* https://globalwellnessinstitute.org/industry-research/wellness-real-estate-communities-research/.

——. 2019. *Move to be Well: The Global Economy of Physical Activity.* https://globalwellnessinstitute.org/industry-research/global-economy-physical-activity/.

Gorski, M. T. and C. A. Roberto. 2015. Public Health Policies to Encourage Healthy Eating Habits: Recent Perspectives. *Journal of Healthcare Leadership* 7, 81–90. https://doi.org/10.2147/JHL.S69188.

Grosso, G., F. Bella, J. Godos, S. Sciacca, D. Del Rio, S. Ray, and E. L. Giovannucci. 2017. Possible Role of Diet in Cancer: Systematic Review and Multiple Meta-analyses of Dietary Patterns, Lifestyle Factors, and Cancer Risk. *Nutrition Reviews* 75(6).

GSK Consumer Healthcare. 2017. *GSK Global Pain Index 2017, Global Research Report.* https://www.gsk.com/media/3814/global-pain-index-2017-report.pdf.

Guasch-Ferré, M., A. Satija, S. A. Blondin, M. Janiszewski, E. Emlen, L. E. O'Connor, and M. J. Stampfer. 2019. Meta-Analysis of Randomized Controlled Trials of Red Meat Consumption in Comparison with Various Comparison Diets on Cardiovascular Risk Factors. *Circulation* 139(15).

Guha, A. Undated. Ayurvedic Medicine. *Taking Charge of Your Health & Wellbeing.* https://www.takingcharge.csh.umn. edu/explore-healing-practices/ayurvedic-medicine.

Guthold, R., G. Stevens, L. Riley, and F. Bull. 2018. Worldwide Trends in Insufficient Physical Activity from 2001 to 2016: A Pooled Analysis of 358 Population-based Surveys with 1.9 Million Participants. *The Lancet Global Health* 6. https://doi.org/10.1016/S2214-109X(18)30357-7.

Haapala, E. A., J. Vaisto, and N. Lintu. 2017. Physical Activity and Sedentary Time in Relation to Academic Achievement in Children. *Journal of Science and Medicine in Sport* 20(6). doi: 10.1016/j.jsams.2016.11.003.

Hallal, P. C., L. Bo Andersen, F. Bull, R. Guthold, W. Haskell, and E. Ekelund, 2012. Global Physical Activity Levels: Surveillance Progress, Pitfalls, and Prospects. *The Lancet* 380. https://doi.org/10.1016/S0140-6736(12)60646-1.

Hajek, A., C. Brettschneider, T. Mallon, A. Ernst, S. Mamone, B. Wiese, S. Weyerer, J. W. Jochen, M. Pentzek, A. Fuchs, J. Stein, T. Luck, H. Bickel, D. Weeg, M. Wagner, K. Heser, W. Maier, M. Scherer, S. Riedel-Heller, and K. Hans-Helmut. 2017. The Impact of Social Engagement on Health-related Quality of Life and Depressive Symptoms in Old Age-Evidence from a Multicenter Prospective Cohort Study in Germany. *Health and Quality of Life Outcomes* 15(140). DOI:10.1186/s12955-017-0715-8.

Hämäläinen, P., J. Takala, and T. B. Kiat. 2017. *Global Estimates of Occupational Accidents and Work-Related Illnesses 2017.* Singapore: Workplace Safety and Health Institute. http://www.icohweb.org/site/images/news/ pdf/Report%20Global%20Estimates%20of%20 Occupational%20Accidents%20and%20Work-related%20 Illnesses%202017%20rev1.pdf.

Hanc, M., C. McAndrew, and M. Ucci. 2018. Conceptual Approaches to Wellbeing in Buildings: A Scoping Review. *Building Research and Information.* 10.1080/09613218.2018.1513695.

Harding, K. L., V. M. Aguayo, and P. Webb. 2018. Hidden Hunger in South Asia: A Review of Recent Trends and Persistent Challenges. *Public Health Nutrition* 21(4).

Harvard Health Publishing. 2020. *Exercising to Relax.* https://www.health.harvard.edu/staying-healthy/ exercising-to-relax.

Haushofer, J. and E. Fehr. 2014. On the Psychology of Poverty. *Science* 344(6186). DOI: 10.1126/science.1232491.

Helble, M. and K. Francisco. 2018. The Imminent Obesity Crisis in Asia and the Pacific: First Cost Estimates. In M. Helble and A. Sato, eds. *Wealthy but Unhealthy: Overweight and Obesity in Asia and the Pacific: Trends, Costs, and Policies for Better Health.* Asian Development Bank Institute (ADBI).

Helble, M. and A. Sato, eds. 2018. *Wealthy but Unhealthy: Overweight and Obesity in Asia and the Pacific: Trends, Costs, and Policies for Better Health.* ADBI.

Helliwell, J. F. and S. Wang. 2012. The State of Happiness. In J. F. Helliwell, R. Layard, and J. Sachs, eds. *World Happiness Report 2012.* The Earth Institute of Columbia University.

Helliwell, J. F., H. Huang, and S. Wang. 2019. Changing World Happiness. In J. F. Helliwell, R. Layard, and J. Sachs, eds. *World Happiness Report 2019.* United Nations Sustainable Development Solutions Network.

Hickson, M. and A. Julian. 2018. Consequences of Undernutrition. In M. Hickson, S. Smith, and K. Whelan, eds. *Advanced Nutrition and Dietetics in Nutrition Support.* Wiley Online Library, John Wiley & Sons Ltd.

Huang, R., L. Zhu, L. Xue, L. Liu, X. Yan, J. Wang, B. Zhang, T. Xu, F. Ji, Y. Zhao, J. Cheng, Y. Wang, H. Shao, S. Hong, Q. Cao, C. Li, X. Zhao, L. Zou, D. Sang, H. Zhao, X. Guan, X. Chen, C. Shan, J. Xia, Y. Chen, X. Yan, J. Wei, C. Zhu, and C. Wu. 2020. *Clinical Findings of Patients with Coronavirus Disease 2019 in Jiangsu Province, China: A retrospective, Multi-center Study.* http://dx.doi.org/10.2139/ssrn.3548785.

Institute of Medicine and National Research Council. 2009. Actions for Healthy Eating. In *Local Government Actions to Prevent Childhood Obesity.* The National Academies Press.

International Labour Organization (ILO). 2018. *International Labour Organization Database (ILOSTAT) – Status in Employment, ILO Modelled Estimates.* https://ilostat.ilo.org/data/ (accessed 29 October 2019).

——. 2019. *Safety and Health at the Heart of the Future of Work.* ILO.

Jannasch, F., J. Kröger, and M. B. Schulze. 2017. Dietary Patterns and Type 2 Diabetes: A Systematic Literature Review and Meta-Analysis of Prospective Studies. *The Journal of Nutrition* 147(6).

Japan Sports Agency. 2017. スポーツの実施状況等に関する世論調査 (*Public Opinion Survey on the Implementation Status of Sport*). http://www.mext.go.jp/prev_sports/comp/b_menu/other/__icsFiles/afieldfile/2018/03/30/142346_77_1.pdf.

Jiménez-Pavón, D., A. Carbonell-Baeza, and C. J. Lavie. 2020. Physical Exercise as Therapy to Fight against the Mental and Physical Consequences of COVID-19 Quarantine: Special Focus in Older People. *Progress in Cardiovascular Diseases.* doi: 10.1016/j.pcad.2020.03.009.

Kahneman, D., E. Diener, and N. Schwarz. 1999. *Well-being: The Foundations of Hedonic Psychology*. Russell Sage.

Kang, L., Y. Li, S. Hu, M. Chen, C. Yang, B. X. Yang, Y. Wang, J. Hu, J. Lai, X. Ma, J. Chen, L. Guan, G. Wang, H. Ma, and Z. Liu. 2020. The Mental Health of Medical Workers in Wuhan, China dealing with the 2019 novel coronavirus. *Lancet Psychiatry* 7(3).

Karpati, F. J., C. Giacosa, N. E. Foster, V. B. Penhune, and K. L. Hyde. 2015. Dance and the Brain: A review. *Annals of the New York Academy of Sciences* 1337(1).

Kharas, H. 2017. The Unprecedented Expansion of the Global Middle Class: An Update. *Brookings Global Economy & Development Working Paper* 100. Brookings Institution. https://www.brookings.edu/wp-content/uploads/2017/02/global_20170228_global-middle-class.pdf.

Kharas, H. and K. Hamel. 2018. *A Global Tipping Point: Half the World Is Now Middle Class or Wealthier*. Brookings Institution. https://www.brookings.edu/blog/future-development/2018/09/27/a-global-tipping-point-half-the-world-is-now-middle-class-or-wealthier/.

Klick, J. and T. Stratmann. 2008. Do Spa Visits Improve Health: Evidence from German Micro Data. *Eastern Economic Journal* 34.

Koch, S., T. Kunz, S. Lykou, and R. Cruz. 2014. Effects of Dance Movement Therapy and Dance on Health-related Psychological Outcomes: A metaanalysis. *The Arts in Psychotherapy* 41(1).

Kohl, H. W., C. L. Craig, E. V. Lambert, S. Inoue, J. R. Alkandari, G. L. Sonja Kahlmeier, and Lancet Physical Activity Series Working Group. 2012. The Pandemic of Physical Inactivity: Global Action for Public Health. *The Lancet* 380. https://doi.org/10.1016/S0140-6736(12)60898-8.

Korczak, D. J., S. Madigan, and M. Colasanto. 2017. Children's Physical Activity and Depression: a Meta-analysis. *Pediatrics* 139(4). doi: 10.1542/peds.2016–2266.

Lathia, N., G. M. Sandstrom, C. Mascolo, and P. J. Rentfrow. 2017. Happier People Live More Active Lives: Using Smartphones to Link Happiness and Physical Activity. *PLOS One* 12(1).

Lear, S. A. et al. 2017. The Effect of Physical Activity on Mortality and Cardiovascular Disease in 130 000 people from 17 High-income, Middle-income, and Low-income Countries: the PURE study. *The Lancet*. DOI: http://dx.doi.org/10.1016/S0140-6736(17)31634-3.

Li, Y. 2017. *Closing the Mental Health Treatment Gap in [the People's Republic of] China*. https://asialink.unimelb.edu.au/stories/archive/bridging-the-mental-health-treatment-gap-in-china.

Liang, W., W. Guan, C. Li, Y. Li, H. Liang, Y. Zhao, X. Liu, L. Sang, R. Chen, C. Tang, T. Wang, W. Wang, Q. He, Z. Chen, S. Wong, M. Zanin, J. Liu, X. Xu, J. Huang, J. Li, L. Ou, B. Cheng, S. Xiong, Z. Xie, Z. Ni, Y. Hu, L. Liu, H. Shan, C. Lei, Y. Peng, L. Wei, Y. Liu, Y. Hu, P. Peng, J. Wang, J. Liu, Z. Chen, G. Li, Z. Zheng, S. Qiu, J. Luo, C. Ye, S. Zhu, L. Cheng, F. Ye, S. Li, J. Zheng, N. Zhang, N. Zhong, and J. He. 2020. Clinical Characteristics and Outcomes of Hospitalised Patients with COVID-19 Treated in Hubei (epicenter) and outside Hubei (non-epicenter): A Nationwide Analysis of [the People's Republic of] China. *European Respiratory Journal*. In press. https://doi.org/10.1183/13993003.00562-2020.

Liu, S., L. Yang, C. Zhang, Y. Xiang, Z. Liu, S. Hu, and B. Zhang. 2020. Online Mental Health Services in [the People's Republic of] China during the COVID-19 outbreak. *The Lancet Psychiatry* 7(4). https://doi.org/10.1016/S2215-0366(20)30077-8.

Lu, W., E. McKyer, C. Lee, P. Goodson, M. Ory, and S. Wang. 2014. Perceived Barriers to Children's Active Commuting to School: a Systematic Review of Empirical, Methodological and Theoretical Evidence. *International Journal of Behavioral Nutrition & Physical Activity* 11(140). https://doi.org/10.1186/s12966-014-0140-x.

Macfarlane, D. J. and Tomkinson, G. R. 2007. Evolution and Variability in Fitness Test Performance of Asian Children and Adolescents. *Medicine & Sport Science* 50. https://doi.org/10.1159/000101358.

Madjdian, D. S., F. Azupogo, S. J. Osendarp, H. Bras, and I. D. Brouwer. 2018. Socio-cultural and Economic Determinants and Consequences of Adolescent Undernutrition and Micronutrient Deficiencies in LLMICs: A Systematic Narrative Review. *Annals of the New York Academy of Sciences* 1416(1).

Maghsoudi, Z., R. Ghiasvand, and A. Salehi-Abargouei. 2016. Empirically Derived Dietary Patterns and Incident type 2 diabetes mellitus: A Systematic Review and Meta-analysis on Prospective Observational Studies. *Public Health Nutrition* 19(2).

Magyar, J. L., and C. L. M. Keyes. 2019. *Defining, Measuring, and Applying Subjective Well-being.* In *Positive Psychological Assessment: A Handbook of Models and Measures* edited by M. W. Gallagher and S. J. Lopez. American Psychological Association. https://doi.org/10.1037/0000138-025.

Maher, C. A., M. Toohey, and M. Ferguson. 2016. Physical Activity Predicts Quality of Life and Happiness in Children and Adolescents with Cerebral Palsy. *Disability and Rehabilitation* 38(9).

Maruyama, T. Forthcoming. Enriching the Lives of Seniors in Japan—Ikigai Healthy Ageing Policy. In C. Goh, G. Bodeker, and K. Kariippanon, eds. *Healthy Ageing in Asia.* Taylor & Francis.

Mayo Clinic. 2020. Meditation: A Simple, Fast Way to Reduce Stress. https://www.mayoclinic.org/tests-procedures/meditation/in-depth/meditation/art-20045858.

Miller, R. and P. Blair. 2009. *Input-Output Analysis: Foundations and Extensions*. Oxford: Cambridge University Press.

Mintz, L. 2020. Coronavirus Recovery: How long does it take, and am I immune after having Covid-19? *The Telegraph*. https://www.telegraph.co.uk/health-fitness/body/coronavirus-recovery-qa-long-does-take-immune-having-covid-19/.

Morning Consult. 2020. *How the Coronavirus Outbreak is Impacting Public Opinion*. https://morningconsult.com/form/coronavirus-outbreak-tracker/.

Mozaffarian, D., S. Angell, T. Lang, and J. Rivera. 2018. Role of Government Policy in Nutrition – Barriers to and Opportunities for Healthier Eating. *BMJ* 361. https://doi.org/10.1136/bmj.k2426.

Narici, M., G. De Vito, M. Franchi, A. Paoli, T. Moro, G. Marcolin, B. Grassi, G. Baldassarre, L. Zuccarelli, G. Biolo, F. G. di Girolamo, N. Fiotti, F. Dela, P. Greenhaff, and C. Maganari. 2020. Impact of Sedentarism due to the COVID-19 Home Confinement on Neuromuscular, Cardiovascular and Metabolic Health: Physiological and Pathophysiological Implications and Recommendations for Physical and Nutritional Countermeasures. *European Journal of Sport Science*. https://doi.org/10.1080/17461391.2020.1761076.

National Public Radio. 2020. *Most Americans say U.S. "Doing Enough" to prevent coronavirus spread*. https://www.npr.org/sections/health-shots/2020/02/04/802387025/poll-most-americans-say-u-s-doing-enough-to-prevent-coronavirus-spread.

Ndanuko, R. N., L. C. Tapsell, K. E. Charlton, E. P. Neale, and M. J. Batterham. 2016. Dietary Patterns and Blood Pressure in Adults: A Systematic Review and Meta-Analysis of Randomized Controlled Trials. *Advances in Nutrition* 7(1).

NDTV. 2018. China's 'Dancing Aunties' Take Over Public Places in Jitterbug Craze. https://www.ndtv.com/offbeat/chinas-dancing-aunties-take-over-public-places-in-jitterbug-craze-1927165.

Nidich, S., R. J. Nidich, J. Salerno, B. Hadfield, and C. Elder. 2015. Stress Reduction with the Transcendental Meditation Program in Caregivers: A Pilot Study. *International Archives of Nursing and Health Care* 1(2).

Niles, B. L., D. L. Mori, C. P. Polizzi, A. P. Kaiser, A. M. Ledoux, and C. Wang. 2016. Feasibility, Qualitative Findings and Satisfaction of a Brief Tai Chi mind–body Programme for Veterans with Post-traumatic Stress Symptoms. *BMJ Open* 6(11).

Norris, R., D. Carroll, and R. Cochrane. 1992. The Effects of Physical Activity and Exercise Training on Psychological Stress and Well-being in an Adolescent Population. *Journal of Psychosomatic Research* 36(1).

Office for National Statistics. 2020. *Personal and Economic Well-being in Great Britain.* https://www.ons.gov.uk/peoplepopulationandcommunity/wellbeing/bulletins/personalandeconomicwellbeingintheuk/may2020.

Panchal, N., R. Kamal, K. Orgera, C. Cox, R. Garfield, L. Hamel, C. Muñana, and P. Chidambaram. 2020. *The Implications of COVID-19 for Mental Health and Substance Use.* https://www.kff.org/coronavirus-covid-19/issue-brief/the-implications-of-covid-19-for-mental-health-and-substance-use/.

Patel, V., S. Saxena, C. Lund, G. Thornicroft, F. Baingana, P. Bolton, D. Chisholm, P. Collins, J. Cooper, J. Eaton, H. Herrman, M. Herzallah, Y. Huang, M. Jordans, A. Kleinman, M. Medina-Mora, E. Morgan, U. Niaz, O. Omigbodun, M. Prince, A. Rahman, B. Saraceno, B. Sarkar, M. De Silva, I. Singh, D. Stein, C. Sunkel, and J. UnÜtzer. 2018. Lancet Commission on Global Mental Health and Sustainable Development. *The Lancet* 392(10157).

Pedersen, B. K. and B. Saltin. 2015. Exercise as Medicine— Evidence for Prescribing Exercise as Therapy in 26 Different Chronic Diseases. *Scandinavian Journal of Medicine & Science in Sports* 25(S3). https://doi.org/10.1111/sms.12581.

Pierce, M., H. Hope, T. Ford, S. Hatch, M. Hotopf, and A. John. 2020. *Mental Health Before and During the COVID-19 Pandemic: A Longitudinal Probability Sample Survey of the UK Population.* DOI:https://doi.org/10.1016/S2215-0366(20)30308-4.

Pinto-Sanchez, M. I., A. Ford, C. Avila, E. Verdu, S. Collins, D. Morgan, P. Moayyedi, and P. Bercik. 2015. Anxiety and Depression Increase in a Stepwise Manner in Parallel With Multiple FGIDs and Symptom Severity and Frequency. *The American Journal of Gastroenterology* 110(7).

Powell, K. E., A. E. Paluch, and S. N. Blair. 2011. Physical activity for health: What kind? How much? How intense? On top of what? *Annual Review of Public Health* 32(1). https://doi.org/10.1146/annurev-publhealth-031210-101151.

Pryce-Jones, J. 2010. *Happiness at Work: Maximizing Your Psychological Capital for Success.* Chichester, United Kingdom: John Wiley & Sons Ltd.

Puerto Valencia, L. M., A. Weber, H. Spegel, R. Bögle, A. Selmani, S. Heinze, and C. Herr. 2019. Yoga in the Workplace and Health Outcomes: A Systematic Review. *Occupational Medicine* 69(3). doi:10.1093/occmed/kqz033.

Rees, B., F. Travis, D. Shapiro, and R. Chant. 2014. Significant Reductions in Posttraumatic Stress Symptoms in Congolese Refugees Within 10 days of Transcendental Meditation Practice. *Journal of Traumatic Stress* 27.

Republic of Korea Ministry of Culture, Sports, & Tourism. 2017. 국민생활체육참여실태조사 2017 National Sports Participation Survey 2017. https://www.sports.re.kr/front/board/boardFileUseDown.do?board_seq=74&con_seq=2848&file_seq=1606.

Richards, J., X. Jiang, P. Kelly, J. Chau, A. Bauman, and D. Ding. 2015. Don't Worry, be Happy: cross-sectional associations between physical activity and happiness in 15 European countries. *BMC Public Health* 15(53).

Ritter, M. and K. G. Lowe. 1996. The Effectiveness of Dance/Movement Therapy. *The Arts in Psychotherapy* 23(3).

Roscoe, L. J. 2009. Wellness: A Review of Theory and Measurement for Counselors. *Journal of Counselling and Development* 87(2).

Rossi, R., V. Socci, D. Talevi, S. Mensi, C. Niolu, F. Pacitti, A. Di Marco, A. Rossi, A. Siracusano, and G. Di Lorenzo. 2020. COVID-19 Pandemic and Lockdown Measures Impact on Mental Health among the General Population in Italy. *Frontiers in Psychiatry*. https://www.frontiersin.org/articles/10.3389/fpsyt.2020.00790/full.

Schwingshackl, L., G. Hoffmann, A.-M. Lampousi, S. Knüppel, K. Iqbal, C. Schwedhelm, and H. Boeing. 2017. Food groups and Risk of Type 2 Diabetes Mellitus: A Systematic Review and Meta-analysis of Prospective Studies. *European Journal of Epidemiology* 32(5).

Schwingshackl, L., M. Neuenschwander, G. Hoffmann, A. E. Buyken, and S. Schlesinger. 2019. Dietary Sugars and Cardiometabolic Risk Factors: A Network Meta-analysis on Isocaloric Substitution Interventions. *The American Journal of Clinical Nutrition* 111(1).

Seligman, M. E., A. C. Parks, and T. Steen. 2004. A Balanced Psychology and a Full Life. *Philosophical Transactions of the Royal Society of London. Series B, Biological Sciences* 359(1449).

Shi, L., L. Zheng-An, J. Que, X. Huang, L. Liu, M. Ran, Y. Gong, K. Yuan, W. Yan, Y. Sun, J. Shi, Y. Bao, and L. Lu. 2020. Prevalence of and Risk Factors Associated with Mental Health Symptoms among the General Population in [the People's Republic of] China during the Coronavirus Disease 2019 Pandemic. *JAMA Network Open* 3(7). doi:10.1001/jamanetworkopen.2020.14053.

Sievert, K., M. Lawrence, A. Naika, and P. Baker. 2019. Processed Foods and Nutrition Transition in the Pacific: Regional Trends, Patterns and Food System Drivers. *Nutrients* 11(6).

Sims, J., K. Hill, S. Davidson, J. Gunn, and N. Huang. 2006. Exploring the Feasibility of a Community-based Strength Training Program for Older People with Depressive Symptoms and its Impact on Depressive Symptoms. *BMC Geriatrics* 6(18).

Stiglitz, J., A. Sen, and J.-P. Fitoussi. 2009. *Report by the Commission on the Measurement of Economic Performance and Social Progress.* Commission on the Measurement of Economic Performance and Social Progress.

Straatmann, V. S., A. J. Oliveira, M. Rostila, and C. S. Lopes. 2016. Changes in Physical Activity and Screen Time Related to Psychological Well-being in Early Adolescence: Findings from Longitudinal Study. *BMC Public Health* 16(977).

Suterwala, A. M., C. D. Rethorst, T. J. Carmody, T. L. Greer, B. D. Grannemann, M. Jha, and M. H. Trivedi. 2016. Affect Following First Exercise Session as a Predictor of Treatment Response in Depression. *The Journal of Clinical Psychiatry* 77(8). doi: 10.4088/JCP.15m10104.

Tan, B., N. Chew, G. Lee, M. Jing, Y. Goh, L. Yeo, K. Zhang, H. Chin, A. Ahmad, F. Khan, G. Shanmugam, B. Chan, S. Sunny, B. Chandra, J. Ong, P. Paliwal, L. Wong, R. Sagayanathan, J. Chen, A. Ng, H. Teoh, C. Ho, R. Ho, and V. Sharma. 2020. Psychological Impact of the COVID-19 Pandemic on Health Care Workers in Singapore. *Annals of Internal Medicine*. https://doi.org/10.7326/M20-1083.

The Lancet. 2019. Globally, One in Five Deaths are Associated with Poor Diet. *ScienceDaily.* www.sciencedaily.com/releases/2019/04/190403193702.htm.

Tomkinson, G. R., Lang, J. J., and M. S. Tremblay. 2019. Temporal Trends in the Cardiorespiratory Fitness of Children and Adolescents Representing 19 High-income and Upper Middle-income Countries between 1981 and 2014. *British Journal of Sports Medicine* 53(8). https://doi.org/10.1136/bjsports-2017-097982.

Tomkinson, G., D. Macfarlane, S. Noi, D. Kim, Z. Wang, Zhengzhen, and R. Hong. 2012. Temporal Changes in Long-distance Running Performance of Asian Children between 1964 and 2009. *Sports Medicine* 42(4). https://doi.org/10.2165/11599160-000000000-00000.

Tomljenović, H., D. Begić, and Z. Maštrović. 2016. Changes in Trait Brainwave Power and Coherence, State and Trait Anxiety after Three-month Transcendental Meditation (TM) Practice. *Psychiatria Danubina* 28(1).

Trivedi, M. H., T. L. Greer, T. S. Church, T. J. Carmody, B. D. Grannemann, D. I. Galper, A. L. Dunn, C. P. Earnest, P. Sunderajan, S. S. Henley, and S. N. Blair. 2011. Exercise as an Augmentation Treatment for Nonremitted Major Depressive Disorder: A Randomized, Parallel Dose Comparison. *The Journal of Clinical Psychiatry* 72(5). doi:10.4088/JCP.10m06743.

Tyson, P. 2001. The Hippocratic Oath Today. *PBS.* https://www.pbs.org/wgbh/nova/article/hippocratic-oath-today/.

Uddin, R., S. Mandic, and A. Khan. 2019. Active Commuting to and from School among 106,605 Adolescents in 27 Asia-Pacific Countries. *Journal of Transport & Health* 15. https://doi.org/10.1016/j.jth.2019.100637.

United Nations. 2018. *World Urbanization Prospects: The 2018 Revision—Key Facts*. https://esa.un.org/unpd/wup/Publications/Files/WUP2018-KeyFacts.pdf.

———. 2019. World Population Prospects 2019. https://population.un.org/wpp/ (accessed 15 January 2020).

———. 2020. *Policy Brief: COVID-19 and the Need for Action on Mental Health*. https://unsdg.un.org/resources/policy-brief-covid-19-and-need-action-mental-health.

United Nations World Tourism Organization (UNWTO). 2020. *Impact of COVID-19 on Global Tourism Made Clear as UNWTO Counts the Cost of Standstill*. https://www.unwto.org/news/impact-of-covid-19-on-global-tourism-made-clear-as-unwto-counts-the-cost-of-standstill.

Verghese, J., R. B. Lipton, M. J. Katz, M. Katz, C. Hall, C. Derby, G. Kuslamsky, A. Ambrose, M. Sliwinski, and H. Buschke. 2003. Leisure Activities and the Risk of Dementia in the Elderly. *The New England Journal of Medicine* 348(25). doi:10.1056/NEJMoa022252.

Wang, D., B. Hu, C. Hu, F. Zhu, X. Liu, J. Zhang, B. Wang, H. Xiang, Z. Cheng, Y. Xiong, Y. Zhao, Y. Li, X. Wang, and Z. Peng. 2020. Clinical Characteristics of 138 Hospitalized Patients with 2019 Novel Coronavirus–Infected pneumonia in Wuhan, [People's Republic of] China. *Journal of the American Medical Association*. 323. doi:10.1001/jama.2020.1585 pmid:32031570.

World Health Organization (WHO). 1948. *Constitution of World Health Organization: Principles*. https://www.who.int/about/mission/en/.

———. 2005. *Preventing Chronic Diseases: A Vital Investment – Misunderstanding #4*. https://www.who.int/chp/chronic_disease_report/part1/en/index11.html.

———. 2006. *Health Promotion Glossary Update*. WHO.

———. 2010. *Global Recommendations on Physical Activity for Health*. WHO.

———. 2016. Fiscal Policies for Diet and Prevention of Noncommunicable Diseases. *Technical Meeting Report (5–6 May 2015, Geneva, Switzerland)*. WHO.

———. 2018a. Investing in noncommunicable disease control generates major financial and health gains. *WHO News Release*. https://www.who.int/news-room/detail/16-05-2018-investing-in-noncommunicable-disease-control-generates-major-financial-and-health-gains.

———. 2018b. *Fact Sheet: Noncommunicable diseases*. http://www.who.int/en/news-room/fact-sheets/detail/noncommunicable-diseases.

——. 2019. *Sanitation Fact Sheet*. 14 June. https://www.who.int/
    news-room/fact-sheets/detail/sanitation.

——. 2020a. *Coronavirus disease (COVID-19) Advice for the Public:
    Myth Busters*. https://www.who.int/emergencies/diseases/
    novel-coronavirus-2019/advice-for-public/myth-busters.

——. 2020b. Global Health Observatory Data Repository. https://apps.
    who.int/gho/data/view.main.HWF11v (accessed 6 July 2020).

Wu, D., T. Shu, X. Yang, J. Song, M. Zhang, C. Yao, W. Liu, M. Huang,
    Y. Yu, Q. Yang, T. Zhu, J. Xu, J. Mu, Y. Wang, H. Wang, T. Tang,
    Y. Ren, Y. Wu, S. Lin, Y. Qiu, D. Zhang, Y. Shang, and X. Zhou.
    2020. Plasma Metabolomic and Lipidomic Alterations
    Associated with COVID-19. *National Science Review*.
    https://doi.org/10.1093/nsr/nwaa086.

Xiang, M., Z. Zhang, and K. Kuwahara. 2020. Impact of COVID-19
    on Children and Adolescents' Lifestyle Behavior Larger
    than Expected. *Elsevier Public Health Emergency Collection*.
    doi:10.1016/j.pcad.2020.04.013.

Xiao, H., Y. Zhang, D. Kong, S. Li, and N. Yang. 2020. The Effects
    of Social Support on Sleep Quality of Medical Staff Treating
    Patients with Coronavirus Disease 2019 (COVID-19) in
    January and February 2020 in [the People's Republic of] China.
    Medical Science Monitor. 26:e923549.

Yang, J., Y. Zheng, X. Gou, K. Pu, Z. Chen, Q. Guo, R. Ji, H. Wang,
    Y. Wang, and Y. Zhou. 2020. Prevalence of Comorbidities in the
    Novel Wuhan Coronavirus (COVID-19) Infection: A Systematic
    Review and Meta-analysis. *International Journal of Infectious
    Diseases* 94. https://www.sciencedirect.com/science/article/
    pii/S1201971220301363.

Yates, M. 2018. Out of the Shadows: Mental Health in Asia Pacific.
    Perspectives from Emerging Markets. https://social.
    eyeforpharma.com/column/out-shadows-mental-health-asia-
    pacific.

Yoshimura, M., E. Kurokawa, T. Noda, Y. Tanaka, K. Hineno,
    Y. Kawai, and M. Dillbeck. 2015. Disaster Relief for the
    Japanese Earthquake–Tsunami of 2011: Stress Reduction
    through the Transcendental Meditation Technique.
    Psychological Reports 117(1). doi:10.2466/02.13.PR0.117c11z6.

Zandifar, A. and R. Badrfam. 2020. Iranian Mental Health during
    the COVID-19 epidemic. *Asian Journal of Psychiatry* 51.
    https://doi.org/10.1016/j.ajp.2020.101990.

Zhang, Z. and W. Chen. 2019. A Systematic Review of Measures
    for Psychological Well-being in Physical Activity Studies
    and Identification of Critical Issues. *Journal of Affective
    Disorders* 256.

Zhang, C., L. Yang, S. Liu, S. Ma, Y. Wang, Z. Cai, H. Du, R. Li,
    L. Kang, J. Zhang, Z. Li, and B. Zhang. 2020. Survey of
    Insomnia and Related Social Psychological Factors among
    Medical Staff Involved in the 2019 Novel Coronavirus Disease
    Outbreak. *Frontiers of Psychiatry* 11. https://www.frontiersin.
    org/articles/10.3389/fpsyt.2020.00306/full.

3

ECONOMIC TRENDS AND PROSPECTS IN DEVELOPING ASIA

Central Asia

The COVID-19 pandemic has weakened growth prospects in Central Asia from projections made in *Asian Development Outlook 2020*, where a grimmer economic outlook prevails in 2020 for all countries and in 2021 for several, including Kazakhstan, the subregion's largest economy. Inflation projections are revised upward, reflecting supply-side constraints from lockdown and other restrictive measures, as well as currency depreciation in some countries. The revised forecast for the weighted average current account deficit in the subregion is wider for both 2020 and 2021.

Subregional assessment and prospects

As the COVID-19 pandemic worsens, 2020 growth projections for Central Asia are progressively revised down from 2.8% growth in *ADO 2020* and 0.5% contraction in the June *ADO Supplement* to 2.1% contraction in this *Update* (Figure 3.1.1). Growth projections for 2021 are also reduced, from 4.2% in *ADO 2020* and the *Supplement* to 3.9%. Weakness in the first half of this year prompts lower 2020 growth projections for every economy in the subregion, and 2021 growth projections are revised down for Armenia, Azerbaijan, Kazakhstan, and the Kyrgyz Republic.

Looking first at hydrocarbon exporters, the projection for Kazakhstan in 2020 is lowered from 1.8% growth in *ADO 2020* to 3.2% contraction, the economy having shrunk at an annual rate of 1.8% in the first half of the year, mainly from a decline in services as strict quarantine measures returned in July. The growth forecast for 2021 is reduced from 3.6% to 2.8%. Azerbaijan's projection for 2020 is cut from marginal 0.5% growth to 4.3% contraction after lockdowns and lower oil prices brought 2.7% shrinkage in the first half of the year. Its 2021 growth forecast is revised down from 1.5% to 1.2%. The Turkmenistan growth forecast for 2020 is nearly halved, from 6.0% to 3.2%, the government having reported growth slowing in the first half of the year from 6.2% a year earlier to 5.9%, and with restrictive policies expected to bite harder later in the year.

Figure 3.1.1 GDP growth, Central Asia

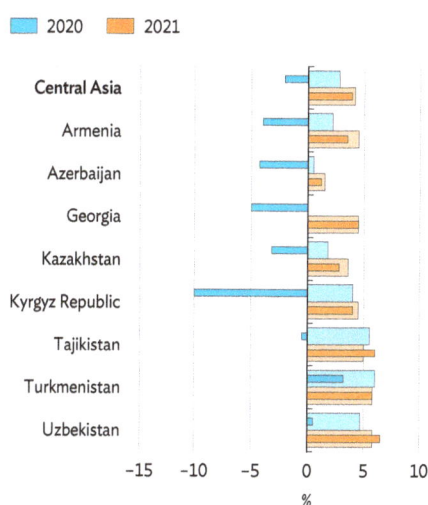

Note: Lighter colored bars are *ADO 2020* forecasts.
Source: *Asian Development Outlook* database.

The subregional assessment and prospects were written by Kenji Takamiya. Kazakhstan was written by Genadiy Rau, and the other economies by Muhammadi Boboev, Grigor Gyurjyan, Jennet Hojanazarova, George Luarsabishvili, Gulkayr Tentieva, Nail Valiyev, and Begzod Djalilov. All authors are in Central and West Asia Department of ADB.

In Uzbekistan, projected growth for 2020 is slashed from 4.7% to 0.5% after first-half expansion slowed from 6.0% in 2019 to 0.2%, and after investment, a major growth driver before the pandemic, shrank by 12.8%.

Turning to hydrocarbon importers, the 2020 projection for Armenia is slashed from 2.2% growth to 4.0% contraction, with economic activity reversing from 7.0% expansion in the first half of 2019 to 5.7% contraction a year later and weakness expected to continue for the rest of this year. The 2021 growth forecast is adjusted downward from 4.5% to 3.5%. For Georgia, projected zero growth in 2020 is revised down to 5.0% contraction as broadly lower output is estimated to have shrunk the economy by 5.8% in the first half of the year, reversing 4.8% growth in the same period of 2019. Georgia's 4.5% growth forecast for 2021 is unchanged from *ADO 2020*. In the Kyrgyz Republic, the projection is slashed from 4.0% growth to 10.0% contraction in 2020 after a 5.3% decline in the first half of the year reversed 6.4% growth in 2019, and with the pandemic expected to worsen in the coming months. The growth forecast for 2021 is trimmed from 4.5% to 4.0%. Tajikistan's projection for 2020 is revised down from 5.5% growth to 0.5% contraction after the pandemic and its consequences more than halved expansion in the first half of this year, from 7.5% a year earlier to 3.5%. The revised forecast for 2021 is, at 6.0%, higher than 5.0% in *ADO 2020* but lower than 7.0% in the June *Supplement*.

Projected inflation in the subregion as a whole is revised up for 2020 from 7.6% in *ADO 2020* and 8.0% in the June *Supplement* to 8.3% in this *Update*, and for 2021 from 6.3% in *ADO 2020* to 6.6%. Relative to *ADO 2020*, inflation projections are higher in 2020 for Azerbaijan, Georgia, Kazakhstan, the Kyrgyz Republic, and Tajikistan, and in 2021 for Georgia, Kazakhstan, the Kyrgyz Republic, and Tajikistan (Figure 3.1.2). One main reason is supply-side constraints from lockdown and other restrictive policies, which outweigh effects of lower demand. Another is currency depreciation in some countries.

The projected weighted average current account deficit for the subregion in 2020 is revised up from the equivalent of 3.8% of GDP in *ADO 2020* to 6.3% in this *Update*, and in 2021 from 2.4% to 3.9% (Figure 3.1.3). This reflects forecasts for larger deficits in Georgia, Tajikistan, and Uzbekistan in both years, and in the Kyrgyz Republic in 2020 and Kazakhstan in 2021. In Azerbaijan, a deficit is now forecast for 2020 and a smaller surplus for 2021. These revisions reflect in part lower remittances but mainly sluggish exports of goods and services because of some oil production cuts and declining tourism.

Figure 3.1.2 Inflation, Central Asia

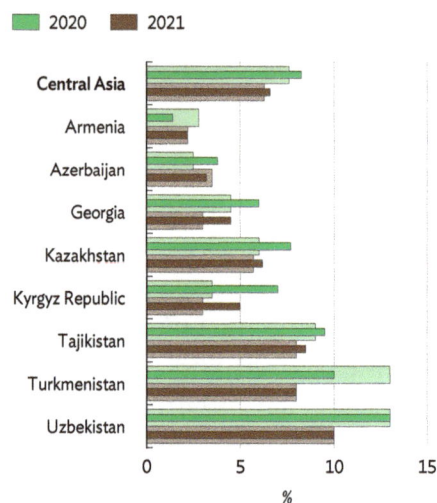

Note: Lighter colored bars are *ADO 2020* forecasts.
Source: *Asian Development Outlook* database.

Figure 3.1.3 Current account balance, Central Asia

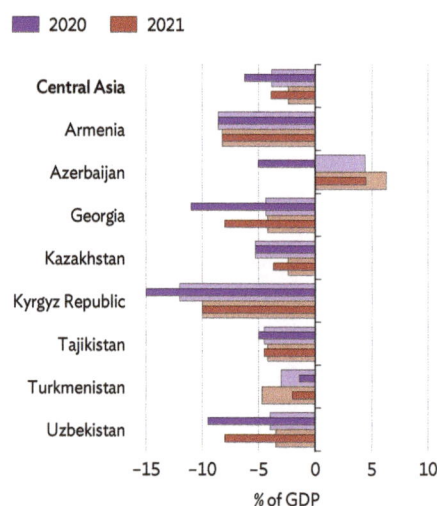

Note: Lighter colored bars are *ADO 2020* forecasts.
Source: *Asian Development Outlook* database.

Kazakhstan

Stringent measures to contain COVID-19 severely hurt services, triggering contraction in the first half of 2020 despite moderate gains in industry and agriculture. With weaker net exports and stalling private consumption and investment, despite sizable fiscal stimulus, this *Update* projects marked GDP contraction in 2020 and some recovery in 2021. As currency depreciation boosts prices despite the contraction, this *Update* revises up projections for inflation in 2020 and 2021 from *ADO 2020*. Despite some oil price recovery, the current account deficit is still seen widening in 2020 but narrowing in 2021 with further recovery in commodity prices and output.

Updated assessment

Reflecting the impact of COVID-19, the economy contracted at an annual rate of 1.8% in the first half of 2020, reversing 4.1% growth in the same period of last year (Figure 3.1.4). Services declined by 5.6% as strict quarantine measures cut transportation by 14.6% and trade by 10.6%. Industry grew by 3.1% as import substitution programs helped manufacturing expand by 4.8%. Mining rose by 2.2% as oil and gas production increased by 1.6% despite weaker oil prices, but only because early output gains offset production cuts in May and June agreed with the Organization of the Petroleum Exporting Countries and other major oil producers (OPEC+). Agriculture expanded by 2.4% as livestock production grew by 2.5% and crops by 0.5%. Growth in construction remained strong at 11.2%, supported by state housing and infrastructure programs.

A massive crisis-induced economic support program estimated to equal 9% of GDP mitigated economic contraction by targeting infrastructure, manufacturing, and small and medium-sized enterprises while enhancing social protection. In the first quarter of 2020, the unemployment rate remained historically low at 4.8%, but pandemic-induced quarantine measures caused 45.7% of the labor force to be temporarily suspended or laid off in March and April (Figure 3.1.5).

Demand-side data, available for only the first quarter of 2020, show consumption growth slowing somewhat from 4.7% in the first quarter of 2019 to 3.3% as private consumption grew by only 1.0% but public consumption surged by 14.2%. Despite public infrastructure spending, overall investment fell by 5.0%, with lower spending on machinery and equipment. Imports declined faster than exports. As the government declared a state of emergency from mid-March to mid-May, about 4.5 million people who lost their incomes under pandemic-containment restrictions received a support payment equal to one or two monthly minimum wages, depending on when they applied, which is believed to have bolstered consumption in the second quarter of 2020.

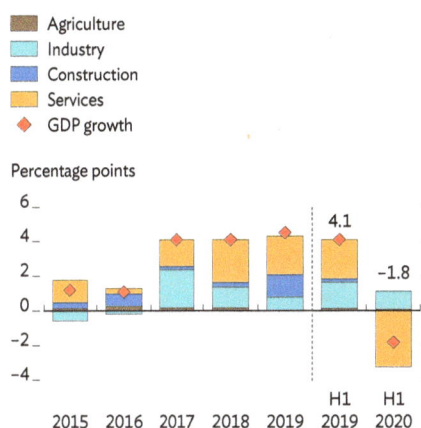

Figure 3.1.4 Supply-side contributions to growth

Agriculture
Industry
Construction
Services
GDP growth

Percentage points

GDP = gross domestic product, H1 = first half.
Source: Republic of Kazakhstan. Ministry of National Economy. Committee on Statistics.

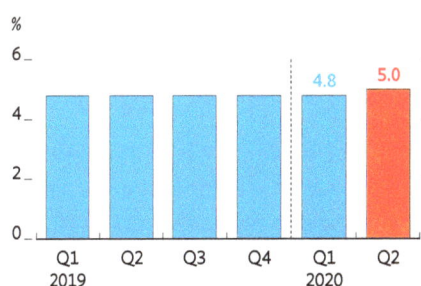

Figure 3.1.5 Unemployment rate

Q = quarter.
Source: Republic of Kazakhstan. Ministry of National Economy. Committee on Statistics.

Average inflation in the first 7 months of 2020 accelerated from 5.1% in the same period a year earlier to 6.5%, reflecting increases of 10.1% for food, 5.4% for other goods, and 3.0% for services (Figure 3.1.6). Many staple food items saw double digit price increases, despite government control measures. Disrupted supply chains and notable currency depreciation more than offset weakening consumer demand under the pandemic, raising prices. A shift in the second quarter toward supporting economic activity limited the ability of monetary policy to help contain inflation.

The government substantially revised the state budget in April 2020 to address the adverse effects of COVID-19 and low commodity prices. A crisis-response program boosted expenditure by 9.7% despite a projected 21.3% drop in tax revenue (Figure 3.1.7). Budget transfers from the National Fund of the Republic of Kazakhstan, the sovereign wealth fund, are projected to rise by 76.7% to $10.8 billion to finance most of the higher outlays. In the first 6 months of 2020, budget revenue fell by 10.8% to equal 23.7% of GDP, with value-added tax revenue dropping by 13.0%. Expenditure rose by 23.8% to equal 24.8% of GDP, with increases of 44.8% for health care, 35.5% for education, and 13.9% for social programs, leaving a budget deficit equal to 1.1% of GDP.

The National Bank of Kazakhstan, the central bank, acted repeatedly in the first 7 months of 2020. In March, it temporarily raised the policy rate by 275 basis points to 12.0% to reduce pressure on the currency, which was depreciating on news of a sharp oil price decline and the spread of COVID-19. To stimulate economic activity, it lowered the rate to 9.5% in April, and then to 9.0% in July, reflecting greater coordination with the government's economic development objectives.

Broad money reversed a 6.1% decline in the first half of 2019 to grow by 6.2% in the first half of this year as total credit grew by 0.5% and deposits by 5.7% (Figure 3.1.8). Lending to firms remained stagnant, but consumer credit grew modestly. Foreign currency deposits rose by 5.2% to account for 41.6% of all deposits, while deposits in tenge, the national currency, rose by 6.1%. Official figures from a recently established agency for the regulation and development of financial markets show the share of nonperforming loans rising from 8.1% at the end of 2019 to 9.0% in June 2020.

In the first half of 2020, the tenge fluctuated sharply, the average rate against the US dollar was 6.7% below the average in the same period of 2019 (Figure 3.1.9). The central bank reported net interventions of $1.6 billion to support the currency. The sovereign wealth fund used $5.2 billion in foreign exchange to buy tenge, and in March the government ordered state companies to sell foreign currency revenue on the domestic market.

Figure 3.1.6 Monthly inflation

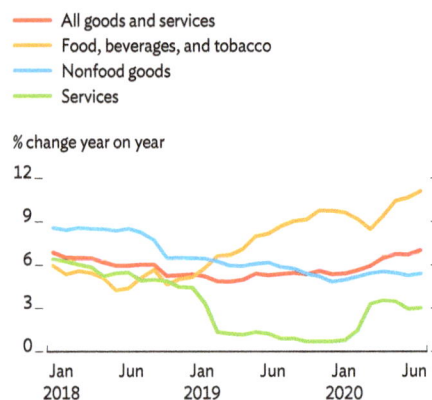

— All goods and services
— Food, beverages, and tobacco
— Nonfood goods
— Services

% change year on year

Source: Republic of Kazakhstan. Ministry of National Economy. Statistics Committee.

Figure 3.1.7 Fiscal indicators

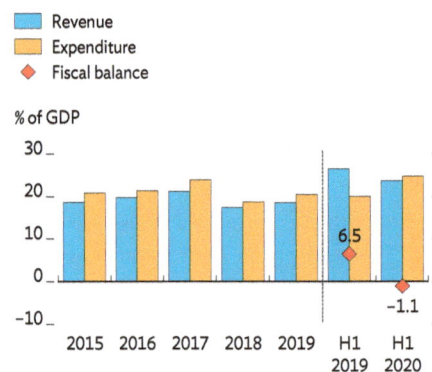

■ Revenue
■ Expenditure
◆ Fiscal balance

% of GDP

GDP = gross domestic product, H1 = first half.
Sources: Ministry of Finance; Ministry of National Economy.

Figure 3.1.8 Broad money

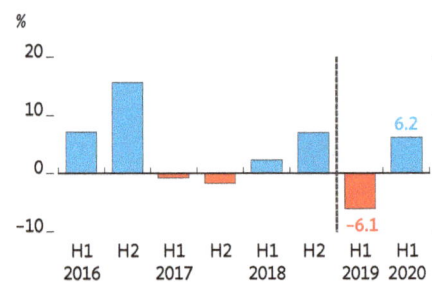

%

H = half.
Note: Broad money growth refers to percent changes from December of previous year.
Source: National Bank of the Republic of Kazakhstan.

Preliminary estimates for the first half of 2020 indicate a sharp fall in profit repatriation by foreign direct investors. This contributed to a current account surplus of $2.1 billion, equal to 1.2% of GDP, despite the merchandise trade surplus shrinking by 12.3%. Merchandise exports contracted by 10.7% as lower prices cut the value of oil and gas exports by 8.5%. Merchandise imports shrank by 9.7%, and imports of capital goods by 15.8%. With extractive industries becoming less attractive, foreign direct investment plunged by 37.5% to $1.5 billion.

Gross foreign exchange reserves reached $32.9 billion in June 2020, reflecting a higher valuation for gold, which constitutes 65.5% of holdings, and providing cover for 8.3 months of imports (Figure 3.1.10). External debt was $152.7 billion, equal to 83.2% of GDP. Intercompany debt, primarily for oil and gas projects, declined to $97.3 billion, or 53.0% of GDP, of which $18.4 billion comes due in 2020. Public sector external debt decreased to $29.4 billion, or 16.0% of GDP, of which $3.0 billion is due in 2020. In the first half of 2020, net receipts to the sovereign wealth fund were 85% above those in the same period of 2019, as a sixfold rise in investment income more than offset a 31.2% decline in tax revenue from oil companies and a substantial decline in privatization earnings. However, a 72.0% rise in budget transfers during this period reduced sovereign wealth fund assets to an estimated $57.7 billion.

Prospects

Kazakhstan reintroduced strict social distancing and quarantine measures in early July 2020 and maintained them until mid-August to reduce the spread of COVID-19. The health crisis and efforts to contain it have dampened growth prospects for 2020 and 2021.

On the supply side, quarantine measures will continue to have their greatest adverse impact on services, particularly catering, transportation, and hospitality. Growth prospects for mining remain limited under continued participation in the OPEC+ agreement, weak oil prices, and a slowdown for projects to expand the Tengiz and Kashagan oil fields. However, government support programs are expected to boost manufacturing and agriculture.

On the demand side, consumption is projected to grow by 1.1% in 2020 solely on social support measures and rising public expenditure. In 2021, consumption growth is forecast to accelerate to 1.4% as private consumption recovers. Despite substantial government support for infrastructure development, total investment is projected to slow by 2.9%, more than earlier forecast because of the dampening effect on foreign direct investment from a global recession deeper than foreseen. Weak exports are projected to push net exports

Figure 3.1.9 Exchange rates

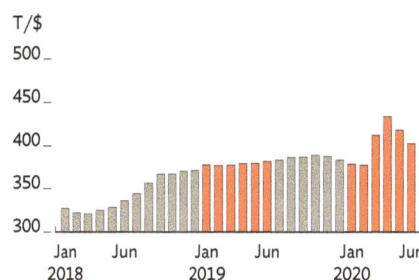

Source: Republic of Kazakhstan. Ministry of National Economy. Statistics Committee.

Figure 3.1.10 Reserves and assets

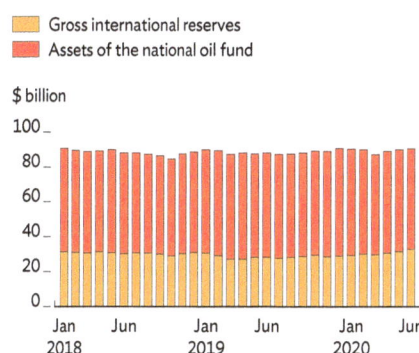

Source: National Bank of the Republic of Kazakhstan.

of goods and services into negative territory, as in 2016. In view of the impact of policies to contain the pandemic, this *Update* forecasts 3.2% contraction in 2020, followed by gradual recovery in 2021.

Inflationary pressure has intensified from currency depreciation and expansionary fiscal and monetary policy, though it should ease under announced price controls for staple foods and continued restraint on utility prices, as well as declining real incomes and economic contraction. Accordingly, this *Update* raises projections for inflation in both years from *ADO 2020*, though inflation should diminish in 2021 as the pandemic recedes.

After substantial revision of the 2020 state budget in April, expenditure is now projected to equal 24.0% of GDP, revised up from 20.6% in *ADO 2020*. The revenue projection is raised from 17.1% of GDP to 19.4%, reflecting a sharp rise in planned transfers from the sovereign wealth fund, which are now forecast to provide 34.0% of budget receipts. Thus, the budget deficit projection is widened from 3.5% of GDP to 4.6%, or from 8.7% to 11.2% excluding petroleum revenue. The non-oil deficit projected for 2021 rises from 8.2% of GDP to 10.5% in view of the government's continued social support and countercyclical economic programs. Public debt is now forecast to reach the equivalent of 27.0% of GDP at the end of 2020 and 29.0% at the end of 2021.

The merchandise trade surplus projection is cut to $6.7 billion for 2020, as exports will be slashed by curtailed oil export volume under the OPEC+ agreement on production. The forecast for imports is also reduced, reflecting lower domestic income and capital expenditure. The trade surplus is expected to recover in 2021 to $13.1 billion on higher oil prices and production. With deficits in services and primary income expected to persist, this *Update* maintains the current account deficit forecast for 2020 and expands it for 2021. The outlook for external debt, international reserves, and sovereign wealth fund assets remains unchanged.

Accumulated international reserves will allow the government to stimulate economic activity and thus soften the impact of the pandemic. However, anticipated subsequent waves of COVID-19 pose substantial downside risks to the outlook, as they could trigger major problems in banking, manufacturing, and other areas of the economy.

Table 3.1.1 Selected economic indicators, Kazakhstan (%)

	2019	2020			2021		
		ADO 2020	ADOS	Update	ADO 2020	ADOS	Update
GDP growth	4.5	1.8	-1.2	-3.2	3.6	3.4	2.8
Inflation	5.3	6.0	7.9	7.7	5.7	6.2	6.2
CAB/GDP	-3.6	-5.3	...	-5.3	-2.4	...	-3.7

... = unavailable, ADO = *Asian Development Outlook* (April), ADOS = *ADO Supplement* (June), CAB = current account balance, GDP = gross domestic product.
Source: ADB estimates.

Other economies

Armenia

Under COVID-19, the economy reversed 7.0% growth a year earlier to contract by 5.7% in the first half of this year. Agriculture grew by only 1.8%, with livestock and crops weak. Industry excluding construction fell by 2.0% as declines in manufacturing, electricity, and water supply outweighed gains in mining and quarrying. Lockdown from mid-March to mid-May postponed investment projects, slashing construction by 30.4%. Services contracted by 4.4% almost across the board.

On the demand side, private consumption fell by 9.5%, hurt by economic restrictions, weaker consumer sentiment, and lower incomes and remittances. Public consumption grew by 14.2% as the government raised current expenditure. Investment plunged by 30.7%, reflecting lower inventories and a 19.6% drop in fixed capital formation. The deficit in net exports narrowed further as imports shrank more than exports. With the pandemic expected to persist through 2020, this *Update* projects recession in 2020 and, with modest recovery expected in Armenia's trade partners, positive growth in 2021 but less than forecast in *ADO 2020*.

Fiscal policy has been expansionary in 2020 with higher outlays for health care, social protection, and economic support. To counter COVID-19, the government introduced stimulus equal to 2.3% of GDP. That, along with weak revenue, prompted a higher government projection for the 2020 fiscal deficit, from the equivalent of 2.3% of GDP to 5.6%.

Inflation has been low, with weak demand at home and abroad, low oil prices, and a fairly stable exchange rate. Average annual inflation slowed from 1.9% a year earlier to 0.7% in January–July 2019 as prices rose by 1.3% for services but only 0.3% for food and 0.8% for other goods. In July, inflation was 1.5% year on year, below the central bank's 2.5%–5.5% target and prompting in June a refinancing rate cut of 100 basis points to 4.5%. With inflation in the first 7 months below expectations, this *Update* cuts its forecast for 2020 from *ADO 2020* but keeps its 2021 forecast in anticipation of recovery in domestic demand and commodity prices.

The current account deficit narrowed from the equivalent of 10.4% of GDP in the first quarter of 2019 to 7.5% a year later as smaller deficits in goods, services, and income more than offset a smaller surplus in transfers. Exports of goods fell by 1.0% and imports by 3.6%, narrowing the trade deficit from 14.1% of GDP a year earlier to 12.5%. Global disruption from COVID-19 is expected for the rest of 2020, further weakening trade, remittances, and tourism. However, after reduction of the estimated current account deficit for 2019, this *Update* retains its projections for 2020 and 2021.

Table 3.1.2 Selected economic indicators, Armenia (%)

	2019	2020			2021		
		ADO 2020	ADOS	*Update*	*ADO 2020*	ADOS	*Update*
GDP growth	7.6	2.2	–3.5	–4.0	4.5	3.5	3.5
Inflation	1.4	2.8	1.2	1.4	2.2	2.5	2.2
CAB/GDP	–7.2	–8.6	...	–8.6	–8.2	...	–8.2

... = unavailable, ADO = *Asian Development Outlook* (April), ADOS = *ADO Supplement* (June), CAB = current account balance, GDP = gross domestic product.
Source: ADB estimates.

Azerbaijan

The economy reversed 2.4% growth in the first half of 2019 to contract by 2.7% in the same period of this year, reflecting low oil prices amid the COVID-19 pandemic and lockdowns that lasted from March to May and introduced again in July. The petroleum industry shrank by 2.5%, and the rest of the economy by 2.9%, though fiscal stimulus equal to 4.3% of GDP for health care, social protection, and support to business limited the contraction. A 3.1% decline in industry reflected weak mining as Azerbaijan cut oil production by 4.5% under an agreement with the Organization of the Petroleum Exporting Countries and other major oil producers (OPEC+), though gas output rose by 14.9%. Construction shrank by 14.5% because of the pandemic and a 22.2% cut in public investment. Services fell by 3.0% as tourism-dependent services plunged by half and weak domestic demand curtailed retail trade by 1.9%. Growth in agriculture slowed from 13.0% in the first half of 2019 to 2.2% a year later as drought and the pandemic disrupted crop production.

On the demand side, private consumption reversed 2.4% expansion in the first quarter of 2019 to slip by 0.4% a year later. Overall consumption is expected to drop sharply as mobility restrictions and weakening income persist throughout 2020. With the pandemic and cuts to oil production expected to continue in the coming months, this *Update* forecasts deeper contraction in 2020 than projected in *ADO 2020* and more gradual recovery in 2021 as demand and oil prices revive.

Average inflation in the first half of 2020 rose from 2.5% a year earlier to 3.0%. Food prices climbed by 5.5% as consumers stockpiled and supply tightened, but prices for other goods increased by only 1.3% and for services by 1.0%. In June, the central bank reduced its policy rate by 25 basis points to 7.0%, citing low inflation, while still accepting income-yielding deposits from banks to soak up liquidity and thus contain inflation and avoid downward pressure on the Azerbaijan manat. With food price inflation likely to continue, this *Update* raises the inflation forecast for 2020 while reducing it for 2021 as lockdowns and supply chain disruption end.

The current account surplus narrowed to 6.0% of GDP in the first quarter 2020 and is expected to have become negative in the first half. While slack demand cut imports by 35.0% in the first half of 2020, lower oil prices and production slashed export earnings by 23.0% and the halving of tourism widened the deficit in services. Slowdown in the Russian Federation and Turkey cut remittances, weakening income and transfers. With OPEC+ cuts expected to reduce exports further this year, this *Update* projects the current account dipping into deficit for the first time since 2016 and returning to surplus in 2021 as oil prices and external demand recover.

Table 3.1.3 Selected economic indicators, Azerbaijan (%)

	2019	2020			2021		
		ADO 2020	ADOS	Update	ADO 2020	ADOS	Update
GDP growth	2.2	0.5	−0.1	−4.3	1.5	1.2	1.2
Inflation	2.6	2.5	2.8	3.8	3.5	3.5	3.2
CAB/GDP	9.1	4.4	...	−5.1	6.3	...	4.5

... = unavailable, ADO = Asian Development Outlook (April), ADOS = ADO Supplement (June), CAB = current account balance, GDP = gross domestic product.
Source: ADB estimates.

Georgia

Real GDP reversed 4.8% growth in the first half of 2019 to contract by an estimated 5.8% in the first half of this year. Industry including construction fell by 4.2% year on year, with manufacturing down by 3.5%. Services shrank by 6.8%, with declines of 4.0% in transportation and storage, 6.2% in wholesale and retail trade, and 22.9% in accommodation and food services. Agriculture posted a small gain of 0.3%. The unemployment rate rose by about a percentage point from mid-2019 to 11.9%.

On the demand side, private consumption contracted by 3.3%, while restrictions to contain COVID-19 cut private investment by 1.9%. Public consumption recorded a small decline of 0.9%, and public investment 0.8%, but both are expected to strengthen in the rest of 2020 and support private consumption and investment following the announcement of fiscal stimulus equal to 7.5% of GDP. In view of the adverse effects of COVID-19 on the economy and the investment climate, this *Update* forecasts contraction in 2020 but rebound in 2021 equal to the *ADO 2020* forecast, based on expected recoveries in tourism, other foreign inflows, private consumption, investment, and net exports.

A possible government standstill following parliamentary elections in October could further reduce growth forecasts, as could prolonged disruption of tourism and external demand and supply chains, sharply driving down consumer and business confidence and causing widespread liquidity crunches to recur.

Inflation accelerated from 3.6% in the first half of 2019 to 6.4% a year later, reflecting price increases of 13.6% for food, 4.3% for other goods, and 2.2% for services. Core inflation reached 6.6%, and the producer price index rose by 10.1%. The Georgian lari depreciated by 4.4% year on year in real effective terms as inbound tourism and foreign direct investment plunged, though the National Bank of Georgia, the central bank, intervened to smooth the decline. Despite rising inflation, the central bank cut its policy rate to 8.0% in August 2020 to support economic activity and provide additional liquidity, bank deposits having fallen by 3.2% in the first half of 2020 as savings shrank. With rising producer prices and notable currency depreciation, this *Update* raises inflation forecasts for 2020 and 2021.

The current account deficit nearly doubled in the first quarter of 2020, from a record low equal to 5.9% of GDP a year earlier to 11.0%, as a 29.8% decline in receipts from tourism cut exports of services by 15.6% while service imports fell by only 3.1%. The trade deficit deepened by 11.4% as exports of goods fell by 6.2% while imports rose by 1.2% despite a sharp plunge in vehicle imports for re-export. Current transfers rose by 12.3% even as remittances fell by 4.6% in the first half—26.6% down from the Russian Federation. With sharp declines in net services and income projected for all of 2020, this *Update* sharply raises its projections for current account deficits in 2020 and 2021.

Table 3.1.4 Selected economic indicators, Georgia (%)

	2019	2020			2021		
		ADO 2020	ADOS	Update	ADO 2020	ADOS	Update
GDP growth	5.1	0.0	–5.0	–5.0	4.5	5.0	4.5
Inflation	4.9	4.5	5.0	6.0	3.0	3.5	4.5
CAB/GDP	–5.0	–4.4	...	–11.0	–4.2	...	–8.0

... = unavailable, ADO = Asian Development Outlook (April), ADOS = ADO Supplement (June), CAB = current account balance, GDP = gross domestic product.
Source: ADB estimates.

Kyrgyz Republic

GDP growth at 7.0% in January–July 2019 reversed to contraction by 6.1% in the same period of 2020. The economy is expected to fare even worse in the next 5 months because of the direct health effects of the COVID-19 pandemic and a consequent lockdown and border trade disruption. This *Update* therefore projects that real GDP will contract deeply in 2020, double the projection in the June *ADO Supplement,* as production falls almost across the board. Assuming that growth elsewhere in Central Asia and in the Russian Federation picks up in 2021, the Kyrgyz economy could grow next year by almost as much as forecast in *ADO 2020.*

In the same period, industry plunged from 20.6% growth year on year to contraction by 0.9%. Manufacturing contracted by 0.5%, mining by 4.2%, and construction by 8.9%. In the service sector, wholesale and retail trade shrank by 17.6%, transportation by 30.7%, and hospitality by 44.8%. Agriculture, by contrast, grew by 1.8% as livestock production rose by 1.5%.

Inflation accelerated from an average of 0.1% in the first 7 months of 2019 to 5.7% a year later. The main reason was a 4.9% increase in food prices as border closures disrupted food supply, while prices for other goods fell by 0.8% and prices for services were unchanged from December 2019. The National Bank of the Kyrgyz Republic, the central bank, raised its policy rate by 0.75 percentage points to 5.00% in February 2020 to stem currency depreciation and inflationary pressure. The Kyrgyz som nevertheless depreciated by 13.1%, from Som69.5 to the dollar at the beginning of this year to Som78.2 at the end of August. The central bank is pursuing a managed float, intervening only to smooth excess volatility. To this end, it sold foreign exchange worth $227 million, which is 60% more than its intervention last year. This *Update* projects inflation in 2020 at double the rate projected in *ADO 2020,* slowing in 2021 but still much higher than earlier forecast.

The trade deficit in the first 6 months of 2020 was $656.8 million. Exports are estimated to have grown by 2.4% year on year, mainly on strong exports of higher-priced gold. Imports are observed to have shrunk by 32.2%, notably reflecting lower imports of machinery and equipment, apparel, and sugar. Remittances shrank by over 13% as migrants returned home, most of them having lost their jobs in the Russian Federation. This *Update* projects a larger current account deficit in 2020 than forecast in *ADO 2020* but retains the earlier forecast for a narrower deficit in 2021.

Table 3.1.5 Selected economic indicators, Kyrgyz Republic (%)

	2019	2020			2021		
		ADO 2020	ADOS	Update	ADO 2020	ADOS	Update
GDP growth	4.5	4.0	−5.0	−10.0	4.5	4.0	4.0
Inflation	1.1	3.5	7.0	7.0	3.0	5.0	5.0
CAB/GDP	−11.3	−12.0	...	−15.0	−10.0	...	−10.0

... = unavailable, ADO = Asian Development Outlook (April), ADOS = ADO Supplement (June), CAB = current account balance, GDP = gross domestic product.
Source: ADB estimates.

Tajikistan

Growth slowed from 7.5% in the first half of 2019 to 3.5% in the same period of 2020, reflecting the pandemic and consequent responses, as well as declining remittances, external trade, and foreign direct investment. Expansion in industry moderated from 12.5% to 9.2% as mining contracted by 1.8% and growth in electricity generation decelerated to 3.0%, though manufacturing rose by 14.0%. Unfavorable weather slowed growth in agriculture from 10.8% to 8.2%. With remittances falling by 14.8% in the first half of 2020, services reversed a 0.9% rise in the first half of last year to contract by 4.8%. To mitigate the economic impact of COVID-19, the government approved in March countercyclical assistance equal to 4.5% of GDP, nearly half of it earmarked to support firms affected by the pandemic.

On the demand side, fixed investment fell by 4.6%, but net exports rose by 14.6%. With further constraint on private consumption expected under the continuing pandemic and declining remittances, and with the Rogun electric power project proceeding more slowly than expected, this *Update* forecasts contraction in 2020 but a strong pickup in 2021 as economic activity recovers in trade partners.

Inflation was little changed from an average of 8.7% in the first half of 2019 to 8.4% a year later as moderate credit growth offset the effects of 6.4% currency depreciation, restrictions on food exports by neighboring countries, and seasonal supply shocks. Prices rose by 12.4% for food, 3.9% for other goods, and 5.0% for services, prompting the government to impose price controls on medical supplies and key consumer goods. To support the economy, the National Bank of Tajikistan, the central bank, reduced reserve requirements on 1 April and cut the policy interest rate from 12.75% to 11.75% on 1 May and further to 10.75% on 3 August. Despite weak demand, this *Update* raises inflation forecasts from *ADO 2020* for both 2020 and 2021 in light of salaries and pensions set to rise by 15% in September, a widening fiscal deficit, and greater exchange rate flexibility.

The trade deficit narrowed by 14.6% in the first half of 2020 as higher sales abroad of precious and semiprecious gems and metals sharply raised export growth from 8.0% a year earlier to 14.6%. Imports fell by 3.9% with disruption to trade and supply chains, as well as lower disposable income and slow progress on the Rogun project. In the first half of 2020, Tajikistan received $300.8 million in pandemic-related concessional loans and grants from development partners to help cover financing needs. However, with remittances projected to fall by as much as 35% this year from 2019, this *Update* projects wider current account deficits in 2020 and 2021 than forecast in April.

Table 3.1.6 Selected economic indicators, Tajikistan (%)

	2019	2020			2021		
		ADO 2020	ADOS	Update	ADO 2020	ADOS	Update
GDP growth	7.5	5.5	–3.6	–0.5	5.0	7.0	6.0
Inflation	8.0	9.0	10.0	9.5	8.0	8.5	8.5
CAB/GDP	–2.3	–4.5	...	–5.0	–4.2	...	–4.5

... = unavailable, ADO = Asian Development Outlook (April), ADOS = ADO Supplement (June), CAB = current account balance, GDP = gross domestic product.
Source: ADB estimates.

Turkmenistan

Growth is reported to have slowed from 6.2% in the first half of 2019 to 5.9% in the first half of 2020. Industry is estimated to have been the main source of growth, with hydrocarbon output and processing reportedly stable and with chemicals, textiles, food, and other industries supported by import substitution. Record wheat harvests boosted agriculture, with cotton likely to meet the government's production goals in the second half of the year. Services contracted, however, as government measures imposing stringent travel restrictions and quarantines sharply cut retail and other trade, transport, catering, tourism, and hospitality.

On the demand side, public investment and net exports supported growth whereas weakening household income constrained private consumption. This *Update* reduces the *ADO 2020* growth projection for 2020 but not for 2021.

Supplemented by price controls on selected goods and services, monetary policy continued to focus on controlling inflation by limiting cash in circulation. However, further depreciation on the parallel market reportedly raised prices for food and other goods, as did import cuts and resulting shortages, while the official exchange rate stayed unchanged. With depressed consumption for the rest of this year, this *Update* trims the inflation projection for 2020 from *ADO 2020* while maintaining the forecast for 2021.

Lower gas exports required 2020 state budget revision, and the International Monetary Fund cut its revenue projection from 13.7% of GDP to 11.8%. With government response to the pandemic, outlays are still projected to equal 14.0% of GDP, widening the fiscal deficit to 2.3% of GDP. In 2021, anticipated export recovery is forecast to raise revenue to 12.6% of GDP, narrowing the fiscal deficit to 0.5% of GDP.

The volume of gas exports to the People's Republic of China is estimated to have fallen by 13.7% year-on-year as of July 2020. However, with the gradual easing of trade and transport restrictions and revived natural gas shipments as the economy of the People's Republic of China rebounds, export performance has begun to recover in recent months, and this trend is expected to continue through 2021. In view of this recovery and with stringent controls on imports, particularly in 2020, this *Update* narrows its projections for current account deficits in both years.

Table 3.1.7 Selected economic indicators, Turkmenistan (%)

	2019	2020			2021		
		ADO 2020	ADOS	Update	ADO 2020	ADOS	Update
GDP growth	6.3	6.0	3.2	3.2	5.8	5.8	5.8
Inflation	13.4	13.0	8.0	10.0	8.0	8.0	8.0
CAB/GDP	5.1	-3.0	...	-1.4	-4.7	...	-2.0

... = unavailable, ADO = Asian Development Outlook (April), ADOS = ADO Supplement (June), CAB = current account balance, GDP = gross domestic product.
Source: ADB estimates.

Uzbekistan

The government reported growth falling from 6.0% in the first half of 2019 to 0.2% in the same period of 2020. COVID-19 and weak demand reversed 4.8% expansion in industry a year earlier with 1.9% contraction as slowing natural gas and copper production caused mining and quarrying to plunge by 20.1%. Manufacturing, however, rose by 2.2%. A pandemic-induced lockdown turned last year's 12.7% growth in services into 0.7% decline, with cuts of 8.0% in transport and 17.4% in catering and accommodation moderated by gains of 0.7% in trade and 35.9% in financial services. Slower expansion in commercial facilities and housing slashed growth in construction from 23.7% to 7.3%. Growth in agriculture rose slightly from 2.4% to 2.8% as ample water supply boosted livestock and crop production.

On the demand side, pandemic-related disruption to supplies of equipment and other inputs cut investment by 12.8%, reversing 58.9% growth a year earlier. Net exports remained negative, but deficits narrowed by 4.0% for goods and 14.8% for services. To support the economy, the government created an Anti-Crisis Fund equal to 1.5% of GDP, including aid for small and medium enterprises. After a phased easing, the government lifted the lockdown altogether in August to facilitate business recovery. Despite these measures, this *Update* sharply reduces the *ADO 2020* growth projection for 2020 while raising the *ADO 2020* forecast for 2021.

Inflation rose slightly in the first 7 months of 2020 from 13.7% a year earlier to 13.9%. Pandemic-related disruptions raised food price inflation from 15.8% to 17.7%, while inflation for other goods slowed from 10.0% to 9.6% and for services from 14.0% to 13.7%. In April 2020, the central bank cut its policy rate from 16.0% to 15.0% after inflation in March fell 1.3 percentage points below forecast to 13.6% year on year. Meanwhile, Uzbek sum depreciation year on year against the US dollar rose from 2.5% in the first half of 2019 to 6.7% a year later. With demand sluggish and energy tariffs unlikely to change in 2020, this *Update* retains earlier projections for inflation in 2020 and 2021.

The current account deficit widened from the equivalent of 6.8% of GDP in the first half of 2019 to 7.7% a year later as travel restrictions and weakness in the Russian Federation cut remittances by about 6.0%, while exports of goods fell by 19.7% with lower demand and prices for natural gas and copper. Supply chain disruptions cut imports of goods by 14.1%, with notable declines in imports for construction and industry. Exports of services dropped by 38.6%, and imports by 28.4%. With continued weakness in exports and remittances, this *Update* projects a wider current account deficit in 2020, narrowing in 2021 as exports and remittances recover.

Table 3.1.8 Selected economic indicators, Uzbekistan (%)

	2019	2020			2021		
		ADO 2020	ADOS	*Update*	*ADO 2020*	ADOS	*Update*
GDP growth	5.6	4.7	1.5	0.5	5.8	6.5	6.5
Inflation	14.6	13.0	13.0	13.0	10.0	10.0	10.0
CAB/GDP	–5.6	–4.0	...	–9.5	–3.5	...	–8.0

... = unavailable, ADO = *Asian Development Outlook* (April), ADOS = *ADO Supplement* (June), CAB = current account balance, GDP = gross domestic product.
Source: ADB estimates.

East Asia

East Asia contracted in the first half of 2020 under COVID-19 and its far-reaching effects. The GDP forecast for the whole year is downgraded from the *ADO 2020* projection in April, but recovery in 2021 is now expected to be more robust. Inflation has been stable, and reduced demand is likely to keep it below earlier forecasts. Subregional current account surpluses show little change from earlier projections as lower imports offset lower exports.

Subregional assessment and prospects

The economies of East Asia contracted in aggregate in the first half of 2020, underperforming forecasts in *ADO 2020*. In the People's Republic of China (PRC), GDP fell by 1.6% in the first half, stemming from steep contraction in the first quarter because of COVID-19, followed by recovery in the second quarter as epidemic control measures proved largely effective. Most other economies in the subregion also contracted in the first quarter, mainly from COVID-19, but in Taipei,China accommodative policies moderated some of the pandemic impact, allowing that economy to expand by 0.8% in the first half.

Subregional inflation remained subdued in the first half of 2020. In the first 7 months, inflation in the PRC averaged 3.7%, driven by higher food prices. Inflation in Mongolia accelerated temporarily in the first quarter but moderated in the second to average 4.9% in the first half. In the rest of the subregion, inflation was low because of weak demand, generally in line with expectations.

Available information suggests that East Asia's current account surplus was stable in the first half of 2020 and close to the *ADO 2020* forecast. In the PRC, the current account surplus widened to equal 1.3% of GDP in the first half as the deficit in services shrank, mainly in line with plummeting outbound tourism, while the merchandise trade surplus remained broadly unchanged as imports and exports both fell.

Figure 3.2.1 GDP growth, East Asia

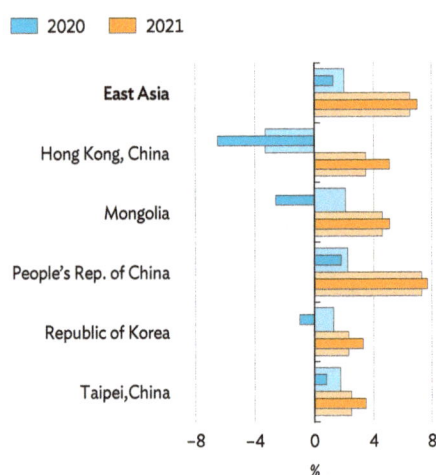

Note: Lighter colored bars are *ADO 2020* forecasts.
Source: *Asian Development Outlook* database.

The section on the PRC was written by Dominik Peschel, Jian Zhuang, and Wen Qi, and the part on other economies by Shiela Camingue-Romance, Matteo Lanzafame, Declan Magee, Nedelyn Magtibay-Ramos, Donghyun Park, Irfan Qureshi, Bold Sandagdorj, and Michael Timbang, consultant. All authors are in the East Asia and Economic Research and Regional Cooperation departments of ADB. Subregional assessment and prospects were written by Eric Clifton, consultant, Economic Research and Regional Cooperation Department.

In Hong Kong, China, declines in the service surplus and net inflow of primary income, only partly offset by a smaller deficit in goods, pushed the current account into a first-quarter deficit equal to 1.4% of GDP. Elsewhere, Taipei,China and the Republic of Korea enjoyed current account surpluses, while Mongolia experienced a deficit.

Subregional GDP growth is forecast to slow from 5.4% in 2019 to 1.3% in 2020 before recovering to 7.0% in 2021 (Figure 3.2.1). Growth in the PRC is expected to accelerate in the second half of the year to bring growth in the whole of 2020 to 1.8% and in 2021 to 7.7%. Taipei,China is projected to expand by 0.8% in 2020, supported by accommodative policies. The remaining three economies in the subregion—Hong Kong, China; Mongolia; and the Republic of Korea—are forecast to contract this year but return to growth in 2021, rejoining the PRC and Taipei,China.

Inflation in East Asia is forecast at 2.6% in 2020 and 1.7% in 2021, lower than projected in *ADO 2020* because of sharply reduced economic activity (Figure 3.2.2). Inflation in the PRC is now forecast to average 3.0% in 2020, below the *ADO 2020* projection, as consumer demand recovers only slowly. In Mongolia, inflation is forecast at 5.6% in 2020 and 8.2% in 2021. Elsewhere in the subregion, 2021 inflation is expected to be subdued.

The subregional current account surplus is forecast to equal 2.0% of aggregate GDP in 2020 and 2021 (Figure 3.2.3). The only economy in the subregion not expected to achieve a surplus in both years is Mongolia, where the current account deficit is forecast to widen to equal 14.1% of GDP in 2020, with lower exports and tourism receipts, then narrow in 2021 as the subregional economy recovers, demand revives for mineral commodities, and the country gradually opens up for exports. The PRC current account surplus is forecast to rise to the equivalent of 1.5% of GDP in 2020 before moderating to 1.3% in 2021. Notably, Taipei,China is expected to run surpluses equal to 10% of GDP in 2020 and 12% in 2021.

Downside risks to the growth outlook substantially outweigh upside risks. The biggest risk is from feared new waves of COVID-19 infections within the subregion or elsewhere, either way likely hindering international trade and any tourism rebound. Another risk is a possible worsening of geopolitical tensions, which could hobble recovery.

Figure 3.2.2 Inflation, East Asia

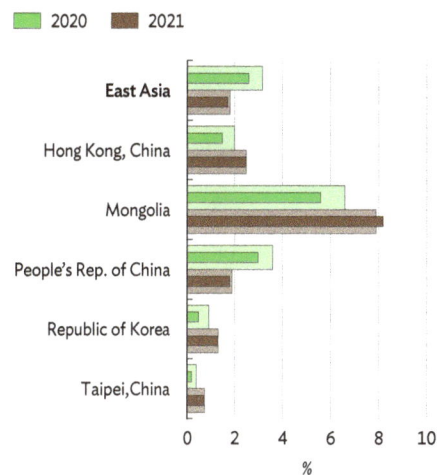

Note: Lighter colored bars are *ADO 2020* forecasts.
Source: *Asian Development Outlook* database.

Figure 3.2.3 Current account balance, East Asia

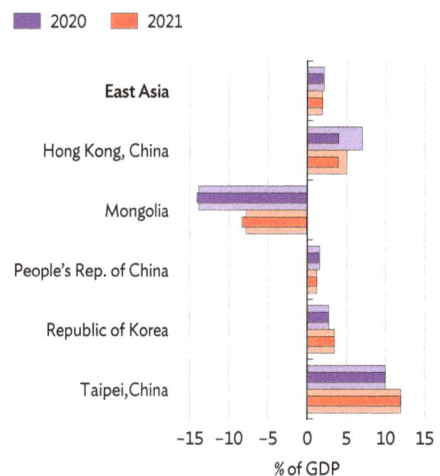

Note: Lighter colored bars are *ADO 2020* forecasts.
Source: *Asian Development Outlook* database.

People's Republic of China

Thanks to strong monetary and fiscal policy support, the economy rebounded from deep contraction in the first quarter (Q1) of 2020 with respectable growth in Q2. Earlier *ADO 2020* growth forecasts are revised down for 2020 but up for 2021, reflecting the expectation that recovery in domestic demand and the global economy will be protracted. Inflation is projected lower in both years as food prices gradually normalize and other prices remain subdued. The current account will stay in surplus, broadly in line with earlier forecasts.

Updated assessment

GDP shrank by 1.6% in the first half (H1) of 2020, sharply reversing 6.3% growth in the same period of 2019. The decline stemmed from contraction by 6.8% in Q1, under the COVID-19 emergency, followed by 3.2% recovery in Q2 as epidemic control measures proved largely effective (Figure 3.2.4).

On the demand side, consumption—a key driver of growth in 2019, contributing 3.6 percentage points in H1 of that year—began to drag on the economy in H1 2020, deducting 2.9 points from growth (Figure 3.2.5). This development reflected a sharp decline in household consumption and retail sales. While household income reversed 6.5% real growth in H1 2019 to decline by 1.3% a year later, real household consumption plunged from 5.2% growth to 9.3% contraction. In the first 7 months of 2020, retail sales fell by more than 18 percentage points, from an estimated 6.5% expansion to contraction estimated at 12.0% in real terms.

In H1 2020, investment contributed 1.5 percentage points to growth, partly on rising industrial inventories as manufacturing picked up but domestic demand remained lackluster. Fixed asset investment fell in nominal terms from 5.7% growth in the first 7 months of 2019 to 1.6% decline a year later (Figure 3.2.6). Reflecting heightened uncertainty, manufacturing investment dropped by 10.2%. Growth in infrastructure could not fully offset a sharp decline in Q1, leaving a 1.0% decrease in the first 7 months of 2020, during which real estate investment expanded by 3.4%.

As the merchandise trade surplus narrowed slightly with a decline in international trade, net exports subtracted 0.2 percentage points from growth in H1 2020, reversing a 1.1 point contribution in the same period of 2019, when the merchandise trade surplus expanded notably as a result of lower imports.

On the supply side, services reversed 7.0% growth in H1 2019 to shrink by 1.6% a year later and subtract from growth (Figure 3.2.7). Accommodation and catering were hard hit by COVID-19, as were wholesale and retail trade, while information technology and financial services performed well. Industry including mining and construction was down in H1 2020 from 5.8% growth a year earlier to 1.9% decline,

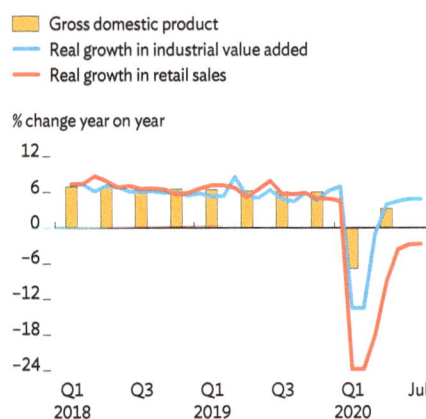

Figure 3.2.4 Economic growth

☐ Gross domestic product
— Real growth in industrial value added
— Real growth in retail sales

% change year on year

Q = quarter.
Sources: National Bureau of Statistics; ADB estimates.

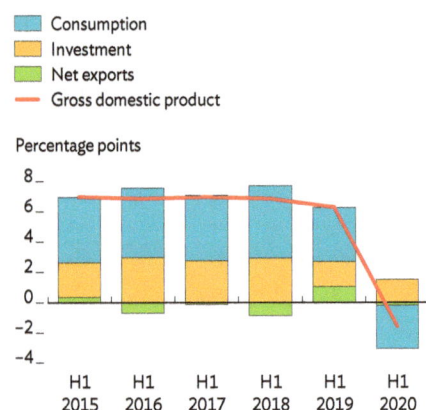

Figure 3.2.5 Demand-side contributions to growth

☐ Consumption
☐ Investment
☐ Net exports
— Gross domestic product

Percentage points

H1 = first half.
Source: National Bureau of Statistics.

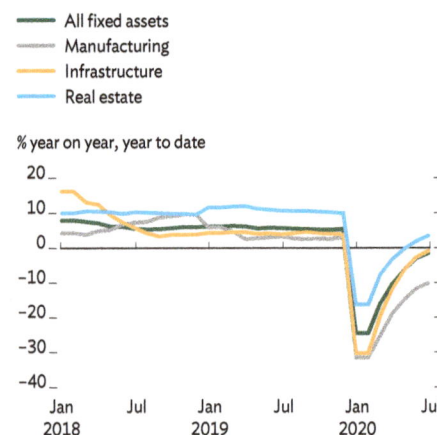

Figure 3.2.6 Growth in fixed asset investment

— All fixed assets
— Manufacturing
— Infrastructure
— Real estate

% year on year, year to date

Source: National Bureau of Statistics.

with automobiles, general equipment, and textiles falling substantially. In the first 7 months of 2020, industry value added reversed 5.8% expansion a year earlier to decline by 0.4%. Construction plunged in Q1 2020 but rebounded sharply in Q2 as public infrastructure investment picked up notably. In agriculture, pig farming still struggled to recover from African swine fever, slowing expansion in the sector from 3.0% to 0.9%, for a negligible contribution to GDP growth.

The labor market was under pressure from mobility restrictions to contain COVID-19 and weaker economic growth. Labor market expansion slowed, creating 1.96 million fewer new urban jobs in the first 7 months of 2020 than a year earlier. The surveyed urban unemployment rate shot up from 5.2% in December 2019 to 6.2% in February and then eased to 5.7% in July, at least partly because the urban labor force shrank as some migrants did not return to cities after the lunar new year holiday for lack of jobs. Similarly unreflected in labor market statistics is underemployment. Many state-owned enterprises do not lay off workers in an economic downturn but temporarily reduce their working hours and wages. As statistics continue to count these workers as employed, the extent of such reductions is unknown, and the actual adverse effect of COVID-19 on the labor market has very likely been more pronounced than the surveyed unemployment rate suggests.

In the first 7 months of 2020, food prices continued to push up average consumer inflation, to 3.7%, while other prices remained subdued (Figure 3.2.8). Pork price inflation peaked in February but has remained high. Meanwhile, tight vegetable supply caused by COVID-19 and heavy rain and flooding helped push up food prices by 15.8% on average in the first 7 months. Nonfood price inflation softened, however, by a full percentage point to 0.6% on average as domestic demand weakened. Average producer prices declined by 2.0%, notably reversing a marginal increase of 0.3% a year earlier. Prices for newly constructed homes in the top 70 cities were, on average, 5.4% higher in the first 7 months of 2020 than a year earlier, with increases most pronounced in second- and third-tier cities (Figure 3.2.9).

The fiscal deficit is set to increase significantly. The 2020 annual budget, approved in May, mobilizes additional resources for economic support under COVID-19. The fiscal deficit is expected to widen from the equivalent of 2.8% of GDP in 2019 to more than 3.6% this year. In addition, the government-managed funds budget, which is separate from the general government budget, includes this year an increase in the new local government special bond quota from CNY2.15 trillion in 2019 to CNY3.75 trillion, in addition to central government special bonds worth CNY1 trillion. The budget to fund social security is expected to show a deficit of at least CNY500 billion in 2020, even after taking into account a CNY585 billion surplus carried over from 2019.

Figure 3.2.7 Supply-side contributions to growth

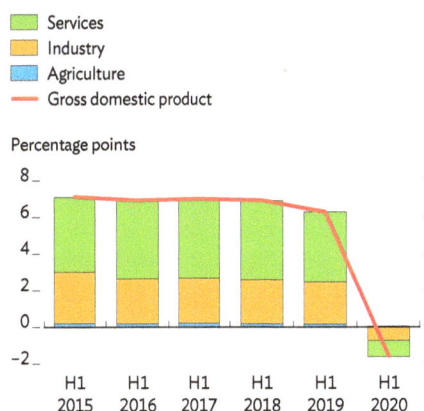

Percentage points

H1 = first half.
Source: National Bureau of Statistics.

Figure 3.2.8 Monthly inflation

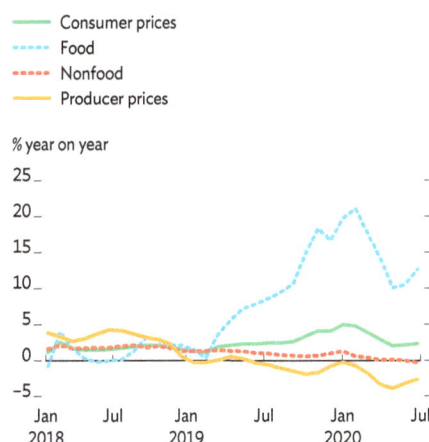

% year on year

Source: National Bureau of Statistics.

Figure 3.2.9 Price increase for newly constructed homes

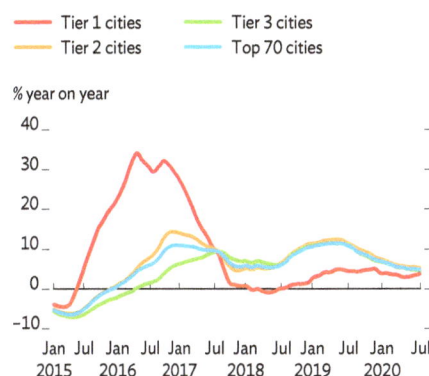

% year on year

Note: Tier 1 cities are Beijing, Guangzhou, Shanghai, and Shenzhen; tier 2 has 31 provincial capitals and larger municipalities; and tier 3 has 35 other cities.
Sources: National Bureau of Statistics; ADB estimates.

Fiscal policy in H1 2020 concentrated on mitigating the adverse effects of COVID-19 (Box 3.2.1). Support came mainly from tax relief and the temporary waiving of social security contributions, as well as from higher local government special bond issuance to finance public infrastructure investment (Figure 3.2.10). Suppressed by lower economic growth, tax relief, and lower fees, fiscal revenue fell by 10.8% in H1 2020, with collection of value-added tax—the most important source of tax revenue—declining the most, by 19.1%. Fiscal expenditure decreased by 5.8% as local governments had to reduce spending in line with falling revenue. In sum, the deficit in the consolidated government budget, which comprises central and local governments, expanded by a percentage point from a year earlier, to equal 4.4% of GDP in H1 2020 (Figure 3.2.11).

Monetary policy was loosened in February 2020 in response to COVID-19 as the People's Bank of China, the central bank, took several targeted measures (Box 3.2.1). Interest rates in the secured interbank market fell, notably following liquidity injections by the central bank (Figure 3.2.12). To reduce financing costs for the real economy, the central bank cut the 1-year medium-term lending facility rate twice in H1 2020 by a total of 30 basis points to 2.95% (Figure 3.2.13). Reductions in the reserve requirement ratio for banks freed funds for credit expansion.

Total social financing—a broad credit aggregate that includes bank loans, shadow bank lending, government and corporate bonds, and equity financing—was up by 12.9% at the end of July 2020 from a year earlier (Figure 3.2.14). While shadow bank finance outstanding declined by 4.0%, bank loans outstanding increased by 13.3% as lending was expanded to stabilize the economy following the COVID-19 shock. Government bonds outstanding were up by 16.5% as their issuance picked up rapidly in H1 2020 in tandem with increased government financing needs and higher annual quotas for local government special bonds. In line with faster growth in total social financing, growth in broad money (M2) year on year accelerated from 8.1% at the end of July 2019 to 10.7% a year later.

In the first 7 months of 2020, merchandise exports declined by 4.1% while imports fell by 5.7% (Figure 3.2.15). Exports had plunged at the start of 2020 under COVID-19 disruption but then recovered somewhat on a massive increase in global demand for personal protective equipment that fueled a sharp rise in exports of textiles and fabrics, plastic articles, and medical instruments. Geographically, exports to the US declined by 7.2% and to Japan by 3.0%.

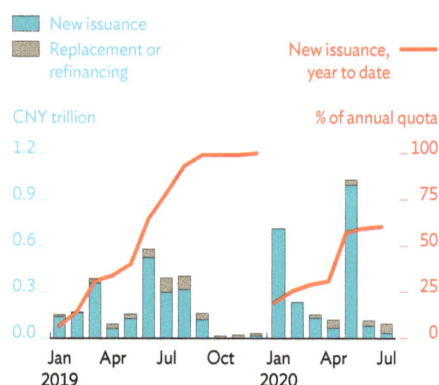

Figure 3.2.10 Local government special bond issues

Sources: Ministry of Finance; ADB estimates.

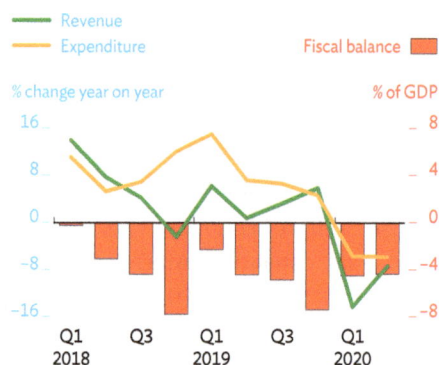

Figure 3.2.11 General government fiscal revenue and expenditure

GDP = gross domestic product, Q = quarter.
Sources: Ministry of Finance; ADB estimates.

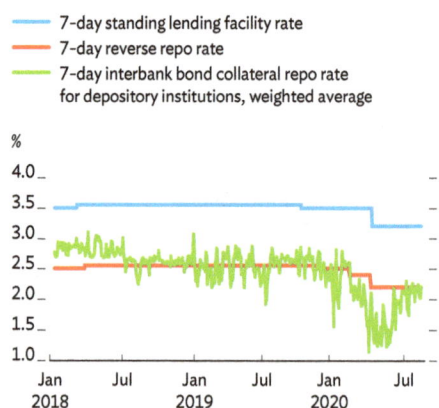

Figure 3.2.12 Short-term policy and interbank rates

Sources: People's Bank of China; National Interbank Funding Center.

Box 3.2.1 Policy responses to COVID-19

The PRC has adopted an array of fiscal and monetary policy measures since February 2020 to stabilize the economy in the face of the COVID-19 pandemic.

Fiscal policy measures
Besides tax incentives for companies critical to epidemic prevention and control, the government temporarily reduced taxes and fees. Key measures included

i.   temporary exemption from the value-added tax for small-scale taxpayers in Hubei Province and a rate cut from 3% to 1% for those in other provinces;
ii. deferral of income tax payments for qualified small companies and individually owned businesses to early 2021;
iii. extension of the period allowed for the tax-related carryover of losses to enterprises in eligible industries that incurred high losses from the pandemic;
iv. temporary exemptions from value-added tax for enterprises in services hit hard by the pandemic;
v.   temporary exemption from social security contributions for eligible enterprises; and
vi. industry-specific support, in particular incentives for eligible car sales, higher tax rebate rates for exporters, and fee reductions for the logistics, shipping, and aviation industries.

Monetary and macro-financial policies
The central bank cut policy rates, injected liquidity into the banking system, and widened the use of special relending instruments. Key measures included

i.   liquidity injections via reverse repos and, to provide banks with longer-term liquidity, medium-term facilities;
ii. cuts in the reserve requirement ratio totaling 100 basis points for small- and medium-sized banks and additional targeted ratio cuts by 50–100 basis points for midsize and large banks that meet inclusive financing criteria supporting small and micro businesses, as well as yet another ratio cut for qualified joint-stock banks by 100 points;

iii. reducing the 1-year medium-term lending facility rate by 30 basis points and the targeted medium-term lending facility rate by 20 points;
iv. reducing 7- and 14-day reverse repo rates by 30 basis points;
v.   cutting rates in the relending facility by 50 basis points and in the rediscounting facility by 25 points;
vi. expanding relending and rediscount facilities by an initial CNY1.8 trillion to support agriculture, manufacturers of medical supplies and daily necessities, and micro, small, and medium-sized enterprises; and
vii. introducing a new credit support instrument, whereby the central bank uses CNY400 billion to purchase 40% of qualified local banks' new loans to micro and small enterprises until June 2021, and a CNY40 billion program to support further extension of the repayment period for qualified loans by subsidizing 1% of the loan principal.

Further, the government

i.   encouraged lending to micro, small, and medium-sized enterprises—which frequently struggle to obtain bank credit for lack of collateral and because of the segment's higher default rates—in part by increasing the target for growth in large banks' lending to micro and small firms;
ii. allowed payment delays for qualified loans, with deadlines extended to the end of March 2021;
iii. eased requirements for loan-loss provisioning and increased tolerance for nonperforming loans, to allow banks to increase their lending despite weaker economic growth;
iv. allowed local governments to use CNY200 billion in proceeds from local government special bond issues to recapitalize qualified small and midsized banks; and
v.   delayed the implementation of asset management reform set in 2018 to avoid a tightening of financial conditions.

Exports to Southeast Asia grew by 2.1%, somewhat faster than those to the European Union (excluding the United Kingdom), which increased by 0.8%. The decline in merchandise imports was across the board, reflecting lower domestic demand for investment goods such as machinery, a drop in household consumption that sharply contracted car imports, and lower imports for processing and assembly for reexport as global trade took a hit.

The surplus in the current account increased from 0.9% of GDP in H1 2019 to 1.3% a year later as the service deficit shrank by 40.9% in line with plummeting outbound tourism, while the merchandise trade surplus remained broadly unchanged as imports and exports both fell (Figure 3.2.16). COVID-19 had an adverse impact on foreign direct investment, which declined from the equivalent of 0.5% of GDP in H1 2019 to 0.3% a year later as inflows declined but outflows remained virtually stable.

By the end of July 2020, the renminbi had depreciated by 0.9% from the end of 2019 in nominal effective terms, against a trade-weighted basket of currencies, and by 0.2% in real effective terms, taking inflation into account. In nominal terms, it depreciated by 0.1% against the US dollar in the first 7 months of 2020 (Figure 3.2.17).

Prospects

In H2 2020, GDP growth is expected to accelerate further from 3.2% in Q2. Fiscal policy will continue to support growth, especially infrastructure investment, but ongoing weak fiscal revenue will limit increases in government spending. Monetary policy is expected to stay largely accommodative, but concern over financial stability will likely prevent any further easing. While the service sector is expected to recover further, lackluster domestic household consumption and external headwinds will continue to weigh on recovery. GDP is now forecast to grow by 1.8% in 2020, revised down from 2.3% forecast in *ADO 2020*, before rebounding to 7.7% in 2021, or 0.4 percentage points higher than forecast earlier (Figure 3.2.18).

On the demand side, consumption is expected to recover only gradually. Consumer staples should stay largely resilient. Discretionary spending will likely continue to be depressed, however, by only slow growth in disposable income and ongoing economic uncertainty—though faster growth and a brightening outlook could boost consumer confidence. The local housing market is expected to be a driver of growth in H2 2020, which should support purchases of housing-related consumer goods. At the same time, any easing of local housing market restrictions will be allowed only to the extent that home prices avoid a new cycle of massive price increases.

Infrastructure investment is expected to remain strong throughout the remainder of 2020, supported by ongoing local government special bond issues (Figure 3.2.10). Indeed, investment is expected to be the main driver of growth in the remainder of 2020, with consumption dragging on growth this year but recovering further in 2021 and regaining its role as the main driver of growth, especially with a likely gradual easing of public infrastructure investment.

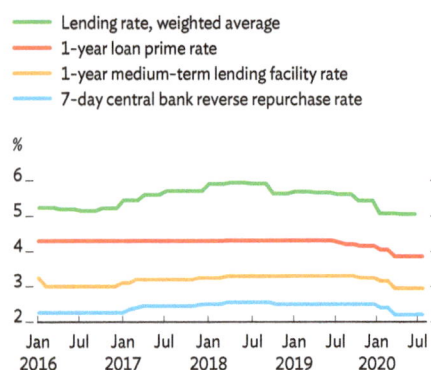

Figure 3.2.13 Banking lending and policy rates

- Lending rate, weighted average
- 1-year loan prime rate
- 1-year medium-term lending facility rate
- 7-day central bank reverse repurchase rate

Sources: People's Bank of China; National Interbank Funding Center.

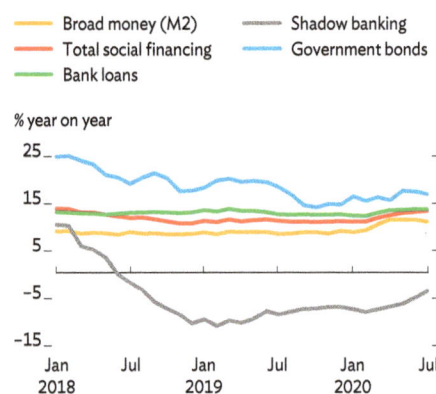

Figure 3.2.14 Growth in broad money, credit outstanding, and government bonds outstanding

- Broad money (M2)
- Total social financing
- Bank loans
- Shadow banking
- Government bonds

Note: Shadow banking comprises entrust loans, trust loans, and banks' acceptance bills.
Sources: People's Bank of China; ADB estimates.

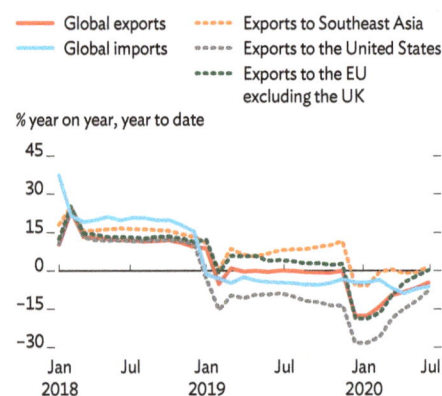

Figure 3.2.15 Growth in PRC exports, by region or country, and imports

- Global exports
- Global imports
- Exports to Southeast Asia
- Exports to the United States
- Exports to the EU excluding the UK

EU = European Union, PRC = People's Republic of China, UK = United Kingdom.
Note: Data for January and February combined in 2020.
Sources: General Administration of Customs; ADB estimates.

As the deficit in service trade is forecast to narrow more than the merchandise trade surplus moderates, net exports will increase in 2020, continuing to contribute to growth this year before dragging on growth in 2021 as imports of goods and services outgrow exports.

On the supply side, recovery in services will remain burdened by restrained household demand as the labor market improves only gradually. While construction and some upstream industries, especially steel and cement, will benefit from buoyant housing demand and substantial government infrastructure investment, recovery in manufacturing as a whole will be limited by tepid domestic demand and protracted weakness in exports, though high-tech manufacturing and innovative industries will continue to profit from government support. Growth in agriculture is expected to normalize after suffering in 2020 from heavy rain and flooding in the middle of the year.

Consumer price inflation is now forecast to average 3.0% in 2020, lower than projected in *ADO 2020*, as consumer demand recovers only slowly (Figure 3.2.19). While food prices are expected to remain volatile, pork prices should normalize toward the end of 2020, allowing average consumer price inflation to retreat to 1.8% in 2021, slightly lower than the *ADO 2020* projection. Despite forecast increased demand for construction materials owing to the pickup in housing and infrastructure construction, average producer prices are projected to decline in 2020 before recovering in 2021.

Fiscal policy is expected to stay supportive in the remainder of 2020. Fiscal revenue declined faster in H1 than officially projected in May 2020, and expenditure increased less. Fiscal revenue will likely improve alongside higher economic growth in H2 2020, and expenditure will pick up moderately. As a result, the fiscal deficit is expected to exceed the equivalent of 3.6% of GDP by a considerable margin, though the government will aim to limit the budget deficit by continuing to control fiscal expenditure. Public debt should nevertheless rise notably given the sizeable increase in new special government bond issues. General government debt climbed 5.2 percentage points to equal 54.2% of GDP at the end of 2019 and is expected to rise by nearly twice as much this year (Figure 3.2.20).

Support will come as well from the high volume of local government special bond issues, which is likely to remain elevated in 2021. The central government mandated in late July that the remaining quota for new special bonds in 2020 should be issued by the end of October. This way, it retains from November the option of issuing part of next year's quota this year.

Figure 3.2.16 Balance of payments

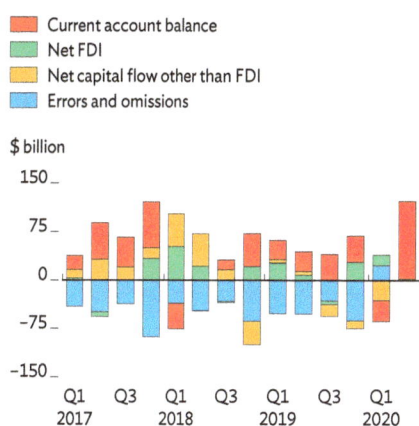

FDI = foreign direct investment, Q = quarter.
Note: For Q2 2020, data only for the current account and FDI.
Sources: State Administration of Foreign Exchange; ADB estimates.

Figure 3.2.17 Renminbi exchange rates

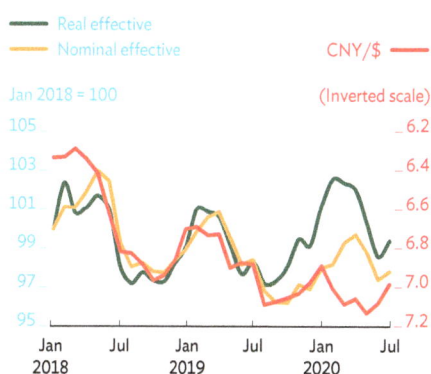

Sources: Bank for International Settlements; People's Bank of China; ADB estimates.

Table 3.2.1 Selected economic indicators, People's Republic of China (%)

	2019	2020			2021		
		ADO 2020	ADOS	Update	ADO 2020	ADOS	Update
GDP growth	6.1	2.3	1.8	1.8	7.3	7.4	7.7
Inflation	2.9	3.6	3.3	3.0	1.9	1.9	1.8
CAB/GDP	1.0	1.6	...	1.5	1.2	...	1.3

... = unavailable, ADO = *Asian Development Outlook* (April), ADOS = *ADO Supplement* (June), CAB = current account balance, GDP = gross domestic product.
Sources: National Bureau of Statistics; ADB estimates.

Local governments face a significant structural budget imbalance, as spending requirements frequently exceed weak fiscal revenue, leaving no scope for substantive increases in fiscal expenditure to stimulate the economy. Since 2018, tax cuts, especially to value-added tax, have slowed growth in local government fiscal revenue—until COVID-19 slashed revenue and forced spending reductions. Partial compensation came from increases in local government special bond allocations and stepwise broadening of the permitted use of their proceeds. Following increased pressure from the COVID-19 crisis, the central government even allowed local governments the exceptional use of some of these proceeds to recapitalize qualified small and medium-sized banks.

Monetary policy is expected to stay accommodative in the remainder of 2020 but without much further easing. While the central bank will probably keep interest rates in the interbank market moderate by providing sufficient liquidity to banks, it will avoid excessive rate declines to squelch opportunities for financial arbitrage. Targeted cuts to the reserve requirement ratio remain likely, freeing up additional funds for banks to lend. Also, a further small reduction in the medium-term lending facility rate is expected because the economic recovery remains fragile.

It is noteworthy that cuts to policy lending rates during the crisis have been only gradual in the PRC. Narrowing the spread between bank lending rates and deposit rates reduces banks' net interest margins and thereby their profitability. Many smaller local banks, especially in economically weak areas, do not have sufficient buffers to cope with a sizable increase in nonperforming loans (NPLs). Hence, financial stability is increasingly a concern that the central bank needs to take into consideration when reducing policy lending rates. In addition, a sharp reduction in short-term policy lending rates can be expected to bleed into long-term rates. In particular, effective mortgage rates could moderate, though this would fuel home price increases against the agenda of the government.

Ongoing expansion of bank loans despite deteriorating credit quality will mean more NPLs. At the end of June 2020, the NPL ratio stood at 1.94%, which was 13 basis points higher than a year earlier (Figure 3.2.21). The ratio is expected to rise further, especially in 2021, when deferred loan repayments come due—along with repayment of recently increased lending, usually with a loan tenor of 1 year, to micro and small firms, some of which will likely have gone out of business by then. Similarly, corporate revenue and profit still have to recover from the shock suffered in Q1 2020.

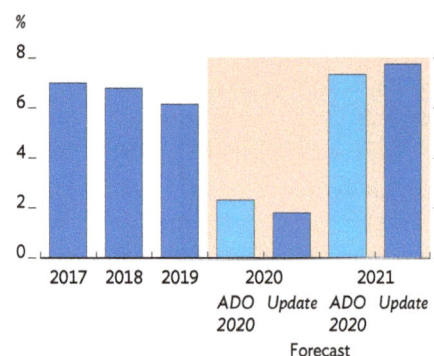

Figure 3.2.18 GDP growth

Source: Asian Development Outlook database.

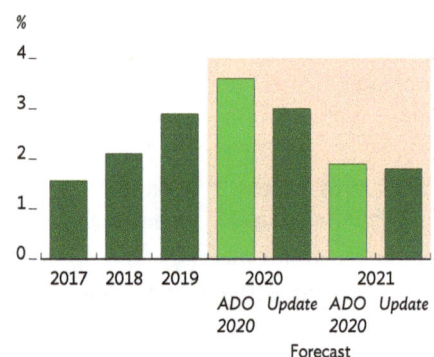

Figure 3.2.19 Inflation

Source: Asian Development Outlook database.

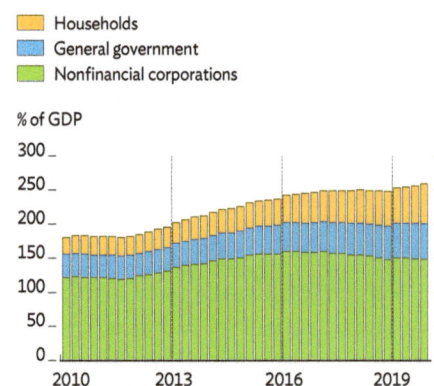

Figure 3.2.20 Debt structure

- Households
- General government
- Nonfinancial corporations

Source: Bank for International Settlements.

External trade is expected to remain lackluster in the remainder of 2020, with merchandise exports underperforming last year. In 2021, exports will be hampered by a tepid and protracted recovery globally, and by the rapid accumulation of new debt worldwide, which will likely weigh on future external demand. Imports of investment goods are expected to stay in 2020 below last year's level as most manufacturers delay investment in light of ongoing uncertainty, though commodity imports will benefit from a pickup in industry. Assuming a much smaller deficit in service trade in 2020 owing to ongoing travel restrictions, the current account surplus is forecast to widen to the equivalent of 1.5% of GDP in 2020, a bit less than forecast in *ADO 2020*, before moderating to 1.3% in 2021, or 0.1 percentage points more than earlier forecast.

Capital inflow into PRC bond and equity markets is expected to continue (see the policy challenge in *ADO 2020* for details). The PRC bond market is expected to benefit from a wider spread in yields since US Treasury yields fell sharply in March 2020 (Figure 3.2.22). At the same time, foreign direct investment inflow is expected to remain subdued as persistent uncertainty delays investment.

Besides COVID-19, risks to the outlook stem from a possible intensification of the trade conflict with the US or, domestically, mounting credit risk for banks, especially against a backdrop of many local banks' weak capitalization. Another domestic risk is intensifying fiscal revenue pressure on local governments. Besides limiting their capacity to stimulate the economy, insufficient revenue undercuts their ability to expand expenditure in line with rising need.

Figure 3.2.21 Problematic bank loans by category

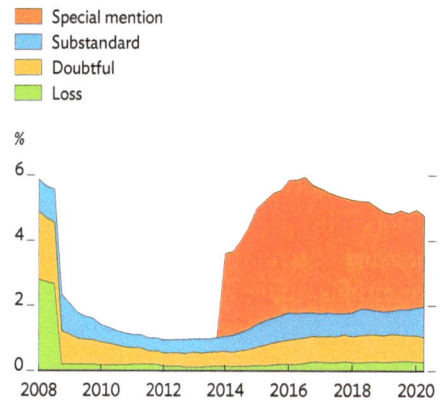

Note: Data on special-mention loans, a category one notch above substandard, started in 2014.
Source: China Banking and Insurance Regulatory Commission.

Figure 3.2.22 Difference in government bond yields

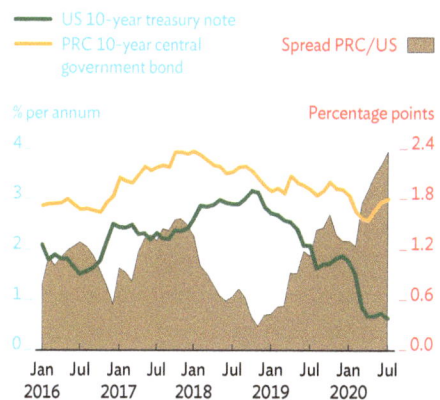

PRC = People's Republic of China, US = United States.
Sources: PRC National Interbank Funding Centre; US Federal Reserve Board; ADB estimates.

Other economies

Hong Kong, China

GDP plunged by 9.0% year on year in the first half of 2020, the steepest fall on record, as the COVID-19 pandemic hit the external sector and, added to local political tensions, battered domestic demand. Despite a massive cash handout from the government, private consumption expenditure dropped by 12.4% in the first half as social distancing measures disrupted commerce and worsening labor market conditions undermined consumer confidence. An ongoing decline in fixed investment deepened to 18.6% as a highly fluid outlook stymied construction. Meanwhile, exports of goods declined by 6.0%, weighed down by moderating growth in the People's Republic of China and weaker global trade. Service exports contracted sharply by 41.5%, with inbound tourism, cross-border transport, and commercial services disrupted and down. Imports also plummeted amid weaker economic activity, by 12.2%, but net exports remained negative in the period.

On the supply side, services dropped by 9.0% in the first quarter of 2020 almost across the board as the COVID-19 pandemic upended regional supply chains, related trade services, and transportation. The fall in manufacturing also deepened, to 4.6%, and in construction to 12.1%, but agriculture, fishing, mining, and quarrying grew by 2.3%.

The COVID-19 pandemic and global recession will continue to dampen economic sentiment. Established drivers of growth, notably exports and tourism, are likely to remain subdued this year. Gradual recovery is expected starting in the second half of the year as a relief package equal to about 10% of GDP is rolled out. Nevertheless, this *Update* downgrades the *ADO 2020* GDP forecast for 2020 to much deeper contraction. It significantly upgrades the growth forecast for 2021 but mainly to accommodate a base effect.

Headline consumer price inflation slowed to 0.7% year on year in June 2020, subdued by softer increases for pork and private housing rentals. Consumer price pressures are likely to ease in the near term in light of subdued local and global economic prospects and recent strengthening of the local dollar. This *Update* therefore cuts the *ADO 2020* inflation forecast for 2020 but maintains it for 2021.

A narrower surplus in services and lower net inflow of primary income were only partly offset by a decrease in the goods deficit, summing to a current account deficit equal to 1.4% of GDP in the first quarter of 2020. In light of this and of recent external economic developments, current account surpluses in both 2020 and 2021 are now projected narrower than forecast in *ADO 2020*.

The primary downside risk to the outlook is any renewed outbreak of COVID-19 or local political tensions.

Table 3.2.2 Selected economic indicators, Hong Kong, China (%)

	2019	2020			2021		
		ADO 2020	ADOS	Update	ADO 2020	ADOS	Update
GDP growth	-1.2	-3.3	-6.5	-6.5	3.5	5.1	5.1
Inflation	2.9	2.0	1.5	1.5	2.5	2.5	2.5
CAB/GDP	6.1	7.0	...	4.0	5.0	...	4.0

... = unavailable, ADO = *Asian Development Outlook* (April), ADOS = *ADO Supplement* (June), CAB = current account balance, GDP = gross domestic product.
Source: ADB estimates.

Mongolia

GDP contracted by 9.7% in the first half (H1) of 2020 mainly because COVID-19 substantially reduced exports and capital inflows. Lower external demand shrank mining output as crude oil plunged by 77.5% and coal by 57.4%. Declines in mining, manufacturing, construction, transportation, trade, and services dragged down GDP growth, leaving agriculture as the only positive contributor. On the demand side, consumption, boosted by increased government expenditure, contributed 5.0 points to growth, while investment dragged growth down by 8.7 points and net exports by 6.0 points.

The budget recorded a deficit equal to 11.5% of GDP in H1 2020 as revenue fell by 21.4% and expenditure increased by 37.0%, mainly on COVID-19 response. In the full year, the deficit is expected to reverse a 2019 surplus equal to 1.4% of GDP with a 9.9% deficit, raising concerns for macroeconomic stability. Average annual inflation fell from 7.1% in H1 2019 to 6.1%—further below the 8% target set by the Bank of Mongolia, the central bank— as high food inflation was tempered by reduced domestic demand and prices for transportation and recreation. Faltering exports drove the current account deficit up by 19.8% in H1 2020.

Gross international reserves fell to provide cover for only 5.2 months of imports as net inflows of foreign direct investment declined, government-guaranteed corporate bonds were fully repaid, and the central bank intervened to contain Mongolian togrog depreciation against US dollar, which reached 4.3% in the first 8 months. To support growth, it cut its policy rate by 200 basis points to 9.0% and eased regulations on asset classification and on loan repayment and restructuring. Bank credit nevertheless contracted by 4.1% year on year. Nonperforming loans and loans past due rose to 14.6% of the total, indicating asset quality deterioration.

Some signs of recovery in the PRC and significant rebounding of copper and gold prices in July and August implies that exports and mining output will pick up in the second half—indicating cautious optimism compared to early this year. The economy is forecast to contract in 2020 as a whole, however. Fiscal space for stimulus is in short supply this year, and exchange rate concerns rule out any further policy rate cut. Growth will recover in 2021 above the *ADO 2020* forecast as regional economies rebound.

Weak demand will keep inflation this year lower than earlier forecast, but revived demand and imported inflation will push it higher. The current account deficit will be larger than forecast in both 2020 and 2021 as substantial declines in exports and tourism receipts dwarf a fall in imports, but the deficit will narrow in 2021 as exports and the economy recover.

An external downside risk to the outlook would be delayed economic recovery globally or regionally as pandemic containment drags on. Domestic risks include unemployment, potentially unstable finances, and inconsistent macroeconomic policy deepening pressure on the balance of payments.

Table 3.2.3 Selected economic indicators, Mongolia (%)

	2019	2020			2021		
		ADO 2020	ADOS	*Update*	*ADO 2020*	ADOS	*Update*
GDP growth	5.1	2.1	-1.9	-2.6	4.6	4.7	5.1
Inflation	7.3	6.6	6.4	5.6	7.9	8.2	8.2
CAB/GDP	-13.1	-13.9	...	-14.1	-7.8	...	-8.3

... = unavailable, *ADO* = *Asian Development Outlook* (April), *ADOS* = *ADO Supplement* (June), CAB = current account balance, GDP = gross domestic product.
Source: ADB estimates.

Republic of Korea

GDP contracted by 0.7% year on year in the first half of 2020 as COVID-19 took its toll on domestic and external demand. Private consumption was hit hard, contracting by 4.4% as the unemployment rate climbed to 4.3% in the second quarter and consumer confidence remained weak despite an early exit from community quarantine restrictions. Easier social distancing rules in April unleashed pent-up demand, causing surges in retail and car sales and in domestic travel in the second quarter—which quickly stopped as COVID-19 cases climbed again. Efforts to lessen pandemic impact boosted government spending by 6.5%.

Despite lower private construction, private investment expanded by 2.5% year on year in the first half on increased investment in facilities and intellectual property, fueled by expansion in the logistics and digital economy even as corporate retrenchment and closures worsened. Government investment picked up by a robust 13.0% on increased public construction. Net exports shrank by 5.9% as both exports and imports slowed.

On the supply side, all sectors contracted in the first half of 2020: industry by 0.9% with weak exports, services by 0.6%, and agriculture by 3.0% following last year's strong harvest.

Consumer price inflation remained muted at 0.5% year on year in the first 7 months of the year, held below the central bank's revised target of 2.0% by declining global fuel prices and subdued domestic demand. Food prices rose by 2.6%, spurred by government measures to stimulate consumer spending. To support growth, the central bank cut its policy interest rate from 0.7% in March to 0.5% in May. With COVID-19 expenditure, the fiscal deficit rose to equal a record 9.8% of GDP in the first quarter of 2020.

Merchandise exports plunged by 13.1% in the first 6 months of 2020, and merchandise imports shrank by 9.8%, slashing the current account surplus by 15.3% to the equivalent of 2.5% of GDP. The deficit in the service account worsened on lower net travel receipts, and primary and secondary income fell sharply on reduced dividend and investment income. The local currency depreciated by 0.9% against the dollar from January to June, reflecting global investors' flight to safety.

GDP is now projected to contract in 2020 but grow strongly in 2021 as the world economy recovers. A third *supplement*ary budget, worth $29 billion, was approved in July, raising the whole stimulus package to $230 billion, which should boost domestic activity. Inflation is projected to remain muted in 2020 with both demand and commodity prices subdued, and then pick up in 2021, as forecast in *ADO 2020*, on stronger growth. With the export slump, the current account surplus will continue to narrow this year, as earlier projected. Uncertainty about COVID-19 remains the biggest risk to forecasts.

Table 3.2.4 Selected economic indicators, Republic of Korea (%)

	2019	2020 ADO 2020	2020 ADOS	2020 Update	2021 ADO 2020	2021 ADOS	2021 Update
GDP growth	2.0	1.3	−1.0	−1.0	2.3	3.5	3.3
Inflation	0.4	0.9	0.5	0.5	1.3	1.3	1.3
CAB/GDP	3.7	2.8	...	2.8	3.5	...	3.5

... = unavailable, ADO = Asian Development Outlook (April), ADOS = ADO Supplement (June), CAB = current account balance, GDP = gross domestic product.
Source: ADB estimates.

Taipei,China

GDP growth slowed from 2.2% in the first half (H1) of 2019 to 0.8% in H1 2020 under the COVID-19 pandemic, which affected demand both at home and abroad. Private consumption contracted by 3.3%, subtracting 1.7 percentage points from growth as confidence waned and unemployment ticked up, but government consumption increased to add 0.1 points to growth. Gross capital formation rose by 9.2% on higher investment in plant and machinery, contributing 2.1 points to growth. As soft domestic demand pushed down imports, higher exports of electronic components tempered contraction in all exports, such that net exports added 0.3 points to growth.

On the supply side, growth was driven by a 4.8% increase in industrial output in H1 2020, compared to a contraction in H1 2019. Services meanwhile contracted by 0.4% as tourist arrivals sank, and agriculture grew only marginally.

The GDP growth forecast for 2020 is revised down from *ADO 2020* because private consumption contracted in the second quarter more than expected. Domestic and external demand are projected to pick up gradually in H2 of this year as consumer confidence surveys and the manufacturing purchasing managers' index both suggest a bottoming out. Expansion this year will be further supported by planned fiscal stimulus equal to 5.6% of GDP. Growth is forecast to revive strongly in 2021, higher than projected in *ADO 2020* to accommodate a base effect. GDP will be buoyed by rebounds in domestic and external demand and by accommodative monetary and fiscal policies.

The consumer price index fell to an average of 0.2% in H1 2020, with food inflation decelerating to 1.2%. Core inflation excluding volatile food and energy prices ticked down to a marginal 0.1% as domestic demand weakened, transportation and communication prices fell steeply in tandem with lower crude oil and gasoline prices, and as intense competition lowered communication prices. The forecast for inflation is revised down for 2020 but kept unchanged for 2021 as domestic demand and global commodity markets are expected to strengthen in H2 of this year and in 2021.

The current account surplus widened to equal 13.0% of GDP in H1 2020. However, as the trade surplus is projected to hold steady—with imports of machinery, industrial parts, and transportation equipment expected to remain strong thanks to robust public investment—forecasts for the current account surplus are unchanged from *ADO 2020* for both years.

Risks to the outlook tilt mostly to the downside. The main risks are a prolonged global COVID-19 pandemic and increased trade tensions between the US and the People's Republic of China, either of which would adversely affect this highly trade-dependent economy.

Table 3.2.5 Selected economic indicators, Taipei,China (%)

	2019	2020			2021		
		ADO 2020	ADOS	Update	ADO 2020	ADOS	Update
GDP growth	2.7	1.8	0.8	0.8	2.5	3.5	3.5
Inflation	0.6	0.4	0.2	0.2	0.8	0.8	0.8
CAB/GDP	10.7	10.0	...	10.0	12.0	...	12.0

... = unavailable, ADO = *Asian Development Outlook* (April), ADOS = *ADO Supplement* (June), CAB = current account balance, GDP = gross domestic product.
Source: ADB estimates.

South Asia

As COVID-19 continues to spread in South Asia, the subregional economy is projected to contract in 2020 but resume growth in 2021. The forecast for India is downgraded to wider contraction in fiscal year 2020 after a more-than-expected decline in the first quarter. Inflation projections are raised for both years, mainly on higher inflation in India. Current account deficits are now forecast narrower than in *ADO 2020* after domestic demand slackened.

Subregional assessment and prospects

Aggregate GDP in South Asia is projected to contract by 6.8% in 2020, the forecast downgraded from 4.1% growth in *ADO 2020*, and lesser contraction by 3.0% in the June *ADO Supplement*, as the pandemic spreads in the subregion, requiring sustained containment measures. If the pandemic dissipates before the end of 2020, the subregional economy is projected to grow in 2021 by 7.1%, stronger than forecast in *ADO 2020* or the *ADO Supplement* (Figure 3.3.1). Subregional forecasts reflect heavy weighting for India, which provides nearly 80% of the South Asian economy.

The Indian economy contracted by 23.9% from a year ago in the first quarter of fiscal year 2020 (FY2020, ending 31 March 2021), much worse than expected. Weakness before the pandemic and constrained fiscal space left it vulnerable to shocks, and the continuing spread of COVID-19 has prevented quick normalization. As headline inflation stayed above the medium-term target range of 2%–6% for 4 consecutive months, and as core inflation accelerated, the Reserve Bank of India, the central bank, has maintained the policy interest rate at a low 4% since June 2020, after two cuts, late in March and May, totaling 115 basis points. The Indian economy is projected to contract by 9.0% in FY2020. With economic activity expected to normalize more fully next year, the economy is seen to grow by 8.0% in FY2021.

Figure 3.3.1 GDP growth, South Asia

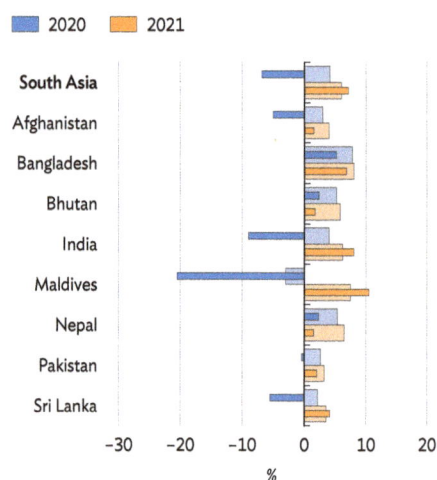

Note: Lighter colored bars are *ADO 2020* forecasts.
Source: *Asian Development Outlook* database.

The subregional assessment and prospects were written by Lei Lei Song. The section on Bangladesh was written by Jyotsana Varma, Soon Chan Hong, and Barun K. Dey; India by Lei Lei Song and Shalini Mittal; Pakistan by Kiyoshi Taniguchi and Ali Khadija; and other economies by Eshini Ekanayake, Abdul Hares Halimi, Manbar Singh Khadka, Kanokpan Lao-Araya, Tshering Lhamo, and Masato Nakane, as well as consultants Abdulla Ali, Macrina Mallari, and Thilina Panduwawala. Authors are in the Central and West Asia and South Asia departments of ADB.

This *Update* also downgrades growth forecasts for the other seven South Asian economies. With only the last quarter of the fiscal year affected by COVID-19, Bangladesh, Bhutan, and Nepal managed to grow in FY2020 (ended 30 June 2020 in Bangladesh and Bhutan and mid-July 2020 in Nepal) but not as much as *ADO 2020* projected. FY2020 growth in Bangladesh and Bhutan was likely the lowest in many decades, and in Nepal lower than any recent year other than FY2016, when the country was devastated by a huge earthquake. Pakistan's economy contracted marginally in FY2020 (ended 30 June 2020). To the extent that the pandemic still affects these economies in FY2021, their recovery will likely be muted, prompting revisions of their growth projections down from *ADO 2020*.

With the impact of COVID-19 spanning almost the whole of this calendar year in Afghanistan, Maldives, and Sri Lanka, 2020 growth projections have been revised to deep contraction. Heavy reliance on tourism renders Maldives and Sri Lanka especially vulnerable. Assuming a tourism rebound next year as the advanced economies recover, this *Update* revises up 2021 growth projections for Maldives and Sri Lanka. It revises down the 2021 growth projection for Afghanistan as it continues to struggle with a difficult security and political situation.

Inflationary pressures in South Asia appear to be rising, largely because of food prices forced up by supply chain disruption. The projection for subregional average inflation in 2020 is revised up from 4.1% in *ADO 2020* to 5.2% to accommodate a higher inflation forecast of 4.5% for India following elevated inflation in April–July. In three other South Asian economies, *ADO 2020* inflation projections are now considered too low, but forecasts are revised down for Bhutan, Maldives, and Sri Lanka on account of depressed demand and for Pakistan as reform takes hold. The forecast for average subregional inflation in 2021 is revised slightly higher, from 4.4% to 4.5%, as economies normalize and demand recovers (Figure 3.3.2).

Combined current account deficits are now forecast narrower, revised from the equivalent of 0.7% of subregional GDP to 0.5% in 2020, and from 1.3% to 0.9% in 2021, as almost every economy in South Asia is now expected to have a smaller current account deficit than forecast in *ADO 2020* because of sluggish domestic demand (Figure 3.3.3). The forecast for Afghanistan's current account surplus including grants rises on new international commitments for COVID-19 emergency response, as well as falling imports. Large current account deficits in Bhutan and Maldives are now seen narrowing more significantly with lower imports for investments. In Bangladesh, current account deficits in both years are still expected to narrow from FY2019 but are now projected wider than in *ADO 2020* following revisions to projections for exports and remittances.

Figure 3.3.2 Inflation, South Asia

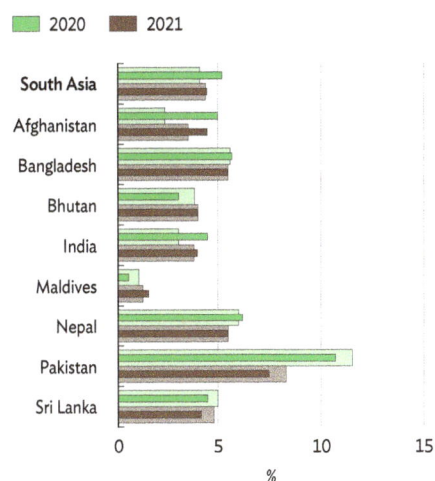

Note: Lighter colored bars are *ADO 2020* forecasts.
Source: *Asian Development Outlook* database.

Figure 3.3.3 Current account balance, South Asia

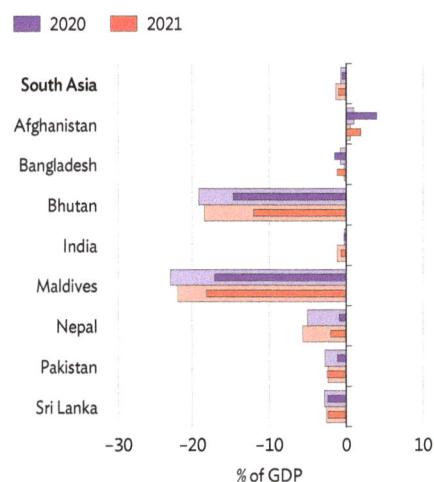

Note: Lighter colored bars are *ADO 2020* forecasts.
Source: *Asian Development Outlook* database.

Bangladesh

After years of steady advances, GDP growth declined in fiscal year 2020 (FY2020, ended 30 June 2020) as the COVID-19 pandemic upended economic activity globally. Disruption to supply chains pushed inflation slightly higher but remained under control, and the current account deficit narrowed. Assuming prudent macroeconomic management and proper implementation of timely announced stimulus packages to mitigate the impact of COVID-19, GDP growth is expected to pick up, inflation to moderate, and current account deficit to narrow further in FY2021.

Updated assessment

GDP grew by 5.2% in FY2020, according to preliminary official estimates. This is significantly less than the *ADO 2020* projection published in April and down from 8.2% growth achieved in FY2019 (Figure 3.3.4). The spread of COVID-19 globally, especially in major trade partners, affected the Bangladesh economy in the final quarter of FY2020. Containment measures enforced by the government from 26 March limited the movement of people and goods within the country and across borders, further impairing economic performance. Exports and imports contracted significantly, and remittances, which grew by more than 20% in the first 8 months, were hit hard in March–May 2020. Moreover, mobility constraints substantially cut back consumer demand. Consumers' uncertainty and lack of confidence scuttled plans for business expansion and investment, further constraining domestic demand.

On the supply side, mobility restrictions disrupted the production and supply of goods and services. Growth in agriculture slowed to 3.1% in FY2020 as farmers faced a shortage of seasonal workers for the harvest, and as pandemic-induced export restrictions hampered poultry, crab, shrimp, and fish production. Industry growth declined sharply to 6.5%, tracking lower garment exports during a global economic slowdown before the pandemic and, with the onset of the pandemic, the postponement or cancellation of export orders from key destinations. Growth in services slowed to 5.3% as wholesale and retail trade and transport services struggled under mobility restrictions.

Consumer inflation accelerated from 5.5% year on year in June 2019 to 6.0% in June 2020 with food inflation rising from 5.4% to 6.5% but nonfood inflation slowing from 5.7% to 5.2%. Overall inflation remained under control, though marginally above *ADO 2020* projections, at an average of 5.7% in FY2020 (Figure 3.3.5). Supply chain disruption created some upward pressure on nonfood inflation in the third quarter of the fiscal year, and pushed up food inflation in the fourth quarter, but these pressures were countered by a bumper food crop and substantially lower international commodity prices.

Figure 3.3.4 Supply-side contributions to growth

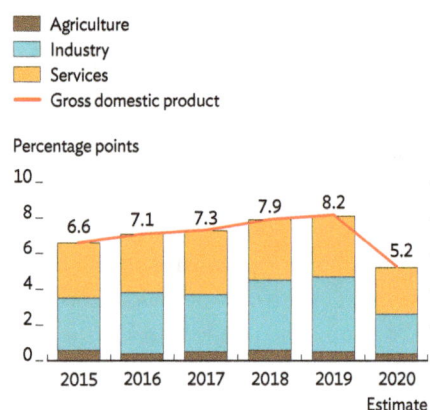

Note: Years are fiscal years ending on 30 June of that year.
Sources: Bangladesh Bureau of Statistics. http://www.bbs.gov.bd; ADB estimates.

Figure 3.3.5 Monthly inflation

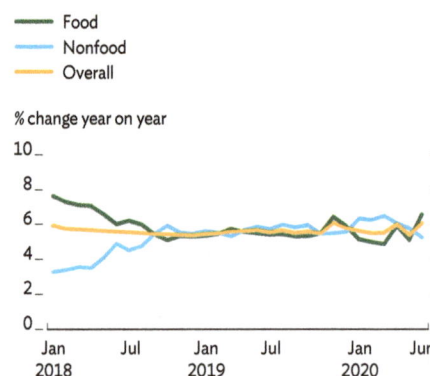

Source: Bangladesh Bank. 2020. *Monthly Economic Trends.* July. https://www.bb.org.bd.

Broad money growth accelerated from 9.9% in FY2019 to 12.6% in FY2020 in line with a monetary program target of 13.0% for the fiscal year set by Bangladesh Bank, the central bank (Figure 3.3.6). Growth in credit to the private sector slowed from 11.3% to 8.6%, falling away from the target of 14.8% as economic activity plunged at home and abroad. Growth in credit to the government accelerated from 19.4% to 55.5%, well above the program target of 37.7%, on borrowing to sustain necessary expenditure in the face of a severe revenue shortfall and to fund COVID-19 related measures, including expanded cash and food transfers to the poor, as well as continued efforts to confine sales of higher-yielding national savings certificates to intended beneficiaries. After relying heavily on bank borrowing until February 2020, the government started requiring autonomous state entities to deposit cash beyond their needs into the government account, making these funds available for budget expenditure. To counter COVID-19 impacts, the central bank reduced its main policy repo rate by 75 basis points to 5.25% in the fourth quarter of FY2020 (Figure 3.3.7).

As in the past, the revised budget for FY2020 set highly ambitious growth targets for revenue, at 38.2%, and spending, at 28.1%. Initial estimates indicate that budget revenue increased only slightly during the year and fell as a percentage of GDP from 9.9% in FY2019 to 9.0% due to the COVID-19 pandemic, while expenditure increased by 10.7%, inching up from 15.4% of GDP to 15.5%. Despite pandemic-related spending on health care and the initiation of stimulus packages, fiscal pressures eased as spending on development projects was reprioritized, lower fuel prices reduced energy subsidies to generate savings, and, as mentioned above, autonomous state entities handed over revenue supplements. The deficit is estimated equal to 6.5% of GDP, crossing above the customary ceiling of 5.0%.

Exports fell by 17.1% in FY2020, reflecting weaker income and trade globally in the first 8 months of the fiscal year, followed by a sharper pandemic-induced trade downturn (Figure 3.3.8). Garment exports, accounting for about 83% of all exports, declined sharply by 18.1%. Other exports including leather and leather products fell by 10.6%, the decline mitigated by raw jute and jute products.

Imports declined by 8.6%, notably reflecting sharply reduced imports of capital goods, garment industry inputs, and fertilizer. Moreover, the government declaration of a general holiday from 26 March to 30 May prompted the idling of nearly all industries and construction projects, which curtailed import requirements. Rice imports were small following a good harvest.

The trade deficit widened moderately to $17.9 billion in FY2020 because the $4.7 billion decline in import payments offset much of the $6.8 billion reduction in exports receipts.

Figure 3.3.6 Growth of monetary indicators

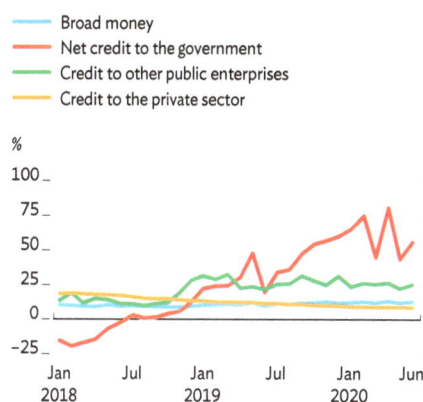

Note: Years are fiscal years ending on 30 June of that year.
Source: Bangladesh Bank. 2020. *Major Economic Indicators, Monthly Update*. July. https://www.bb.org.bd.

Figure 3.3.7 Interest rates

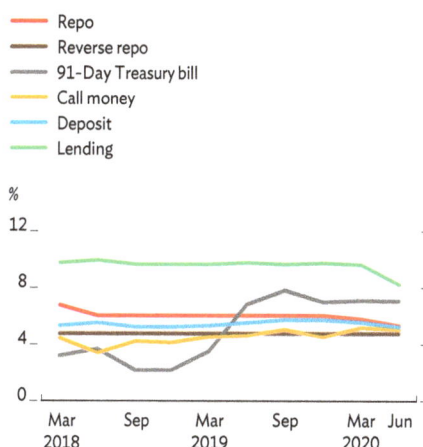

Source: Bangladesh Bank. 2020. *Major Economic Indicators, Monthly Update*. July. https://www.bb.org.bd.

Figure 3.3.8 Exports and export growth

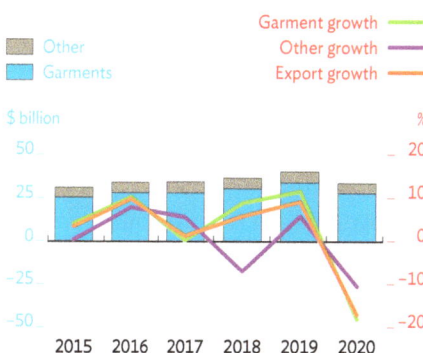

Note: Years are fiscal years ending on 30 June of that year.
Source: Export Promotion Bureau.

Remittance growth was strong from the beginning of FY2020 until February 2020, contracted in March–May under the COVID-19 pandemic, and recovered in June to reach a record inflow of $18.2 billion, up by 10.9% from FY2019 (Figure 3.3.9). This strong result was driven mainly by a 2% cash incentive for remittances from the start of FY2020 and the relaxation of documentation requirements late in the fiscal year. Buoyant remittances take most of the credit for narrowing the current account deficit from $5.1 billion in FY2019, or 1.7% of GDP, to $4.8 billion in FY2020, or 1.5% of GDP (Figure 3.3.10).

The surplus in the combined capital and financial account, adjusted for errors and omissions, ballooned from $5.3 billion in FY2019 to $8.5 billion in FY2020 despite net foreign direct investment inflow falling by 31% to $1.8 billion. With net financial inflow far exceeding the current account deficit, gross foreign exchange reserves in the central bank increased by $3.3 billion to $36.0 billion, covering for 7.2 months of imports of goods and services (Figure 3.3.11).

By severely depressing the economy, COVID-19 created a large financing gap that the government is filling by borrowing from COVID-19 support facilities offered by multilateral financial institutions and from other development partners. These inflows helped to boost foreign exchange reserves and underpinned government finances in the fourth quarter of FY2020. Despite the expectation of sizeable COVID-19 related borrowing, public debt remains relatively low, posing little risk of debt distress.

The Bangladesh taka depreciated by 0.5% against the US dollar in FY2020. The central bank sold some $835 million to commercial banks to meet demand for foreign exchange and lessen excessive market volatility (Figure 3.3.12). Taking into account inflation differentials, the taka appreciated by 6.9% year on year in real effective terms at the end of June 2020.

Prospects

GDP growth is projected at 6.8% in FY2021, revised down from *ADO 2020* because COVID-19 and its impacts are lingering longer than expected, and government stimulus packages have had little time to take hold (Figure 3.3.13). With cautious reopening of the economy since May 2020 and subdued global economic conditions, recovery is expected to be gradual in the first 2 quarters of FY2021. Then a strong manufacturing base will enable more rapid recovery in tandem with projected strengthening of growth in the advanced economies and import demand from them. As factories gradually accelerate production, growth in exports and imports will revive. After the slowdown in March–April 2020, remittances started to recover, firming private consumption. The restoration of consumer confidence, along with government stimulus packages, will boost private and public investment.

Figure 3.3.9 Remittances

Note: Years are fiscal years ending on 30 June of that year.
Source: Bangladesh Bank. https://www.bb.org.bd.

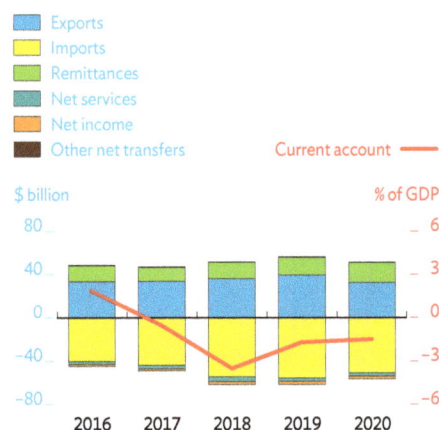

Figure 3.3.10 Current account components

Note: Years are fiscal years ending on 30 June of that year.
Source: Bangladesh Bank. http://www.bb.org.bd.

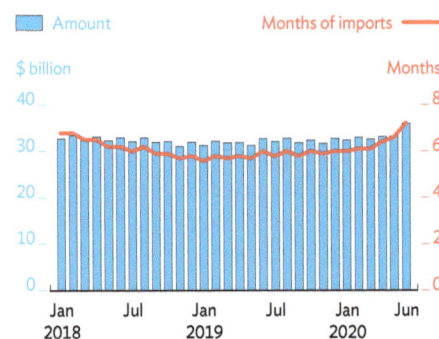

Figure 3.3.11 Foreign exchange reserves

Source: Bangladesh Bank. 2020. *Monthly Economic Trends.* July. https://www.bb.org.bd.

The main downside risk to the forecast would be a prolonged pandemic in Bangladesh or its export markets.

The authorities announced a stimulus package in April 2020 amounting to Tk1.03 trillion, equal to 3.7% of GDP, that includes support for health care, cash and food transfers for the vulnerable, comprehensive support for agriculture, wage support for export industries, subsidies on interest payments for working capital loans, strengthened export facilitation, and liquidity support for refinance schemes to implement stimulus packages. Most stimulus package spending will occur in FY2021.

Growth in agriculture is projected rising to 3.5% in FY2021, aided by government subsidies for seed, fertilizer, innovation, farm mechanization, and irrigation, and by central bank refinancing facilities to provide working capital for small and medium-sized farms affected by the pandemic. Growth in industry is forecast at 10.3%, assuming improved consumer demand, strong export growth following recovery in major export markets, and expected growth in private investment. Supported by sustained growth in agriculture and industry, services are expected to grow by 5.5%.

Inflation is projected steady at 5.5% in FY2021, as forecast in *ADO 2020*, considering a good crop outlook and favorable international commodity prices. Consumer caution and underutilized production capacity should calm any fear that fiscal and monetary stimulus may drive up prices.

Monetary policy will continue to be expansionary and accommodative in FY2021 toward achieving the government growth target while containing inflation. As in the past, the central bank will adjust sector-specific support policies and programs as needed. As part of its expansionary policy, it reduced its main policy repo rate by 50 basis points to 4.75% in its *FY2021 Monetary Policy Statement* in July. Broad money is targeted to grow by 15.6% to June 2021, domestic credit by 19.3%, credit growth to the public sector by 44.4%, and private sector credit by 14.8%. A monetary policy regime based on the policy interest rate, intended to strengthen monetary policy transmission, is under development, and its adoption is deferred until after the COVID-19 pandemic. The main risks to the achievement of monetary goals are uncertainty surrounding COVID-19, natural calamities, any worsening of nonperforming loans, and unexpected inflationary pressure.

With focus shifting to economic recovery, the FY2021 budget aims to raise revenue collection to the equivalent of 11.9% of GDP and spending to 17.9%. Current spending is targeted to grow by 13.2% over the FY2020 revised budget—mostly for higher pay and allowances, interest payments, and subsidies—and development spending by 6.3%, primarily for high-priority development projects to enhance growth.

Figure 3.3.12 Exchange rates

Source: Bangladesh Bank. 2020. *Monthly Economic Trends.* July. https://www.bb.org.bd.

Figure 3.3.13 GDP growth

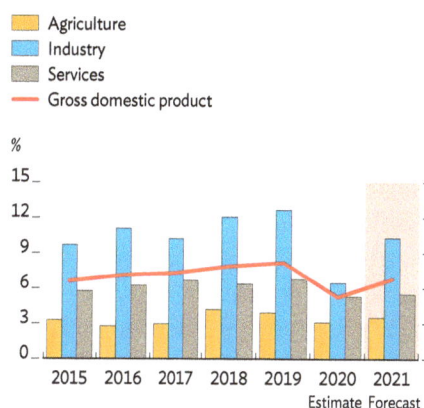

Note: Years are fiscal years ending on 30 June of that year.
Sources: Bangladesh Bureau of Statistics. http://www.bbs.gov.bd; ADB estimates.

Table 3.3.1 Selected economic indicators, Bangladesh (%)

	2019	2020			2021		
		ADO 2020	ADOS	Update	ADO 2020	ADOS	Update
GDP growth	8.2	7.8	4.5	5.2	8.0	7.5	6.8
Inflation	5.5	5.6	5.6	5.7	5.5	5.5	5.5
CAB/GDP	–1.7	–0.8	...	–1.5	–0.3	...	–1.1

... = unavailable, ADO = *Asian Development Outlook* (April), ADOS = ADO Supplement (June), CAB = current account balance, GDP = gross domestic product.
Note: Years are fiscal years ending on 30 June of that year.
Sources: Bangladesh Bureau of Statistics. http://www.bbs.gov.bd; Bangladesh Bank. http://www.bb.org.bd; ADB estimates.

The budget deficit is targeted lower at 6.0% of GDP, nearly 60% of it financed domestically. To further reduce reliance on sales of national savings certificates, an effort begun in FY2019, banks are expected to provide 77% of domestic financing and 23% from nonbank sources, mostly national savings certificates.

While the revenue target is more measured than in previous years, fully achieving it will still be a challenge, considering the impact of COVID-19 on tax revenue. As most stimulus will be implemented through this budget, along with large priority projects, government expenditure must rise. Consequently, the budget deficit is likely to be somewhat higher, equal to 6.2% of GDP, requiring greater reliance on external lines of credit, which are ample (Figure 3.3.14).

Exports are expected to grow by 8.0% in FY2021, with gradual recovery in the first half accelerating in the second along with the expected upturn in the global economy. Export recovery will be aided by government stimulus measures and efforts to improve the business climate, as well as using duty-free trade opportunities extended by People's Republic of China. Potential exists for signing other free or preferential trade agreements.

Imports are expected to grow by 5.0% as the readymade garment industry returns to normal operations and requires substantial imports of input materials. In addition, the accelerated implementation of large infrastructure projects should boost imports of capital equipment and materials. Despite government subsidies to agriculture this year and efforts to expand arable area and mechanization, rice imports may need to be larger than earlier expected to replace harvest that may be lost to floods.

Growth in remittances is likely to moderate to 4.5% in FY2021 as job opportunities for migrants shrink in traditional job markets in the Persian Gulf and Southeast Asia. In addition, net repatriation of workers may continue as host countries adapt to changed economic circumstances. The trade deficit will be broadly stable as both exports and imports increase. The current account deficit is thus expected to equal 1.1% of GDP in FY2021, somewhat above the *ADO 2020* forecast but lower than the FY2020 outcome.

Figure 3.3.14 Fiscal indicators

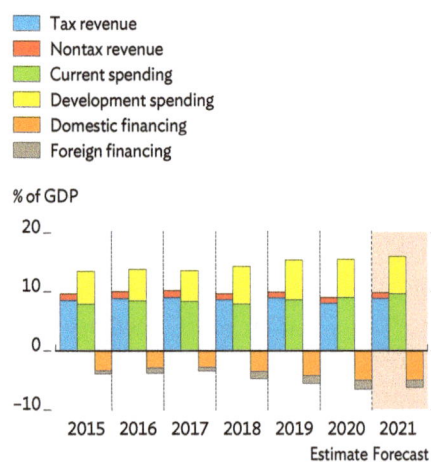

- Tax revenue
- Nontax revenue
- Current spending
- Development spending
- Domestic financing
- Foreign financing

Note: Years are fiscal years ending on 30 June of that year.
Sources: Ministry of Finance. https://www.mof.gov.bd; ADB estimates.

India

The economy contracted more than expected in the first quarter (Q1) of fiscal year 2020 (FY2020, ending 31 March 2021) and is expected to contract in the whole fiscal year. The FY2020 inflation projection is revised up on elevated food prices. Growth and inflation projections for FY2021 will be higher than April forecasts in *ADO 2020* as the economy rebounds. The earlier forecast is retained for the FY2020 current account deficit but narrowed for FY2021 as economic activity resumes more gradually than foreseen.

Updated assessment

GDP contracted by 23.9% year on year in Q1 FY2020 under one of the strictest lockdowns in the world. The unexpectedly deep decline was the worst among large economies in the same quarter and the first since India began publishing quarterly GDP reports in 1996. Contraction was across the board, with most segments of the economy falling by double digits. The collapse in growth was cushioned by healthy expansion in agriculture and double-digit growth in government spending. Imports fell much more than exports to yield positive net exports, which contributed 5.5 percentage points to GDP growth. Structural issues and cyclical factors had already slowed economic growth gradually over the past 2 years.

Industry declined by 38.1%, with manufacturing, mining, and construction all contracting in the range of 40%–50% (Figure 3.3.15). Electricity, gas, water, and other utilities fell much less, by 7.0%, as people stayed at home. Services were hit hard by 20.6% contraction as trade, hotels, and transport together shrank by 47.0%. Financial, real estate, and professional services also contracted but by only 5.3%, while public administration and defense services retrenched by 10.3% as the government directed resources to COVID-19 containment. Agriculture grew by 3.4% in a less restricted rural environment and thanks to a good monsoon and government support for farmers' income.

Private consumption fell by 26.7% as people stayed at home, and precautionary savings rose (Figure 3.3.16). Government consumption, on the other hand, grew by 16.4%. Reflecting bleak private investor sentiment, gross fixed capital formation contracted by 47.1% even as the government increased its capital expenditure despite falling revenue. Exports contracted by 17.1% and imports by 38.5%, turning net exports positive for the first time since Q4 FY2004.

High food prices kept consumer price inflation above the target range of 2%–6%, averaging 6.7% in the first 4 months of FY2020 (Figure 3.3.17). Food inflation averaged 8.5% after surging to 10.0% in April on lockdown-induced supply chain disruption. While fuel prices fell in rural areas along with global oil prices, hikes in excise duties pushed urban fuel prices

Figure 3.3.15 Supply-side contributions to growth

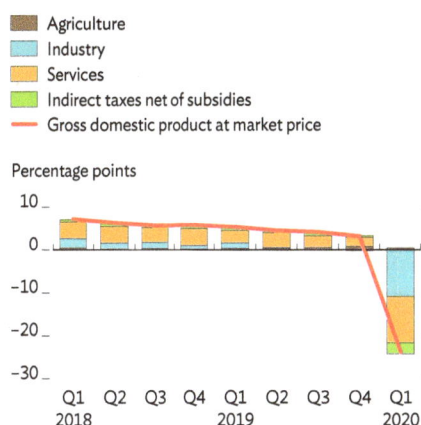

Legend:
- Agriculture
- Industry
- Services
- Indirect taxes net of subsidies
- Gross domestic product at market price

Percentage points

Q = quarter.
Note: Years are fiscal years ending 31 March of the next year. Sector data are in basic prices.
Sources: Ministry of Statistics and Programme Implementation. http://www.mospi.nic.in; CEIC Data Company (accessed 31 August 2020).

Figure 3.3.16 Demand-side contributions to growth

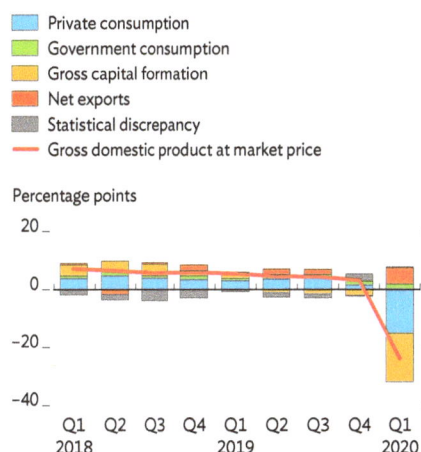

Legend:
- Private consumption
- Government consumption
- Gross capital formation
- Net exports
- Statistical discrepancy
- Gross domestic product at market price

Percentage points

Q = quarter.
Note: Years are fiscal years ending 31 March of the next year.
Sources: Ministry of Statistics and Programme Implementation. http://www.mospi.nic.in; CEIC Data Company (accessed 31 August 2020).

up in June and July. Core inflation accelerated from 4.1% in Q4 FY2019 to 5.1% in the first 4 months of FY2020, driven largely by higher prices for transport, communication, and personal care.

Following initial relief measures in late March, when the national lockdown started, the central government announced in mid-May a full support package, the March–May combined effort worth ₹21 trillion. In addition to supporting health care, the package includes social protection measures such as support for employee provident funds, free food and gas for poor households and migrants, affordable rental housing for migrants, and an increased allocation to the rural employment guarantee program. In June, the government introduced an employment guarantee program for migrant workers and prolonged free food distribution until November. Together, these initiatives effectively protected the most vulnerable groups—the poor, the elderly, the disabled, and women— through a national financial inclusion platform called Pradhan Mantri Jan Dhan Yojana. Credit guarantees were provided for small and medium-sized enterprises, street vendors, and farmers, the last group also receiving subsidies on loan interest. This indirect fiscal support equaled 5.6% of GDP. Included in the package were liquidity injections by the Reserve Bank of India, the central bank, equal to 4.0% of GDP.

The fiscal package initiates a series of reforms such as portable ration cards, usable in different jurisdictions; an equity fund of funds, or investment pool, to mobilize and provide equity funding for micro, small, medium-sized enterprises; legal amendments to ensure that farmers receive competitive prices; and an infrastructure fund for agriculture.

As the economy contracted, central government tax revenue shrank by 29.5% in the first 4 months of FY2020, and nontax revenue and nondebt capital receipts fell by more than half from the same period a year earlier (Figure 3.3.18). The central government spent 34.7% of the FY2020 budget in the first 4 months, outpacing FY2019. The central government had planned to increase borrowing by an amount equal to 2.0% of GDP to reach ₹12.0 trillion this fiscal year. In FY2019, before the pandemic struck India, the fiscal deficit rose to equal 4.6% of GDP, prompting the central government to invoke in February 2020 an escape clause under the Fiscal Responsibility and Budget Management Act that enabled it to budget the FY2020 deficit at 3.5% of GDP.

Transfers to state governments were sustained at ₹1.8 trillion in the first 4 months of FY2020, only slightly less than a year earlier despite sharply falling gross tax revenue, to ease pressure on their finances. In late May, the central government raised borrowing limits for states from the equivalent of 3% of gross state domestic product to 5%, with the bulk of the increase subject to clearly specified reform

Figure 3.3.17 Inflation

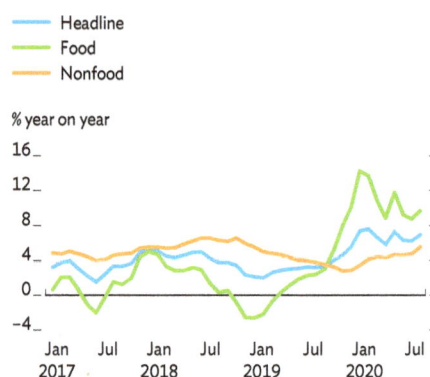

Source: CEIC Data Company (accessed 20 August 2020).

Figure 3.3.18 Fiscal revenue and expenditure

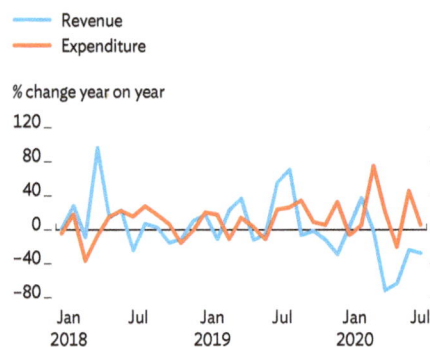

Source: CEIC Data Company (accessed 1 September 2020).

Figure 3.3.19 Interest rates

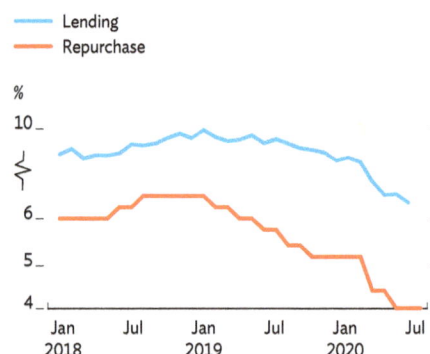

Source: CEIC Data Company (accessed 20 August 2020).

that is both measurable and feasible. In Q1 FY2020, states borrowed ₹1.6 trillion, twice as much as in the same period of either of the past 2 fiscal years. States' market borrowings, which finance more than 85% of their fiscal deficits, reached ₹6.3 trillion in FY2019, equal to 3.0% of GDP.

The central bank cut its policy rates by 115 basis points in a span of 3 months—by 75 basis points in late March, immediately after the national lockdown started, and by 40 points in late May—bringing the repo rate down to 4.00%, its lowest ever (Figure 3.3.19). With consumer inflation above the target range, the central bank maintained its policy rates in August despite a contracting economy. Meanwhile, it continued to roll out liquidity and regulatory measures, such as long-term repurchase operations to sustain small and medium-sized nonbanking financial companies and microfinance institutions, a plan to resolve stressed assets, and special open market operations that included simultaneously selling short-term government securities and purchasing long-term securities. The yield curve steepened as the spread between 10-year government bonds and 91-day Treasury bills more than doubled by 285 basis points from March to August 2020, but it has since eased by 20 points after the central bank launched special open market operations.

Thanks to government and central bank measures, growth in nonfood credit (which excludes public sector loans for procuring crops from farmers) was, at 6.7% at the end of July, unchanged from the end of March (Figure 3.3.20). Growth in credit to agriculture increased to 5.4%. While credit to micro, small, and medium-sized enterprises continues to contract, growth in credit to large enterprises more than doubled to 1.4%. Supported by government guarantees, credit to the service sector—particularly tourism, real estate, and nonbanking financial companies—grew by double digits. The share of nonperforming loans in all bank loans improved from 9.3% in September 2019 to 8.5% at the end of March (Figure 3.3.21).

Merchandise exports contracted by 23.9% year on year in the first 4 months of FY2020 but were overshadowed by a 42.7% decline in merchandise imports reflecting bleak domestic demand (Figure 3.3.22). Gold imports contracted by 79.7% despite rising gold prices and the metal's attraction in uncertain times. Merchandise trade recorded in June its first surplus since 2002, which still left a small deficit in April–July. The trade surplus in services grew by double digits in Q1 FY2020 as imports contracted more than exports. All trade—imports and exports of goods and services—contracted in FY2019 in line with a synchronized slowdown at home and abroad. With its last quarter turning a surplus, the FY2019 current account deficit shrank to the equivalent of 0.8% of GDP.

Figure 3.3.20 Bank credit

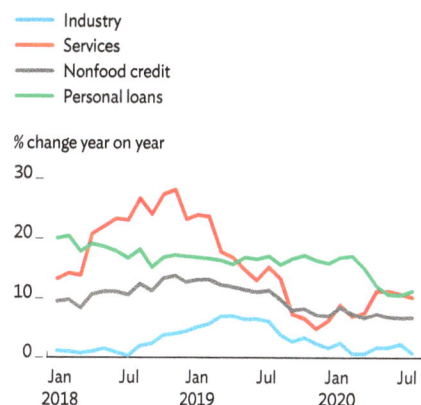

Note: Nonfood credit excludes public sector loans for procuring crops from farmers.
Source: Centre for Monitoring Indian Economy Pvt. Ltd (accessed 31 August 2020).

Figure 3.3.21 Nonperforming loans

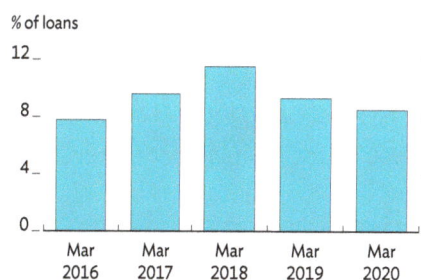

Source: Reserve Bank of India. https://rbi.org.in/ (accessed 21 August 2020).

Figure 3.3.22 Trade indicators

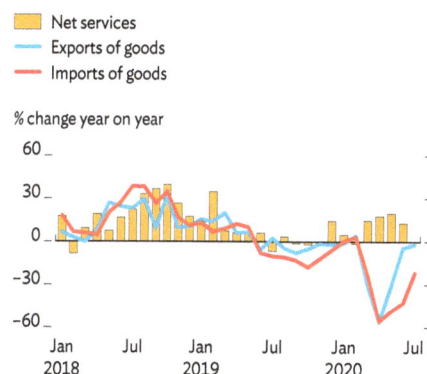

Sources: Centre for Monitoring Indian Economy Pvt. Ltd; CEIC Data Company (accessed 28 August 2020).

Net inflow of foreign direct investment fell by almost half in April and May to $4.4 billion from the year-earlier period, after increasing by 9.8% to $43.3 billion in the whole of FY2019. India remains an attractive investment destination, however, with a major Indian tech firm selling since March stock worth almost $15 billion to 10 global investors and Google announcing in July investment worth $10 billion in India over the next 5–7 years. After outflow totaling $15.9 billion in March, net foreign portfolio inflow turned positive in the first 5 months of FY2020 as stock markets rebounded strongly (Figure 3.3.23). Foreign exchange reserves increased to a record high of $541.4 billion as of the end of August (Figure 3.3.24).

After depreciating by 4.4% against the US dollar in March 2020, the Indian rupee bounced back to appreciate by 3.4% from April to August (Figure 3.3.25). In real effective terms based on consumer prices, the rupee depreciated by 2.1% in Q1 from the previous quarter, despite rising domestic prices.

The lockdown sparked unexpected reverse migration to the countryside. With no urban jobs, social security, or housing, millions of migrant workers returned to their villages during the lockdown, some perhaps carrying COVID-19 to rural areas. The central and state governments quickly stepped in to provide food, transport, and shelter. Even as the economy starts to unlock, uncertainty about urban job markets and deficient social benefits and housing may keep migrant workers away and starve factories of labor, hampering economic normalization.

Prospects

COVID-19 is spreading rapidly in India. Confirmed cases surpassed 4 million in early September, and the virus has penetrated deep into rural areas. Many states and districts have implemented local lockdowns, and the resumption of economic activity has been slow. This *Update* assumes a protracted pandemic and only gradual economic normalization that may be interrupted by surges of new cases to the end of FY2020.

Economic activity is therefore unlikely to resume fully within the remaining 3 quarters of FY2020. With local lockdowns and risk-averse consumers, private consumption may continue to languish. Despite real interest on savings having turned negative, precautionary savings are likely to rise in response to pandemic worries. Rural consumption may benefit, however, from rural employment guarantees and other social protection. So far in FY2020, interventions have generated 1.9 billion person-days of work for 132.8 million active workers, a 44.8% increase over the same period of FY2019. Meanwhile, investment will continue to contract as investors are deterred by heightened risk and declines in public capital expenditure. Lockdowns drove down the value of projects announced or completed in Q1 FY2020 to historic lows (Figure 3.3.26).

Figure 3.3.23 Stock prices

Source: Bloomberg (accessed 1 September 2020).

Figure 3.3.24 Gross international reserves

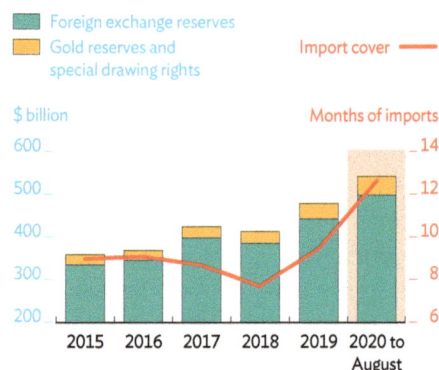

Note: Years are fiscal years ending on 31 March of the next year.
Sources: CEIC Data Company (accessed 4 September 2020); ADB estimates.

Figure 3.3.25 Exchange rates

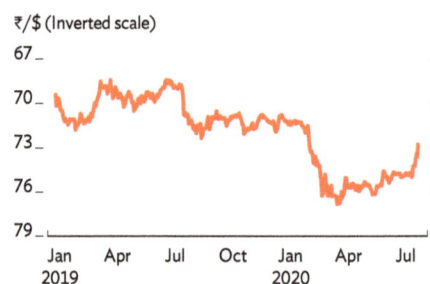

Source: Bloomberg (accessed 1 September 2020).

Several high-frequency indicators improved in Q2 FY2020. After falling to historic lows in April, the purchasing managers' index for manufacturing bounced back to 52.0 in August and for services to 41.8 (Figure 3.3.27). Electricity generation in August was only 2.6% lower than a year earlier, improving on a 18.1% decline in Q1. August also saw freight traffic grow by 3.9% year on year and steel production recovery but not to that extent (Figure 3.3.28). Consumers' confidence in the current situation declined in July, but their expectations for the future inched up (Figure 3.3.29). Google mobility in retail and recreation improved from a mere 13% of normal in April 2020 to 58% in August, and workplace mobility has doubled since mid-April as offices reopened. The number of e-way bills, registering interstate shipments by road of goods worth more than ₹50,000, recovered from a record low of 8.6 million in April to 47.4 million in August, higher than before the lockdown.

Agriculture is expected to continue to prosper with a good monsoon, higher minimum support prices, and ample labor. Farm tractor sales rebounded by double digits in June and July after contracting by 80.1% in April. Cultivated area reported sown in June was double a year earlier, and area with sowing completed was higher. Major ordinances issued in June to reform agriculture markets will ensure competitive prices to farmers and boost rural incomes.

On balance, the economy is expected to contract by 9.0% in FY2020, more than projected in the June *ADO Supplement*. Growth year on year is expected to remain negative for the next 2 or possibly 3 quarters. Economic activity may start to resume more fully from early FY2021, with growth expected to rebound, albeit gradually, to 8.0% in FY2021, higher than forecast in either *ADO 2020* or the *Supplement*.

With revenue falling sharply and expenditure rising to fight the pandemic and support the economy, the central government's fiscal deficit is expected to rise dramatically in FY2020. A contracting economy similarly strains state finances as their own revenue takes a hit. In addition, transfers from the center, constituting 40% of states' revenue, will decline further.

The highest priority is to contain the pandemic with robust testing and tracking and to shore up treatment capacity in tandem with developing vaccines as rapidly as possible and preparing for their efficient and equitable delivery. India currently conducts over 1 million COVID-19 tests daily, which bodes well for containing the pandemic and reopening the economy. Meanwhile, protecting the poor, preserving jobs, and reviving the economy require more direct support for the vulnerable, such as extending conditional cash transfers to other low-income groups, and for businesses, particularly micro, small, medium-sized enterprises.

Figure 3.3.26 Investment projects

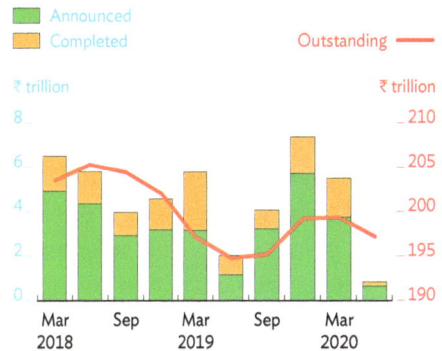

Source: Centre for Monitoring Indian Economy Pvt. Ltd.

Figure 3.3.27 Purchasing managers' indexes

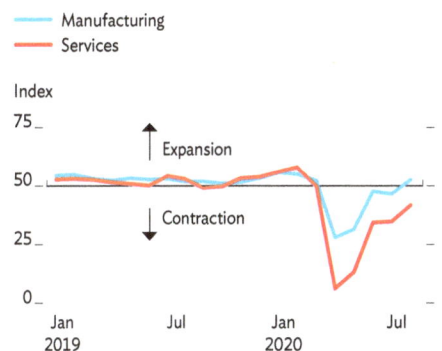

Note: Nikkei, Markit.
Source: Bloomberg (accessed 3 September 2020).

Figure 3.3.28 Selected high-frequency indicators

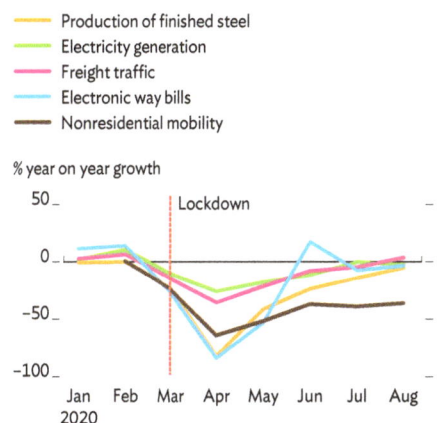

Note: Nonresidential mobility is expressed as percentage change from a baseline derived from median values during the 5-week period from 3 January to 6 February 2020.
Sources: CEIC Data Company; CMIE and Google COVID-19 Community Mobility Reports (accessed 10 September 2020).

The government has announced ambitious initiatives in a wide range of areas to foster a more robust recovery sooner rather than later: notably agriculture market reform discussed above, upgrading industrial park infrastructure, and implementing the National Infrastructure Pipeline. Their careful coordination under government agencies promises to promote foreign direct investment, attract global supply chains to India, and spawn opportunities for India to create modern manufacturing hubs.

With government action constrained by fiscal weakness, the central bank is expected to play a key role in reviving credit flows and keeping borrowing costs low. In its *Financial Stability Report*, published on 24 July, it estimates as its optimistic scenario nonperforming loans reaching 12.5% of all loans outstanding at the end of FY2020. As nonperforming loans rise, policy makers must be aware of unintended risks to the financial sector posed over the medium term by some monetary and regulatory measures. With its loan moratorium closing on 31 August, the central bank introduced a one-off plan allowing lenders to restructure loans to support borrowers hit by COVID-19 but otherwise sound. Under strict conditions requiring borrowers to shoulder some of the loss and otherwise behave responsibly, and providing a clear timetable, borrowers may reach agreements with lenders to reschedule repayment, avail themselves of a moratorium on loan repayment, or lower interest rates on existing loans.

Inflation is expected to ease in the remainder of FY2020 as an anticipated bumper harvest tames food inflation and depressed economic activity exerts little price pressure. Global oil prices lower than last year will continue to pass through to the domestic economy, even when the government hikes excise taxes. Headline inflation is forecast to average 4.5% in FY2020 and decline somewhat to 4.0% in FY2021 as food inflation falls, with both revised projections higher than in *ADO 2020*.

Depressed global demand and border closures will shrink exports of goods and services in FY2020. Import of goods and services will contract further because of subdued domestic demand, low oil import bills, and tensions with the People's Republic of China (PRC), leaving only a small trade deficit in FY2020. Despite lower remittances, the current account deficit will shrink to the equivalent of 0.3% of GDP in FY2020, as forecast in *ADO 2020* (Figure 3.3.30). Exports of goods and services are expected to recover in FY2021 as global growth rebounds. Imports will pick up too, likely at a slower pace as India lags global recovery but enough to double the small current account deficit to 0.6% of GDP in FY2021, still narrower than forecast in *ADO 2020*.

Figure 3.3.29 Consumer confidence

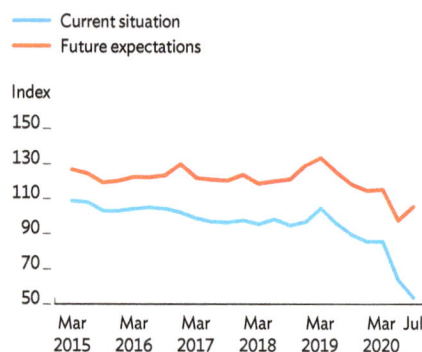

Source: Reserve Bank of India. https://www.rbi.org.in (accessed 22 August 2020).

Figure 3.3.30 Current account indicators

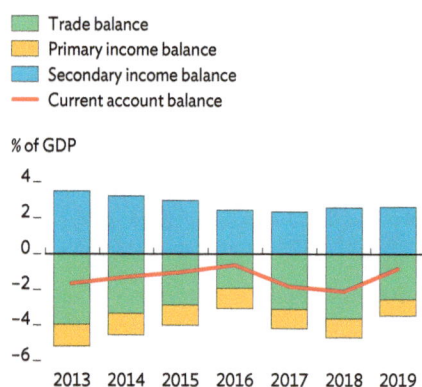

Note: Years are fiscal years ending on 31 March of the next year.
Source: CEIC Data Company (accessed 27 August 2020).

Table 3.3.2 Selected economic indicators, India (%)

	2019	2020			2021		
		ADO 2020	ADOS	Update	ADO 2020	ADOS	Update
GDP growth	4.2	4.0	-4.0	-9.0	6.2	5.0	8.0
Inflation	4.8	3.0	3.0	4.5	3.8	4.0	4.0
CAB/GDP	-0.8	-0.3	...	-0.3	-1.2	...	-0.6

... = unavailable, ADO = *Asian Development Outlook* (April), ADOS = *ADO Supplement* (June), CAB = current account balance, GDP = gross domestic product.
Note: Years are fiscal years ending on 31 March of the next year.
Source: ADB estimates.

Net capital inflow is expected to remain positive in the whole of FY2020 as foreign investors adjust to the new normal (Figure 3.3.31). PRC investment in India, having grown rapidly in recent years, may be deterred by bilateral tensions, but India will remain a preferred destination for foreign direct investment. Pandemic disruption presents opportunities for India to attract foreign investors as global supply chains adjust to a new landscape.

Any early deployment of vaccines poses an upside risk to the outlook, but most risks tilt to the downside. The future course of the pandemic is unknown and may seriously dent India's growth potential. Significantly higher public and private debt could constrain investment in infrastructure and new technology, and a proliferation of nonperforming loans caused by the pandemic could further weaken the financial sector and its ability to support economic growth.

Figure 3.3.31 Portfolio capital flows

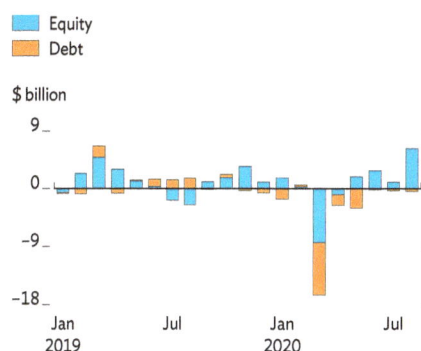

Source: Security and Exchange Board of India.
https://www.fpi.nsdl.co.in (accessed 1 September 2020).

Pakistan

GDP contracted in fiscal year 2020 (FY2020, ended 30 June 2020) in the wake of the COVID-19 pandemic and the economic consequences of containment measures. Rising food prices pushed inflation into double digits, but the current account deficit eased considerably as merchandise imports fell steeply because of containment disruptions, lower oil prices, and local currency depreciation. Growth is forecast to recover in FY2021 as economic sentiment improves with the expected subsiding of COVID-19 and the resumption of structural reform. Inflation will ease somewhat with lower food and oil prices, but the current account deficit will widen as imports expand.

Updated assessment

Real GDP at factor cost contracted by 0.4% in FY2020 as the COVID-19 pandemic severely battered economic activity, erasing gains achieved in the first half of the fiscal year and reversing 1.9% growth in FY2019. Containment restrictions, including the suspension of travel and the closure of nonessential businesses, induced concurrent demand and supply shocks that significantly reduced output (Figure 3.3.32).

On the supply side, agriculture remained largely unaffected as its growth accelerated from 0.6% in FY2019 to 2.7% in FY2020 despite a severe locust infestation that damaged the harvests of many crops, most notably cotton. Higher water availability enabled increased production of wheat, rice, and maize, as did government subsidies for fertilizer and an uptick in agriculture credit disbursement. Industry contracted by 2.6% in FY2020 as shutdowns and supply chain disruptions related to COVID-19 exacerbated other adverse factors affecting the sector since FY2019, notably double-digit inflation, higher import duties on nonessential items, the high cost of working capital imposed by high interest rates until the third quarter of FY2020, and rising costs for energy and other inputs as the Pakistan rupee depreciated, though by only a moderate 6.3% year on year against the US dollar, as of June 2020.

Large-scale manufacturing, which accounts for about half of the industry sector, deepened 2.6% contraction in FY2019 to contract by 10.2% in FY2020, with exceptionally large decreases occurring after the onset of the pandemic and spreading across the board. Particularly pronounced declines in FY2020 were by 43.8% for automobiles, 20.1% for coke and petroleum products, 34.8% for electronics, and 10.4% for textile. By contrast, construction expanded by 8.1% on higher public development spending. With the marked fall in industry, closure of nonessential businesses, and suspension of travel and transport, the service sector reversed 3.8% expansion in FY2019 to contract by 0.6% in FY2020.

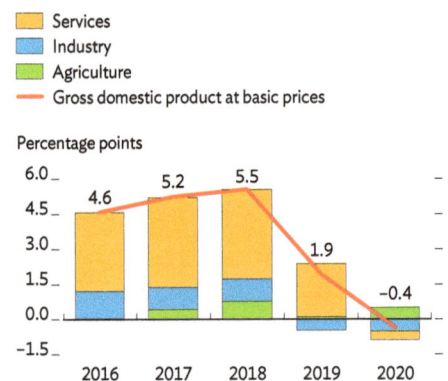

Figure 3.3.32 Supply-side contributions to growth

Note: Years are fiscal years ending on 30 June of that year.
Source: Ministry of Finance. *Pakistan Economic Survey 2019–20.* http://www.finance.gov.pk.

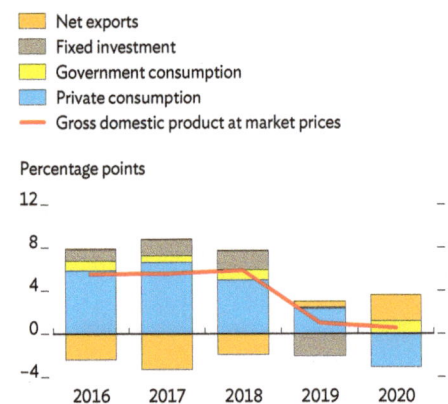

Figure 3.3.33 Demand-side contributions to growth

Note: Years are fiscal years ending on 30 June of that year.
Source: Ministry of Finance. *Pakistan Economic Survey 2019–20.* http://www.finance.gov.pk.

On the demand side, private consumption, which provides 79.0% of GDP, weakened in the second half of FY2020 in response to lost income from a domestic lockdown and heightened uncertainty about the duration and financial impact of the pandemic, trimming growth by 3.2 percentage points (Figure 3.3.33). By contrast, public consumption edged up to 12.6% of GDP and contributed 1.2 points to growth. A fiscal stimulus package equal to 3.0% of GDP was introduced to mitigate the health and economic impacts of the COVID-19 pandemic. Fixed investment stagnated in FY2020 as uncertainty caused by the pandemic cut investment by the private sector and public enterprises, offsetting the rise in government investment on development projects. Net exports contributed 2.5 percentage points to growth as imports dropped substantially in the wake of global trade disruption, rupee depreciation, higher import duties on nonessential items, and restrained economic activity at home.

Inflation jumped from 6.8% in FY2019 to 10.7% in FY2020, led by food inflation, which averaged 13.6% in urban areas and 15.9% in rural, primarily reflecting food supply shocks (Figure 3.3.34). Other factors were an increase in utility prices, the knock-on effect of currency depreciation, and transport strikes during the first 3 quarters of FY2020. In the last quarter of FY2020, average inflation took a downward trajectory as overall domestic demand was subdued and domestic gasoline prices fell when a huge decline in international oil prices was passed on to consumers.

As inflationary pressures eased, the State Bank of Pakistan, the central bank, cut its policy rate by a cumulative 625 basis points from March to June 2020 to 7.0% (Figure 3.3.35). It also introduced additional measures to support economic recovery against the backdrop of the COVID-19 pandemic, notably concessional loans for businesses to protect employment, a relaxation of conditions limiting subsidized credit schemes for exporters, a higher regulatory ceiling on banks' lending to small and medium-sized enterprises, and new concessional loans for manufacturing and medical support industries. Outstanding credit to the private sector nevertheless declined marginally from the equivalent of 17.6% of GDP in FY2019 to 16.4% in FY2020, even as the money supply increased by 16.4%.

The consolidated fiscal deficit of the federal and provincial governments fell from the equivalent of 9.1% of GDP in FY2019 to an estimated 8.1% in FY2020, following fiscal consolidation gains of the first 3 quarters, before the COVID-19 shock (Figure 3.3.36). Fiscal revenue is estimated at 15.0% of GDP in FY2020, up by 2.1 percentage points from the previous year. This mainly reflected tax revenue declining by 0.4 percentage points from the previous year and nontax revenue increasing almost threefold to equal 3.7% of GDP in FY2020, largely on

Figure 3.3.34 Monthly inflation

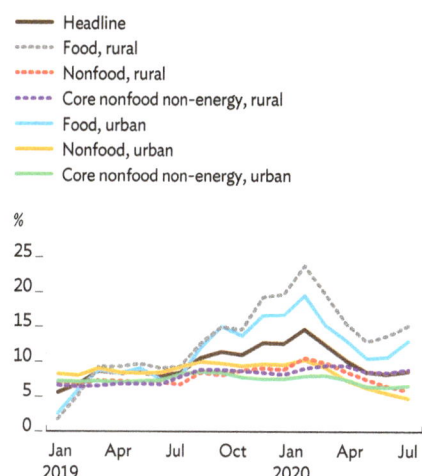

Source: State Bank of Pakistan. *Economic Data.*
http://www.sbp.org.pk.

Figure 3.3.35 Interest rates

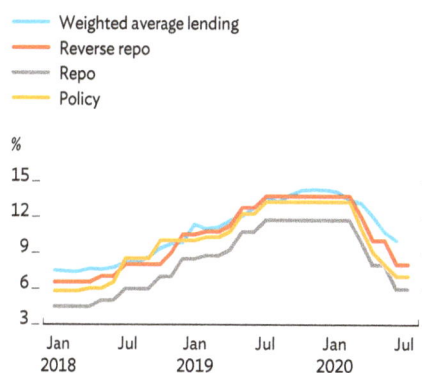

Sources: State Bank of Pakistan. *Economic Data.*
http://www.sbp.org.pk (accessed 28 July 2020);
Monetary Policy Information Compendium May 2020.

Figure 3.3.36 Government budget indicators

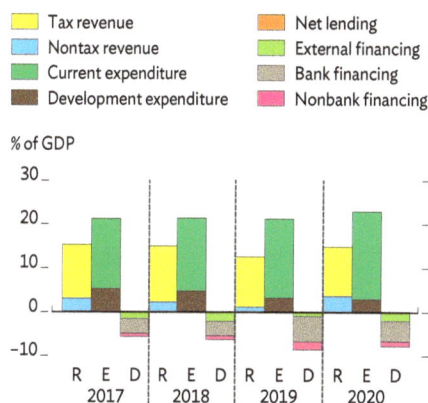

D = deficit, E = expenditure, R = revenue.

Note: Years are fiscal years ending on 30 June of that year.
FY2020 is provisional.

Sources: Ministry of Finance, Budget in Brief FY2019–2020
and Summary of Consolidated Federal & Provincial
Budgetary Operations (July 2019–March 2020).

higher central bank profits, which are transferred to the Treasury, and the receipt of the telecommunication license fee. On the expenditure side, spending increased from 22.0% of GDP in FY2019 to 23.1% in FY2020 on account of increased interest payments and a fiscal stimulus package to mitigate economic losses from the COVID-19 pandemic. Public sector development spending remained stable at around 2.6% in FY2020, supporting construction and other business activities.

The fiscal deficit was financed largely through domestic borrowing, which provided 73.5% of total financing, 57.5% from the banks and 16.0% from other sources. External borrowing financed 26.5% of the deficit while planned privatization receipts did not materialize in FY2020 (Figure 3.3.37). Government borrowing from commercial banks equaled 5.2% of GDP in FY2020, as direct budget financing from the central bank was discontinued. Gross public debt reached an estimated 86.8% of GDP in FY2020 with high fiscal deficit and GDP contraction, negating significant fiscal consolidation gains made in the first 9 months of FY2020 under an International Monetary Fund (IMF) stabilization program. Rollover risk of the public debt was reduced with the shift in debt profile towards longer tenors. Consequently, average time to maturity of domestic debt held by other than central bank increased to 2.7 years in FY2020 from 1.5 years in FY2019.

The current account deficit eased significantly from the equivalent of 4.8% of GDP in FY2019 to 1.1% in FY2020 as almost all import categories recorded steep reductions in the wake of the COVID-19 pandemic (Figure 3.3.38). The deficit in merchandise trade narrowed by 27.9% as the global slowdown, lower oil prices, and rupee depreciation drove down merchandise imports by 18.2%. Following the onset of the pandemic, merchandise exports reversed the rising trend seen at the beginning of FY2020 to decline by 7.2% in the whole fiscal year. Concurrently, the service trade deficit shrank by 43.0% as suspended travel and transport caused service imports to drop by 24.3%. Despite lower international oil prices, remittances from workers overseas, many of them in the Persian Gulf, remained robust, growing by 6.3% in FY2020 despite volatility month to month—contracting by 50.7% in May, for example, and expanding by 32.2% in June. Net inflows of foreign direct investment almost doubled to $2.6 billion in FY2020 with the renewal of telecommunication licenses and increased flows into the energy industry, while the rising trend in foreign portfolio investment witnessed from July 2019 to February 2020 reversed as foreign investors offloaded local government securities with the unfolding of COVID-19 global pandemic.

Disbursement from multilateral and bilateral development partners increased considerably to support government stabilization efforts and mitigate the adverse impact of the

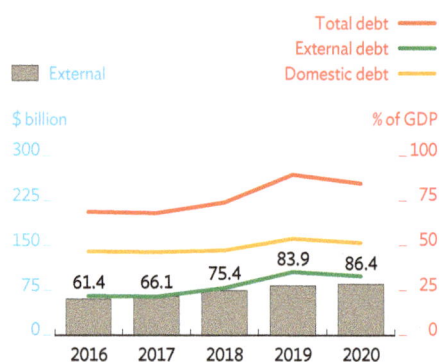

Figure 3.3.37 Public debt

Note: Years are fiscal years ending on 30 June of that year. FY2020 is provisional based on data for the first 9 months.
Source: State Bank of Pakistan. *Economic Data.* http://www.sbp.org.pk (accessed 28 July 2020).

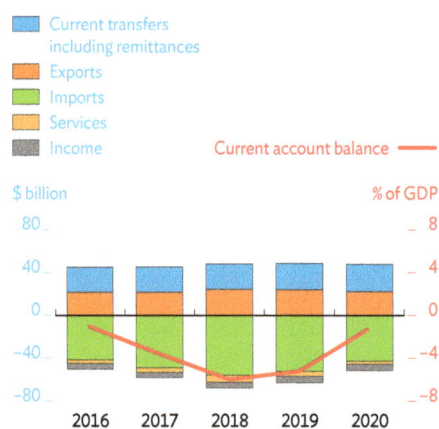

Figure 3.3.38 Current account components

Note: Years are fiscal years ending on 30 June of that year.
Source: State Bank of Pakistan. http://www.sbp.org.pk (accessed 28 July 2020).

COVID-19 pandemic. This included one-off emergency assistance worth $1.4 billion under the IMF Rapid Financing Instrument to meet urgent financial needs stemming from the COVID-19 pandemic. Buoyed by these inflows, international reserves reached $12.1 billion at the end of FY2020, improving import coverage to 2.9 months (Figure 3.3.39).

Prospects

Broad economic recovery is projected for FY2021, with GDP growth estimated to rebound to 2.0%, albeit lower than forecast in *ADO 2020*. This forecast assumes that the COVID-19 impact will subside by the end of 2020—the end of the second quarter of FY2021—allowing global conditions to normalize and economic sentiment to improve. It also assumes the resumption of structural reform under an ongoing IMF Extended Fund Facility program to address macroeconomic imbalances. The government has proposed detailed economic stimulation measures in its FY2021 budget. In addition to reallocating PRs7 billion from the Federal Public Sector Development Programme budget to COVID-19 response, the proposed budget raises allocations for initiatives that provide social protection to the disadvantaged. The flagship Ehsaas program will be scaled up from PRs190 billion in FY2020, or 2.3% of government expenditure, to PRs230 billion in FY2021, or 2.6%. With support from development partners, the government has been deploying the Benazir Income Support Programme to further counter the detrimental impacts of the COVID-19 pandemic.

On the supply side, agriculture is expected to continue to lend impetus to GDP growth. Crop damage from a severe locust infestation in FY2020 prompted several budgetary measures, including an agriculture emergency program worth PRs13.7 billion to support investment and expansion in agriculture and livestock rearing. Growth in industry is forecast to improve in FY2021, led predominantly by construction and small-scale manufacturing. In addition to the normalization of global economic conditions, improved market sentiment, and stronger business and consumer confidence expected with the easing of the COVID-19 pandemic by the end of the first half of FY2021, a relatively low policy rate should facilitate the financing of industrial initiatives. Spurred by improved growth in agriculture and industry, coupled with an expected improvement in domestic demand overall, services should also contribute to growth in FY2021.

Inflation is projected to slow to 7.5% in FY2021, lower than the April forecast in *ADO 2020* driven by the expected economic recovery, but tempered by expenditure reform, and the government's decision to stop borrowing from the central bank, which should help slow growth in the money supply

Figure 3.3.39 Gross official reserves and exchange rate

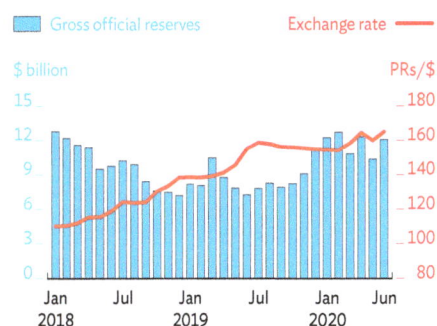

Source: State Bank of Pakistan. http://www.sbp.org.pk (accessed 28 July 2020).

Table 3.3.3 Selected economic indicators, Pakistan (%)

	2019	2020			2021		
		ADO 2020	ADOS	Update	ADO 2020	ADOS	Update
GDP growth	1.9	2.6	−0.4	−0.4	3.2	2.0	2.0
Inflation	6.8	11.5	11.0	10.7	8.3	8.0	7.5
CAB/GDP	−4.8	−2.8	...	−1.1	−2.4	...	−2.4

... = unavailable, ADO = *Asian Development Outlook* (April), ADOS = *ADO Supplement* (June), CAB = current account balance, GDP = gross domestic product.

Note: Years are fiscal years ending on 30 June of that year.

Source: ADB estimates.

to 14.2% in FY2021. An upside risk to the inflation forecast is global oil prices rising higher than currently projected in FY2021. A greater risk would be electricity tariff increases currently under consideration to improve cost recovery in the industry and help bring down government subsidies.

The fiscal deficit is forecast to decline to the equivalent of 7.0% of GDP in FY2021. Revenue is projected to increase, reflecting ambitious revenue-mobilization targets following initiatives to withdraw tax exemptions, rationalize tax concessions, and broaden the tax base. This forecast depends on COVID-19 risks subsiding and rapid economic recovery to pre-COVID norms. Fiscal expenditure is projected to increase only slightly as the anticipated curtailment of some current expenditures such as subsidies somewhat compensates for higher development and social sector spending, which will continue to rise to support growth and economic recovery.

The current account deficit is anticipated to remain contained at the equivalent of 2.4% of GDP in FY2021, unchanged from the *ADO 2020* forecast. Exports are expected to grow in FY2021 with the likely pickup in economic activity in Pakistan's major trade partners, and as Pakistan's exports become more competitive thanks to government measures to reduce business costs. Imports will rebound from a low base in FY2020 and, more importantly, in response to economic recovery in FY2021—and despite higher tariffs on imports of nonessential goods. Remittances should continue to cushion the current account deficit but will likely be lower than in FY2020 with the layoff of Pakistani workers overseas, in particular in the Persian Gulf, as economic activity remains soft globally (Figure 3.3.40).

Continued improvement is anticipated in the balance of payments and foreign reserve position in FY2021. This prospect owes to a flexible, market-determined exchange rate regime adopted in early 2019, which significantly improved the FY2020 external position; the anticipated containment of fiscal and current account deficits; debt service suspension granted by the Group of 20; and increasing foreign direct investment (Figure 3.3.41). Pakistan's public debt is expected to revert to a downward trajectory as the IMF stabilization program improves prospects for fiscal consolidation, and assuming rapid economic recovery from the COVID-19 shock. However, the economic outlook is subject to unusually potent downside risks in light of uncertainty about the duration and magnitude of the COVID-19 pandemic, the persistence of containment measures, and more than expected fall in remittances.

Figure 3.3.40 Remittances

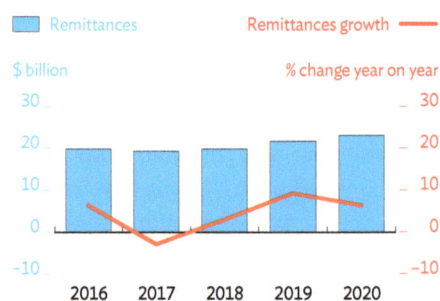

Note: Years are fiscal years ending on 30 June of that year.
Source: State Bank of Pakistan. http://www.sbp.org.pk (accessed 28 July 2020).

Figure 3.3.41 Exchange rates

Source: State Bank of Pakistan. http://www.sbp.org.pk (accessed 28 July 2020).

Other economies

Afghanistan

In the first half of 2020, the economy was beset by COVID-19 on top of continued security and political challenges. Border closures and lockdowns in the major cities disrupted trade and transportation, undermining industry and services. Household consumption declined, confidence waned, and investment fell sharply, as did remittance inflow as thousands of Afghans returned from Iran and Pakistan. These developments drove up unemployment and suppressed business activity and regional trade, and thus government revenue.

These factors will likely shrink GDP in 2020—a significant downward revision from the *ADO 2020* forecast for sustained though modest growth. An expected rebound in 2021 should bring low but positive growth, assuming that peace talks are successful and enable improved security and political stability.

Average inflation over the first 6 months of 2020 more than doubled from 2.5% a year earlier to 5.3% as food inflation jumped threefold on shortages caused by trade restrictions, border closures, and possibly hoarding, though nonfood inflation remained subdued at 0.8%. These results and the expectation that shortages will persist inform inflation forecasts, that are revised up from those published in *ADO 2020*.

As trade, economic activity, and customs revenue faltered under the pandemic, domestic fiscal revenue declined in tandem in the first half of this year. It is projected to fall in the full year from the equivalent of 13.6% of GDP in 2019 to 10.0%. With expenditure rising as revenue drops, the fiscal deficit is forecast to reach 4.0% of GDP in 2020. Fiscal support commitments from development partners amount to 2.0% of GDP, leaving the other half of the gap to be financed domestically.

In the first half of 2020, exports declined by 28% from the same period of last year alongside faltering remittances. Imports also fell, by 24%, and higher external grant inflow widened the current account surplus. In June 2020, international reserves exceeded $9 billion for the first time ever, providing cover for 15 months of imports. This occurred despite continued US dollar auctions by Da Afghanistan Bank, the central bank, that managed to stabilize the exchange rate. The current account surplus is projected to be higher than forecast in *ADO 2020* in both 2020 and 2021 in light of declining imports and large COVID-19 grant commitments from development partners.

Risks to the forecast—high uncertainty about every major factor: the persistence of the pandemic, security and political developments, international grant inflow, and weather— tilt to the downside. On the positive side, if intra-Afghan

Table 3.3.4 Selected economic indicators, Afghanistan (%)

	2019	2020			2021		
		ADO 2020	ADOS	Update	ADO 2020	ADOS	Update
GDP growth	3.0	3.0	−4.5	−5.0	4.0	3.0	1.5
Inflation	2.3	2.3	5.0	5.0	3.5	4.5	4.5
CAB/GDP	8.6	1.0	...	4.0	0.5	...	2.0

... = unavailable, ADO = *Asian Development Outlook* (April), ADOS = *ADO Supplement* (June), CAB = current account balance, GDP = gross domestic product.

Note: Years are fiscal years ending on 20 December of that year.

Source: ADB estimates.

peace negotiations succeed and bring a speedy political settlement—and consequently stronger commitment from development partners at their next conference, expected in November 2020—the economy should recover more rapidly and improve prospects for peaceful economic development.

Bhutan

The COVID-19 pandemic is taking a heavy toll, disrupting supply chains for critical imports and exports. All types of economic activity were stymied by border and air closures in March 2020—which shut down the large tourism industry—and other measures to contain the virus. An exodus of expatriate workers to India left severe shortages of labor and skills.

With most constraints expected to persist, forecasts for growth in fiscal year 2020 (FY2020, ended 30 June 2020) and FY2021 are substantially downgraded from April forecasts in *ADO 2020*, both years now projected to underperform FY2018 and FY2019. Growth will likely be further depressed by the imposition of a nationwide lockdown on 11 August, and could even result in a contraction if such episodes recur until a vaccine becomes available.

Absent official GDP data, supply-side indicators covering most of FY2020 indicate that agriculture grew by 3.9% on continued government support, and hydropower generation surged by 27.0%, markedly boosting export sales. Manufacturing contracted by 5.3%, and construction by 3.9%, as both industries suffered supply disruption and labor shortages. Expansion in the large service sector slowed from 9.1% in FY2019 to 3.8%.

On the demand side, growth in consumption expenditure slipped to 0.6%. Private spending declined as income and credit use weakened and containment measures limited activity, but strong expansion in government current expenditure kept overall consumption afloat. Fixed investment underpinned growth in FY2020 as government capital spending increased substantially in the first 9 months of FY2020. Statistically, though, net exports were the largest contributor to growth, mainly reflecting lower imports.

Fiscal policy is expansionary to counter downdraft from the COVID-19 pandemic. Fiscal expenditure soared by 44.0% in FY2020 and is slated to expand by a further 8.0% in FY2021. Policy is for the National Resilience Fund to sustain individual livelihoods and welfare while the Economic Contingency Plan fosters employment and growth by underpinning three critical areas: tourism, construction, and agriculture. As government revenue slows in tandem with economic growth, fiscal deficits are forecast to widen to the equivalent of 6.2% of GDP in FY2020 and 7.4% in FY2021.

Table 3.3.5 Selected economic indicators, Bhutan (%)

	2019	2020			2021		
		ADO 2020	ADOS	Update	ADO 2020	ADOS	Update
GDP growth	4.4	5.2	2.4	2.4	5.8	1.7	1.7
Inflation	2.8	3.8	2.8	3.0	4.0	4.0	4.0
CAB/GDP	-22.6	-19.1	...	-14.6	-18.4	...	-11.9

... = unavailable, ADO = *Asian Development Outlook* (April), ADOS = *ADO Supplement* (June), CAB = current account balance, GDP = gross domestic product.

Notes: Years are fiscal years ending on 30 June of that year. There may have been new developments in the economy and data updates since the data cut-off.

Source: ADB estimates.

Monetary policy is accommodative, featuring interest payment waivers, deferred loan repayment, and concessional loans for agriculture and small enterprises. Risks to growth forecasts hinge mainly on developments in India but also on any further lockdowns in Bhutan.

The *ADO 2020* inflation projection is slightly downgraded for FY2020, mainly in line with weaker domestic demand, but retained for FY2021, aligned as it is with the projection for India. Current account deficits in FY2020 and FY2021 are now forecast well below earlier projections in light of marked slower forecast growth, a likely attendant decline in import demand, and expected higher electricity exports.

Maldives

After a strong start in January 2020, tourist arrivals plunged from February and disappeared in the second quarter after Maldives closed to visitors on 27 March in response to the COVID-19 pandemic. Arrivals contracted by 55.6% year on year in the first half (H1) as those from the People's Republic of China, the largest single market, dropped by 75.8% and those from Europe by 44.9%. Bed-nights, a proxy for tourism earnings, plummeted by 49.6%.

Lost income markedly weakened private consumption, as COVID-19 containment measures begun in February. Construction was likewise weak, as evidenced by imports of building materials declining by 36.2% year on year in H1. With revenue down, the government suspended most new investment projects and prioritized expenditure to counter COVID-19. It estimated that GDP fell by 5.9% year on year in the first quarter of 2020.

Maldives reopened to visitors on 15 July—hoping that its "one island one resort" model, featuring enhanced health safeguards, would give it a competitive edge—but weak demand means few airlines will likely resume flights until October, leaving arrivals forecast to plunge this year by 65%–70%. The GDP forecast is consequently downgraded for 2020 but revised up for 2021 on improved prospects for global recovery. The main downside risks to the forecast are a persistent COVID-19 pandemic and a weaker global economy, either one dampening tourism. This could further imperil fiscal and debt sustainability, given Maldives' very high public debt and meager foreign exchange reserves.

The average index of consumer prices sagged by 1.6% year on year in H1 2020 as lockdown weakened demand, telecoms gave away some services from March, and households received electricity and water utility subsidies as COVID-19 relief. Though inflation is expected to pick up in H2 as containment eases and tourism revives, the *ADO 2020* inflation forecast is trimmed for 2020. It is revised up for 2021 on expected improvement in domestic demand.

Table 3.3.6 Selected economic indicators, Maldives (%)

	2019	2020			2021		
		ADO 2020	ADOS	*Update*	*ADO 2020*	ADOS	*Update*
GDP growth	5.9	–3.0	–11.5	–20.5	7.5	13.7	10.5
Inflation	0.2	1.0	1.0	0.5	1.2	1.2	1.5
CAB/GDP	–26.3	–23.0	...	–17.0	–22.0	...	–18.0

... = unavailable, ADO = *Asian Development Outlook* (April), ADOS = *ADO Supplement* (June), CAB = current account balance, GDP = gross domestic product.
Source: ADB estimates.

The trade deficit narrowed by 25.9% year on year in H1 2020 as imports fell by more than 27% across the board, but the service trade surplus markedly weakened as travel receipts dried up. The COVID-19 shock created a large external financing gap, for which the government turned to the Rapid Credit Facility of the International Monetary Fund and substantial financing lines from other development partners. Gross foreign reserves, which include foreign exchange deposits in commercial banks, slid during H1 by 6.8% to $702.3 million. Usable reserves plunged by 51.7% to $152.6 million, or cover for only 1.1 months of imports. Despite the collapse in tourism receipts expected in 2020, earlier forecasts for current account deficits are narrowed, mainly in line with lower imports for construction.

Nepal

After strong growth in recent years, the economy is faltering under measures to contain COVID-19, declining exports, remittances and tourist income, and pervasive uncertainty. At the end of March 2020, the authorities imposed a national lockdown, closed the borders, and canceled all flights. Mobility restrictions were lifted on 22 July after infections waned but reimposed in the Kathmandu valley and other parts of the country beginning in mid-August after a spike in cases. International flights resumed on 1 September mainly to repatriate Nepalis stranded abroad, but international tourism remains closed for the time being.

Official preliminary estimates show GDP growth in fiscal year 2020 (FY2020, ended 15 July 2020) fell well below the *ADO 2020* forecast as exports slowed, government spending weakened, and stringent and prolonged containment measures crimped activities. Growth for FY2021 is revised below the *ADO Supplement* forecast primarily due to a longer than anticipated period to contain COVID-19 and because India, Nepal's predominate trade partner, is forecast to contract sharply in a fiscal year that coincides with 3 quarters of FY2021. Containment measures may ease over time, and the major advanced economies may rebound in 2021, but with little boost to growth in Nepal.

In FY2020, floods and pest infestation halved growth in agriculture from 5.1% a year earlier to 2.6%, while industry growth plunged from 7.7% to 3.2% and services from 7.3% to 2.0%. On the demand side, growth came mainly from 4.2% higher private consumption expenditure, likely in the period before mid-March, facilitated by remittances—still sizeable despite shrinkage—as fixed investment tumbled by 15.1% because of slumping private investment and implementation woes that curtailed government investment. The drop in capital formation was mostly offset, however, by a decline in imports that improved net exports.

Table 3.3.7 Selected economic indicators, Nepal (%)

	2019	2020			2021		
		ADO 2020	ADOS	Update	ADO 2020	ADOS	Update
GDP growth	7.0	5.3	2.3	2.3	6.4	3.1	1.5
Inflation	4.6	6.0	6.6	6.2	5.5	6.5	5.5
CAB/GDP	-7.7	-5.0	...	-0.9	-5.6	...	-1.9

... = unavailable, ADO = *Asian Development Outlook* (April), ADOS = *ADO Supplement* (June), CAB = current account balance, GDP = gross domestic product.
Note: Years are fiscal years ending 15 July of that year.
Source: ADB estimates.

Average inflation increased considerably from the year earlier to slightly exceed the *ADO 2020* forecast as average food inflation accelerated to 8.2% because of weak agriculture, disrupted distribution, and higher prices for Indian imports. Nonfood inflation eased to 4.6%, holding overall inflation in check. Inflation in FY2021 is revised below the *ADO Supplement* forecast, with a good harvest expected to ease food prices and subdued non-food prices on weak domestic demand.

The FY2020 current account deficit fell well below the *ADO 2020* forecast as weak domestic demand drove down imports. The small deficit masked a worrisome 3.4% decline in workers' remittances, which have recently exceeded 20% of GDP on average and financed needed imports. The small current account deficit and greater financial inflow lifted gross foreign exchange reserves by over 20% to $11.6 billion, or cover for 12.7 months of imports of goods and services. The FY2021 current account deficit will remain well below the *ADO 2020* forecast as markedly slower growth shrinks investment for a second year. Financial uncertainty has prompted Nepal to use support facilities provided by the International Monetary Fund and other multilateral development banks.

Sri Lanka

GDP contracted by 1.6% year on year in the first quarter of 2020 as agriculture fell by 5.6%, manufacturing by 4.1% in line with a decline in garment exports, and construction by 16.0% as investment expenditure plunged. Expansion in services was supportive but eased to 3.1% on lower household consumption expenditure. Expanded government consumption by 28.8% helped to stabilize the economy. Unemployment reached a 10-year high of 5.7% in the first quarter, a rate last seen at the end of the civil conflict in 2009.

The forecast for 2020 GDP is revised from June *Supplement* to a reduced contraction of 5.5%. While the impact of the lockdown due to COVID-19 on economic activity during the second quarter of the year will be significant, a faster recovery than earlier anticipated in the second half of the year is expected. A strict lockdown introduced in mid-March arrested the spread of the virus, allowing containment measures to be gradually eased from late April and economic activity to resume. The economy is showing stronger-than-expected signs of recovery as the manufacturing purchasing managers' index expanded for the second consecutive month to 64.6 in July, and that for services reached 51.4. In the near term, the government's focus of boosting domestic production is likely to support employment and growth. Meanwhile, a strong mandate for the President's party in the general election in August is expected to enable the policy clarity needed to underpin growth.

Table 3.3.8 Selected economic indicators, Sri Lanka (%)

	2019	2020			2021		
		ADO 2020	ADOS	Update	ADO 2020	ADOS	Update
GDP growth	2.3	2.2	−6.1	−5.5	3.5	4.1	4.1
Inflation	4.3	5.0	4.0	4.5	4.8	4.2	4.2
CAB/GDP	−2.2	−2.8	...	−2.4	−2.6	...	−2.3

... = unavailable, ADO = Asian Development Outlook (April), ADOS = ADO Supplement (June), CAB = current account balance, GDP = gross domestic product.
Source: ADB estimates.

On the monetary policy front, the Central Bank of Sri Lanka lowered policy rates by 200 basis points and substantially boosted bank liquidity through open market operations. Domestic credit grew by 12.4% up until July 2020, driven by credit to the government and state-owned enterprises, while private sector credit grew by a marginal 0.6%. An expanded credit scheme and credit guarantee system for small- and medium-sized enterprises, and a sharp fall in bank lending rates since July, may spark stronger private credit expansion in the second half of the year.

However, the tight fiscal space limits options to boost growth in 2020. Cash transfers and the expansion of existing social protection schemes provided some relief, but their scale, scope, and duration provided only a limited stimulus to the economy. In the first half of the year, tax revenue fell by 28.4% year on year following tax cuts implemented in late 2019 and a fall in economic activity under COVID-19. Recurrent expenditure increased by 10.5% while capital spending fell by 43.5%, but the deficit nevertheless ballooned by 41.0% year on year. The government has projected capital expenditure to fall to 2.8% of GDP in 2020, the lowest since 1950. The deficit was financed mainly by the central bank and state-owned captive funds. Sri Lanka suffered a sovereign downgrade to B– for its elevated deficits and large debt refinancing needs.

The forecast for GDP growth in 2021 is maintained to accommodate a low base this year and with the expectation of higher growth in the major advanced economies as they return to normal. GDP will nevertheless remain below its pre-COVID-19 level.

The inflation forecast for 2020 is revised up from the *Supplement* after tight food supply and higher import tariffs pushed food inflation to an average of 11.9% in the first 8 months of 2020, more than double the Colombo consumer price average of 4.8%. The inflation forecast for 2021 is unchanged from the *Supplement*.

Import and capital export controls were introduced to counter pressure on reserves and the exchange rate in the wake of high exchange rate volatility in March and April, stabilizing the Sri Lanka rupee at 2.5% depreciation in the year to August. The trade deficit shrank by 8.9% in the first half of 2020 as imports contracted by 20.0%—with sharp declines for fuel, textile intermediates, and investment goods—and exports by 26.7%. Remittance inflows that provide much needed financing for the trade deficit fell by 5.5% till end July but has picked up since May, likely due to returning migrants transferring their savings, and an election related bump as seen historically. Similarly, tourist earnings too fell by 54.9% during the same period. Yet, current account deficit forecasts are trimmed for 2020 and 2021 reflecting a larger-than-expected contraction in imports and a better recovery in exports. Foreign exchange reserves declined moderately from $7.6 billion at the start of the year to $7.1 billion in July.

Southeast Asia

Southeast Asia is hard hit by the COVID-19 pandemic. The forecast for aggregate GDP in 2020 is contraction—the first subregional contraction since the Asian financial crisis of 1997–1998. Growth is expected to return in 2021, rebounding higher than forecast in April in *ADO 2020*. Inflation will decelerate as economies contract and global oil prices decline. Subregional current account surpluses are now forecast smaller than in April, but with differences largely erased in 2021.

Subregional assessment and prospects

Economies in Southeast Asia took a beating as they battled COVID-19. The larger economies slumped in the second quarter of 2020 with double-digit GDP contraction in Malaysia, the Philippines, Singapore, and Thailand under stringent travel restrictions and quarantines beginning in March. Border closures disrupted tourism, transportation, and trade. Most governments have since relaxed these restrictions, and some economies have started to show signs of recovery. However, rising infections in Indonesia and the Philippines and recent outbreaks in Myanmar, Timor-Leste, and Viet Nam suggest that recovery will be slow—a disappointment for Viet Nam in particular after a long stretch with no local transmission. Further, recovery is tethered to improvement in demand from the major advanced economies.

The subregional GDP forecast is revised down for 2020 from 1.0% growth in *ADO 2020* to 3.8% contraction, but the growth forecast is revised up for 2021 from 5.2% to 5.5%. Forecasts are downgraded since April for all 11 economies, only 3 of them likely to remain in positive territory: Brunei Darussalam on petrochemical exports, Myanmar on agricultural exports, and Viet Nam on telephone and electronic products. All Southeast Asian economies are expected to grow more strongly in 2021 with domestic stimulus and global recovery.

Figure 3.4.1 GDP growth, Southeast Asia

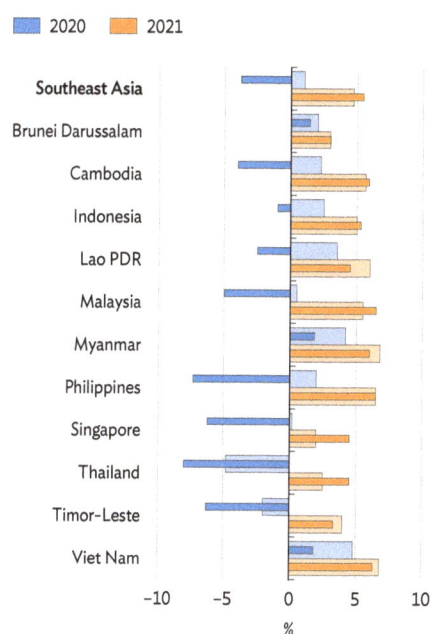

Note: Lighter colored bars are *ADO 2020* forecasts.
Source: *Asian Development Outlook* database.

The subregional assessment and prospects were written by Thiam Hee Ng and Dulce Zara. The section on Indonesia was written by Emma Allen and Priasto Aji; Malaysia by Thiam Hee Ng and Maria Theresa Bugayong; the Philippines by Cristina Lozano and Teresa Mendoza; Thailand by Chitchanok Annonjarn; Viet Nam by Cuong Minh Nguyen, Nguyen Luu Thuc Phuong, and Chu Hong Minh, and the other economies by Poullang Doung, David M. Freedman, Kavita Iyengar, Soulinthone Leuangkhamsing, Rattanatay Luanglatbandith, Eve Cherry Lynn, Pilipinas Quising, Shiu Tian, Mai Lin Villaruel, and Dulce Zara. Authors are in the Southeast Asia and Economic Research and Regional Cooperation departments of ADB.

All economies experienced broad declines in consumption, investment, and trade in the first half of 2020. With little debt, most governments loosened fiscal policy aggressively to minimize the impact of COVID-19, making government consumption the bulwark against economic collapse. Fiscal measures included cash transfers to vulnerable groups, wage subsidies and loan guarantees to small businesses, and public spending on curbing COVID-19 transmission. Household consumption slumped in most economies under job losses, pay cuts, mandatory leave, high household debt, and lower remittances. The number of poor people spiked as unemployment ballooned. Stymied by an uncertain and restrictive environment, investment nosedived in most economies in the first half of 2020. Capital spending fell as private sector plans were put on hold, particularly in construction, while public spending prioritized immediate COVID-19 needs.

In the first half of 2020, strong demand for work-from-home electronics boosted exports from Cambodia, Malaysia, Singapore, and Viet Nam. Meanwhile, exports from Thailand contracted sharply under weaker external demand and supply chain disruption. The slowdown in Thailand is expected to drag growth in neighboring countries. Countries heavily dependent on tourism, notably Cambodia and Thailand, are unlikely to recover quickly, and exporters to major economies like the US, the euro area, and Japan must await recovery in these markets.

The dour economic outlook for the subregion is accompanied by a downward revision for subregional inflation this year from 1.9% forecast in *ADO 2020* to 1.0%. Downgrades are made for Indonesia, Malaysia, Myanmar, Singapore, Thailand, Timor-Leste, and Viet Nam to accommodate weaker demand, lower global oil prices, and subdued domestic food prices. The inflation forecast for this year is unchanged for Cambodia, slightly up for the Philippines but raised for Brunei Darussalam and the Lao People's Democratic Republic (PDR) due to rising food prices. Import price hikes as the local currency weakens compounded higher inflation in the Lao PDR. Inflation in 2021 is now forecast slightly higher, revised up from 2.2% in *ADO 2020* to 2.3%.

Forecasts for 2020 current account balances in the subregion are mixed. Since *ADO 2020* in April, no change is seen for Myanmar; improvement for Brunei Darussalam, Indonesia, the Lao PDR, and Viet Nam; and smaller surpluses or larger deficits for Cambodia, Malaysia, the Philippines, Singapore, Thailand, and Timor-Leste as demand for exports languishes.

With inflation benign, central banks have cut interest rates and capital reserve requirements to support faltering economies, and governments have rolled out large fiscal stimulus measures. Risks to the subregional outlook come mostly from COVID-19 as, in the absence of effective vaccines, a lingering pandemic or new waves of infections would slow recovery—as would slower global growth.

Figure 3.4.2 Inflation, Southeast Asia

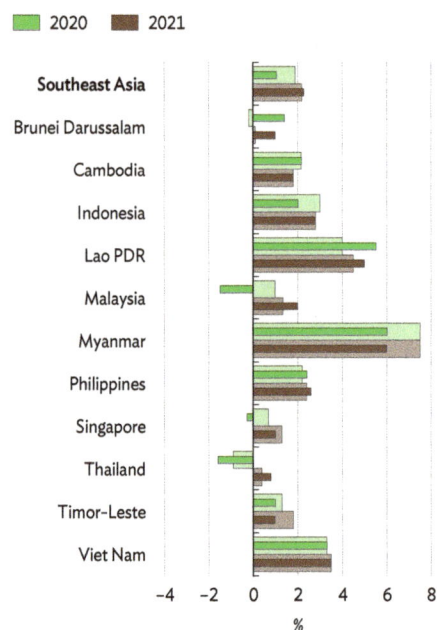

■ 2020   ■ 2021

Note: Lighter colored bars are *ADO 2020* forecasts.
Source: *Asian Development Outlook* database.

Figure 3.4.3 Current account balance, Southeast Asia

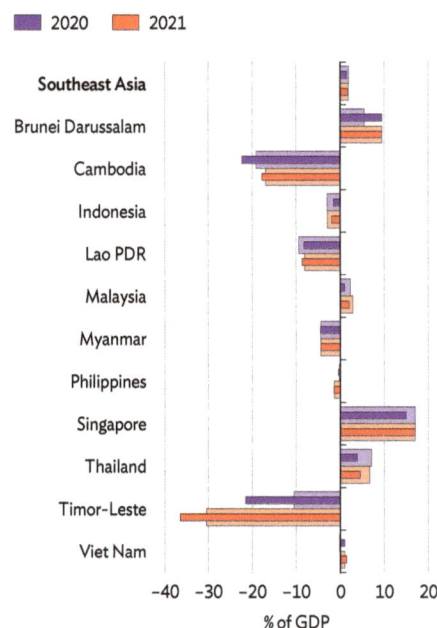

■ 2020   ■ 2021

Note: Lighter colored bars are *ADO 2020* forecasts.
Source: *Asian Development Outlook* database.

Indonesia

The 2020 growth forecast for Indonesia is revised down from the *ADO 2020* projection after COVID-19 broadly worsened conditions. The pandemic has stifled domestic activity and external demand, causing consumption, investment, and trade to decline across the board. Growth is forecast to rebound in 2021 as the global economy recovers and as domestic reform spurs an investment-led recovery. Subdued domestic demand will see both inflation and the current account deficit moderate this year before rising marginally next year.

Updated assessment

Indonesia's economy contracted in the second quarter of 2020 for the first time since the Asian financial crisis of 1997–1998, buffeted by shocks to both supply and demand from the COVID-19 pandemic. Real GDP slid from 3.0% growth in the first quarter of 2020 to 5.3% contraction in the second quarter, with declines recorded across consumption, investment, and trade. Comparing first halves, GDP reversed 5.1% growth in 2019 with 1.3% contraction this year (Figure 3.4.4).

Domestic consumption contracted as households cut their spending and the government lagged in redirecting expenditure from general activities to pandemic response. Household spending, especially on tourism and dining out, fell as mobility was restricted and job and income losses undermined confidence (Figure 3.4.5). Families' purchasing power was extended somewhat as the government scaled up public services to households, notably for health care and education, though this effort was undercut as government consumption disbursement suffered delays.

Fixed investment collapsed, as did imports of investment inputs, as construction projects were postponed and business sentiment withered under worsening uncertainty. Fixed capital formation fell from 4.8% growth in the first half of 2019 to 3.5% contraction in the first half of 2020 (Figure 3.4.6). Purchases of new vehicles, machinery, and equipment were delayed, and international travel declined, contracting imports by 9.6%.

Demand for Indonesia's exports shrank apace with lockdowns around the world (Figure 3.4.7). Exports of services contracted as business and tourism abruptly halted, while earnings from export commodities such as palm oil and coal fell with the closure of factories. With natural resources accounting for a large share of Indonesia's exports, growth in mining and quarrying also performed poorly. Export earnings from metal ores were constrained by new requirements that raw materials undergo some domestic processing before export—requirements that cannot yet be met.

Lower growth spanned sectors. Growth in agriculture was subdued in the first half of 2020 as poor crop management continued to hold down yields (Figure 3.4.8).

Figure 3.4.4 Demand-side contributions to growth

- Private consumption
- Government consumption
- Gross fixed capital formation
- Stocks
- Net exports
- Statistical discrepancy
- Gross domestic product

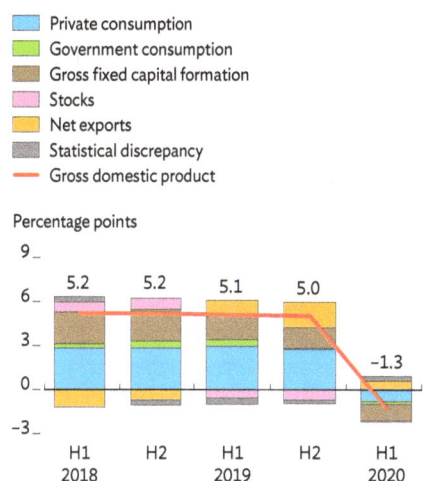

H = half.
Source: CEIC Data Company (accessed 28 August 2020).

Figure 3.4.5 Contributions to household consumption growth

- Food and beverages
- Clothing, footwear, and maintenance
- Housing and household supplies
- Health and education
- Transport and communications
- Restaurants and hotels
- Others
- Household consumption expenditure

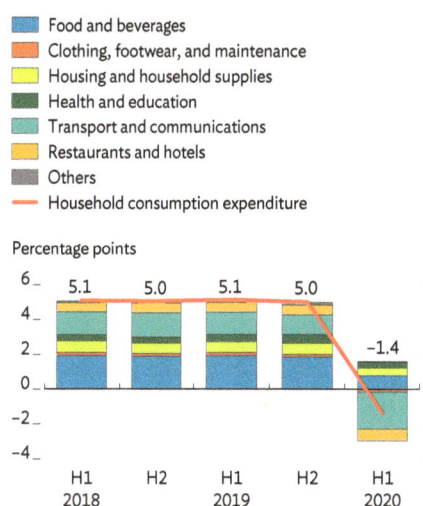

H = half.
Source: CEIC Data Company (accessed 28 August 2020).

Food crop production stagnated, while growth in plantation output moderated. Terms of trade deteriorated for farmers in the first half of 2020 as the prices they received for crops declined while those they paid for inputs remained stable.

The decline of industry was rapid. Manufacturing contracted by 2.1% in the first half of 2020 as both import-intensive and export-oriented industries collapsed under shrinking demand at home and abroad. As private investment slowed and public infrastructure projects were put on hold, construction contracted by 1.3%.

Visitor arrivals plunged by 60.0% in the first half as travel restrictions prompted travelers for both business and leisure to postpone their trips. Tourism ground to a halt, accommodation contracted by 24.3% in the first half of 2020, and restaurant trade declined by 6.8% in the same period. Consumption was seriously disrupted, driving down wholesale and retail trade. Demand for new automobiles fell as the middle class postponed spending.

Transportation and storage services reversed 5.7% growth in the first half of 2019 to contract sharply by 15.1% in the same period a year later as measures were introduced to limit movement (Figure 3.4.9). Air transport services contracted for a sixth quarter running, while storage services declined in line with shrinking imports and exports of goods.

Information and communication services remained buoyant, growing by 10.3% in the first half of 2020 as online services expanded rapidly to accommodate more people working from home. Growth in financial and insurance services remained steady at 5.9% as capital movement in Indonesia's financial markets picked up in line with fluctuations in global risk sentiment. Financial asset transfers increased, with securities sold and new bonds issued. From January to August 2020, cumulative portfolio outflow stood at $8.9 billion. Bond yields sharply increased in March, but this trend had largely reversed by the end of the first half after Bank Indonesia, the central bank, responded swiftly and market sentiment recovered.

With the slowdown in household and business spending, headline inflation softened to average 2.3% from January to August 2020 (Figure 3.4.10). Inflation for price-volatile goods declined rapidly in the first 8 months of the year, but core inflation remained stable, and inflation in administered prices accelerated as electricity tariffs were adjusted up for households not covered by subsidies. Mobility restrictions reduced demand for goods and services alike, slowing inflation for public transport fares, food, and accommodation. Prices fluctuated for personal care items, such as sanitizer, while fees for health care and information services remained stable.

The current account deficit was more than halved from $14.8 billion in the first half of 2019 to $6.6 billion a year later as the trade surplus widened and payments to foreign

Figure 3.4.6 Contributions to fixed capital growth

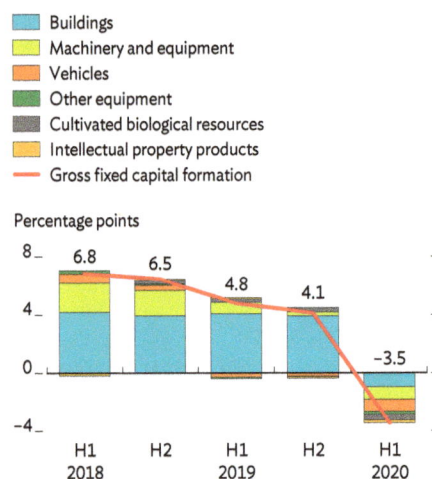

Legend:
- Buildings
- Machinery and equipment
- Vehicles
- Other equipment
- Cultivated biological resources
- Intellectual property products
- Gross fixed capital formation

Percentage points

Values: 6.8, 6.5, 4.8, 4.1, −3.5

H1 2018, H2, H1 2019, H2, H1 2020

H = half.
Source: CEIC Data Company (accessed 28 August 2020).

Figure 3.4.7 Contributions to trade growth

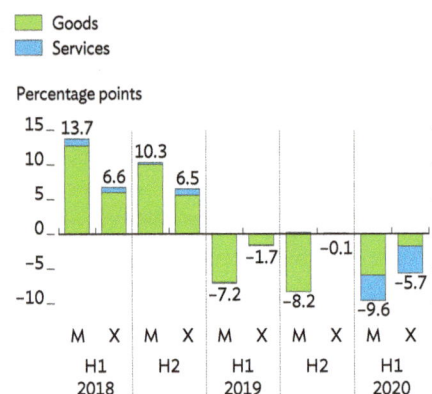

Legend:
- Goods
- Services

Percentage points

Values: 13.7, 6.6, 10.3, 6.5, −7.2, −1.7, −8.2, −0.1, −9.6, −5.7

M X H1 2018, M X H2, M X H1 2019, M X H2, M X H1 2020

H = half, M = imports, X = exports.
Source: CEIC Data Company (accessed 28 August 2020).

Figure 3.4.8 Supply-side contributions to growth

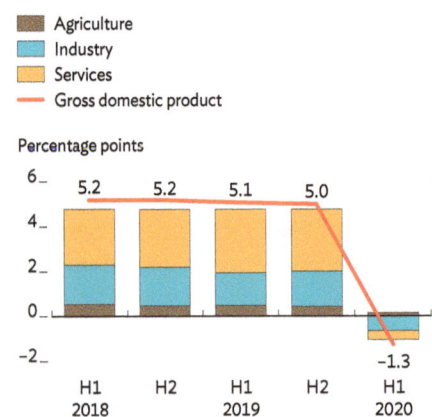

Legend:
- Agriculture
- Industry
- Services
- Gross domestic product

Percentage points

Values: 5.2, 5.2, 5.1, 5.0, −1.3

H1 2018, H2, H1 2019, H2, H1 2020

H = half.
Source: CEIC Data Company (accessed 28 August 2020).

investors declined (Figure 3.4.11). With domestic demand slowing, imports of goods fell by 14.5%, more than offsetting 6.2% contraction in exports. With business weak, lower profit remittances shrank the deficit in the income account.

Net outflow of portfolio investment in the first quarter turned to net inflow in the second quarter as financial markets became less nervous, leaving a financial account surplus of $7.5 billion in the first half of 2020. Government issues of global bonds in the second quarter helped reverse portfolio outflow suffered in the first quarter. Net direct investment inflow was $7.4 billion in the first half of 2020, albeit smaller than $11.9 billion in the same period of last year.

The narrowing current account deficit and the rebound in capital flows left a small surplus of $700 million in the balance of payments in the first half of the year (Figure 3.4.12). Official reserves thus rose to $137.0 billion at the end of August, cover for 9.0 months of imports and external debt service.

As negative sentiment in February and March roiled markets, the central bank cut its policy 7-day reverse repurchase rate four times by a total of 100 basis points to 4.0% and relaxed liquidity to prop up credit. By the end of the second quarter, the stock market and the exchange rate had both stabilized and even regained some value that had been lost in the first quarter. From January to August, the Jakarta composite index lost 16.8%, and the rupiah depreciated by 4.5% against the US dollar.

Prospects

Continuing disruption from COVID-19 will have severe implications for growth. Negative business and consumer sentiment will hold down domestic demand in the near term. Uncertain recovery in Indonesia's trade partners will similarly dampen export prospects. Growth forecasts are therefore revised down from those in *ADO 2020*. GDP is forecast to contract by 1.0% this year and grow by 5.3% next year as the global economy recovers and domestic investment reform spurs recovery. Subdued domestic demand will moderate inflation and the current account deficit.

The number of COVID-19 cases continued to rise in August, with the epicenter of the outbreak on Java, the central island that generates approximately 60% of GDP. Pervasive social restrictions are being relaxed only slowly and will continue to depress household spending in the near term. The government's expanded household social assistance programs will help to prop up incomes and essential spending, but they cannot offset all of the decline in private consumption. As workers were laid off and furloughed, the social security agency reported that, from January to July, 4.9 million beneficiaries temporarily withdrew from the program, presumably because their employment had been suspended.

Figure 3.4.9 Contributions to growth of transportation and storage

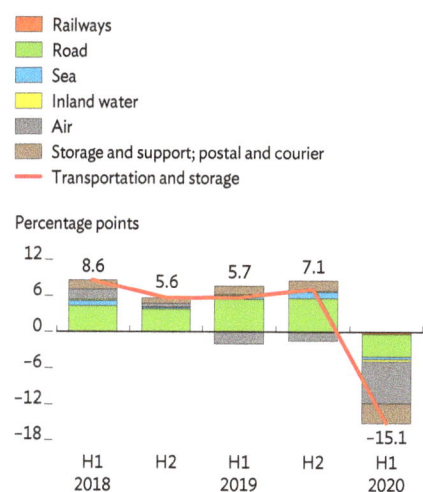

- Railways
- Road
- Sea
- Inland water
- Air
- Storage and support; postal and courier
- Transportation and storage

H = half.
Source: CEIC Data Company (accessed 28 August 2020).

Figure 3.4.10 Monthly inflation

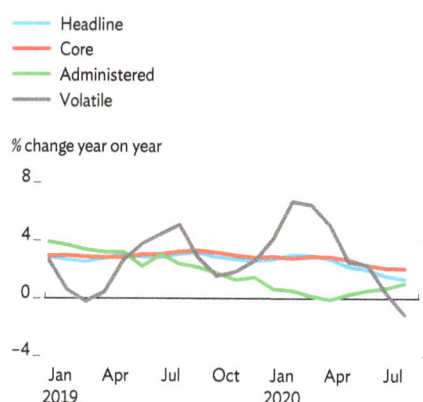

- Headline
- Core
- Administered
- Volatile

Source: CEIC Data Company (accessed 28 August 2020).

Figure 3.4.11 Current account balance

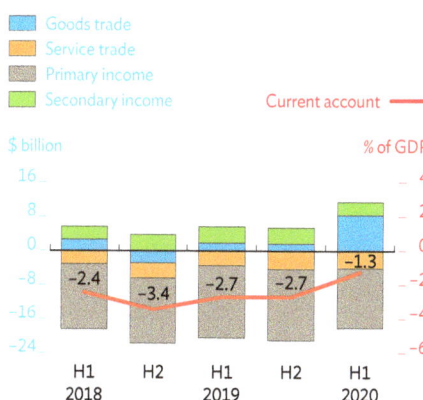

- Goods trade
- Service trade
- Primary income
- Secondary income
- Current account

H = half.
Source: CEIC Data Company (accessed 28 August 2020).

In March, the number of people living below the national poverty line increased to 26.4 million, the first reversal of a downward trend in the poverty rate since 2015 (Figure 3.4.13).

Business sentiment will remain subdued as long as demand weakness persists both domestically and globally, postponing investment. However, the release of some pent-up domestic demand lifted the manufacturing purchasing mangers' index above the threshold of 50 in August for the first time since February, indicating future growth (Figure 3.4.14). Confidence should also rise as the government provides interest subsidies and working capital guarantees to commercial banks. This assistance, when passed on to bank customers, should support credit growth and financing for investment and business operations. Investment is expected to be further spurred in 2021 by the resumption of public infrastructure projects, including renewable energy, and the expansion of new private investment in tradable goods, after business climate reforms gain traction in the second half of next year.

Export and import volumes are expected to remain depressed in the rest of 2020 as global demand languishes and adverse domestic conditions persist. Global commodity prices continue to be weak, and growth in Indonesia's trade partners is halting. However, exports should improve in 2021 in line with recovery in the major advanced economies.

With drought in the dry season and prices for plantation commodities stubbornly low, growth in agriculture will be minimal this year and next. Manufacturing and construction will suffer as factories close and projects are postponed. Services will continue to shrink as consumers hold off on retail and tourism purchases. However, spending on telecommunications and digital services should be strong as more people work from home. Frontline services that are integral to pandemic response, such as health care and social work, will be bolstered by government spending this year and next.

The government has relaxed conditions for access to subsidies for tuition fees and public health services, but domestic demand remains weak, holding down inflation. Hotels and restaurants have cut prices to stimulate consumption. Core inflation has steadily declined, and so has headline inflation thanks to deft supply management that has kept food prices stable. The 2020 inflation projection is therefore revised down from 3.0% average in *ADO 2020* to 2.0%. As household and business spending recovers in 2021, inflation is expected to accelerate to 2.8%, the rate earlier forecast.

Figure 3.4.12 Balance of payments

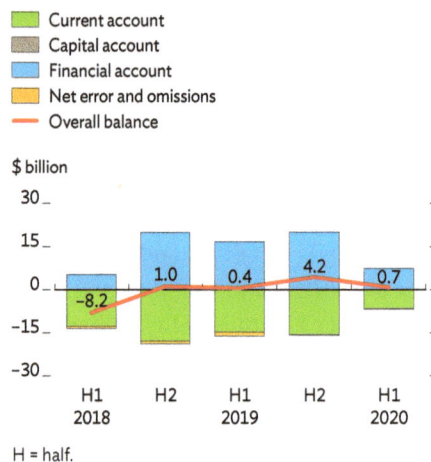

H = half.
Source: CEIC Data Company (accessed 28 August 2020).

Figure 3.4.13 Poverty incidence

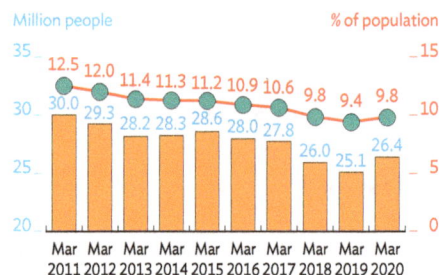

Source: Statistics Indonesia.https://www.bps.go.id (accessed 1 September 2020).

Figure 3.4.14 Manufacturing purchasing managers' index

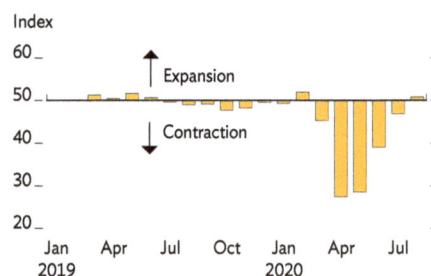

Note: A purchasing managers' index reading <50 signals deterioration, >50 improvement.
Source: Markiteconomics. https://www.markiteconomics .com (accessed 1 September 2020).

The current account deficit is set to narrow to the equivalent of 1.5% of GDP in 2020, half the *ADO 2020* forecast of 2.9%. Weak domestic demand should keep merchandise imports shrinking faster than exports. Import declines have been most notable in capital goods and machinery, the result of weak consumer confidence, cautious bank lending, and postponed public and private investment. The lower goods deficit will offset deterioration in the service balance as international tourism declines. As the economy recovers in 2021, import demand should recover apace, and the current account deficit should rise to 2.0% of GDP.

To boost the economy and maintain external stability, the central bank has eased selected macroprudential regulations and agreed to finance $38.6 billion of the government's expanded expenditure program, partly by purchasing $26.7 billion in government bonds and, if necessary, more of the issue as the buyer of last resort. The government has earmarked the financing for public services such as health care, social safety nets, and food security, and for supporting enterprises. Government bond purchases by the central bank will help the government meet over half of the country's additional financing needs, thus avoiding excessive crowding out in the bond market while reducing Indonesia's reliance on foreign capital inflow in the near term.

Fiscal policy is expected to remain accommodative in 2020, with a proposed deficit target equal to 1.8% of GDP revised up to 6.3%. Revenue collection reached over half of the revised annual target in July and was expected to stabilize thereafter. In the same month, public spending hit about 40% of the annual target and was expected to speed up in the coming months. Disbursement of expenditure on COVID-19 reached only 28.3% of the target by the end of August, but the government is determined to ramp up spending in the remainder of the year. The budget proposed for next year preserves growth support with a fiscal deficit equal to 5.5% of GDP and priority on public spending for social assistance, health care, and economic assistance to mitigate the impact of the pandemic.

Under prevailing uncertainty, risks to the outlook tilt heavily to the downside. A resurgence of infections either locally or globally, and consequent prolongation of subdued consumer confidence, could delay recovery. It is therefore critical that measures continue to contain the pandemic and promote economic recovery, and that pending domestic reform reach completion.

Table 3.4.1 Selected economic indicators, Indonesia (%)

	2019	2020			2021		
		ADO 2020	ADOS	Update	ADO 2020	ADOS	Update
GDP growth	5.0	2.5	–1.0	–1.0	5.0	5.3	5.3
Inflation	2.8	3.0	2.0	2.0	2.8	2.8	2.8
CAB/GDP	–2.7	–2.9	...	–1.5	–2.9	...	–2.0

... = unavailable, ADO = *Asian Development Outlook* (April), ADOS = *ADO Supplement* (June), CAB = current account balance, GDP = gross domestic product.
Source: ADB estimates.

Malaysia

The worldwide spread of COVID-19 and travel restrictions in the first half of 2020 spell GDP contraction in the full year, not marginal growth as projected in April. Collapsing oil prices and economic contraction will bring deflation this year. The current account will remain in surplus but be narrower than previously forecast. Growth is expected to rebound in 2021 as activity gradually returns to normal. Inflation will likely return next year but remain low, and the current account surplus will widen.

Updated assessment

GDP contracted by 8.3% year on year in the first half of 2020, a sharp reversal of 4.7% expansion in the same period of last year (Figure 3.4.15). After growing by 0.7% in the first quarter (Q1) of 2020, GDP plunged by 17.1% in Q2. Weakness all around reflected measures taken both globally and domestically to contain the spread of COVID-19, including restrictions in Malaysia on movement and nonessential economic activity from 18 March 2020. Exports and imports of goods and services registered double-digit declines as demand collapsed at home and abroad.

Private consumption, which had grown by an annual average of 7.0% since 2012 to provide 59.0% of total demand in 2019, continued that trend with 6.7% growth in Q1 2020 but then plummeted by 18.5% in Q2 for a 6.0% decline in the first half of the year. Stimulus measures implemented in the period—notably cash transfers, employee provident fund withdrawals, tax payment deferral, and a moratorium on loan payment—helped to cushion the drop in consumption spending. With movement restrictions gradually relaxed toward the end of Q2 (Figure 3.4.16), private consumption remained weak as retrenchment, pay cuts, and mandatory unpaid leave continued to weigh on incomes and private spending. Public consumption, by contrast, strengthened, from a 3.2% increase in the first half of 2019 to 3.6% in the same period of this year. Investment remained sluggish, stymied by disruption and uncertainty stemming from COVID-19. Gross fixed capital formation declined further from 2.0% contraction in the first half of 2019 to contract by 17.3% in the first half of this year. Private investment plunged by 15.2% after mobility restrictions temporarily halted project implementation. Slower production and disruption to global value chains drove down the business confidence index and consequently investment. Public investment, which had been on a downtrend since Q4 2017, plunged by 24.2% in the first half of this year. Despite the government's announcement that the implementation of several large infrastructure projects would continue, the imposition of travel restrictions delayed large ongoing construction projects.

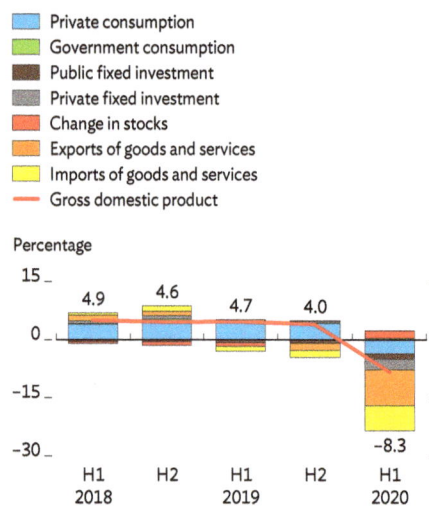

Figure 3.4.15 Demand-side contributions to growth

- Private consumption
- Government consumption
- Public fixed investment
- Private fixed investment
- Change in stocks
- Exports of goods and services
- Imports of goods and services
- Gross domestic product

H1 = first half.
Sources: Haver Analytics; Bank Negara Malaysia. 2020. Monthly Statistical Bulletin. August. http://www.bnm.gov.my (accessed 25 August 2020).

Figure 3.4.16 Stringency and mobility restrictions

Notes: The stringency index is the average score of nine indicators of containment and closure, with 0 the least stringent and 100 the most. Average mobility is the change in visits or time spent outside of the residence in places divided into five categories, compared with baseline days or the median value during the 5-week period from 3 January to 6 February 2020, before mobility restrictions became widespread.
Sources: Hale, T., S. Webster, A. Petherick, T. Phillips, and B. Kira. 2020. *Oxford COVID-19 Government Response Tracker*. Blavatnik School of Government. https://www.bsg.ox.ac.uk/research/research-projects/coronavirus-government-response-tracker; Google LLC. *Google COVID-19 Community Mobility Reports*. https://www.blog.google/technology/health/covid-19-community-mobility-reports?hl=en (both accessed 21 August 2020).

The decline in output was across the board following the imposition of movement restrictions in Q1 2020, and as supply disruption continued under less stringent restrictions in force in Q2 2020. Services reversed 6.3% growth in the first half of 2019 to contract by 6.7% a year later as the lockdown substantially affected wholesale and retail trade, food and beverage services, accommodation, and transportation. The only service segments that grew in the period were information and communication, insurance, and government services. Meanwhile, industrial output declined by 6.1% in the first 6 months of the year, with the largest contraction in construction, by 25.9%. Contraction in mining worsened from 0.3% in the first half of 2019 to 11.0% a year later; manufacturing, following 4.2% growth a year earlier, contracted by 8.7%. Agriculture reversed strong 5.1% growth in the first half of last year to contract by 3.9% in the same period of this year, though palm oil output recovered in Q2 (Figure 3.4.17).

Inflation has been muted since the onset of the pandemic. After rising by 1.4% year on year in the first 2 months of 2020, prices started to fall in March, bringing average deflation by 0.9% in the first 7 months (Figure 3.4.18). By component in the consumer price index, prices for food and non-alcoholic beverages increased by 1.2% year on year in the period, but prices for transportation declined by 9.9%, for nondurable goods by 4.4%, and for clothing and footwear by 1.1%.

The unemployment rate worsened from 3.3% in the first half of 2019 to 4.3% under the lockdown, workplace closures, and layoffs. Tourism and related businesses were the hardest hit, retrenching workers or shortening their work hours and pay to cut costs (Figure 3.4.19).

Trade declined as lockdowns and other restrictions globally took their toll, weakening demand from Malaysia's main trade partners and undermining commodity prices. Following modest declines in Q1 2020, exports and imports alike fell by double digits in Q2. By value, merchandise exports contracted by almost 14.0% in the first 6 months of 2020 to an estimated $83.8 billion. Sluggish investment and lower demand in Malaysia caused imports to decline as well, from $82.4 billion a year earlier to an estimated $71 billion. As imports shrank from a smaller base, the trade surplus narrowed from close to $15 billion in the first half of last year to $13 billion in the first half of 2020.

The service deficit expanded to an estimated $4.8 billion in the first half of 2020, the worst on record as COVID-19 restrictions brought international travel almost to a complete halt. The primary income deficit narrowed on higher direct investment from abroad, and the secondary income deficit narrowed as well with lower outward remittances. In sum, the current account surplus shrank from the equivalent of 4.3% of GDP in the first half of 2019 to 2.5% a year later.

Figure 3.4.17 Supply-side contributions to growth

Agriculture
Industry
Services
Imports duties
Gross domestic product

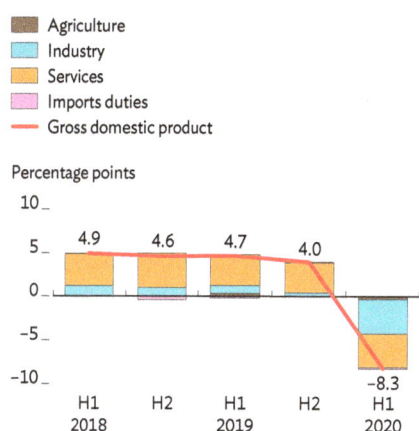

H1 = first half.
Sources: Haver Analytics; Bank Negara Malaysia. 2020. Monthly Statistical Bulletin. August. http://www.bnm.gov.my (accessed 25 August 2020).

Figure 3.4.18 Monthly inflation

Overall
Core inflation

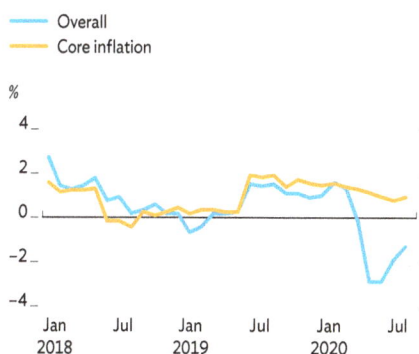

Sources: Haver Analytics; Bank Negara Malaysia. 2020. Monthly Statistical Bulletin. August. http://www.bnm.gov.my (accessed 25 August 2020).

Figure 3.4.19 Labor indicators

Average monthly wage per person, manufacturing
Unemployment rate

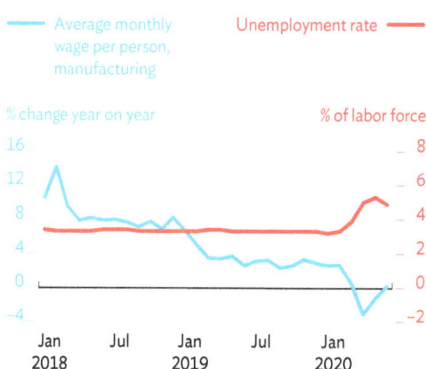

Source: Haver Analytics (accessed 25 August 2020).

Portfolio investment recorded large outflow in Q1 2020 but staged a strong recovery in Q2 as investors flocked back to Malaysian bonds. Factoring in other investment outflows, the financial account recorded an outflow of $7.8 billion. International reserves stood at $103.5 billion at the end of June 2020, enough to finance 6.4 months of imports.

Four stimulus packages totaling RM295 billion were announced, including an estimated RM45 billion in additional fiscal expenditure. The first economic stimulus package was announced on 27 February 2020. As the COVID-19 outbreak worsened and businesses were required to close unless providing essential services or support for them, three more fiscal packages were announced. The packages included relief measures for households and vulnerable businesses. A strong focus on employment protection was evidenced by wage subsidies and financial support to vulnerable businesses, particularly small and medium-sized enterprises, to help them maintain cashflow.

Bank Negara Malaysia, the central bank, has reduced its policy rate four times so far this year—on 22 January, 3 March, 5 May, and 7 July—by a cumulative 125 basis points to 1.75%. The reductions were expected to ease debt-servicing burdens and financing costs for households, small and medium-sized enterprises, and corporations. The central bank also lowered the statutory reserve requirement ratio for commercial banks by 100 basis points to 2.0%, effective on 20 March 2020. Further, to support financial intermediation, it allowed banks to apply Malaysian government securities and investment issues toward compliance with the statutory reserve requirement.

Prospects

The economy will continue to be dragged down by the adverse effects of the pandemic on consumption, exports, and investment. Measures to contain the spread of the virus by restricting travel and business activity weigh on household spending. However, with restrictions relaxed from mid-June, some recovery is expected in the second half of 2020. The release of pent-up demand is already showing in wholesale and retail trade, which picked up strongly in June. Yet concern about a possible resurgence of the virus will limit the extent to which economic activity is able to return to pre-pandemic levels.

Government fiscal stimulus and liquidity support, equal in total to 20.0% of GDP, is expected to boost domestic demand, but weak labor market conditions under persistent layoffs and pay cuts will still dampen consumer spending. Private investment is expected to contract sharply because of nagging uncertainty about how long the pandemic will last and the long-term impact of measures taken to contain COVID-19.

Table 3.4.2 Selected economic indicators, Malaysia (%)

	2019	2020			2021		
		ADO 2020	ADOS	Update	ADO 2020	ADOS	Update
GDP growth	4.3	0.5	-4.0	-5.0	5.5	6.5	6.5
Inflation	0.7	1.0	-1.5	-1.5	1.3	2.5	2.0
CAB/GDP	3.4	2.3	...	1.0	2.9	...	2.0

... = unavailable, ADO = Asian Development Outlook (April), ADOS = ADO Supplement (June), CAB = current account balance, GDP = gross domestic product.
Source: ADB estimates.

The government has announced that it will continue to implement large investments, but public investment is nevertheless likely to shrink this year. With COVID-19 containment measures lasting longer than expected when *ADO 2020* was published in April, and the global economy plunging into sharp recession, this *Update* revises down the forecast for GDP growth in 2020 from projections in both *ADO 2020* and the June *ADO Supplement* to contraction by 5.0% this year. A rebound by 6.5% is forecast for 2021 (Figure 3.4.20).

By sector, growth in agriculture should revive in the near term. Palm oil yield and production are expected to recover with better weather. Mining is expected to continue to struggle, however, under low global oil prices. Manufacturing will face headwinds from much weaker demand, both at home and internationally. In Q2, manufacturers were hit hard by a change in restrictions under which only essential industries were allowed to operate, and only at reduced capacity. However, with COVID-19 restrictions now relaxed, some companies have restarted operations, and manufacturing has picked up strongly. One bright spot in manufacturing has been the production of medical and pharmaceutical goods, exports of which have increased by 22.2% in the first half of the year, on strong global demand, in particular for rubber gloves (Figure 3.4.21).

In the service sector, hospitality and retail businesses have been particularly hard hit by the lockdown and people's general reluctance to go out during the pandemic. Hotels, restaurants, and transportation services are expected to languish as international travel continues to be highly restricted. While travel restrictions within Malaysia have been removed, domestic tourism is not expected to make up for the loss of international tourist arrivals. Growth in other services will also suffer, with some segments perhaps facing permanently lost demand. However, others—notably information technology and financial and digital services—will gain ground in the world left behind by COVID-19. While some workers in shrinking segments will find jobs in expanding areas, others will likely face unemployment or reduced working hours. Reflecting concerns about rising unemployment, the government has decided that foreign workers will now be allowed only in construction and agriculture, in particular plantation agriculture.

The deflationary trend may gradually ease toward the end of 2020 as the economy recovers. However, as oil prices likely remain relatively low, and as the pace of recovery likely remains weak, inflation will stay muted, with deflation in the whole year forecast at 1.5%. Next year, as the economy picks up and global oil prices stabilize, inflation is expected to return, projected at 2.0% (Figure 3.4.22).

Figure 3.4.20 GDP growth

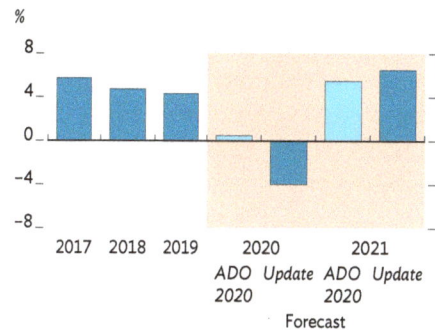

Source: *Asian Development Outlook* database.

Figure 3.4.21 Growth of selected exports

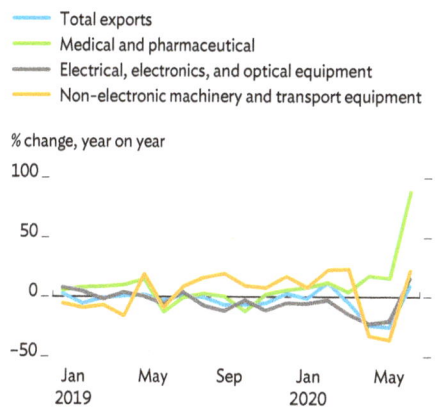

Source: ADB estimates using data from CEIC Data Company and Haver Analytics (accessed 24 August 2020).

Figure 3.4.22 Inflation

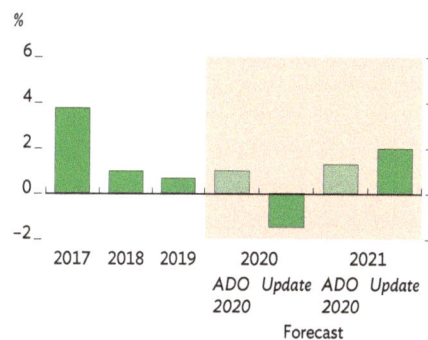

Source: *Asian Development Outlook* database.

External demand is forecast to remain weak as the global economy slows, and exports will shrink further as Malaysia's key markets are affected. Lower petroleum production because of plant maintenance and depressed oil prices is expected to significantly reduce earnings from oil and gas exports. Travel and tourism receipts are not expected to recover anytime soon, with most countries maintaining travel restrictions as the number of COVID-19 cases continues to climb globally. Slowdowns hitting domestic investment and exports will suppress imports of capital and intermediate goods. In sum, the current account surplus is projected to shrink to the equivalent of 1.0% of GDP in 2020, then widen to 2.0% in 2021, both downward revisions from *ADO 2020* (Figure 3.4.23).

With the economy headed into a recession this year, expansionary fiscal policy will need to continue beyond 2020 to keep consumption strong and stimulate business investment. As additional support to businesses and individuals, the government recently announced a 3-month extension of the moratorium on loan repayment when the current blanket moratorium expires in September, but with the extension limited to those who have lost jobs and remained unemployed. Others who have suffered salary reduction will be eligible for lower loan repayment.

While providing extensive support to people and businesses, the government is mindful of its rising fiscal deficit—projected to jump from the equivalent of 3.4% of GDP in 2019 to 6.1% in 2020—and its rising ratio of debt to GDP. The budget for 2021 is currently being prepared for presentation to Parliament in November alongside the Twelfth Malaysia Plan, 2021–2025. Ensuring a path back to sustainable fiscal balances will be key to Malaysia's medium-term economic prospects.

Muted price pressures will enable the central bank to continue to pursue accommodative monetary policy throughout 2020 and 2021 and so strengthen consumer and business confidence and support growth. The bank reiterated in its announcement of the overnight policy rate reduction in July that it stood ready to use policy levers to facilitate recovery.

The economic outlook is vulnerable to external risks, in particular heightened volatility in international financial markets or a faltering global economic recovery. Another risk is uncertainty about how much global economic weakening will hamper growth in private investment. A resurgence of COVID-19 cases could require more restrictions on economic activity and thus delay recovery. A key domestic risk would be further weakening of the job market, which could curtail household spending.

Figure 3.4.23 Current account balance

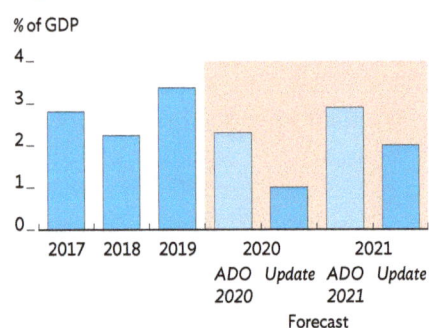

Source: *Asian Development Outlook* database.

Philippines

The growth projection for 2020 is downgraded after steep contraction in private consumption and investment drove a sharp recession in the first half (H1) of 2020. Widespread and stringent lockdowns to contain the spread of COVID-19 in the community impeded economic activity. The economic contraction may have bottomed out in May or June and a net 7.5 million jobs were restored by July as the government eased its community quarantine measures across the country. As government fiscal measures to support growth gain traction, and assuming the virus is contained, the economy will recover slowly in H2 2020 and meet the *ADO 2020* growth forecast for 2021. The outlook is for continued modest inflation and small current account deficits.

Updated assessment

The economy fell into recession with GDP contracting by 0.7% year on year in the first quarter (Q1) of 2020 and by 16.5% in Q2. These drops brought the H1 decline to 9.0% in the first recession in the Philippines since 1998, during the Asian financial crisis (Figure 3.4.24). All demand components shrank except government consumption. Community quarantine measures from mid-March to suppress COVID-19 transmission, most notably in Luzon, substantially restricted movement and commerce (Figure 3.4.25). Luzon is the country's largest island, with over half of the population and contributing over 70% of GDP.

Household consumption, providing three-fourths of GDP, fell by 15.5% in Q2 for a 7.8% decline in H1 2020. The unemployment rate more than tripled from 5.1% in April 2019 to 17.7% in April 2020, when lockdowns were widespread and at their most strict (Figure 3.4.26). Job losses that left 7.3 million unemployed in April were largely in services—mainly trade, transport, accommodation, restaurants, and entertainment—but also in industry, especially manufacturing. Lower-income and semi-skilled workers, most of them employed only informally, were hit hard because few had the option to work from home. Young workers were another seriously affected group as the share of youth not in employment, education and training (NEET) rose from 18.7% a year earlier to 25.3% in April 2020.

With movement and business restrictions gradually relaxed in June in most areas, including Metro Manila and other parts of Luzon, business resumed and a net of 7.5 million jobs were restored by July 2020. Services sector recorded additional 3.4 million jobs, agriculture 2.1 million and industry 2.0 million between April and July 2020. The unemployment rate consequently fell to 10.0% in July.

Figure 3.4.24 Demand-side contributions to growth

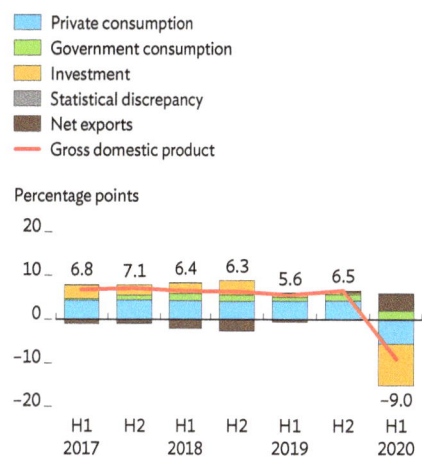

- Private consumption
- Government consumption
- Investment
- Statistical discrepancy
- Net exports
- Gross domestic product

Percentage points

H = half.
Source: CEIC Data Company (downloaded 24 August 2020).

Figure 3.4.25 Stringency and mobility restrictions

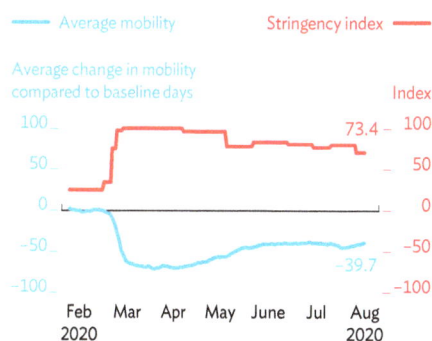

Average mobility   Stringency index

Average change in mobility compared to baseline days   Index

Notes: Stringency Index refers to the average score of 9 containment and closure policy indicators. A value equals 0 means less stringent and 100, the most stringent. Average mobility pertains to the average change in visitors or time spent in 5 categorized places, excluding to residence, compared to baseline days, or the median value from the 5-week period from 3 January to 6 February 2020 when widespread restrictions in mobility have not yet taken place.

Sources: Hale, T., S. Webster, A. Petherick, T. Phillips, and B. Kira. 2020. *Oxford COVID-19 Government Response Tracker.* Blavatnik School of Government. https://www.bsg.ox.ac.uk/research/research-projects/coronavirus-government-response-tracker; Google LLC. *Google COVID-19 Community Mobility Reports.* https://www.blog.google/technology/health/covid-19-community-mobility-reports?hl=en (both accessed 21 August 2020).

Remittances from workers overseas were 4.2% lower year on year in H1. They fell steeply in April and May before recovering somewhat in June—but notably not from seafarers, who contribute a fifth of all remittances. Their remittances continued to show double-digit declines. That said, the decline in remittances overall was much less than widely feared.

GDP contraction also came from investment, which plunged by 53.5% year on year in Q2 for a 36.6% decline in H1. Private investment slumped in Q2 with outlays for industrial machinery and transport equipment 62.1% lower and for private construction 46.8% lower. Public construction slipped by a marginal 0.9% in Q2.

Government spending growth picked up significantly to 22.1% in Q2, bringing H1 expansion to 15.6% toward offsetting declines in other components of GDP. Large increases in spending on social assistance, wage subsidies, and health care helped to mitigate the worst effects of the pandemic on incomes of the poor and middle class families.

Exports of goods and services in real terms declined by 37.0% year on year in Q2 for a 21.4% decline in H1 as external demand weakened, supply chains were disrupted, and international tourism collapsed because of travel restrictions. Imports fell even more as demand dried up for consumer and investment goods and for components for export-oriented manufacturing. Net exports thus contributed positively to GDP growth.

On the supply side, community quarantine measures caused service and industry output to contract (Figure 3.4.27). Services contributed the most to GDP contraction, falling by 15.8% in Q2 for an 8.2% decline in H1. Travel bans and border closures severely hit tourism, transportation, and trade. Industry also fell sharply, by 22.9% in Q2 and 13.5% H1, with losses in manufacturing and construction. After a slight decline in Q1, agriculture managed 1.6% growth in Q2 on higher production of major crops, including rice.

Inflation remained low at 2.4% in August, averaging 2.5% in the first 8 months of 2020. Food inflation stayed subdued, and low global oil prices helped contain inflation.

Bangko Sentral ng Pilipinas, the central bank, cut its policy rates by another 50 basis points on 26 June 2020, bringing the overnight reverse repurchase rate to a record low of 2.25% (Figure 3.4.28). Further, it reduced the reserve requirement ratio by 200 basis points in April for big banks. Consequently, growth in domestic liquidity (M3) picked up from 11.5% year on year in December 2019 to 14.5% in July 2020.

GDP contraction shrank budget revenue by 6.1% year on year in H1 2020, and with expenditure excluding interest increasing by 29.5%, the fiscal deficit increased from the equivalent of 0.5% of GDP a year earlier to 6.5%, as expected. Tax revenue was 11.9% lower but partly offset by higher dividend remittance from corporations owned or controlled by the government.

Figure 3.4.26 Unemployment

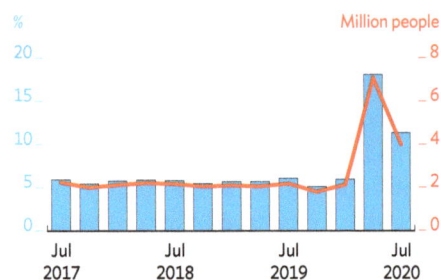

Source: CEIC Data Company (downloaded 4 September 2020).

Figure 3.4.27 Supply-side contribution to growth

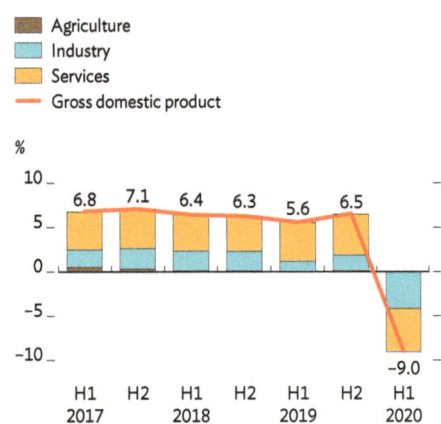

Source: CEIC Data Company (downloaded 4 September 2020).

Figure 3.4.28 Inflation and interest rate

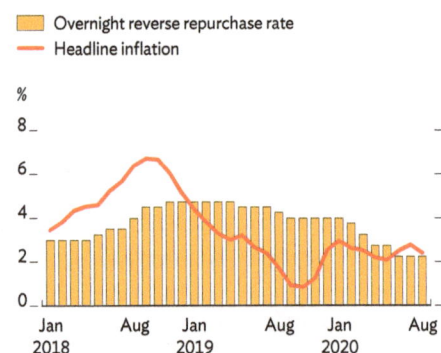

Source: CEIC Data Company (downloaded 4 September 2020).

The current account surplus equaled 0.1% of GDP in Q1 2020, reversing a 2.0% deficit in Q1 2019. Merchandise exports fell in US dollar terms by 4.3%, while imports declined by 10.3%, narrowing the merchandise trade deficit from 14.5% of GDP a year earlier to 11.6%. Exports of services, especially tourism, declined significantly. While net inflow of foreign direct investment shrank, portfolio investment reversed to net outflow. In sum, the balance of payments fell from a surplus equal to 4.5% of GDP in Q1 2019 to a 0.1% deficit.

Foreign exchange reserves stood at $98 billion in July 2020, providing cover for more than 8 months of service and income payments and imports of goods. The ratio of external debt to GDP trended lower to 21.4% at the end of March 2020. The Philippine peso appreciated by 4.7% against the US dollar in the year to August.

Prospects

The GDP outlook for 2020 is revised down to 7.3% contraction (Figure 3.4.29). The purchasing managers' index suggests, as do sales of cement and vehicles, that economic contraction may have bottomed out in May or June. Consumer confidence and business sentiment are expected to slowly recover in the second half of 2020 as the government's fiscal stimulus measures gain traction, community quarantine restrictions are further eased, and unemployment falls further. The growth forecast for next year is maintained at 6.5%, assuming that the virus is contained, fiscal support bolsters economic activity, and the global economy recovers in parallel.

Quarantines are being eased in phases contingent on how the number of local transmissions changes. Broad lockdowns of entire regions may yield to more focused lockdowns in smaller areas such as provinces, cities, or municipalities. In Metro Manila and nearby provinces, quarantine restrictions have been eased, restoring some public transportation and other businesses.

Employment will continue to recover and unemployment to gradually fall below 10% by the first semester of 2021, as the economy continues to open up and recovers, and the labor market retains flexibility. However, a larger share of these new jobs may be in the informal sector reflecting lower quality jobs. Public caution and social distancing measures will constrain household expenditure, particularly on travel and recreation. While digital e-commerce platforms see new opportunities, other businesses may take some time to adapt before resuming full operations under new health and safety protocols.

The outlook for remittances is weak. The government reported over 600,000 repatriated overseas workers as of mid-August, with more expected to return home. About 18% of overseas workers are in sales or other services, making them especially vulnerable to dismissal.

Figure 3.4.29 GDP growth

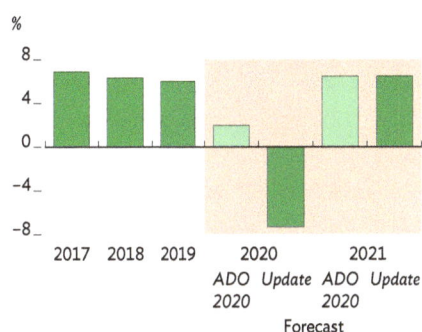

Source: *Asian Development Outlook* database.

Table 3.4.3 Selected economic indicators, Philippines (%)

	2019	2020			2021		
		ADO 2020	ADOS	Update	ADO 2020	ADOS	Update
GDP growth	6.0	2.0	–3.8	–7.3	6.5	6.5	6.5
Inflation	2.5	2.2	2.2	2.4	2.4	2.4	2.6
CAB/GDP	–0.1	–0.3	...	–0.5	–1.4	...	–1.5

... = unavailable, ADO = *Asian Development Outlook* (April), ADOS = ADO Supplement (June), CAB = current account balance, GDP = gross domestic product.
Source: ADB estimates.

Private investment will slump this year with demand weak at home and abroad. Firms are deferring capital expenditure, shrinking imports of capital goods in H1. Growth in loans for production has slowed since April, to 5.9% year on year in July. A weaker external environment will weigh heavily on investor sentiment. Net inflow of foreign direct investment fell by 25.6% year on year in the first 5 months of 2020, though growth was recorded in May. Weak private investment is partly countered by accelerated public infrastructure spending, which soared by 44.5% year on year in June.

The purchasing managers' index—an indicator of business sentiment—has stayed in contractionary territory since March, though improved in recent months suggesting the worst appeared to be over in June (Figure 3.4.30). Some other indicators appear to improve as restrictions ease. Contraction in merchandise exports year on year lessened in July, as did manufacturing (Figure 3.4.31). The pace of import contraction also broadly eased, notably for raw materials and intermediate goods.

Policy support in response to COVID-19 has mitigated weakness in private domestic demand. The government rolled out in Q2 a package of income support to families, relief for small businesses, and support to agriculture. About a third of the package is for emergency cash transfers to affected workers and to poor and vulnerable households in general, and other funding extends wage subsidies, soft loans, and credit guarantees to small businesses. With government spending and transfers to individuals comprising a significant share of the package, the Asian Development Bank estimates high fiscal multiplier effects.

An additional fiscal support package for implementation in September includes (i) further support to the health-care system, (ii) skill training and digital education programs, (iii) cash subsidies to low-income households, (iv) assistance to displaced workers and cash-for-work programs, (v) assistance to local governments, and (vi) support to agriculture, tourism, transportation, and other critically affected sectors. Further, the package provides a 60-day grace period for loan payments due on or before the end of 2020 and infuses additional capital into government financial institutions, which will act as wholesale banks to fund a substantial portion of loans that other commercial banks will retail to businesses.

As regulatory relief for finance, the central bank has relaxed terms for using its financing facilities, allowed banks to draw down their regulatory buffers, and reduced penalties for reserve deficiencies. To encourage loans to smaller businesses, it started counting new loans to micro, small, and medium-sized enterprises toward compliance with reserve requirements, temporarily reducing the credit risk weight of such loans and assigning zero risk weight to those with government guarantees.

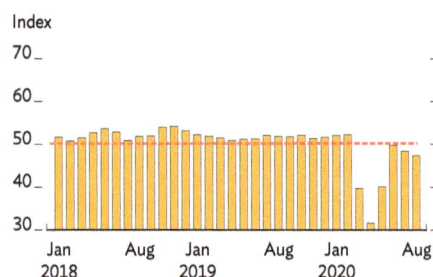

Figure 3.4.30 Manufacturing purchasing managers' index

Note: Above 50 indicates expansion, below 50 indicates contraction.
Source: IHS Markit.

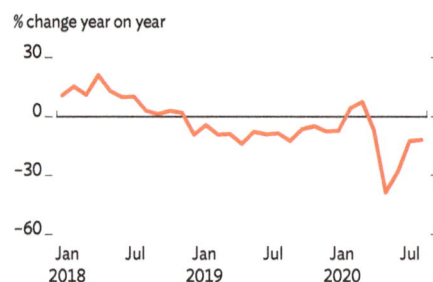

Figure 3.4.31 Manufacturing volume of production index

Source: Philippine Statistics Authority.

Budget deficit targets have been raised to equal 9.6% of GDP this year and 8.5% in 2021, well up from 3.2% planned for both years before the pandemic. The proposed 2021 budget is 9.9% higher than this year's budget, featuring increases for social services and infrastructure investment. The infrastructure budget is rising from the equivalent of 4.2% of GDP in 2020 to 5.4% in 2021, with an updated program to consider project readiness and priorities in line with the pandemic, notably boosting health-care and digital infrastructure.

The Philippines entered the crisis with room for fiscal policy support. Tax reform had increased the ratio of tax to GDP from 13.0% in 2015 to 14.5% in 2019. The fiscal deficit averaged only 2.4% in 2015–2019, and the ratio of government debt to GDP fell to a record low of 39.6% in 2019. Debt rose to equal 48.1% of GDP at the end of June 2020 on higher borrowing to fund programs to address the pandemic. Investment-grade credit ratings have been affirmed by Fitch Ratings, Moody's Investors Service, and Standard & Poor's despite economic headwinds. To facilitate economic recovery, the government is pushing to reduce corporate income tax rates, extend incentives tailored to investors, allow banks to dispose of nonperforming loans and assets through asset management companies, and enable government banks to form a special holding company to infuse equity into strategically important companies facing insolvency, subject to strict conditions.

Inflation forecasts are revised up slightly to 2.4% for 2020 and 2.6% in 2021 as global oil prices stabilize (Figure 3.4.32). With inflation within the 2%–4% target, monetary policy is expected to remain expansionary. Following policy rate cuts from February to June this year amounting to 175 basis points, the central bank maintained the rates in its meeting in August 2020, allowing earlier rate reductions to feed through the economy as it reopens. Further cuts to the reserve requirement ratio are likely to free up more funds for banks to lend.

The forecast for the current account deficit in 2020 is revised from the equivalent of 0.3% of GDP to 0.5%. A weakening 2020 outlook for the major advanced economies will continue to weigh heavily on exports of goods and services, as well as remittances. For a fifth consecutive month in July, merchandise exports continued to fall (though less sharply) and, in the first 7 months of 2020, tourist arrivals fell by 73% year on year. The contraction in imports has eased after plunging in April and May.

The forecast for slow recovery in the second half of 2020 and stronger growth in 2021 is subject to downside risks. Recurring or worsening COVID-19 outbreaks pose the risk of containment becoming longer and more stringent, which would again impede economic activity. Disappointing global recovery would weigh heavily on trade, investment, and worker remittances.

Figure 3.4.32 Inflation

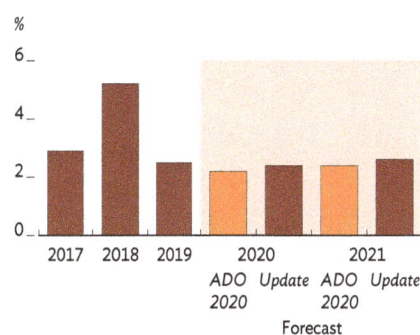

Source: *Asian Development Outlook* database.

Thailand

The economic outlook is grim in the near term. Results in the first half show the economy contracting more than anticipated in April in *ADO 2020*, despite some positive results from expansionary fiscal and monetary policy. Deflation is forecast deeper this year than was projected in April but is no longer persisting into next year. The current account surplus will likely narrow sharply this year but recover somewhat in 2021. Risks to the outlook, primarily from external headwinds, tilt to the downside.

Updated assessment

The COVID-19 pandemic caused deep economic contraction in the first half of 2020, following the implementation of a national lockdown on 26 March. It dragged GDP down from 2.7% growth year on year in the first half of 2019 to 6.9% contraction in the same period of this year (Figure 3.4.33). Exports of goods and services contracted by 17.6% in US dollars terms. Merchandise exports shrank by 7.0% year on year in the first half of 2020, in line with weaker external demand and disruption to global and regional supply chains. Key export categories that contracted sharply were automobiles and auto parts, rubber and rubber products, air-conditioners and parts, and petroleum products.

Exports categories that expanded were agricultural products and processed food such as frozen and processed fruit and vegetables, pet food, cassava, and canned and processed seafood, but their increases were insufficient to offset sharp drops in the other categories. By export destination, shipments to the advanced economies collapsed, down by 16.8% to the European Union, 9.6% to Australia, and 9.3% to Japan. Shipments to other markets were also down, by 9.1% to Southeast Asia, 8.9% to the Middle East, and a staggering 39.7% to India. The only major export market to expand was the People's Republic of China, where the easing of restrictions and resumption of economic activity allowed shipments to grow by 5.8%.

International tourist arrivals remained muted in the second quarter of 2020 under restrictions on inbound travel to Thailand. In the first half of the year, arrivals plunged by 66.2%, dragging down exports of services by 49% in real terms and severely affecting employment in tourism and related businesses (Figure 3.4.34).

Private investment shrank by 10.2% year on year in the first half of 2020 in response to contraction in demand, both domestic and external, though some public–private partnership projects were little affected. Private consumption fell by 2.1%, with spending down across the board as unemployment rose and purchasing power and consumer confidence weakened.

Figure 3.4.33 Demand-side contributions to growth

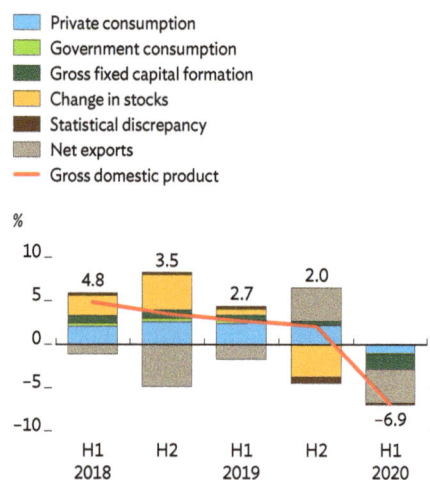

- Private consumption
- Government consumption
- Gross fixed capital formation
- Change in stocks
- Statistical discrepancy
- Net exports
- Gross domestic product

H = half.
Source: Office of the National Economic and Social Development Council. http://www.nesdc.go.th (accessed 26 August 2020).

Figure 3.4.34 Tourism indicators

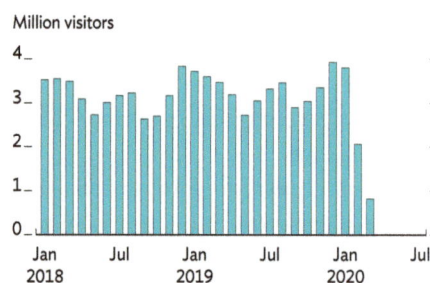

Sources: Bank of Thailand. http://www.bot.or.th; CEIC Data Company (both accessed 26 August 2020).

Economic disruption undermined merchandise imports, which contracted by 9.9% in the half from a year earlier, affecting consumer goods, raw materials, intermediate goods, and capital goods.

Higher public expenditure partly cushioned the adverse economic effects of the pandemic. The government accelerated disbursement and reallocated budget shares toward alleviating the impact of COVID-19 and supporting the economy, launching three relief packages together worth the equivalent of 12% of GDP. The packages aimed to provide relief to vulnerable households—including affected informal workers, farm families, the elderly, and children under 6 years old in low-income households—as well as to small and medium-sized enterprises hurt by containment measures, and to support post COVID-19 economic recovery. Benefits include cash handouts to affected households, soft loans, and tax relief and debt restructuring for firms and households. Public consumption nevertheless declined by 0.7% in the first half of 2020, partly because of delay in passing the budget. Meanwhile, public investment expanded by 1.2%, slightly narrowing fiscal space but not affecting fiscal stability. The ratio of public debt to GDP rose from 41.1% at the end of fiscal year 2019 (ending 30 September 2019) to 44.8% at the end of June 2020, mainly from increased borrowing to fund COVID-19 relief programs.

Growth suffered across all sectors in the first half of the year (Figure 3.4.35). Agriculture stagnated as harvests of rice, sugarcane, maize, cassava, and oil palm declined under drought. Manufacturing plunged by 7.4% year on year in response to softening domestic and external demand for manufactures, notably motor vehicles and food products, and for nonmetallic minerals such as clay, cement, and concrete products for manufacturing production. Services declined by 6.7% with a steep drop in foreign tourist arrivals and the implementation of containment restrictions. To boost tourism, the government introduced in July a B22.4 billion promotion campaign under the slogan *We Travel Together* that subsidizes until October 2020 domestic flight fares, accommodation up to 5 nights (subsidizing 40% of normal accommodation rate, up to 3,000 baht per night), and other services including food (subsidy capped at 900 baht during weekdays and 600 baht during weekends per person), aiming to benefit 5 million registered Thai travelers with hotel accommodation and eating out, and 2 million with reduced airfare.

Dampened aggregate demand and energy prices further suppressed already low inflation. Headline inflation, at 0.9% in the first half of 2019, reversed to 1.1% deflation as core inflation fell from 0.6% to 0.3% (Figure 3.4.36). Also tamping down inflation were government measures to contain the cost of living for households during the pandemic. Inflation was thus below the lower bound of the monetary policy target of 1.0%–3.0%

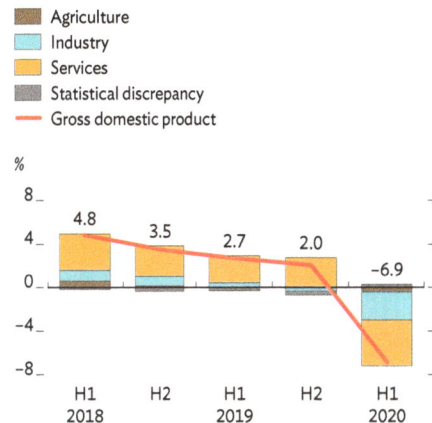

Figure 3.4.35 Supply-side contributions to growth

H = half.
Source: Office of the National Economic and Social Development Council. http://www.nesdc.go.th (accessed 26 August 2020).

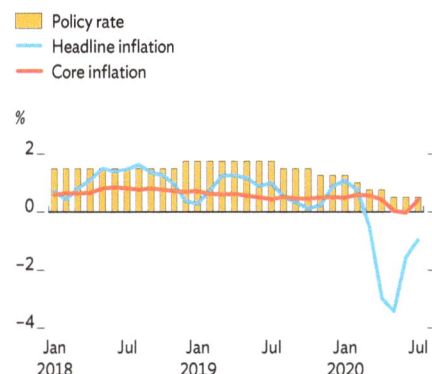

Figure 3.4.36 Inflation and policy interest rate

Source: CEIC Data Company (accessed 26 August 2020).

in 2020, prompting the Bank of Thailand, the central bank, to issue an open letter on 3 July 2020 to explain how and within what time frame headline inflation was expected to move up into the target range. At the same time it projected that, from July 2020 to June 2021, deflation would persist at an average of 0.9%. The labor market suffered as the number of jobless claims filed with the social security system rose significantly.

Externally, the current account surplus shrank in the first half of 2020 from a year earlier with exports of goods and services contracting sharply. The capital and financial accounts posted surpluses as funds were repatriated from abroad. Meanwhile, nonresident net flows turned negative as portfolio investment fell (Figure 3.4.37). The external payments position remained sustainable, though, with international reserves providing cover for 11.4 months of imports, or equal to 3.8 times short-term external debt.

After *ADO 2020* was published, the central bank cut the policy rate in May by a further 0.25 basis points, from 0.75% to 0.50%, having concluded that monetary policy needed to become more accommodative to support a sagging economy. Financial conditions in Thailand became more accommodative overall. Commercial bank lending rates declined substantially in line with the policy rate. Corporate financing accelerated as more businesses needed liquidity buffers. Financial markets remained resilient, with ample capital fund and loan-loss provision to cushion any economic volatility that may accompany COVID-19.

Prospects

Thailand has contained COVID-19 relatively well, permitting the gradual relaxation of lockdown measures and allowing domestic economic activity to resume. However, COVID-19 impacts on the economy have been more severe than expected in *ADO 2020*, and economic recovery remains elusive. GDP is therefore forecast to contract by 8.0% this year, well beyond the April forecast of contraction by 4.8%. The rebound next year is now expected to feature 4.5% growth, revised up from 2.5% growth anticipated in April (Figure 3.4.38). Deflation will persist this year under a sharp decline in energy prices as the global economy languishes. Deflation is further entrenched by government measures to reduce electricity and water utility charges.

External demand is likely to continue to be weak in the near term. Even with trade partners gradually recovering as the COVID-19 situation allows them to relax containment measures, economic activity is projected to remain significantly below pre-pandemic norms in many countries. Thailand's earnings from exports of goods and services are now projected to contract more deeply in dollar terms in 2020, by 22.3%, then rebound to 7.6% growth in 2021.

Figure 3.4.37 Balance of payments

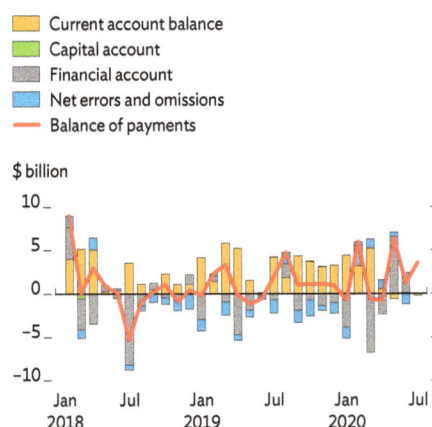

- Current account balance
- Capital account
- Financial account
- Net errors and omissions
- Balance of payments

Source: CEIC Data Company (accessed 26 August 2020).

Figure 3.4.38 GDP growth

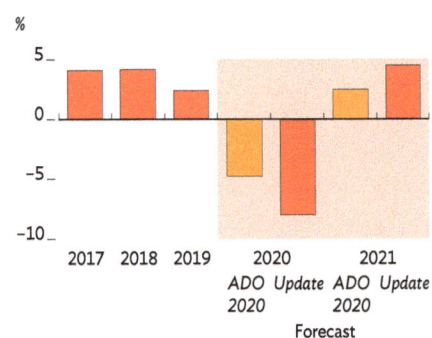

Source: *Asian Development Outlook* database.

Deeper export contraction will weigh on private consumption and investment. Private investment is now expected to contract in 2020 more than forecast in April. Weak demand at home and abroad, lots of excess production capacity, and persistent uncertainty about the course of the COVID-19 pandemic will undermine business confidence and hamper investment this year. Investment to produce automobiles, machinery, and equipment is unlikely to expand as long as consumers continue to stay away from durable goods. Hotel, restaurant, and transportation services will continue to suffer as economic activity languishes, even with more relaxed lockdown measures. Some businesses may choose not to reopen as long as sales look unlikely to cover operating costs. Private investment is forecast to decline substantially by 12.1% in 2020 and then recover with 4.0% growth next year.

Private consumption is expected to decline in 2020 more than anticipated in April under containment measures and a marked decline in income. While the gradual relaxation of these measures could improve domestic economic activity before too long, private consumption is expected to grow only slowly in 2021 because households will remain cautious about spending. Moreover, households are expected to have more vulnerable finances given rising unemployment and an elevated burden of household debt.

Public expenditure seems to be almost the only economic driver this year. Public consumption is now expected to expand by 3.8%, revised up from 2.4% in *ADO 2020*, thanks to speedy disbursement of relief spending. Meanwhile, public investment is projected to expand, especially on infrastructure projects for state-owned enterprises, and this will be key to sustaining the economy to the forecast horizon. Especially likely to expand is infrastructure investment to support the digital economy, including accelerated investment in the 5G network following a successful auction in the first quarter of 2020, as households and businesses alike turn to technology to ease their isolation under movement restrictions.

On the supply side, the forecast for agriculture is revised down to 2.5% decline from 0.5% expansion projected in April as drought has reduced harvests more than anticipated. Prices will nevertheless fall for agricultural goods, mainly with a decline in rubber prices as a result of sharply falling external demand. Manufacturing will continue to be hampered by weak demand, both external and domestic, in particular for such major products as vehicles, air-conditioners, garments, and steel. Industry is thus projected to contract by 5.3% this year but rebound with growth at 2.3% next year.

Services are now projected to recover more slowly than anticipated in *ADO 2020*, with COVID-19 and its consequences in other countries more prolonged than expected.

Table 3.4.4 Selected economic indicators, Thailand (%)

	2019	2020			2021		
		ADO 2020	ADOS	Update	ADO 2020	ADOS	Update
GDP growth	2.4	−4.8	−6.5	−8.0	2.5	3.5	4.5
Inflation	0.7	−0.9	−1.3	−1.6	0.4	0.7	0.8
CAB/GDP	7.0	7.1	...	3.9	6.7	...	4.5

... = unavailable, ADO = *Asian Development Outlook* (April), ADOS = *ADO Supplement* (June), CAB = current account balance, GDP = gross domestic product.
Source: ADB estimates.

Moreover, public concerns over reopening the country to visitors may slow progress in welcoming back foreign tourists. The government is expected to maintain travel restrictions for foreign tourists until sometime toward the end of this year. The number of foreign tourists is projected to plunge from almost 40 million in 2019 to 7 million this year. Tourism may pick up in the latter half of this year, mainly from domestic tourists and at least partly thanks to domestic tourism stimulus. However, domestic tourism may be insufficient to offset the decline in foreign tourism, which provided 65% of all tourism receipts last year.

With the economy expected to contract, prices will continue to decline. The forecast for headline inflation in 2020 is adjusted down from 0.9% deflation in *ADO 2020* to 1.6% deflation. Core inflation will remain low in line with muted demand. Inflation should return in 2021 to the positive territory, though, forecast at 0.8% but still a bit short of the target range set by the central bank (Figure 3.4.39).

Forecasts for merchandise imports are revised down from *ADO 2020* in tandem with weakening domestic demand and declining merchandise exports, which undermine demand for manufacturing components. The trade balance surplus is projected to shrink. The forecast for the current account surplus is revised down to 3.9% in 2020. Instead of narrowing in 2021, the surplus is now forecast to widen somewhat to 4.5% as exports recover (Figure 3.4.40). The capital and financial accounts are expected to be in balance as resident repatriation is unlikely to offset nonresident outflow.

Risks to the forecasts tilt to the downside. The outlook for the Thai economy depends largely on the COVID-19 situation globally and regionally. It will underperform the projection if the global economy recovers more slowly than anticipated. Worsening global trade protectionism or heightened geopolitical tensions could disrupt supply chains and price stability.

Domestically, a second wave of COVID-19 could trigger another round of lockdowns and disruption to domestic economic activities. The rising risk of businesses and households defaulting on loans could undermine the outlook for private consumption and investment. Recovery in tourism may be delayed by slow progress in reopening the country to international tourists. Finally, heightened domestic political tensions could further unsettle an economy already struggling to cope with the impacts of the COVID-19 pandemic.

Figure 3.4.39 Inflation

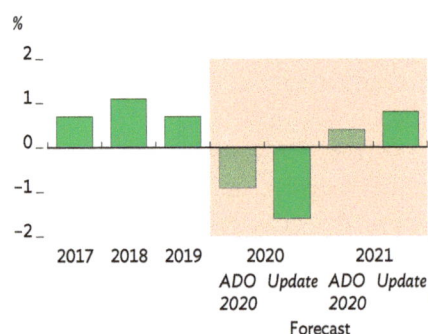

Source: *Asian Development Outlook* database.

Figure 3.4.40 Current account balance

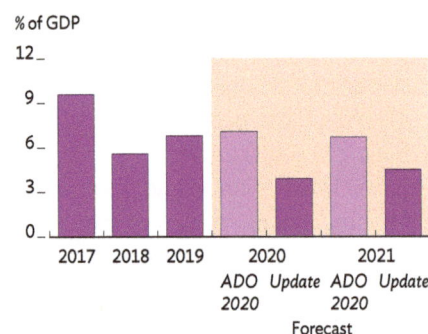

Source: *Asian Development Outlook* database.

Viet Nam

After being well contained domestically in the first half (H1) of 2020, COVID-19 re-emerged in July. Projected GDP growth in 2020 is revised down from the *ADO 2020* forecast in April, mainly to reflect lower domestic consumption and external demand than earlier projected. Growth is expected to revive in 2021, supported by accelerated public investment, increased trade with the European Union and the People's Republic of China (PRC), and the reallocation of global value chains to Viet Nam. Inflation is forecast to rise little this year or next, as earlier forecast.

Updated assessment

Growth plunged from 3.7% year on year in Q1 2020 to 0.4% in Q2, dragging down growth in H1 2020 to 1.8%, the lowest rate since 2011 (Figure 3.4.41). On the supply side, growth in services fell from 6.7% in H1 2019 to 0.6% a year later as international tourist arrivals shrank by 56.0%, slashing the contribution of services to GDP growth from 2.5 percentage points a year earlier to 0.2 points. Domestic tourism started to recover in May and June but was halted by the COVID-19 resurgence in July (Figure 3.4.42).

Growth in agriculture was halved from 2.3% in H1 2019 to 1.2% a year later because of falling demand for exports but also the worst drought in 4 decades, salinity intrusion in the Mekong Delta, and livestock hit by African swine fever. Farming output expanded by only 0.8%, forestry by 2.1%, and fisheries by 2.4%.

Growth in industry and construction plunged from 8.9% a year earlier to 3.0%. Growth in export-oriented manufacturing tumbled from 11.2% to 5.0%, while output in mining and quarrying contracted by 5.4%. Restricted mobility and weak demand dragged down construction growth from 7.9% in H1 2019 to 4.5% a year later. The purchasing managers' index, in which a reading below 50 indicates future contraction, fell further from 47.6 in July to 45.7 in August, the lowest reading since May. August output and new orders fell even more than in July (Figure 3.4.43).

The slowdown was reflected in lower incomes and spending. Growth in private consumption fell from 7.2% in H1 2019 to a marginal 0.2% in H1 2020. Retail sales contracted by 2.7% month on month in August and 0.02% in the first eight months over the same period a year earlier. Public consumption, on the other hand, was propped up by government spending, enabling it to accelerate from 5.6% growth in H1 2019 to 6.1% a year later. The slowdown closed firms and unemployed workers. In the first 8 months of 2020, nearly 34,300 enterprises suspended operations, a 71.0% increase year on year.

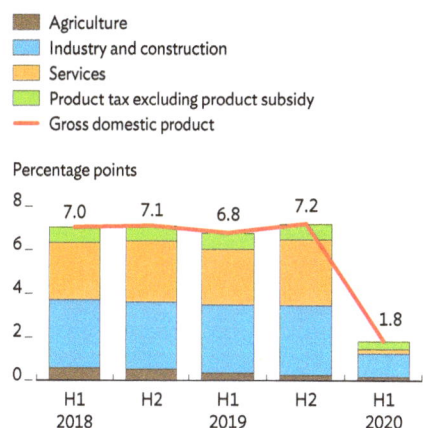

Figure 3.4.41 Supply-side contributions to growth

- Agriculture
- Industry and construction
- Services
- Product tax excluding product subsidy
- Gross domestic product

Percentage points

H = half.
Source: General Statistics Office of Viet Nam.

Figure 3.4.42 Visitor arrivals

Number   Growth

Million persons   %

H = half.
Source: General Statistics Office of Viet Nam.

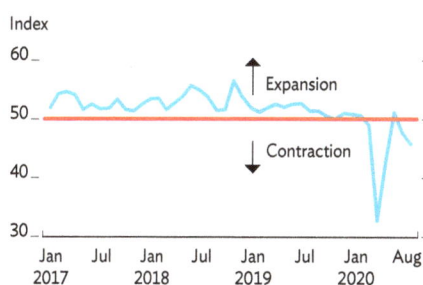

Figure 3.4.43 Purchasing managers' index

Index

Expansion

Contraction

Sources: HSBC; HCMC Securities Corporation.

In the same period, 7.8 million people lost their jobs, and unemployment rose to its highest rate in 10 years. Average individual income dropped by 5.1% in H1 2020 compared with the same period in 2019.

Investment was subdued. Growth in gross domestic investment slowed from 7.1% in H1 2019 to 1.9% a year later as foreign investment contracted. From January to August, foreign investment registration was $19.5 billion, down by 13.7% year on year (Figure 3.4.44). As disbursement of foreign direct investment contracted by 5.1% year on year in the 8-month period, public investment disbursement jumped by 30.4% to an estimated $11.0 billion.

The weak economy kept average inflation at 4.2% in H1, the lowest average recorded since the beginning of the year. In the year to August, average inflation fell further to 4.0% (Figure 3.4.45).

The State Bank of Viet Nam, the central bank, cut its policy rates twice, in March and May, by a total of 100–150 basis points. Interest rate caps on Viet Nam dong deposits of less than 6 months fell by 60–75 basis points, and the cap on short-term dong lending rates to priority sectors by 100 basis points. Further, the central bank instructed commercial banks to support affected firms by restructuring debt, lowering interest rates, waiving interest for existing loans, and extending new soft loans. Credit growth nevertheless slowed from 13.4% year on year at the end of June 2019 to an estimated 9.0% a year later (Figure 3.4.46).

Viet Nam's international trade shrank by 0.3% in the first 8 months of 2020, with exports growing by 1.6% but imports contracting by 2.2%. The trade surplus in January–August is estimated at $11.9 billion, nearly four times larger than a year earlier. Exports to the US grew by 19.0% and to the PRC by 13.0%, cushioning the fall in exports to Southeast Asia, Japan, and the Republic of Korea. The trade surplus helped offset a 12.0% reduction in remittances, driving the current account surplus up from the equivalent of 1.8% of GDP in the year-earlier period to 2.5%.

Inflows of foreign direct investment and portfolio investment slumped in H1 2020, dragging the surplus in the financial account down to the equivalent of 1.4% of GDP. At the end of June 2020, the overall balance of payments was a surplus equal to 4.6% of GDP (Figure 3.4.47). Foreign reserves at the end of June were estimated sufficient to cover 3.2 months of imports, down somewhat from 3.6 months at the end of 2019.

Other than during a brief period of volatility in early April, the Viet Nam dong has been stable this year as the US dollar generally weakened and Viet Nam's trade surplus widened on lower domestic demand for imports.

The fiscal balance reversed a surplus equal to 3.2% of GDP in H1 2019 with a deficit estimated at 2.4% in H1 2020.

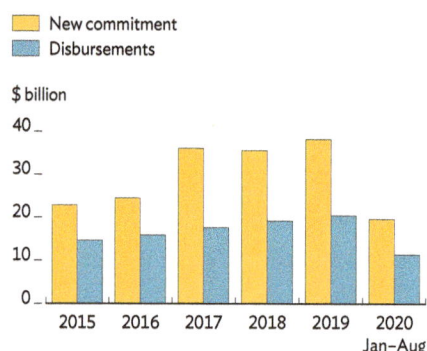

Figure 3.4.44 Foreign direct investment

New commitment
Disbursements

$ billion

Source: General Statistics Office of Viet Nam.

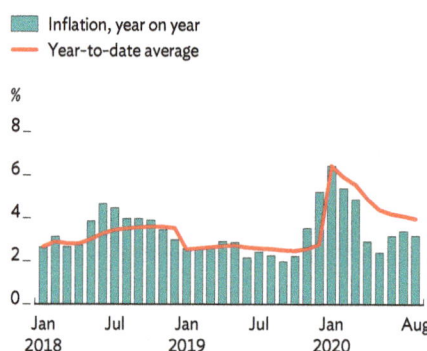

Figure 3.4.45 Monthly inflation

Inflation, year on year
Year-to-date average

%

Source: General Statistics Office of Viet Nam.

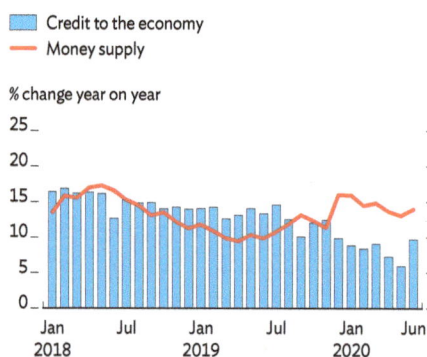

Figure 3.4.46 Credit and money supply growth

Credit to the economy
Money supply

% change year on year

Sources: State Bank of Viet Nam; General Statistics Office; ADB estimates.

Revenue fell by 10.3%, while spending increased by 9.5%, led by outlays for health care, social security, and income support. Fiscal response to the pandemic equal to about 4.0% of GDP was launched in April. By July, 163,000 affected enterprises and household businesses had applied for tax deferral. This number is modest, however, compared with the estimated 700,000 enterprises and 5 million household enterprises in the whole economy.

Prospects

The global downturn and weak domestic conditions, notably worsening unemployment and falling consumption, have hurt the economy more than expected. The outlook is further threatened by a rise in new COVID-19 infections since late July 2020. The growth forecast for 2020 is therefore revised down from 4.8% in *ADO 2020* and 4.1% in the June *ADO Supplement* to 1.8% in this *Update* (Figure 3.4.48).

Domestic consumption is expected to remain weak. Despite recovery in retail sales in July and continuing moderate inflation, consumption will be held back by lower household and corporate incomes, rising unemployment, and more firms suspending operations. The prospect for investment is mixed, with private investment remaining weak and trade-related foreign investment continuing to slide. However, accelerated public investment in H2 2020 will offset these weaknesses. Looking ahead to 2021, investment will be boosted by improving disbursement of public investment, the continuing diversion of production from the PRC to Viet Nam, recovery in the PRC economy, and the implementation of a trade agreement with the European Union to greatly liberalize trade. The Japan External Trade Organization has released a list of 15 Japanese firms to shift their manufacturing from the PRC to Viet Nam. The majority of those moving to Viet Nam make medical equipment while the rest produce semiconductors, phone components, air conditioners, or power modules.

On the supply side, agriculture has been troubled in 2020 by severe weather and will continue to struggle under weak external and domestic demand. Manufacturing will be held back this year by weak exports, restricted mobility, and lower domestic demand in the wake of income and job losses, though it should pick up in 2021. Phones and spare parts, and electronic goods remain the top exports of Viet Nam, accounting for 18% and 16% of total exports respectively. In the first 8 months of 2020, the exports of phones and spare parts, dropped by 5% from a year earlier. Reduced income and restricted mobility will also hamper recovery in domestic and international tourism.

Figure 3.4.47 Balance of payments indicators

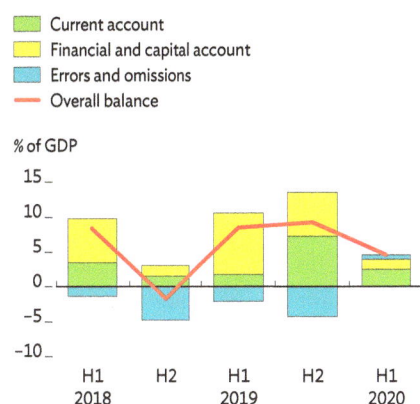

GDP = gross domestic product, H = half.
Sources: State Bank of Viet Nam; General Statistics Office; ADB estimates.

Figure 3.4.48 GDP growth

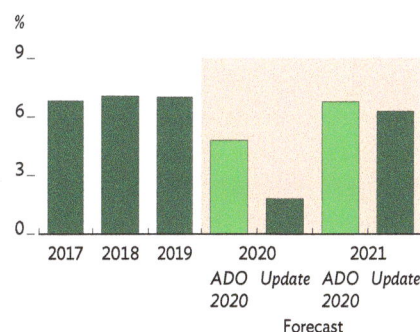

Source: *Asian Development Outlook* database.

Inflation may be pushed up by the higher prices for basic commodities and rising liquidity from accelerated public investment. It should nevertheless remain subdued in 2020, well below the 4.0% central bank's target, as weakness in growth and spending persists (Figure 3.4.49).

Lending will likely remain weak despite central bank measures to support it. For their part, banks may be reluctant to relax lending standards to accommodate firms' weaker balance sheets, fearing an increase in nonperforming loans when the deadline for loan restructuring expires. Credit demand from firms is falling as well, in tandem with weak demand for their products and services. Bank credit is therefore forecast to grow by only 10% this year, well below the central bank's 14.0% annual target.

Unemployment is likely to keep rising. A joint study by the International Labour Organization and the Asian Development Bank projects that Viet Nam will lose 548,000 jobs for youth if the pandemic is prolonged, and 370,000 jobs even if the outbreak is effectively contained.

With tax collection reduced because of lower incomes and export earnings, spending increased on health care and social security, and likely additional fiscal support in 2020, the fiscal deficit is forecast to widen to the equivalent of 6.0% of GDP in 2020, improving to 3.5% in 2021. Disbursement of public investment was slow in H1 2020 but will pick up in H2, helping to keep the economy afloat.

The current account surplus is expected to shrink to the equivalent 1.0% of GDP in 2020 and recover slightly to 1.5% in 2021. Although exports are likely to decline in the rest of the year, imports are expected to decline even more steeply, keeping the trade balance in surplus. This surplus will not be an indicator of economic health, though, as it arises from weakening production and demand. Meanwhile, downward pressure on the current account will likely come from remittances, which are projected to shrink by 18.0% in 2020.

Viet Nam's economic outlook in the near term is difficult, with the global economic downturn and domestic weakness proving worse than expected. However, Viet Nam is showing stronger resilience than most comparable economies, and the economy's outlook over the medium and long term remains positive. Economic fundamentals have not been impaired, and Viet Nam looks likely to benefit from current trends in global patterns of trade, investment, and production.

Figure 3.4.49 Inflation

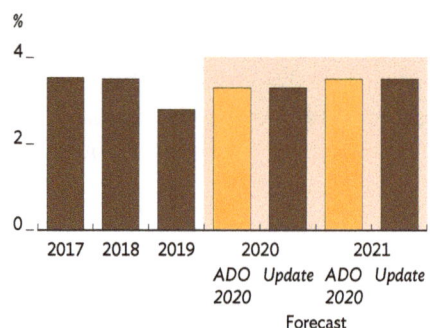

Source: *Asian Development Outlook* database.

Table 3.4.5 Selected economic indicators, Viet Nam (%)

	2019	2020			2021		
		ADO 2020	ADOS	Update	ADO 2020	ADOS	Update
GDP growth	7.0	4.8	4.1	1.8	6.8	6.8	6.3
Inflation	2.8	3.3	3.0	3.3	3.5	3.5	3.5
CAB/GDP	5.0	−0.2	...	1.0	1.0	...	1.5

... = unavailable, ADO = *Asian Development Outlook* (April), ADOS = *ADO Supplement* (June), CAB = current account balance, GDP = gross domestic product.
Source: ADB estimates.

Other economies

Brunei Darussalam

In the first quarter (Q1) of 2020, GDP grew by 2.4% year on year as growth in exports and private consumption more than offset declines in investment and government consumption. Reversing contraction in Q1 2019, exports of goods and services soared 29.1% by volume, primarily on higher exports of petroleum and chemical products as the new Hengyi refinery and petrochemical plant expanded operations, more than offsetting lower exports of crude oil and natural gas. Despite the COVID-19 pandemic, private consumption grew by 2.1%. Government consumption fell by 16.4%, however, as virus containment measures affected some government services, and investment fell by 17.5% with declines in both private and government capital spending.

By sector, growth was driven by 5.3% expansion in industry with new petroleum and chemical production. Services contracted as the COVID-19 outbreak affected many segments, in particular air transport, finance, government services, and hotels and restaurants.

GDP growth is forecast to remain positive in 2020 but at only half the 2019 rate. Restrictions on personal mobility in Brunei Darussalam and abroad will continue to depress demand for crude oil and liquefied natural gas exports, as well as other consumption and investment. Oil production is expected to be further constrained this year and next as Brunei Darussalam adheres to production cuts agreed in April 2020 by the Organization of the Petroleum Exporting Countries and others.

In sum, healthy growth in Q1 is unlikely to be sustained in the remaining 3 quarters, yielding GDP expansion in 2020 somewhat lower than the forecast in *ADO 2020*. However, growth in 2021 is seen improving as forecast in April, driven by increased production and investment at Hengyi and the state-owned Brunei Fertilizer Industries ammonia and urea production plant, as well as by expanded domestic consumption.

An unexpected rise in inflation prompts higher forecasts for this year and next. Consumer prices rose by an average of 1.9% year on year in the first half of 2020, reaching in June 2.5%, the highest rate since 2008. Though mitigated by price subsidies and a currency peg to the Singapore dollar, the rise was led by food, transportation, and miscellaneous goods and services, notably insurance. As these categories are heavily influenced by external trends, inflation is likely to ease only slowly as global conditions improve, yet further in 2021.

In the first 5 months of 2020, exports rose by 21.0% in US dollar terms while imports declined by 3.4% under the pandemic. The current account surplus is thus seen expanding this year mainly on strong growth in exports of petroleum products from the Hengyi plant, which will level off in Q4 2020. The 2021 forecast is for sustained export growth and revived imports to supply petroleum feedstock and inputs for infrastructure investments.

Table 3.4.6 Selected economic indicators, Brunei Darussalam (%)

	2019	2020 ADO 2020	2020 ADOS	2020 Update	2021 ADO 2020	2021 ADOS	2021 Update
GDP growth	3.9	2.0	1.4	1.4	3.0	3.0	3.0
Inflation	-0.4	-0.2	0.4	1.4	0.1	0.4	1.0
CAB/GDP	9.0	5.5	...	9.5	9.5	...	9.5

... = unavailable, ADO = Asian Development Outlook (April), ADOS = ADO Supplement (June), CAB = current account balance, GDP = gross domestic product.
Source: ADB estimates.

Cambodia

Projected growth in 2020 is revised up from the June *ADO Supplement* after strong second-quarter expansion in merchandise exports other than garments, travel goods, and footwear (GTF). COVID-19 continues to depress tourism and GTF exports. Reduced income from exports and remittances will see the current account deficit widen in 2020. As the government has prepared a comprehensive response to the pandemic, GDP growth is forecast to rebound in 2021 slightly above the *ADO 2020* projection, and the current account deficit to narrow. The April forecast for low and stable inflation is retained.

A sharp drop in orders from Europe and North America has temporarily closed about a third of GTF factories, and the pandemic has slowed construction. However, increased production of bicycles and electronics drove exports of manufactures other than GTF 30.3% higher year on year in the first half (H1) of 2020. Growth in industry is projected at 5.1% in 2020, but this hinges on some recovery in GTF exports in H2 and continued strength in higher-value manufacturing.

A collapse in international tourism hit the service sector. After Cambodia closed its land borders and stopped issuing tourist visas in March, international visitor arrivals plunged in the second quarter by 98.1% year on year. As a result, a reported 3,000 businesses had closed by June, and 45,000 workers had been laid off. Gradual reopening is expected in H2, but services are still projected to shrink by 15.1% in the full year. Good progress was achieved in agriculture, with exports rising by 17.4% year on year in H1 2020. The sector—which still employs nearly a third of the Cambodian workforce, especially the poor—is now expected to grow by 2.0%.

A concern has been that COVID-19 could destabilize the financial industry or rapidly deplete foreign exchange reserves. The annualized current account deficit widened to the equivalent of 22.7% of GDP in the first quarter, but capital inflow ensured stable reserves. The National Bank of Cambodia, the central bank, acted quickly in March to ensure bank liquidity and issued guidance on loan restructuring. Bank lending expanded by 6% in H1 2020, led by mortgages.

Growth in the money supply slowed from an average of 22.8% in 2019 to 9.7% year on year in April. Inflation accelerated to 3.6% year on year in January on higher food and fuel prices. Inflation eased in the year to April as fuel prices declined, then revived to 3.2% year on year in June.

Downside risks to the forecasts include unexpectedly deep or persistent weakness in GTF or construction, poor harvests after deficient rainfall in June–July, and further suppression of consumer demand as more households suffer financial distress.

Table 3.4.7 Selected economic indicators, Cambodia (%)

	2019	2020			2021		
		ADO 2020	ADOS	Update	ADO 2020	ADOS	Update
GDP growth	7.1	2.3	-5.5	-4.0	5.7	5.9	5.9
Inflation	1.9	2.1	2.1	2.1	1.8	1.8	1.8
CAB/GDP	-15.0	-19.0	...	-22.3	-16.9	...	-17.8

... = unavailable, ADO = *Asian Development Outlook* (April), ADOS = *ADO Supplement* (June), CAB = current account balance, GDP = gross domestic product.
Source: ADB estimates.

Lao People's Democratic Republic

The COVID-19 outbreak and global economic downturn slowed the economy sharply in the first half (H1) of 2020. While agriculture recovered from last year's severe flood and drought, industry and services were hit hard by slower growth in exports and credit and by fewer tourist arrivals. Recovery over the medium term is expected to be slow.

The economy is now projected to contract by 2.5% in 2020 compared to the 0.5 contraction in the *ADO Supplement*. COVID-19 effects include closed factories, disrupted supply chains, deterred tourists, and reduced consumer spending. Major construction projects and large increases in hydroelectric production are nevertheless projected to sustain industry growth by 1.4% in the full year. Services are projected to contract by 5.5% in 2020. This reflects tourist arrivals falling by 60% in H1 and expected to cease altogether soon, as well as lower numbers for wholesale and retail trade, transportation, and hospitality that are projected to drag consumption down by 17.5%. Agriculture is expected to grow by 1.9% in 2020, somewhat slower than the 2.5% *ADO 2020* projection for lack of rain. Disrupted inflows of foreign direct investment will shrink all investment by 17.5%.

The pandemic is partly to blame for the budget deficit rising from the equivalent of 4.7% of GDP in 2019 to 6.5% in 2020 despite fiscal consolidation efforts. Lower revenue collection and resulting cashflow problems could prove critical in H2, given the government's large public debt burden at 60% of GDP and debt service costs in 2020 estimated at $1.2 billion.

Average inflation tripled from 2.0% year on year in H1 2019 to 5.9% a year later as Lao kip depreciation and high prices for food and imported goods, notably electronics, overwhelmed lower oil prices. Inflation is expected to ease in H2 as demand softens and food production recovers but still exceeds the *ADO 2020* forecast in the whole of 2020.

Exports and imports are expected to contract by 12.0% and 15.8% year on year, respectively in 2020. Gross international reserves nevertheless fell to $946 million at the end of May 2020, or cover for only 1.7 months of imports. Persistent shortages of foreign currency continued to weaken the kip in H1, by 1.6% against the dollar officially and by 5.7% on the parallel market. The current account deficit should narrow this year more than earlier projected on lower oil prices and lower demand for imports, as well as higher electricity exports, but then widen again in 2021.

Growth recovery in 2021 is projected to be U-shaped with the pandemic now expected to subside only slowly. Inflation should fall slightly in 2021 as food prices continue to ease. Risks to the outlook are mainly on the downside: external vulnerability from meager international reserves and rising public debt, continuing pandemic-related losses, and ever-present exposure to natural hazards.

Table 3.4.8 Selected economic indicators, Lao People's Democratic Republic (%)

	2019	2020			2021		
		ADO 2020	ADOS	Update	ADO 2020	ADOS	Update
GDP growth	5.0	3.5	-0.5	-2.5	6.0	4.5	4.5
Inflation	3.3	4.0	5.5	5.5	4.5	5.0	5.0
CAB/GDP	-9.5	-9.4	...	-8.2	-8.1	...	-8.7

... = unavailable, ADO = *Asian Development Outlook* (April), ADOS = *ADO Supplement* (June), CAB = current account balance, GDP = gross domestic product.

Source: ADB estimates.

Myanmar

COVID-19 has slowed economic growth much more than what was forecasted last April in ADO 2020. Demand and supply shocks stemming from the pandemic caused broad and significant contraction in the economy. The GDP growth forecast for fiscal year 2020 (FY2020, ending 30 September 2020) is therefore revised down by more than half. However, growth is still forecast to bounce back in FY2021 almost as dramatically as projected in ADO 2020, supported by stable performance in agriculture, higher government spending, and expansion in the telecommunication industry.

Manufacturing, especially of garments, is affected by both demand and supply shocks. Cuts in new orders, supply delays, and reduction in the manufacturing workforce pushed the purchasing managers' index down to 29.0 in April, its lowest reading ever recorded, before recovering to 48.7 in June. Businesses serving the domestic market resumed operation after the relaxation of COVID-19 containment measures, but weaker external demand and supply have hindered a return to full operation in trade-oriented fields. Moreover, the travel and tourism industry has been severely affected since April. In the first 9 months of FY2020, international tourist arrivals were down by 60.7% year on year. The increasing number of reported COVID-19 cases since late August may trigger stricter containment measures and result in further disruptions in business activities.

Agriculture seems to be less exposed to COVID-19 than other sectors and has been supported by strong domestic and external demand, as well as relatively favorable weather. Growth in agricultural exports—mainly rice, beans, and other pulses— accelerated by 19.5% in the first 3 quarters of FY2020, from October 2019 to June 2020, over the same period of the previous fiscal year. However, exposure to extreme weather events such as flooding still poses risks to growth in the near term.

With sharp contraction in the garment industry, manufacturing exports in the first 3 quarters of FY2020 dropped by 4.4% from the same period a year earlier. However, all merchandise exports rose by 2.7% in US dollar terms in the first half of FY2020 from a year earlier, largely supported by agricultural exports. Meanwhile, imports increased by 9.2%, largely driven by imports of capital and investment goods for government infrastructure projects, widening the trade deficit to $1.8 billion. Approvals of foreign direct investment increased to $4.3 billion in the 3 quarters ending in June 2020 from $3.2 billion in the same period of FY2019. Electric power, real estate development, and manufacturing remained attractive to foreign investors. However, future investment inflows could disappoint expectations due to downside risks from the global economy.

In the first 8 months of FY2020, average inflation decelerated to 7.5% from 7.9% a year earlier, reflecting lower commodity prices and subdued demand. Inflation forecasts for FY2020 and FY2021 are downgraded in light of weak domestic demand.

Table 3.4.9 Selected economic indicators, Myanmar (%)

	2019	2020			2021		
		ADO 2020	ADOS	Update	ADO 2020	ADOS	Update
GDP growth	6.8	4.2	1.8	1.8	6.8	6.0	6.0
Inflation	8.6	7.5	6.0	6.0	7.5	6.0	6.0
CAB/GDP	0.4	-4.5	...	-4.5	-4.5	...	-4.5

... = unavailable, ADO = Asian Development Outlook (April), ADOS = ADO Supplement (June), CAB = current account balance, GDP = gross domestic product.

Note: Years are fiscal years ending 30 September of that year.

Sources: Central Statistical Organization; Central Bank of Myanmar; ADB estimates.

Singapore

The economy contracted in the first half of 2020 by 6.7% year on year. On the demand side, the drop was cushioned by four fiscal stimulus packages amounting to S$92.9 billion, equal to 19.2% of GDP. Despite this support for the fight to contain COVID-19 and its economic consequences, consumption and investment contracted under personal mobility restrictions, delays in implementing public and private projects, and risk aversion in response to COVID-19.

Manufacturing escaped contraction almost alone after the implementation of containment measures from 7 April to 1 June, which included a stay-at-home order and other restrictions on mobility. In the first half of the year, output in the service sector declined by 7.9% year on year as construction fell by 30.2% because restrictions on the movement of foreign workers forced project suspension. Meanwhile, manufacturing grew by 3.7%, largely on expanded production of biomedical goods.

Stringent containment measures curbed consumer demand, slowed the economy, and weakened the labor market. As a result, the first half saw annualized headline deflation by 0.2% and core deflation by 0.1%. A planned hike in the goods and services tax in 2021 was deferred in June because of the COVID-19 crisis, prompting a lower inflation forecast for 2021.

In the first half of 2020, exports contracted by 10.3% year on year as oil exports plunged by 49.5% amid lower international oil prices and economic weakness. Exports other than oil slipped by only 1.8% but further dragged down demand for imported inputs for export production. In sum, the trade surplus in the period narrowed from $14.7 billion to $12.2 billion. The current account surplus narrowed from the equivalent of 16.9% of GDP in first half of 2019 to 15.0% a year later.

With restrictions lifted at the beginning of June, economic activity is expected to recover slowly. From May to June, the manufacturing purchasing managers' index improved from 46.8 to 48.0, and a decline in the business confidence index slowed from 6.2 percentage points to 3.2 points. While information and communication technology businesses will expand as companies increasingly resort to online platforms, growth in most service industries will continue to be weighed down by uncertainty regarding the containment of COVID-19.

While supply chain disruption drives down external demand and trade, the impact is likely to be uneven across different industries. With ongoing downside risks to the outlook, GDP is now expected to contract sharply this year. The GDP growth forecast for 2021 is revised up, however, as most sectors are seen recovering from a low base, though this depends on how well the COVID-19 pandemic is contained domestically and globally.

Table 3.4.10 Selected economic indicators, Singapore (%)

	2019	2020			2021		
		ADO 2020	ADOS	Update	ADO 2020	ADOS	Update
GDP growth	0.7	0.2	−6.0	−6.2	2.0	3.2	4.5
Inflation	0.6	0.7	−0.2	−0.3	1.3	0.8	1.0
CAB/GDP	17.0	17.0	...	15.0	17.0	...	17.0

... = unavailable, ADO = Asian Development Outlook (April), ADOS = ADO Supplement (June), CAB = current account balance, GDP = gross domestic product.

Sources: Ministry of Trade and Industry. *Economic Survey Singapore*; ADB estimates.

Timor-Leste

As public expenditure and private consumption fall, a steeper decline in GDP is now forecast for 2020 than the *ADO 2020* projection in April. GDP shrank by 5.9% in the first quarter of the year. Public spending, which is the main driver of economic growth, was constrained in the first half of 2020 by the parliament's rejection of the budget in January 2020, legally limiting monthly spending allocations to one-twelfth of the previous year's budget. A budget ceiling of $1.49 billion was subsequently approved and is expected to be confirmed in a mid-September vote, leaving the government only 3 months to execute it.

The COVID-19 pandemic and consequent global economic slowdown have not spared Timor-Leste, but its ample Petroleum Fund provides considerable fiscal space with which to shield the economy from external shocks. The fund remains the largest financer of public expenditure and has been effectively used during the COVID-19 emergency, enabling the government to approve a health response and economic stimulus package equal to 9% of GDP. To contain the impact of the crisis on private consumption, the government implemented, among other measures, a wage-support program for registered businesses and cash transfers to households with individual members each earning less than $500 per month.

In the first quarter of 2020, the value of the Petroleum Fund dropped by $660 million in tandem with the US equity market. It then returned to its 2019 value as US bonds recovered in April and May, but revenue from investment income is still expected to decline this year. Domestic revenue maintained robust growth in the first quarter of 2020 but is expected to fall during the rest of the year as the economy slows. Turning to the large offshore oil and gas industry, a fall in revenue from taxes and royalties is similarly expected in 2020 along with lower global oil prices.

The current account deficit widened by 30% year on year in the first quarter of 2020. Service exports, mostly business travel receipts, fell by 18% in the quarter. Coffee exports plunged by 95% in the first half of the year, reflecting a state of emergency at home and disrupted cargo movements abroad. Oil and gas, which account for about 95% of all exports, will continue to suffer as production and global oil prices fall. The trend has raised concerns about the viability of investment in the new Greater Sunrise oil and gas project, delaying the start of drilling operations.

Inflation is still expected to remain low as international food prices decline further and oil prices languish lower than before COVID-19.

Table 3.4.11 Selected economic indicators, Timor-Leste (%)

	2019	2020			2021		
		ADO 2020	ADOS	Update	ADO 2020	ADOS	Update
GDP growth	3.4	-2.0	-3.7	-6.3	4.0	4.0	3.3
Inflation	1.5	1.3	1.3	1.0	1.8	1.8	1.0
CAB/GDP	8.0	-10.5	...	-21.5	-30.4	...	-36.5

... = unavailable, ADO = Asian Development Outlook (April), ADOS = ADO Supplement (June), CAB = current account balance, GDP = gross domestic product.
Source: ADB estimates.

The Pacific

Subregional economic contraction in 2020 is now projected deeper than forecast in either *ADO 2020* or the June *ADO Supplement* as prospects deteriorate under the COVID-19 pandemic, weighed down by Fiji and Papua New Guinea. Recovery in 2021 will depend on how quickly trade and travel restrictions can be safely lifted. Subdued commerce prompts lower inflation forecasts for 2020 and 2021. Sharp reductions in subregional current account surpluses are projected as foreign exchange earnings fall.

Subregional assessment and prospects

The aggregate Pacific economy is forecast to contract by 6.1% in 2020, or 5.8 percentage points deeper than projected in *ADO 2020* and a further 1.8 percentage point downgrade from the June *ADO Supplement*. Growth is weighed down by fading economic activity in Fiji and Papua New Guinea (PNG), the two largest economies in the subregion and the only ADB developing member countries in the Pacific to have recorded COVID-19 cases to date. The forecast contraction would be the first in the Pacific subregion in the past 2 decades.

Fiji's vital tourism industry is at a standstill, with visitor arrivals now projected to remain minimal until the first quarter of 2021 at the earliest. The government is looking to establish a travel bubble with Australia and New Zealand and to attract visitors from these markets with discounts, cash incentives, and tax cuts. However, any return of tourists will likely be determined primarily by health considerations and quarantine requirements. The outlook for other tourism-driven economies in the Pacific—the Cook Islands, Palau, and Vanuatu—is similarly dire, with large contractions projected for this year. The COVID-19 pandemic has likewise affected Samoa and Tonga through tourism, albeit to a lesser extent, and has had implications for remittance inflows. Both economies have also had to contend with public health and extreme weather shocks unrelated to COVID-19.

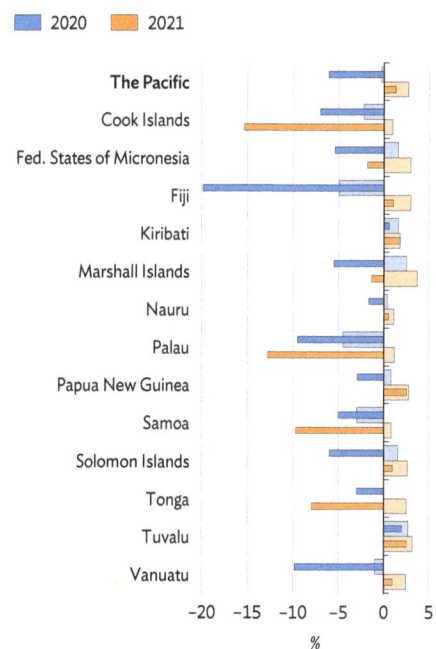

Figure 3.5.1 GDP growth, the Pacific

Note: Lighter colored bars are *ADO 2020* forecasts.
Source: *Asian Development Outlook* database.

The writeup on the Pacific economies was prepared by Jacqueline Connell, Edward Faber, Lily Anne Homasi, Magdelyn Kuari, Rommel Rabanal, Cara Tinio, Isoa Wainiqolo, and James Webb of the Pacific Department of ADB, and by Prince Cruz and Noel del Castillo, consultants to the Pacific Department.

In PNG, the COVID-19 pandemic has been felt mainly through disruption to trade and transport, notably through quarantine requirements on shipments. Cost-cutting measures and weak business profits have affected employment, household incomes, and government revenue. Similar impacts through the trade channel are being experienced in Solomon Islands, where exports of logs and fish have declined. In the Federated States of Micronesia and the Marshall Islands, transportation suffered declines because of severely reduced flight connections and weaker tuna transshipment.

Besides adversely affecting tourism, exports, and remittances, COVID-19 travel restrictions hamper construction on large infrastructure projects across the subregion. Delays in project implementation pushed Nauru into contraction and are slowing growth in Kiribati and Tuvalu.

In anticipation of only cautious recovery, the subregional growth projection for 2021 is adjusted down from 2.7% projected in *ADO 2020* to 1.3% in this *Update*, even taking into account a lower base in 2020. Risks to this outlook remain heavily tilted to the downside. Economic recovery will be determined by progress toward unlocking trade and travel flows without compromising the Pacific's fragile health systems.

Average inflation in the subregion is expected to ease to 2.7% in 2020, as forecast in *ADO 2020* in April. Price pressures remain benign across most of the Pacific amid weak economic activity and soft international commodity prices. However, inflation projections for Solomon Islands and Vanuatu are revised upward substantially, reflecting supply disruption in the wake of Cyclone Harold. The subregional 2021 inflation projection is revised down from 3.8% in *ADO 2020* to 3.1% in line with more downbeat economic growth prospects.

The subregional current account surplus is now expected to be 2.9 percentage points lower than projected in *ADO 2020*, mainly reflecting foreign exchange earnings reduced by weak exports, tourism, and remittances. The PNG current account surplus is expected to be eroded by lower income from both agriculture and mineral exports. Elsewhere, current account deficits are seen to expand as tourism receipts grind to a halt and as exports and remittances contract. In 2021, the regional surplus is projected to be 6.5 percentage points lower than forecast in *ADO 2020* amid expectations of lingering weaknesses affecting foreign exchange inflows.

Figure 3.5.2 Inflation, the Pacific

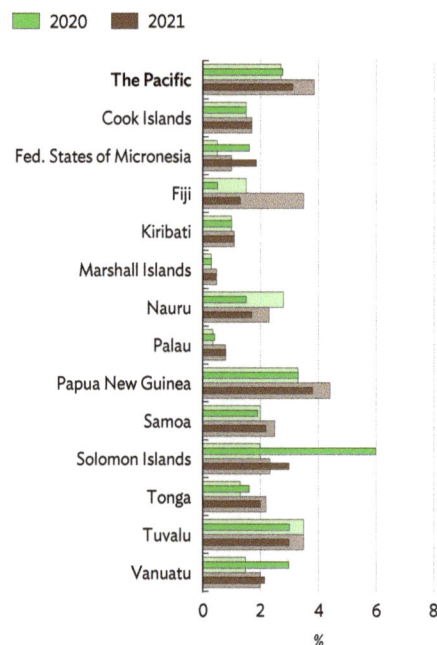

Note: Lighter colored bars are *ADO 2020* forecasts.
Source: *Asian Development Outlook* database.

Figure 3.5.3 Current account balance, the Pacific

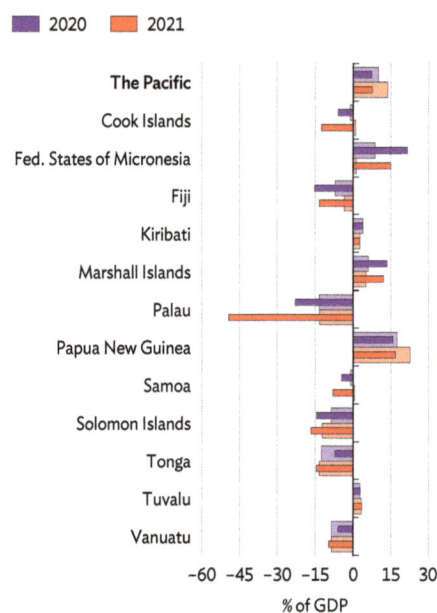

Note: Lighter colored bars are *ADO 2020* forecasts.
Source: *Asian Development Outlook* database.

Fiji

Deepening economic contraction projected for 2020 in *ADO 2020*, and forecast even deeper in the *ADO Supplement*, is further downgraded. The dramatic impact on international tourism from travel restrictions imposed to contain COVID-19 highlights structural impediments to Fiji's economic health: an undiversified economy, reliance on public expenditure to drive economic growth, and the need for fiscal consolidation from fiscal year 2022 (FY2022, ends 31 July 2022). Recovery will likely be prolonged, with business and consumer confidence being fragile and the future course of the COVID-19 pandemic highly uncertain.

ADO 2020 assumed that the global pandemic would be contained by midyear. Recovery in Fiji was to be supported by expansionary monetary policy and a fiscal response package. By June, tourism, which contributes more than one-third of GDP, had ground to a halt, and it was apparent that, even if the virus were to be contained by the end of 2020, economic fallout was likely to continue. This *Update* now projects that international travel disruption will be prolonged and any reopening cautious, with competition for Australian and New Zealand vacationers from those economies' domestic markets.

Fiji aims to attract arrivals in FY2021 by creating a travel bubble and offering discounts, cash incentives, and tax cuts. While these measures should help early recovery, travel decisions are critically based on health considerations and quarantine requirements. COVID-19 was declared contained in Fiji in June after all 18 cases in the country had fully recovered. No community transmission of COVID-19 has since surfaced, though 10 cases were intercepted on arrival in July–August and quarantined.

Fiscal responses to the pandemic since April have included cash incentives and tax cuts. Together with a decline in revenue in line with a slower economy, these measures have resulted in an estimated FY2020 fiscal deficit equivalent to 8.2% of GDP, compared with the 2.7% projected in *ADO 2020*. The deficit projection for FY2021 is revised up to 20.2% from 2.0% in *ADO 2020*. Public debt is consequently expected to continue its climb from the equivalent of 49.3% of GDP at the end of FY2019 to 65.6% a year later and 83.4% at the end of FY2021. These new forecasts starkly contrast with fiscal consolidation that was planned before COVID-19. Weak government revenue and a high debt load will weigh heavily on the economy until tourism recovers.

Low inflation to date comes thanks to a benign global price environment, ample domestic harvests, and weak internal demand. Inflation forecasts, already downgraded for both 2020 and 2021 in the *ADO Supplement*, are further downgraded, but with some revival of inflation still expected in 2021.

Table 3.5.1 Selected economic indicators, Fiji (%)

	2019	2020			2021		
		ADO 2020	ADOS	Update	ADO 2020	ADOS	Update
GDP growth	-1.3	-4.9	-15.0	-19.8	3.0	-0.7	1.0
Inflation	1.8	1.5	1.2	0.5	3.5	3.0	1.3
CAB/GDP	-4.9	-7.1	...	-15.3	-3.6	...	-13.4

... = unavailable, ADO = Asian Development Outlook (April), ADOS = ADO Supplement (June), CAB = current account balance, GDP = gross domestic product.
Source: ADB estimates.

The service trade and income accounts are expected to sink deeper into deficit as the tourism downturn continues because of travel restrictions and the economic impacts of COVID-19 on major source markets. As a result, the current account deficit to GDP ratios for 2020 and 2021 are expected to be substantially higher than predicted earlier. A small reduction in the current account deficit is projected for 2021.

Papua New Guinea

Since *ADO 2020*, the economy has been increasingly battered by the COVID-19 pandemic. The authorities have imposed lockdowns to contain the spread of COVID-19, but these measures have depressed economic activity. Further, combined with falling export revenue as global commodity prices weaken along with external demand, and with the closure of Porgera gold mine, lockdowns have undermined the fiscal position of the government. The economy is now projected to contract in 2020 almost twice as deeply as earlier forecast, and recovery in 2021 is expected to be weaker.

Several industries have been hampered by partial business closures as a result of lockdowns and restrictions on international and domestic travel: transportation, accommodation and food services, real estate, manufacturing, and construction. Agriculture and forestry have also been constrained by disruption to transportation and trade, notably by quarantine requirements on shipments, which have lengthened turnaround times. Domestic demand and household spending have weakened with curtailed business activity and associated cost-cutting measures, most notably layoffs and reduced work hours and salaries.

Production and export of liquefied natural gas are not expected to be significantly affected by COVID-19, but mining and quarrying have been hit by the recent suspension of operations at the Ok Tedi gold and copper mine following a local outbreak of COVID-19. Beyond this suspension, mining and quarrying output overall is now seen to contract by 15% or more in 2020, largely reflecting closure of Porgera, following the government's decision not to renew the operator's license, and by disappointing output from the Lihir gold mine.

The forecast for inflation in 2020 is unchanged as prices track persistently weak economic activity. Recent economic developments have applied both downward and upward pressure on inflation. Downward pressures include weaker domestic demand and government interventions to mitigate the effect of COVID-19, including price regulations on selected consumer goods and a freight subsidy introduced to support shipments of local produce to the capital and ill-served offshore islands. Upward pressures include the reduced supply of goods

Table 3.5.2 Selected economic indicators, Papua New Guinea (%)

	2019	2020			2021		
		ADO 2020	ADOS	Update	ADO 2020	ADOS	Update
GDP growth	5.0	0.8	-1.5	-2.9	2.8	2.9	2.5
Inflation	3.6	3.3	3.3	3.3	4.4	4.4	3.8
CAB/GDP	22.3	17.5	...	15.9	22.6	...	16.8

... = unavailable, ADO = Asian Development Outlook (April), ADOS = ADO Supplement (June), CAB = current account balance, GDP = gross domestic product.
Source: ADB estimates.

under restrictions intended to contain COVID-19 and local currency depreciation. A lesser but still noteworthy upward pressure is accelerated increase in the money supply fueled by a quantitative easing program introduced by the Bank of Papua New Guinea, the central bank.

The forecast for the current account surplus is revised down in line with lower commodity prices, weaker external demand for exports, and disruption caused by transportation bottlenecks. The gold price has increased, but its positive effect will be more than offset by lost gold production from key mines. Imports have similarly slowed as businesses have become cautious and restrictions have reduced trade. Foreign exchange reserves stood at $2.0 billion at the end of March 2020, providing cover for 5.5 months of total imports. The central bank is expected to continue to release foreign exchange slowly into the commercial market to help manage a backlog of foreign exchange orders.

In line with the weaker growth outlook, government revenue is expected to deteriorate further, with the authorities forecasting that revenue in 2020 will fall to the equivalent of 3.4% of GDP, below earlier expectations. Meanwhile, additional expenditure is needed to implement the government's response to the COVID-19 emergency. The shortfall will be funded in part through increased financing from development partners and in part through cuts in expenditure on other budget items.

Solomon Islands

The GDP growth forecast for 2020 is revised down from *ADO 2020* to take into account severe impacts of COVID-19 to date and Tropical Cyclone Harold in early April. The downgrade also accommodates a change in the base year from 2004 to 2012 with an increase in the relative importance of agriculture. Growth in 2021 is also forecast to be lower than projected in *ADO 2020*.

Consumer demand and local business have suffered under measures to keep out COVID-19 as a public emergency curtailed mobility, the suspension of international flights halted tourism, and quarantine measures disrupted incoming cargo. While no cases of COVID-19 have been reported in Solomon Islands, the risk remains that cases could emerge and prompt more stringent containment measures. The public emergency has been extended to 25 November 2020.

COVID-19 and Tropical Cyclone Harold have disrupted agriculture, with follow-on effects on processing industries. By July, log and timber output, which supplied 72% of exports in 2019, was down by 12.6% from a year earlier, and the fish catch, which supplied 11% of exports in 2019, by 51.5%. Other crops were mixed with copra and cocoa expanding on last year but palm oil contracting.

Table 3.5.3 Selected economic indicators, Solomon Islands (%)

	2019	2020			2021		
		ADO 2020	ADOS	Update	ADO 2020	ADOS	Update
GDP growth	1.2	1.5	-6.0	-6.0	2.7	2.5	1.0
Inflation	1.6	2.0	4.5	6.0	2.3	3.0	3.0
CAB/GDP	-9.8	-8.7	...	-14.6	-12.3	...	-16.8

... = unavailable, ADO = *Asian Development Outlook* (April), ADOS = *ADO Supplement* (June), CAB = current account balance, GDP = gross domestic product.
Source: ADB estimates.

The government temporarily scaled down public services as a precaution against COVID-19 and launched two fiscal responses: health-care preparedness and containment spending equivalent of 1.1% of GDP, and economic stimulus equal to 2.6% of GDP to protect jobs and stabilize the economy. With revenue expected to fall, especially from taxes and duties, a fiscal deficit, substantially higher than in 2019, is now projected for 2020, financed by domestic bond issues and assistance from development partners.

The International Monetary Fund (IMF) projects that public debt will rise from the equivalent of 8.9% of GDP in 2019 to 19.2% in 2021. Debt is forecast to rise further to 29.0% by 2025, but the IMF sees debt distress as only a moderate risk.

Consumer prices rose by an average of 6.7% in the first 6 months of 2020, largely on increased demand for domestic goods and from supply-chain disruption caused by COVID-19. Food price inflation ramped up from 1.8% in February to 5.5% in May despite price controls on basic commodities. Prices rose as well for alcoholic beverages and tobacco and for health care consultations but fell for transportation and clothing in line with lower commodity prices. Overall inflation is now expected to ease in the second half of 2020 as economic activity and global commodity prices weaken, but remain higher than earlier projected for the whole year. With supply-chain disruption seen to persist, the higher 2021 inflation forecast in the *ADO Supplement* is retained.

In response to COVID-19, the Central Bank of Solomon Islands reduced commercial banks' cash reserve requirement from 7.5% to 5.0% in June 2020, the same month that the IMF provided $28.5 million to address difficulties in the balance of payments. External reserves dipped in March to $543 million—or 11.3 months of import cover, well above the 6.0-month minimum set by the central bank—and increased to $691 million in August.

The current account deficit is forecast wider than in *ADO 2020* because of disrupted export markets and travel restrictions. Merchandise exports declined by 10.2% year on year in the first quarter of 2020, with logs and timber down by 18.0% and fish by 44.3%, and lower visitor arrivals drove service exports down by 18.4%. Imports also dropped, with goods down by 34.1% and services by 25.8%. The forecast for the 2021 deficit is revised up from *ADO 2020* because higher imports are expected to supply infrastructure projects resumed after COVID-19 while exports of goods and services remain weak.

Vanuatu

Economic contraction is expected to be much sharper than projected in *ADO 2020* in the wake of Tropical Cyclone Harold, and because the impact of COVID-19 on tourism is seen to persist longer than initially predicted.

After a promising start to the year, with cruise ship arrivals in the first quarter jumping by 65.4% year on year, tourism collapsed after international flights and cruise ship arrivals stopped in March 2020 when the government declared a state of emergency. Visitor arrivals, which were previously projected to recover gradually in the second half of 2020, are now expected to remain subdued into 2021.

Compounding COVID-19 challenges, category 5 Cyclone Harold damaged agriculture and infrastructure, particularly in and around Luganville, Vanuatu's second-largest city. This will likely exacerbate projected contraction in agriculture because of a rhinoceros beetle infestation, with follow-on effects on crop-processing industries. The government estimates total damage and losses from the cyclone and the pandemic at the equivalent of more than 54% of GDP.

The budget deficit has been revised from the equivalent of 4.6% of GDP to 11.0%, as outlined in the July *Half Yearly Economic and Fiscal Report*, because of higher COVID-19 stimulus spending and capital investment even as revenue from taxes and duties is estimated lower. Total expenditure rose by 7.2% year on year in the first 6 months of 2020 but reached only 35.0% of its revised budget. Revenue was up by 5.5% on a dramatic 32.2% increase in collections from honorary citizenship programs, generating in the first half of the year a budget surplus equal to 3.5% of GDP.

Forecasts for inflation in 2020 and 2021 are adjusted up from *ADO 2020* but still within the 1%–4% target range of the Reserve Bank of Vanuatu, the central bank. Inflation forecasts were revised up in the *ADO Supplement* to reflect supply chain disruption caused by transport restrictions and cyclone damage. This *Update* revises the 2020 forecast slightly down again because inflation reached only 3.1% in the first quarter of this year despite the index for food rising by 6.7%.

To support the economy, the central bank reduced its key policy interest rate from 2.90% to 2.25% in March and eased commercial banks' capital adequacy requirements.

The central bank reported in July that gross international reserves were sufficient to cover 13.5 months of imports of goods and services, more than triple its minimum threshold of 4.0 months. The forecast for the current account deficit in 2020 is narrower than projected in *ADO 2020* in light of strong inflows from honorary citizenship programs, while imports to supply tourism remain low. The deficit is now expected to widen again in 2021 as imports for reconstruction rise while exports of goods and services remain relatively subdued.

Table 3.5.4 Selected economic indicators, Vanuatu (%)

	2019	2020			2021		
		ADO 2020	ADOS	Update	ADO 2020	ADOS	Update
GDP growth	2.9	-1.0	-9.8	-9.8	2.5	2.0	1.0
Inflation	2.8	1.5	4.0	3.0	2.0	2.2	2.2
CAB/GDP	12.4	-8.7	...	-6.0	-8.6	...	-9.6

... = unavailable, ADO = *Asian Development Outlook* (April), ADOS = *ADO Supplement* (June), CAB = current account balance, GDP = gross domestic product.

Sources: National Statistics Office; International Monetary Fund; ADB estimates.

Central Pacific economies

Growth forecasts for the three Central Pacific economies in 2020 have been downgraded to reflect the impact of international travel bans and weaker economic activity because of the COVID-19 pandemic. Inflation projections for Nauru and Tuvalu are adjusted downward in response to economic weakening and softer global prices but are unchanged for Kiribati reflecting supply-chain disruptions. Current account surplus forecasts for Kiribati are retained and upgraded for Tuvalu.

Kiribati

Growth is still expected, as projected in the June *ADO Supplement*, to slow in 2020 more steeply than forecast in *ADO 2020*. Restrictions on international travel and domestic movement will constrain construction, which relies heavily on foreign experts and imports of raw materials. Travel restrictions are similarly expected to disrupt outbound seafarers and seasonal workers. Lower remittance inflow will reduce household income and domestic demand, and the government estimates that 1,040 jobs, employing 3.7% of Kiribati's working population, will be lost at least temporarily because of COVID-19 impacts on the local economy. Growth is still forecast to recover gradually in 2021, supported by COVID-19 response measures and infrastructure projects funded by the government and development partners.

The projected fiscal deficit in 2020 is revised up from the equivalent of 0.8% of GDP in *ADO 2020* to 9.9% as the government rolls out its COVID-19 response plan. Meanwhile, response restrictions are expected to erode government tax revenue. Fishing revenue in 2020 is projected to be 5%–10% lower than forecast in April because of transshipment delays and restrictions on the movement of observers to monitor the catch. The fiscal forecast for 2021 is unchanged, and the government is expected to achieve a narrower deficit enabled by recovery in domestic revenue, with tax revenue expected to increase by 25.9% and other revenue by 9.3%. These projections assume that government tax reform succeeds and that fisheries recover following the lifting of travel restrictions toward the middle of 2021.

Projections for inflation in 2020 and 2021 are unchanged, the major risks to the forecasts posed by high transportation costs and other costs of supply disruption.

Kiribati is still projected to post a shrinking surplus in its current account in 2020 and 2021, as forecast in *ADO 2020*. Weaker-than-anticipated fishing revenue and an import surge from the stockpiling in 2020 of food, medical, and pharmaceutical essentials is expected to outweigh reduced imports of capital goods.

Table 3.5.5 Selected economic indicators, Kiribati (%)

	2019	2020			2021		
		ADO 2020	ADOS	Update	ADO 2020	ADOS	Update
GDP growth	2.4	1.6	0.6	0.6	1.8	1.8	1.8
Inflation	-1.8	1.0	1.0	1.0	1.1	1.1	1.1
CAB/GDP	7.6	4.0	...	4.0	2.8	...	2.8

... = unavailable, ADO = *Asian Development Outlook* (April), ADOS = *ADO Supplement* (June), CAB = current account balance, GDP = gross domestic product.
Source: ADB estimates.

Nauru

Trade and travel restrictions to combat COVID-19 have
affected supply chains and the Nauru economy, not least
through its biggest infrastructure project. Construction
on the new port relies on foreign workers and imports of
construction materials, the availability of which has been
disrupted. Follow-on impacts can drag down services, the
biggest economic sector. The *ADO 2020* growth forecasts for
fiscal year 2020 (FY2020, ended 30 June 2020) and FY2021
were therefore revised down in the *ADO Supplement*, with
GDP contraction in FY2020, followed by weak recovery in
FY2021. With continuing international travel disruption
and uncertainty about government revenue and its ability
to contain expenditure, the growth forecast for FY2021 is
revised down further.

Even as containment measures restrict arrivals, businesses
and shops in Nauru have generally remained open. Public
administration, which is a major employer and generator of
demand, has continued to operate, helping to prevent sharper
contraction. While government expenditure accelerated
through the year, reflecting the government's fiscal response to
COVID-19, revenue and development partner grants increased
by 17%. The fiscal surplus thus rose to equal 33.1% of GDP.
It was used to reduce arrears and finance contributions to the
national trust fund.

The FY2021 budget projects revenue 22% lower than
in FY2020 but is estimated with considerable uncertainty.
Fishing license fees, which supply some 30% of domestic
revenue, may be affected by a protracted global slowdown or
volatile commodity prices. Arrangements between Australia
and Nauru for the Regional Processing Centre for asylum
seekers, which provides about half of domestic revenue,
are uncertain after 2020.

The inflation estimate for FY2020 and forecast for
FY2021 are adjusted down because of economic weakening.
The government plans to mitigate pandemic impacts on the
supply chain by chartering sea freight services and requiring
the state-owned airline to provide freight services as a
community service obligation.

Tuvalu

The *ADO Supplement* downgraded growth forecasts for both
2020 and 2021, and the lower forecasts are retained in this
Update. Movement restrictions have obstructed supplies
of labor and capital equipment, delaying infrastructure
projects and driving down income from construction jobs.
Further, outbound seasonal workers have been affected
by the challenges posed by cross-border mobilization, and
business inventories have been disrupted by supply-chain
bottlenecks.

Table 3.5.6 Selected economic indicators, Nauru (%)

	2019	2020			2021		
		ADO 2020	ADOS	Update	ADO 2020	ADOS	Update
GDP growth	1.0	0.4	-1.7	-1.7	1.1	0.8	0.5
Inflation	3.9	2.8	1.5	1.5	2.3	1.7	1.7
CAB/GDP	4.9	...	...	...	...	...	...

... = unavailable, ADO = Asian Development Outlook (April),
ADOS = ADO Supplement (June), CAB = current account
balance, GDP = gross domestic product.
Sources: National Statistics Office; International Monetary
Fund; ADB estimates.

Table 3.5.7 Selected economic indicators, Tuvalu (%)

	2019	2020			2021		
		ADO 2020	ADOS	Update	ADO 2020	ADOS	Update
GDP growth	4.1	2.7	2.0	2.0	3.2	2.5	2.5
Inflation	3.3	3.5	3.0	3.0	3.5	3.0	3.0
CAB/GDP	-6.9	2.8	...	2.9	3.4	...	3.5

... = unavailable, ADO = Asian Development Outlook (April),
ADOS = ADO Supplement (June), CAB = current account
balance, GDP = gross domestic product.
Source: ADB estimates.

Despite the absence of any confirmed COVID-19 cases in the country, the government passed a supplementary budget in March 2020 that supports preventive and preparatory measures in response to the pandemic: upgrading medical facilities, ensuring an adequate pool of health-care workers, and helping the private sector acquire sufficient food staples to sustain the population. Tax revenue is now expected to be lower than earlier predicted. Although fishing license revenue will likely be stable in 2020, revenue from customs duties is expected to be lower under restricted international travel, and reduced economic activity is likely to dent revenue from company, consumption, excise, income, and hotel room taxes. Consequently, large fiscal deficits are expected, equal to 24.3% of GDP in 2020 and 7.9% in 2021.

Lower inflation projections published in the *ADO Supplement* for both 2020 and 2021 are retained in line with subdued economic activity brought about by the pandemic.

The current account is projected to remain in surplus in 2020 and 2021, supported in 2020 by stable fishing license revenue and the temporary halt in imports of capital goods for pending construction projects. A wider surplus is expected in 2021 in line with projected improvement in remittance and tourism income as international travel resumes.

North Pacific economies

Although the Federated States of Micronesia (FSM), the Marshall Islands, and Palau have all managed to stay free of COVID-19, extended border closures to avoid bringing in the virus are exacting heavy costs. All three North Pacific economies are now projected to contract in fiscal year 2020 (FY2020, ends 30 September 2020), with the most severe impacts on the tourism-driven economy of Palau. Prospects for recovery in FY2021 depend on how quickly travel restrictions can be eased without risking health security.

Federated States of Micronesia

Following the declaration of a health emergency and the imposition of travel restrictions in January, then by March full border closures across all four states, state and national governments separately developed COVID-19 action plans and began implementing preparedness measures. Economic projections in *ADO 2020* assumed that border closures could be phased out by mid-2020. However, with border closures extended, forecasts for FY2020 and FY2021 were revised down in the *ADO Supplement* to show the COVID-19 pandemic likely causing the FSM economy to contract in both years, largely by constraining trade and travel. The full impact of COVID-19 on the economy has since been revealed as even more severe, so forecasts are revised down again.

Table 3.5.8 Selected economic indicators, Federated States of Micronesia (%)

	2019	2020			2021		
		ADO 2020	ADOS	Update	ADO 2020	ADOS	Update
GDP growth	1.2	1.6	–2.0	–5.4	3.0	–1.5	–1.9
Inflation	–1.0	0.5	0.5	1.6	1.0	1.0	1.9
CAB/GDP	24.8	8.8	...	21.7	1.3	...	15.1

... = unavailable, ADO = *Asian Development Outlook* (April), ADOS = *ADO Supplement* (June), CAB = current account balance, GDP = gross domestic product.
Note: Years are fiscal years ending on 30 September of that year.
Source: ADB estimates.

Adverse impacts are seen to affect transportation, mainly by curtailing flights but also with weaker fish transshipment activity under docking restrictions imposed on foreign-owned vessels.

Further, although tourism is not a large component of the FSM economy, pandemic-related constraints on travel are seen to cause a significant decline in international arrivals, while travel controls imposed by individual states constrain mobility overall. These combined effects are likely to dampen wholesale and retail trade. Construction projects similarly suffer delays under restrictions on specialists' movements and imports of inputs.

A bright spot in the outlook is the fishery industry, which is expected to be largely unaffected by the pandemic. Domestic fishing output is forecast to increase from a low base in FY2019. Earnings from fishing license fees, a major source of government revenue, are seen remaining steady in FY2020 and FY2021 as the FSM has sold all of its allocated vessel-days for 2020 and skipjack tuna prices are projected to rise next year.

Trade and mobility constraints are expected to alter government spending patterns, with budgets unused under the pandemic for official travel for example, reallocated to other critical areas. However, reallocation alone is unlikely to meet the need to strengthen health-care systems and stimulate the economy. Without further assistance from development partners, FSM will need to draw on fiscal buffers or revert to a contractionary fiscal stance. Fiscal strains are especially high for state governments, which depend largely on transfers under the Compact of Free Association with the US.

This *Update* raises *ADO 2020* forecasts for inflation as ongoing trade disruption causes supply bottlenecks. Current account projections for FY2020 and FY2021 likewise see widened surpluses as reduced imports, particularly of capital equipment and materials, likely outweigh declines in exports and other receipts.

Marshall Islands

This *Update* retains *ADO Supplement* forecasts of economic contraction in the Marshall Islands in both FY2020 and FY2021. The June reversal of positive growth forecasts in *ADO 2020* came about in response to economic activity seen constrained by trade and travel restrictions related to the COVID-19 pandemic. Continuing bans on incoming travellers and domestic travel aboard international carriers, in place since January, were reinforced in February by a declaration of a health emergency.

Fisheries are expected to bear the brunt. Local quarantine requirements for fishing vessels continue to affect downstream onshore services such as loining tuna, repairing nets, and transshipping fish.

Table 3.5.9 Selected economic indicators, Marshall Islands (%)

	2019	2020			2021		
		ADO 2020	ADOS	Update	ADO 2020	ADOS	Update
GDP growth	3.8	2.5	-5.5	-5.5	3.7	-1.4	-1.4
Inflation	0.1	0.3	0.3	0.3	0.5	0.5	0.5
CAB/GDP	7.7	6.1	...	13.6	5.1	...	12.3

... = unavailable, ADO = Asian Development Outlook (April), ADOS = ADO Supplement (June), CAB = current account balance, GDP = gross domestic product.
Note: Years are fiscal years ending on 30 September of that year.
Source: ADB estimates.

Trade and travel constraints will hit the Marshall Islands' small hotel and restaurant industry, especially as restaurants depend on visitors for more than half of their business. Further, although projects funded by development partners appear on track in FY2020, construction is expected to decline in FY2021 partly because of shortages of equipment and materials and the restricted mobility of specialists, though some can work remotely. A recent easing of quarantine requirements now allows eligible cargo vessels and fuel tankers to enter Marshall Islands ports, which may mitigate some pandemic impacts.

COVID-19 is similarly limiting mobility within the country. There have been no local lockdowns, but schools have revised their calendars, and public events have been either cancelled or postponed. Weaker demand under diminished movement and social interaction is expected to hit wholesale and retail trade.

The FY2020 budget reduces transfers to the social security system and the Compact Trust Fund, but government operations are otherwise expected to continue as planned despite risks associated with the pandemic and in anticipation of lower revenue.

Inflation projections from *ADO 2020* are maintained, but wider current account surpluses are now forecast as pandemic-related trade restrictions limit imports and narrow the merchandise trade gap.

Palau

Global travel disruption arising from the pandemic has badly damaged the tourism industry. Palau has one of the most tourism-driven economies in the Pacific, as annual tourism receipts provide 40%–50% of GDP. With a tourist profile heavily tilted toward markets in East Asia—in contrast to the dominance of arrivals from Australia and New Zealand in South Pacific destinations—Palau experienced adverse impacts from the COVID-19 pandemic a couple of months before most of its subregional peers. From almost 30% growth year on year in October–January, the first 4 months of FY2020, visitor arrivals fell by 43% in February and 70% in March, before plunging by 99% year on year in April–July.

While the *ADO 2020* outlook optimistically assumed a waning pandemic by midyear, this *Update* reiterates revised projections first presented in the *ADO Supplement*, which take into account the possibility of international travel restrictions extending well into 2021. With minimal arrivals for much of FY2020, economic contraction this year is now expected to more than double the initial projection. Further, with the government's COVID-19 response plan prudently considering extending Palau's closure to international tourism until a vaccine becomes available, arrivals could remain near zero for most of FY2021. The outlook for FY2021 is therefore also revised down, from modest recovery to deepening contraction.

Table 3.5.10 Selected economic indicators, Palau (%)

	2019	2020			2021		
		ADO 2020	ADOS	Update	ADO 2020	ADOS	Update
GDP growth	-1.8	-4.5	-9.5	-9.5	1.2	-12.8	-12.8
Inflation	0.6	0.4	0.4	0.4	0.8	0.8	0.8
CAB/GDP	-26.9	-13.5	…	-23.0	-13.3	…	-49.2

… = unavailable, ADO = *Asian Development Outlook* (April), ADOS = *ADO Supplement* (June), CAB = current account balance, GDP = gross domestic product.
Note: Years are fiscal years ending on 30 September of that year.
Source: ADB estimates.

ADO 2020 inflation projections are unchanged, but the current account is now expected to record much sharper deficits in both FY2020 and FY2021 under the collapse of tourism receipts.

In response to potential impact from the COVID-19 pandemic on businesses and workers, the government established the $20 million Coronavirus Relief One Stop Shop Program to provide temporary assistance to the private sector. Direct relief measures under the program include (i) business loans to cover fixed costs and finance improvements to tourism facilities; (ii) unemployment benefits for workers whose employment has been terminated, suspended, or reduced; (iii) temporary employment schemes administered through the public sector and nongovernment organizations, particularly for non-resident workers; and (iv) expanded lifeline utility services for households affected by COVID-19.

South Pacific economies

Travel bans continue to have disproportionate effects on economies in the South Pacific, all of which rely heavily on international mobility. In the Cook Islands, Niue, and Samoa, the collapse of inbound tourism continues to suppress economic performance despite significant government stimulus, while remittances, mainly from outbound seasonal workers, are more important for Tonga. Recent COVID-19 outbreaks in Auckland and Melbourne will delay economic recovery and the return of easy travel, with significant consequences in the South Pacific.

Cook Islands

When *ADO 2020* was published in April, it was unclear how much COVID-19 would affect Australia and New Zealand, the key tourism markets for the Cook Islands. With the closure of the Cook Islands to all inbound nonresidents on 24 March, the economic outlook deteriorated significantly for fiscal year 2020 (FY2020, ended 30 June 2020 in the Cook Islands, Samoa, and Tonga), as touched on in the *ADO Supplement*. Third-quarter GDP results suggest that the economy was stronger than expected before COVID-19, mitigating the contraction over the whole fiscal year. While this economy is likely to be the first in the Pacific to benefit from a proposed travel bubble, new COVID-19 outbreaks in New Zealand have delayed recommencement of quarantine-free travel with that country. Consequently, the GDP forecast for deep contraction in FY2021 is unchanged from June, with risks heavily weighted on the downside.

Government stimulus measures are supporting economic activity and preventing even larger falls in GDP and household incomes but cannot continue indefinitely. The fiscal deficit is estimated to have equaled 5.0% of GDP in FY2020, smaller than the *ADO 2020* forecast primarily because

Table 3.5.11 Selected economic indicators, Cook Islands (%)

	2019	2020			2021		
		ADO 2020	ADOS	Update	ADO 2020	ADOS	Update
GDP growth	5.3	-2.2	-9.0	-7.0	1.0	-15.4	-15.4
Inflation	0.8	1.5	1.5	1.5	1.7	1.7	1.7
CAB/GDP	3.6	-1.2	...	-6.0	1.1	...	-12.5

... = unavailable, ADO = Asian Development Outlook (April), ADOS = ADO Supplement (June), CAB = current account balance, GDP = gross domestic product.
Note: Years are fiscal years ending on 30 June of that year.
Source: ADB estimates.

most stimulus costs are being incurred in FY2021. This *Update* forecasts the fiscal deficit widening to equal 33.1% of GDP in FY2021 as value-added and company tax receipts fall and payment for wide-ranging stimulus measures comes due. The government warns that cash reserves may run out by FY2022, even when including a recent NZ$15 million grant from New Zealand and potential loans from the Asian Development Bank and the Asian Infrastructure Investment Bank to help finance the fiscal gap. Travel resumption remains the key factor determining the outlook, with 21%–37% of the working-age population at risk of unemployment if international travel does not resume before government stimulus expires.

Lower global commodity prices noted when preparing the *ADO Supplement* suggested that inflation might be more subdued than forecast in *ADO 2020*, but this effect was likely more than offset by import disruption and higher prices for food exports from New Zealand in the second half of FY2020. Prices may have been higher in the fourth quarter, pushing inflation up in FY2020, as forecast in *ADO 2020*. The inflation forecast for FY2021 is unchanged.

The decline in tourism has had a major impact on the current account, the lost income estimated to be greater than savings from a consequent decline in imports. The current account deficit in FY2020 is now estimated to be higher than forecast in *ADO 2020*. It will likely deteriorate further in FY2021, though stepped-up budget assistance from development partners should mitigate the harm to people's well-being.

Samoa

Contraction in FY2020 is estimated in line with the *ADO Supplement* forecast, which was for deeper contraction than projected in *ADO 2020* as the impact of the dual health crises of measles and COVID-19 became more apparent. In June, the expectation was that international reopening would occur around December and that government support would offset some economic losses. However, a cautious approach toward reopening is expected to extend tourism losses well into 2021, with only gradual reopening to visitors and muted arrivals tamping down recovery prospects. This downgrades the economic outlook for FY2021 since the *ADO Supplement*, with GDP now forecast to contract by nearly double the FY2020 rate.

The fiscal deficit in FY2020 is now estimated equal to 7.3% of GDP following a fall in government revenue and simultaneous increase in expenditure. Revenue is expected to fall further in FY2021, expanding the fiscal deficit to 9.8% of GDP.

Inflation in FY2020 is estimated marginally lower than forecast in *ADO 2020* as softer demand under diminished economic activity offsets upward pressure on prices from

Box 3.5.1 COVID-19 impacts on Niue's small, tourism-dependent economy

Like others in the South Pacific, Niue relies heavily on tourism, which has ground to a halt since COVID-19 travel restrictions were imposed early in 2020. The economy is now expected to contract this year. Since late March, passenger flights into Niue have been reduced from their normal twice-weekly schedule to just once every 2 weeks. The number of passengers per flight is restricted to 26 to ensure social distancing, translating into a maximum of 52 monthly arrivals, down from the usual 1,200. As these flights are open only to returning residents and essential workers, tourism has effectively shut down for the time being. After average growth at 14% year on year in January–February, visitor arrivals from New Zealand—which supplies up to 80% of tourists—fell by 63% in March, before plunging by 98% in April–June.

Prospects for economic recovery depend on how quickly inbound tourism can safely resume, perhaps starting with a "travel bridge" to New Zealand, or else Niue's inclusion in a multi-country travel bubble. A critical prerequisite would be further strengthening of the health-care system to permit the implementation of strong protocols for testing, contact tracing, and medical care, responsibility for which will be shared by all parties in any effort to restart international tourism.

Table 3.5.12 Selected economic indicators, Samoa (%)

	2019	2020			2021		
		ADO 2020	ADOS	Update	ADO 2020	ADOS	Update
GDP growth	3.5	–3.0	–5.0	–5.0	0.8	–2.0	–9.7
Inflation	2.2	2.0	2.8	1.9	2.5	2.5	2.2
CAB/GDP	2.3	–1.1	...	–4.7	0.5	...	–8.0

... = unavailable, ADO = *Asian Development Outlook* (April), ADOS = *ADO Supplement* (June), CAB = current account balance, GDP = gross domestic product.
Note: Years are fiscal years ending on 30 June of that year.
Source: ADB estimates.

pandemic-related disruption to supply chains. The projection for FY2021 is revised down to a rate little changed from FY2020 on the expectation that demand will remain weak most of the fiscal year.

The FY2020 current account deficit is estimated much wider than projected in *ADO 2020*. Although remittances grew by an unexpected 4.9% during the period as compared to the previous fiscal year, this was not enough to offset significantly lower earnings from tourism and merchandise exports. The forecast for FY2021 is similarly downgraded from a small surplus previously projected, with the expectation now that earnings from tourism and merchandise exports will remain low, and that remittances will decline as host economies also struggle under COVID-19.

Tonga

Damage to the economy from COVID-19 was foreseen in *ADO 2020* to be offset by continued rehabilitation and recovery projects following Cyclone Gita. However, project delays caused by COVID-19 and damage from Tropical Cyclone Harold have further delayed recovery efforts. Repeated and overlapping economic shocks contracted the economy in FY2020 and significantly downgraded the outlook for FY2021. Long delays until reopening of travel are now deemed likely to undermine both tourism and seasonal labor programs well into 2021, shrinking the economy in FY2021 by nearly triple the FY2020 rate. Particularly important to Tonga is the magnitude of remittance contraction in light of its impact on household consumption.

The fiscal deficit, equivalent to 1.4% of GDP in FY2020, is lower than projected in April due to ample grant support from development partners and a smaller than expected revenue decline. As revenue continues to decline, though, and as pandemic-related expenditure rises, the deficit is projected to widen to 5.5% in FY2021.

Inflation is estimated slightly higher than forecast in *ADO 2020* because of higher prices for imported food. Softer domestic price pressures in FY2021, anticipated in the *ADO Supplement*, are now expected to be offset by continuing price increases for imports, leaving inflation in the current fiscal year between the higher *ADO 2020* forecast and the lower *ADO Supplement* projection.

Thanks to rapid assistance from development partners and resilient remittances, the current account deficit in FY2020 is estimated to be lower than forecast in *ADO 2020* and little changed from FY2019. Tourism and merchandise export earnings are projected to remain weak as long as travel restrictions persist, however, and remittances are likely to drop as seasonal worker programs are disrupted and host economies continue to struggle. Absent offsetting increases in development partner assistance, the FY2021 current account deficit is forecast to double, exceeding the *ADO 2020* forecast.

Table 3.5.13 Selected economic indicators, Tonga (%)

	2019	2020			2021		
		ADO 2020	ADOS	Update	ADO 2020	ADOS	Update
GDP growth	0.7	0.0	–3.0	–3.0	2.5	–4.0	–8.0
Inflation	3.2	1.3	1.3	1.6	2.2	1.8	2.0
CAB/GDP	–6.3	–12.6	...	–7.3	–13.4	...	–14.5

... = unavailable, ADO = *Asian Development Outlook* (April), ADOS = *ADO Supplement* (June), CAB = current account balance, GDP = gross domestic product.
Note: Years are fiscal years ending on 30 June of that year.
Source: ADB estimates.

STATISTICAL APPENDIX

Statistical notes and tables

This statistical appendix presents economic indicators for the 46 developing member economies in the Asian Development Bank (ADB) in three tables: gross domestic product (GDP) growth, inflation, and current account balance as a percentage of GDP. The economies are grouped into five subregions: Central Asia, East Asia, South Asia, Southeast Asia, and the Pacific. The tables contain historical data for 2018–2019 and forecasts for 2020 and 2021.

The data are standardized to the degree possible to allow comparability over time and across economies, but differences in statistical methodology, definitions, coverage, and practice make full comparability impossible. National income accounts are based on the United Nations System of National Accounts, while data on balance of payments use International Monetary Fund accounting standards. Historical data are ADB estimates variously based on official sources, statistical publications and databases, and documents from ADB, the International Monetary Fund, and the World Bank. Projections for 2020 and 2021 are generally ADB estimates based on available quarterly or monthly data, though some projections are from governments.

Most economies report by calendar year. The following report all variables by fiscal year: Afghanistan, Bangladesh, Bhutan, India, Nepal, and Pakistan in South Asia; Myanmar in Southeast Asia; and the Cook Islands, the Federated States of Micronesia, Nauru, Palau, the Republic of Marshall Islands, Samoa, and Tonga in the Pacific.

Regional and subregional averages are provided in the three tables. Averages are computed using weights derived from gross national income (GNI) in current US dollars following the World Bank Atlas method. The GNI data for 2018 are obtained from the World Bank's World Development Indicators Online. Weights for 2018 are carried over to 2021. GNI data for the Cook Islands and Taipei,China are estimated using the Atlas conversion factor.

The following paragraphs discuss the three tables in greater detail.

Table A1: Growth rate of GDP (% per year). The table shows annual growth rates of GDP valued at constant market price, factor cost, or basic price. GDP at market price is the aggregation of value added by all resident producers at producers' prices including taxes less subsidies on imports plus all nondeductible value-added or similar taxes. Constant factor cost measures differ from market price measures in that they exclude taxes on production and include subsidies. Basic price valuation is the factor cost plus some taxes on production, such as those on property and payroll taxes, and less some subsidies such as those related to labor but not to products. Most countries use constant market price valuation. Pakistan uses constant factor costs, and Fiji uses basic prices.

Table A2: Inflation (% per year). Data on inflation rates are period averages. Inflation rates are based on consumer price indexes. The consumer price indexes of the following economies are for a given city only: Cambodia is for Phnom Penh, the Marshall Islands for Majuro, Sri Lanka for Colombo, and Solomon Islands for Honiara.

Table A3: Current account balance (% of GDP). The current account balance is the sum of the balance of trade in merchandise, net trade in services and factor income, and net transfers. Sums are divided by GDP at current prices in US dollars. For Cambodia, official transfers are excluded from the current account balance.

Table A1 Growth rate of GDP (% per year)

	2018	2019	2020			2021		
			April ADO 2020	June ADOS	September Update	April ADO 2020	June ADOS	September Update
Central Asia	4.4	4.9	2.8	−0.5	−2.1	4.2	4.2	3.9
Armenia	5.2	7.6	2.2	−3.5	−4.0	4.5	3.5	3.5
Azerbaijan	1.4	2.2	0.5	−0.1	−4.3	1.5	1.2	1.2
Georgia	4.8	5.1	0.0	−5.0	−5.0	4.5	5.0	4.5
Kazakhstan	4.1	4.5	1.8	−1.2	−3.2	3.6	3.4	2.8
Kyrgyz Republic	3.8	4.5	4.0	−5.0	−10.0	4.5	4.0	4.0
Tajikistan	7.3	7.5	5.5	−3.6	−0.5	5.0	7.0	6.0
Turkmenistan	6.2	6.3	6.0	3.2	3.2	5.8	5.8	5.8
Uzbekistan	5.4	5.6	4.7	1.5	0.5	5.8	6.5	6.5
East Asia	6.1	5.4	2.0	1.3	1.3	6.5	6.8	7.0
Hong Kong, China	2.8	−1.2	−3.3	−6.5	−6.5	3.5	5.1	5.1
Mongolia	7.2	5.1	2.1	−1.9	−2.6	4.6	4.7	5.1
People's Republic of China	6.7	6.1	2.3	1.8	1.8	7.3	7.4	7.7
Republic of Korea	2.7	2.0	1.3	−1.0	−1.0	2.3	3.5	3.3
Taipei,China	2.7	2.7	1.8	0.8	0.8	2.5	3.5	3.5
South Asia	6.1	4.3	4.1	−3.0	−6.8	6.0	4.9	7.1
Afghanistan	2.7	3.0	3.0	−4.5	−5.0	4.0	3.0	1.5
Bangladesh	7.9	8.2	7.8	4.5	5.2	8.0	7.5	6.8
Bhutan	3.8	4.4	5.2	2.4	2.4	5.8	1.7	1.7
India	6.1	4.2	4.0	−4.0	−9.0	6.2	5.0	8.0
Maldives	6.9	5.9	−3.0	−11.3	−20.5	7.5	13.7	10.5
Nepal	6.7	7.0	5.3	2.3	2.3	6.4	3.1	1.5
Pakistan	5.5	1.9	2.6	−0.4	−0.4	3.2	2.0	2.0
Sri Lanka	3.3	2.3	2.2	−6.1	−5.5	3.5	4.1	4.1
Southeast Asia	5.1	4.4	1.0	−2.7	−3.8	4.7	5.2	5.5
Brunei Darussalam	0.1	3.9	2.0	1.4	1.4	3.0	3.0	3.0
Cambodia	7.5	7.1	2.3	−5.5	−4.0	5.7	5.9	5.9
Indonesia	5.2	5.0	2.5	−1.0	−1.0	5.0	5.3	5.3
Lao People's Democratic Republic	6.2	5.0	3.5	−0.5	−2.5	6.0	4.5	4.5
Malaysia	4.8	4.3	0.5	−4.0	−5.0	5.5	6.5	6.5
Myanmar	6.4	6.8	4.2	1.8	1.8	6.8	6.0	6.0
Philippines	6.3	6.0	2.0	−3.8	−7.3	6.5	6.5	6.5
Singapore	3.4	0.7	0.2	−6.0	−6.2	2.0	3.2	4.5
Thailand	4.2	2.4	−4.8	−6.5	−8.0	2.5	3.5	4.5
Timor-Leste	−0.8	3.4	−2.0	−3.7	−6.3	4.0	4.0	3.3
Viet Nam	7.1	7.0	4.8	4.1	1.8	6.8	6.8	6.3
The Pacific	0.4	3.5	−0.3	−4.3	−6.1	2.7	1.6	1.3
Cook Islands	8.9	5.3	−2.2	−9.0	−7.0	1.0	−15.4	−15.4
Federated States of Micronesia	0.2	1.2	1.6	−2.0	−5.4	3.0	−1.5	−1.9
Fiji	3.5	−1.3	−4.9	−15.0	−19.8	3.0	−0.7	1.0
Kiribati	2.3	2.4	1.6	0.6	0.6	1.8	1.8	1.8
Marshall Islands	3.6	3.8	2.5	−5.5	−5.5	3.7	−1.4	−1.4
Nauru	5.7	1.0	0.4	−1.7	−1.7	1.1	0.8	0.5
Niue	6.5	...	...	...	...	...	...	...
Palau	5.8	−1.8	−4.5	−9.5	−9.5	1.2	−12.8	−12.8
Papua New Guinea	−0.8	5.0	0.8	−1.5	−2.9	2.8	2.9	2.5
Samoa	−2.1	3.5	−3.0	−5.0	−5.0	0.8	−2.0	−9.7
Solomon Islands	3.3	1.2	1.5	−6.0	−6.0	2.7	2.5	1.0
Tonga	0.2	0.7	0.0	−3.0	−3.0	2.5	−4.0	−8.0
Tuvalu	4.3	4.1	2.7	2.0	2.0	3.2	2.5	2.5
Vanuatu	2.9	2.9	−1.0	−9.8	−9.8	2.5	2.0	1.0
Developing Asia	5.9	5.1	2.2	0.1	−0.7	6.2	6.2	6.8
Developing Asia excluding the NIEs	6.4	5.6	2.4	0.4	−0.5	6.7	6.6	7.2

... = unavailable, ADOS = ADO Supplement, GDP = gross domestic product, NIEs = newly industrialized economies (Hong Kong, China; the Republic of Korea; Singapore; and Taipei,China).

Table A2 Inflation (% per year)

	2018	2019	2020			2021		
			April ADO 2020	June ADOS	September Update	April ADO 2020	June ADOS	September Update
Central Asia	8.2	7.5	7.6	8.0	8.3	6.3	6.6	6.6
Armenia	2.5	1.4	2.8	1.2	1.4	2.2	2.5	2.2
Azerbaijan	2.3	2.6	2.5	2.8	3.8	3.5	3.5	3.2
Georgia	2.6	4.9	4.5	5.0	6.0	3.0	3.5	4.5
Kazakhstan	6.0	5.3	6.0	7.9	7.7	5.7	6.2	6.2
Kyrgyz Republic	1.5	1.1	3.5	7.0	7.0	3.0	5.0	5.0
Tajikistan	5.4	8.0	9.0	10.0	9.5	8.0	8.5	8.5
Turkmenistan	13.2	13.4	13.0	8.0	10.0	8.0	8.0	8.0
Uzbekistan	17.5	14.6	13.0	13.0	13.0	10.0	10.0	10.0
East Asia	2.0	2.6	3.2	2.9	2.6	1.8	1.8	1.7
Hong Kong, China	2.4	2.9	2.0	1.5	1.5	2.5	2.5	2.5
Mongolia	6.8	7.3	6.6	6.4	5.6	7.9	8.2	8.2
People's Republic of China	2.1	2.9	3.6	3.3	3.0	1.9	1.9	1.8
Republic of Korea	1.5	0.4	0.9	0.5	0.5	1.3	1.3	1.3
Taipei,China	1.3	0.6	0.4	0.2	0.2	0.8	0.8	0.8
South Asia	3.7	5.0	4.1	4.0	5.2	4.4	4.5	4.5
Afghanistan	0.6	2.3	2.3	5.0	5.0	3.5	4.5	4.5
Bangladesh	5.8	5.5	5.6	5.6	5.7	5.5	5.5	5.5
Bhutan	3.6	2.8	3.8	2.8	3.0	4.0	4.0	4.0
India	3.4	4.8	3.0	3.0	4.5	3.8	4.0	4.0
Maldives	−0.1	0.2	1.0	1.0	0.5	1.2	1.2	1.5
Nepal	4.2	4.6	6.0	6.6	6.2	5.5	6.5	5.5
Pakistan	4.7	6.8	11.5	11.0	10.7	8.3	8.0	7.5
Sri Lanka	4.3	4.3	5.0	4.0	4.5	4.8	4.2	4.2
Southeast Asia	2.6	2.1	1.9	1.0	1.0	2.2	2.3	2.3
Brunei Darussalam	1.0	−0.4	−0.2	0.4	1.4	0.1	0.4	1.0
Cambodia	2.5	1.9	2.1	2.1	2.1	1.8	1.8	1.8
Indonesia	3.2	2.8	3.0	2.0	2.0	2.8	2.8	2.8
Lao People's Democratic Republic	2.0	3.3	4.0	5.5	5.5	4.5	5.0	5.0
Malaysia	1.0	0.7	1.0	−1.5	−1.5	1.3	2.5	2.0
Myanmar	5.9	8.6	7.5	6.0	6.0	7.5	6.0	6.0
Philippines	5.2	2.5	2.2	2.2	2.4	2.4	2.4	2.6
Singapore	0.4	0.6	0.7	−0.2	−0.3	1.3	0.8	1.0
Thailand	1.1	0.7	−0.9	−1.3	−1.6	0.4	0.7	0.8
Timor-Leste	−1.8	1.5	1.3	1.3	1.0	1.8	1.8	1.0
Viet Nam	3.5	2.8	3.3	3.0	3.3	3.5	3.5	3.5
The Pacific	4.3	3.0	2.7	2.9	2.8	3.8	3.8	3.1
Cook Islands	0.1	0.8	1.5	1.5	1.5	1.7	1.7	1.7
Federated States of Micronesia	1.7	−1.0	0.5	0.5	1.6	1.0	1.0	1.9
Fiji	4.1	1.8	1.5	1.2	0.5	3.5	3.0	1.3
Kiribati	2.1	−1.8	1.0	1.0	1.0	1.1	1.1	1.1
Marshall Islands	0.8	0.1	0.3	0.3	0.3	0.5	0.5	0.5
Nauru	2.0	3.9	2.8	1.5	1.5	2.3	1.7	1.7
Niue	10.1	...	...	...	...	...	...	...
Palau	2.0	0.6	0.4	0.4	0.4	0.8	0.8	0.8
Papua New Guinea	4.7	3.6	3.3	3.3	3.3	4.4	4.4	3.8
Samoa	3.6	2.2	2.0	2.8	1.9	2.5	2.5	2.2
Solomon Islands	3.5	1.6	2.0	4.5	6.0	2.3	3.0	3.0
Tonga	7.0	3.2	1.3	1.3	1.6	2.2	1.8	2.0
Tuvalu	1.8	3.3	3.5	3.0	3.0	3.5	3.0	3.0
Vanuatu	2.3	2.8	1.5	4.0	3.0	2.0	2.2	2.2
Developing Asia	2.5	2.9	3.2	2.9	2.9	2.3	2.4	2.3
Developing Asia excluding the NIEs	2.6	3.3	3.6	3.2	3.2	2.5	2.5	2.5

... = unavailable, ADOS = ADO Supplement, NIEs = newly industrialized economies (Hong Kong, China; the Republic of Korea; Singapore; and Taipei,China).

Table A3 Current account balance (% of GDP)

	2018	2019	2020		2021	
			April ADO 2020	September Update	April ADO 2020	September Update
Central Asia	−0.3	−1.8	−3.8	−6.3	−2.4	−3.9
Armenia	−6.9	−7.2	−8.6	−8.6	−8.2	−8.2
Azerbaijan	12.9	9.1	4.4	−5.1	6.3	4.5
Georgia	−6.8	−5.0	−4.4	−11.0	−4.2	−8.0
Kazakhstan	−0.1	−3.6	−5.3	−5.3	−2.4	−3.7
Kyrgyz Republic	−12.3	−11.3	−12.0	−15.0	−10.0	−10.0
Tajikistan	−5.0	−2.3	−4.5	−5.0	−4.2	−4.5
Turkmenistan	5.5	5.1	−3.0	−1.4	−4.7	−2.0
Uzbekistan	−7.1	−5.6	−4.0	−9.5	−3.5	−8.0
East Asia	1.1	1.8	2.2	2.0	1.9	2.0
Hong Kong, China	3.7	6.1	7.0	4.0	5.0	4.0
Mongolia	−16.9	−13.1	−13.9	−14.1	−7.8	−8.3
People's Republic of China	0.2	1.0	1.6	1.5	1.2	1.3
Republic of Korea	4.5	3.6	2.8	2.8	3.5	3.5
Taipei,China	11.6	10.7	10.0	10.0	12.0	12.0
South Asia	−2.6	−1.4	−0.7	−0.5	−1.3	−0.9
Afghanistan	13.0	8.6	1.0	4.0	0.5	2.0
Bangladesh	−3.5	−1.7	−0.8	−1.5	−0.3	−1.1
Bhutan	−19.1	−22.6	−19.1	−14.6	−18.4	−11.9
India	−2.1	−0.8	−0.3	−0.3	−1.2	−0.6
Maldives	−28.2	−26.3	−23.0	−17.0	−22.0	−18.0
Nepal	−8.1	−7.7	−5.0	−0.9	−5.6	−1.9
Pakistan	−6.1	−4.8	−2.8	−1.1	−2.4	−2.4
Sri Lanka	−3.2	−2.2	−2.8	−2.4	−2.6	−2.3
Southeast Asia	1.6	2.7	1.9	1.6	1.9	1.8
Brunei Darussalam	7.9	9.0	5.5	9.5	9.5	9.5
Cambodia	−12.2	−15.0	−19.0	−22.3	−16.9	−17.8
Indonesia	−2.9	−2.7	−2.9	−1.5	−2.9	−2.0
Lao People's Democratic Republic	−13.0	−9.5	−9.4	−8.2	−8.1	−8.7
Malaysia	2.2	3.4	2.3	1.0	2.9	2.0
Myanmar	−4.7	0.4	−4.5	−4.5	−4.5	−4.5
Philippines	−2.5	−0.1	−0.3	−0.5	−1.4	−1.5
Singapore	17.2	17.0	17.0	15.0	17.0	17.0
Thailand	5.6	7.0	7.1	3.9	6.7	4.5
Timor-Leste	−12.2	8.0	−10.5	−21.5	−30.4	−36.5
Viet Nam	2.4	5.0	−0.2	1.0	1.0	1.5
The Pacific	14.5	14.5	10.1	7.5	13.9	7.7
Cook Islands	7.1	3.6	−1.2	−6.0	1.1	−12.5
Federated States of Micronesia	20.4	24.8	8.8	21.7	1.3	15.1
Fiji	−8.5	−4.9	−7.1	−15.3	−3.6	−13.4
Kiribati	13.4	7.6	4.0	4.0	2.8	2.8
Marshall Islands	6.5	7.7	6.1	13.6	5.1	12.3
Nauru	−4.5	4.9	...	5.2	...	2.7
Niue	22.7	...	...	...	...	...
Palau	−15.5	−26.9	−13.5	−23.0	−13.3	−49.2
Papua New Guinea	22.8	22.3	17.5	15.9	22.6	16.8
Samoa	0.8	2.3	−1.1	−4.7	0.5	−8.0
Solomon Islands	−3.1	−9.8	−8.7	−14.6	−12.3	−16.8
Tonga	−5.9	−6.3	−12.6	−7.3	−13.4	−14.5
Tuvalu	4.8	−6.9	2.8	2.9	3.4	3.5
Vanuatu	10.2	12.4	−8.7	−6.0	−8.6	−9.6
Developing Asia	0.6	1.4	1.6	1.4	1.4	1.4
Developing Asia excluding the NIEs	−0.4	0.5	0.9	0.8	0.5	0.6

... = unavailable, ADOS = ADO Supplement, GDP = gross domestic product, NIEs = newly industrialized economies (Hong Kong, China; the Republic of Korea; Singapore; and Taipei,China).

www.ingramcontent.com/pod-product-compliance
Lightning Source LLC
Chambersburg PA
CBHW050041220326
41599CB00045B/7246